Contents

Series editors' preface

The International Thomson Business Press Series in Tourism and Hospitality Management is dedicated to the publication of high quality textbooks and other volumes that will be of benefit to those engaged in tourism, hotel and hospitality education, especially at degree and postgraduate level. The series has two principal strands: core textbooks on key areas of the curriculum; and the *Topics in Tourism and Hospitality* series which includes highly focused and shorter texts on particular themes and issues. All the authors in the series are experts in their own fields, actively engaged in teaching, research and consultancy in tourism and hospitality. Each book comprises an authoritative blend of subject-relevant theoretical considerations and practical applications. Furthermore, a unique quality of the series is that it is student oriented, offering accessible texts that take account of the realities of administration, management and operations in tourism and hospitality contexts, being constructively critical without losing sight of the overall goal of providing clear accounts of essential concepts, issues and techniques.

The series is committed to quality, accessiblity, relevance and originality in its approach. Quality is ensured as a result of a vigorous refereeing process, unusual in the publication of textbooks. Accessibility is achieved through the use of innovative textual design techniques, and the use of discussion points, case studies and exercises within books, all geared to encouraging a comprehensive understanding of the material contained therein. Relevance and originality together result from the experience of authors as key authorities in their fields.

The tourism and hospitality industries are diverse and dynamic industries and it is the intention of the editors to reflect this diversity and dynamism by publishing quality texts that enhance topical subjects without losing sight of enduring themes. The Series Editors and Adviser are grateful to Steven Reed of International Thomson Business Press for his commitment, expertise and support of this philosophy.

Series editors
Stephen J. Page
Massey University – Albany
Auckland
New Zealand

Professor Roy C. Wood
The Scottish Hotel School
University of Strathclyde

Series adviser
Professor C. L. Jenkins
The Scottish Hotel School
University of Strathclyde

Preface

Hospitality Accounting was first published – under its original title *Accounting in the Hotel and Catering Industry* – some thirty years ago. Over the last three decades many thousands of students and practitioners have found it an authoritative and comprehensive, yet user friendly, book. In this edition we have retained the basic structure of the previous editions but, otherwise, we have thoroughly updated the text and introduced many important changes with an increased emphasis on student-centred learning.

There are a number of new chapters, starting with Chapter 1 which offers a general introduction to the topic. Chapter 9, Accounting Conventions and Concepts, deals with the regulatory framework of accounting. Chapter 17, Basic Costing, covers the fundamental concepts underlying costing and includes menu costing and pricing. Chapters 18 and 19, entitled Basic Cost Behaviour and Basic Decision accounting, replace Chapter 20 (Fixed and Variable Costs) of the fourth edition and take a more detailed look at these key topics. Chapter 21, entitled The US Uniform System of Accounts for Hotels, introduces the reader to the uniform accounting system which is proving increasingly popular in this country. Chapter 23, Management of Working Capital and Cash Flow Statements, provides an insight into this increasingly important area of study and includes the new structure for cash flow statements. Finally, in Chapter 25, Hospitality Accounting and Computerization by Bruce Braham, we provide an overview of the relevant applications of computerized accounting.

We have also altered the orientation of the book: whilst the first four editions were concerned with, essentially, hotels and restaurants, Hospitality Accounting has a wider outlook. Throughout the text the reader will find references to fast food operations, country clubs, travel agents, etc. – all of which complement the wider concept of the hospitality industry.

We wish to take the opportunity to thank the Hotel Association of New York Inc. for permission to reproduce the Departmental Statement of Income and other schedules and to Bruce Braham for his contribution of Chapter 25 on computerization. We hope that this new edition will prove a worthy successor to the previous editions and demonstrate not only a high degree of relevance to current hospitality accounting practice, but also reflect what is best in the teaching of the subject.

January 1997

Richard Kotas
Michael Conlan

Part I
Book-keeping in the hospitality industry

Introduction to accounting $\boxed{1}$

INTRODUCTION

This chapter looks at the concept of accounting, its nature and uses in society. It highlights the difference between financial accounting and management accounting and examines, from a legal and accounting point of view, the different types of business unit in use today and what effect, if any, it may have on the owners. Finally, it defines the accounting equation and examines its role as a key concept underpinning much of accounting practice.

OBJECTIVES

On completion of this chapter you should be able to:

- understand the need for an effective accounting system;
- list the key types of information that an accounting/recording system will produce;
- differentiate between financial and management accounting;
- list the three different types of business unit available;
- know the key advantages and disadvantages associated with each type of business unit;
- explain the principles underlying the accounting equation;
- understand the duality concept as applied to the accounting equation.

NATURE AND AIMS OF ACCOUNTING

It is widely accepted that since the beginning of time people have kept some form of record of their belongings and, of course, their debts to other people. How these records were kept we are not sure. It may have been scratchings on a stone wall or merely by memory and word of mouth; the only thing of which we can be certain is that records were kept. It's part of human psyche.

Clearly, as social structures developed and bartering/trading increased the need for accurate records also grew. More important perhaps was the evolvement of society away from communal living towards a master/servant or employer/employee relationship. The concept of steward-ship emerged and with it the necessity for an effective recording/account-ing system became more acute. By stewardship we mean the situation where the master entrusts resources and money to a steward or servant who in turn is required to account for them after a given period of time. In those days, just as today, an accurate recording system was important to both master and steward.

The accounting system used today is widely believed to have developed into a coherent system in the late fifteenth century. An Italian monk, Pacioli, is credited as being the father of modern double entry book-keeping/accounting. He published a booklet in 1494 outlining the practice of double entry book-keeping in the city of Venice during that period. This was the first definitive written reference to accounting as a recognizable discipline. Strange as it may seem, the basic principles have not changed much over the years despite the onslaught of modern technology and computer science.

What does an accounting system provide for our society?

The fact that book-keeping/accounting has survived and indeed grown over such a long period suggests that it must be answering an important need in our society. Place yourself in the shoes of any business person and it is not difficult to recognize that without a suitable accounting system there would be chaos in your business world. How would you keep a check on who owes you money, how much money you should have in the bank or the value of your stock at a given time? The list is endless. Without an adequate recording/accounting system it is difficult to see how the majority of businesses would prosper and grow.

What will an effective accounting system do for a business?

The following list is by no means complete but should provide some insight into the topic.

- It should provide an accurate record of all business transactions under-taken by the traders/businesses over a given period and result in a clear record of what they own and what they owe.
- When operated correctly and conscientiously, it will provide an accurate record of the value of goods sold to customers and of course the value of goods bought in from suppliers. This in turn will help to work out a true profit or loss for the period.
- It will provide all relevant information to permit accounting for the stewardship or management of a concern in a fairly objective way.
- It provides useful information to managers which will assist them in improving financial performance and efficiency.
- It provides valuable information to many external users, e.g. potential investors, creditors, banks etc.
- It helps to plan for the future.

Accounting and the hospitality student

This textbook is aimed primarily at students and managers engaged in the hospitality industry, most of whom are from a non-accounting background and sometimes struggle with the subject and therefore fail to recognize its importance to their future and to the business.

Any practising managers in the hospitality field will confirm that a large proportion of the key information crossing their desks each day is in the form of figures and financial statements. The more conversant and at ease one is with financial data the better one is likely to perform in any management role.

This textbook was designed with the hospitality student in mind. It does not seek to make the student into an accountant. It is written to allow the average student to acquire and practise, with relatively little pain, all the basic accounting/financial skills necessary for success in their future management career.

FINANCIAL ACCOUNTING VERSUS MANAGEMENT ACCOUNTING

The accounting function tends to be broken down into two distinct but related strands, i.e. financial and management accounting.

Financial accounting

Financial accounting, in simple terms, tends to revolve around the collection and recording of financial data through the production of key financial statements, e.g. profit and loss accounts, balance sheets, cash flow statements. The information is usually prepared primarily for managers/owners of the business and is used for future planning purposes, budgeting, etc. It is also of keen interest to investors, banks, employees, creditors and the Inland Revenue.

Management accounting

Management accounting used to be referred to as cost accounting because its main impact tended to be on the cost side of a business. However, in modern times the concept has been considerably enlarged and covers the collection of costs, revenues and other accounting data with a view to producing various management reports aimed at assisting management in cost and revenue control, trouble shooting and business decision-making, evaluating business performance and other operational aspects of the business.

TYPES OF BUSINESS UNIT

A business will be one of three principal types, all of which are dealt with in this textbook. These are sole traders, partnerships and limited companies.

At this point it is useful for students to familiarize themselves with the main characteristics of each type.

Sole Traders

As the word suggests, this is where individuals are in business for themselves. Sole ownership of the business rests with the owners although they may have employees. From a legal point of view there is no difference between the business entity and the private assets of the owners themselves. This means, in effect, that should the businesses fail the owners are responsibile for all outstanding debts of the business; and if they cannot pay, the courts may authorize the sale of their private assets, including their homes, in order to meet the debts. If they are not fully paid at this point the courts may arrest part of their wages from any future employment. Clearly there is a serious risk for sole traders should they hit hard times. In addition, there is a limit to the amount of money that an individual can raise and this tends to restrict the size of a sole trader's business.

The financial statements of a sole trader are not governed by any government regulations (unlike a limited company). This affords more privacy to the owner in respect of his business dealings, e.g. no need to declare the levels of his profit or loss for the year.

Partnership

A partnership exists where two or more persons own a business and run it with a view to sharing the profits on some predetermined basis. It is governed by the Partnership Act, 1890.

A partnership has some advantages over a sole trader in that all business risks are shared and it is likely to be able to raise more money, i.e. two or more people introducing capital. However, it also suffers from the main drawback of a sole trader, that is to say, the law does not treat the partnership as a separate legal entity. The partners are said to be jointly and severally liable for the business's debts. Anyone owed money by a partnership can claim payment from any of the partners individually or from all of them jointly. As with the sole trader, if the business or partnership cannot pay the debt, the creditor is entitled to go against the private assets of any or all of the partners, e.g their home, car, etc.

Also there is no legal requirement to publish the accounts of a partnership, thus giving the partners a reasonable level of privacy in their business affairs.

Limited companies

In the early nineteenth century partnerships were common because they facilititated the growth of somewhat larger businesses. By the middle of the nineteenth century the government of the day had put legislation in place to allow the introduction of limited companies. These companies took over from partnerships very quickly and tended to grow into larger organizations. Limited companies are formed by directors following a strict procedure passed by Act of Parliament. Basically, they create shares in the company which are taken up and paid for by shareholders. This is how a limited company raises its capital. The shareholders are the owners of the business but are only liable in law to the value of the shares they own (this is explained more fully in Chapter 16).

A limited company has a separate legal identity of its own quite distinct from the shareholders or persons who formed it. It is sometimes described as a separate legal person, or separate legal entity. A limited company enters a transaction in its own name and those dealing with it can only look to the company and its assets to satisfy payment thereof. They have no recourse to the shareholders or directors of the company. This is one of the most important advantages of being a limited company and is known as 'limited liability'.

On the other hand, all such companies must publish a fairly large amount of information about the company's operation including profits earned and salaries of certain directors and other such sensitive data that many businesses would not willingly disclose.

THE ACCOUNTING EQUATION

We will start our study of accounting by examining the accounting equation. This equation contains the fundamental concept underlying much of accounting practice and underpins all practical aspects of book-keeping and accounting.

The accounting equation is usually written as follows:

$$\text{ASSETS} = \text{LIABILITIES} + \text{CAPITAL}$$

Definition of terms:

- **Assets**. These represent anything of value owned by the business, e.g. buildings, furniture, cars, stocks of food etc.
- **Liabilities**. These represent amounts owed by the company which it is legally bound to pay. Typical examples are debts to suppliers who have sold the company goods on credit.
- **Capital**. One should always think of capital as a form of 'liability'. Capital represents the money invested by the owners of the business. Therefore it is reasonable to say that the business **owes** the capital to the owners, although this is not enforceable in law.

Now that the essential terms have been explained let us return to our study of the accounting equation.

$$\begin{array}{ccc}
\text{ASSETS} & = & \text{LIABILITIES} + \text{CAPITAL} \\
\text{(Things that we OWN)} & = & \text{(Things that we OWE)}
\end{array}$$

This model can be manipulated in a number of ways:

$$
\begin{array}{lcl}
\text{CAPITAL} & = & \text{ASSETS} - \text{LIABILITIES} \\
\text{CAPITAL} + \text{LIABILITIES} & = & \text{ASSETS} \\
\text{ASSETS} - \text{CAPITAL} & = & \text{LIABILITIES}
\end{array}
$$

The total of each side of the equation will at all times equal the total of the other side.

Students should remember that transactions are recorded from the point of view of the business, not from the point of view of the owner or any other person. This is called **the business entity concept**.

Each transaction affects a business in two ways – this is known as the **duality concept**. No matter how many business transactions take place in a given time period, because of the duality concept the assets of that business will always equal its liabilities and capital.

The accounting equation is a simple balance sheet, which demonstrates that what we own must always equal what we owe. (The double sided balance sheets used below are of the American variety, used because they conform more closely to the equation in question. Double sided balance sheets are never used in practice today.)

Consider the following example:

MaryAnne Driscoll started business on 1st Febuary with her savings of £150,000.

	Balance Sheet		
ASSETS	=	*LIABILITIES & CAPITAL*	
Bank A/c	£150,000	Capital	£150,000
		(owing to Owner)	

Note: the dual effect – an increase in an asset (i.e. the business bank a/c goes from zero to £150,000) is matched by an increase in a liability.

On the same day, MaryAnne buys a small take-away shop for £80,000, paid by cheque.

	Balance Sheet		
	£		£
Bank A/c	70,000	Capital	150,000
Shop	80,000		
	150,000		150,000

Note: Increase in one asset matched by decrease in another asset.

Later the business paid out £9,000 by cheque to buy some equipment.

Balance Sheet

	£		£
Bank A/c	61,000	Capital	150,000
Shop	80,000		
Equipment	9,000		
	150,000		150,000

Note: The increase in one asset matched by a decrease in another asset.

Later she bought food on credit from Homepraise Ltd costing £2,000.

Balance Sheet

	£		£
Bank A/c	61,000	Capital	150,000
Shop	80,000	Creditor	2,000
Equipment	9,000		
Stock (food)	2,000		
	152,000		152,000

Note: The increase in an asset matched by an increase in liability.

By the end of the first week MaryAnne had made cash sales of £3,000 and all the food stock had been used.

The above transaction needs to be dealt with in two stages:

Stage 1 Work out profit on sales:

Sales for week	£3,000
Purchases (food)	£2,000
Profit	£1,000

Stage 2 Now complete the statement in the normal way:

Balance Sheet

	£		£
Bank A/c	64,000	Capital	150,000
Shop	80,000	Profit	1,000
Equipment	9,000	Creditors	2,000
	153,000		153,000

Note: The bank account will increase by amount of cash sales. The stock of food a/c will disappear, as all food has been sold. The profit will be placed on the liabilities/capital side, because it represents the amount owed by the business to the owner.

The above exercise is meant to demonstrate in a simple way the workings of the duality concept as it relates to the accounting equation. All aspects of book-keeping and accounting are firmly based on this concept, from double entry to the balance sheet.

SUMMARY

- Accounting/record keeping has been in existence in some form throughout the ages.
- Accounting has evolved considerably over the centuries and now represents an important and clearly defined science.
- It is widely accepted, as a general rule, that businesses could not function adequately without an effective accounting system.
- Accounting systems provide systematic and comprehensive business information, which enables us to control our business i.e what we own/owe/sell/buy/borrow/stock etc. It also facilitates the production of accurate profit and loss figures.
- This textbook is designed with the hospitality student in mind and assumes a non-accounting background.
- Financial accounting tends to be a historical collection/recording of past financial data leading to production of key accounting statements.
- Management accounting is more proactive and usually cost based. Its general aim is to help managers to manage resources more effectively and efficiently, by the production of useful and relevant financial data.
- There are three types of business unit: sole traders, partnerships, and limited companies.
- Sole traders and partnerships leave the owners vulnerable to personal liability for all business debts should the venture fold. Limited company status gives protection to shareholders and directors.
- The accounting equation is the main principle underpinning book-keeping and accounting practice.

PROBLEMS

1. 'An accounting/recording system should be above all useful and effective'. List the kind of data/information that such a system must produce in order to achieve the above objective.

2. 'Financial and management accounting are two different strands of the same thread.' Define each of the these and state which, if any, you believe to be the more useful and why.

3. Describe the different types of business unit available within the UK and state clearly what type of businessman you would envisage engaging in each of the business units and why.

4. Set out the key advantages and disadvantages of (a) a sole trader; (b) a partnership; (c) a limited company.

5. This question is aimed at consolidating your understanding of the accounting equation.

Required:
Using the demonstration model from the text, enter each transaction individually into a balance sheet clearly demonstrating the duality concept or the twin effect of each and every transaction.

- Thomas Kojak commenced trading on 1st June with capital in the bank of £20,000.
- He bought a small snack bar for £6,000 and paid by cheque.
- He secured a loan from the Eastminster Bank for £15,000, which was paid into his bank account.
- He purchased beverages on credit from Vintners Ltd to the value of £850.
- He bought fixtures and fittings to the value of £16,000, paid by cheque.
- During the month, he purchased food on credit from 4 Star Food Wholesalers Ltd to the value of £1,100.
- At the end of June, Thomas sold meals for cash to the value of £3,400 and all the food and beverages bought had been used up.

6. C Hilton started business as a restaurant owner on 1st January 1997. His business transactions for the first week of January were as follows:

Jan 1   Introduced capital of £500,000, opened a bank account.

" 2   Purchased a freehold restaurant for £300,000, paid by cheque.

" 3   Purchased on credit from Hotel Suppliers Ltd the following: kitchen plant £80,000, furniture £30,000.

" 3   Bought food on credit from Fast Foods Ltd to the value of £10,000.

" 4   Sold meals to guests for £20,000 cash which he banked. He used up whole stock of food.

" 5   Purchased food on credit from Fast Foods Ltd for £5,000. Bought food for £1,000, paid by cheque.

" 6   Sold meals for cash £6,000, which he banked.
Sold meals on credit to B Big for £8,000.
(All food bought was used up.)

        C. Hilton paid by cheque amount owed to:
Fast Foods Ltd and Hotel Suppliers Ltd.
He received cheque for amount owed by B Big.

Required:
Prepare a simple style balance sheet for each transaction to demonstrate clearly the duality effect of each transaction on the accounting equation.

Theory and mechanics of double entry $\boxed{2}$

INTRODUCTION

Book-keeping in its simplest form is a method of recording business transactions, e.g. buying and selling goods and services, paying expenses, purchasing equipment etc. expressed in terms of money values.

A good book-keeping system will collect, record, classify and categorize business transactions in a systematic manner.

Any businessman or woman will agree that a clear logical and systematic means of keeping accounts is absolutely necessary to business success. The art of book-keeping has been around in pretty much the same form for at least five hundred years and is practised by businesses all over the world. The method used is the double entry book-keeping system.

OBJECTIVES

On completion of this chapter you should be able to:

• explain the principle of double entry;
• understand what is meant by the ledger;
• enter business transactions into the accounts using double entry;
• close off an account at the end of an accounting period;
• take out a trial balance.

NATURE OF BUSINESS TRANSACTIONS

In the course of any one day, a business will make a number of transactions. It may, for example, buy food, wines and spirits from its suppliers; sell meals, drinks and accommodation to its customers; pay business expenses such as rent, rates, wages and salaries; and perhaps less frequently, buy china, cutlery and equipment.

All such transactions result in a transfer of money (or money's worth, value or benefit) between two parties: the giver and the recipient of value. Thus when a hotel buys food from its suppliers, the giver of value is the supplier and the recipient of value is the hotel. When wages are paid by the hotel, the hotel is the giver and the employees are the recipients of money.

When a meal is served to a customer, the hotel is the giver and the customer the recipient of value.

Hence, it may be said that every business transaction has two aspects: the yielding of a benefit and the receiving of that benefit, and it is impossible to think of one without the other.

We will start by examining some of the documents and underlying principles of double entry and then look at some practical examples.

THE LEDGER

In order to have a systematic record of all transactions it is necessary to keep what is known as the ledger. This is the principal book of account and contains a number of separate ledger accounts, each one drawn up as demonstrated below.

Dr   Cr

Date	Details	F	£	Date	Details	F	£

It will be observed that the ledger account is divided into two identical parts. The left-hand side of the account is known as the DEBIT side (abbreviated to Dr); and the right hand side of the account is known as the CREDIT side (abbreviated to Cr).

The column headed 'F' above means folio column. The folio column is used to cross reference the double entry of a transaction. However, for simplicity purposes we intend to exclude it from the following examples.

The principle of double entry

This principle is the key to successful double entry accounting and states:

FOR EVERY DEBIT ENTRY IN THE LEDGER ACCOUNTS THERE MUST BE A CORRESPONDING CREDIT ENTRY

This is the most important rule in double entry book-keeping which states that in order to have a complete record of all transactions, each transaction must be entered in the ledger twice, once on the debit side of an account and once on the credit side of an account.

Dr   Cr

Date	Details	£	Date	Details	£
	VALUE RECEIVED			VALUE GIVEN	

The above illustration highlights a key rule which should simplify for the student the mechanics of double entry.

It states that **the receiving of value** is entered on the debit side of the relevant account and **the giving of value** on the credit side of another account.

From the point of view of the business there are two aspects to every business transaction, one of receiving something and the other of giving something. Whatever the business is receiving is **debited** in the relevant account, whilst whatever the business is giving is **credited** in a different account.

If we accept the above rule, double entry can be made reasonably simple by placing oneself in the shoes of the business and asking the questions – 'what am I receiving?' and 'what am I giving?'

Take for example the following business transaction:

On 1st February a business purchases food and pays cash £50.

Now ask yourself, from the businesses point of view, what is being received (debit) and what is being given (credit)?

It is clear that the business received food and gave cash. This is entered in the ledger accounts as follows:

Dr			Purchases A/c		Cr
19...		£	19...		£
Feb 1	Cash A/c	50			

Dr			Cash A/c		Cr
19...		£	19...		£
			Feb 1	Purchases A/c	50

Note how transactions are automatically cross referenced. The entry in the Purchases A/c states 'Cash', clearly identifying where the other entry can be found and vice versa with the Cash A/c.

Bearing the above in mind let us examine a number of examples:

On 1st January 19.... a hotel pays wages of £4,000.

The above transaction is entered into the accounts as follows:

Dr			Wages A/c		Cr
19...		£	19...		£
Jan 1	Cash	4,000			

Dr			Cash A/c		Cr
19...		£	19...		£
			Jan 1	Wages	4,000

Note: The cash account of the hotel has given value and is therefore credited.

The wages account represents the labour received from employees and is therefore debited.

On 4th February a hotel bought new lounge furniture for cash £12,000.

Dr		Furniture A/c		Cr
19...		£	19...	£
Feb 4	Cash	12,000		

Dr		Cash A/c		Cr
19...		£	19...	£
			Feb 4 Furniture	12,000

Obviously the business is receiving furniture, therefore we should debit its Furniture A/c and credit the Cash A/c.

On 7th September, 19.... a hotel receives rent of £500 in respect of sublet premises.

Dr		Cash A/c		Cr
19...		£	19...	£
Sept 7	Rent	500		

Dr		Rent Received A/c		Cr
19...		£	19...	£
			Sept 7 Cash	500

Note: the cash account, having received value, is debited; the corresponding credit entry must therefore be made in the rent received account.

All the aforementioned transactions are on a cash basis, which makes double entry relatively straightforward, because once we know what is happening in the cash account – either cash inwards is debited or cash outwards is credited – then the corresponding entry in the other account should be obvious.

We are now going to examine transactions where no cash changes hands at the time of exchange of goods or services

Credit Transactions

A large number of business transactions are 'on credit'. This means that the goods are delivered now and payment is made later. In other words, a period of credit is given.

From a double entry view point, there are two important things to remember about credit transactions:

1. The cash account cannot be involved, as obviously no money is changing hands.
2. One of the accounts for double entry must bear the personal name of an individual or company. The records must show exactly to whom we owe money or who owes money to us.

The following examples illustrate credit transactions.

On 7th April 19... a restaurant bought food on credit from Harrison Ltd for £3,500.
(The key words in the above are 'on credit', this indicates the fact that it is a credit transaction).

Dr		Purchases A/c			Cr
19...		£	19...		£
Apr 7	Harrison Ltd	3,500			

Dr		Harrison Ltd A/c			Cr
19...		£	19...		£
			Apr 7	Purchases	3,500

Food is being received – therefore we debit the Purchases A/c.

But what is being given out by the business in this case? Basically a promise of payment at a future date. Therefore we credit the supplier of goods who has given value.

On 10th of May 19... A restaurant borrows £10,000 from X Finance Company.

Dr		Cash A/c			Cr
19...		£	19...		£
May 10	X Finance Co.	10,000			

Dr		X Finance Co.			Cr
19...		£	19...		£
			May 10	Cash	10,000

Note: The Cash A/c is debited because cash is received and the X Finance Co. A/c is credited, recognizing the promise of payment in the future because they have given us value.

Consideration of the examples given will show that:

- by applying the principle of double entry it is possible to ensure that both aspects of each transaction are reflected in the books of a business;
- a separate account is used for every type of transaction; as a result, at the end of any one period the ledger contains **a systematic and classified summary of all the transactions** for the period concerned; and
- as there is a debit and a credit entry in respect of each transaction, **the sum total of debit entries must be equal to the sum total of the credit entries in the ledger.**

WORKED EXAMPLE

A second illustration is given below, showing how the principle of double entry is applied within a particular business.

On 1st March 19... A Caterer started in business with a capital in cash of £150,000. During March his transactions were as follows:

			£
March	2	Paid quarterly rent in cash	15,000
"	4	Purchased furniture for cash	50,000
"	6	Bought equipment on credit from H & C Ltd	30,000
"	8	Paid wages in cash	6,000
"	11	Bought food on credit from B Blake & Son	12,000
"	14	Sold meals for cash	7,500
"	18	Paid wages in cash	6,500
"	22	Sold meals for cash	5,500
"	26	Paid wages in cash	6,000
"	29	Paid H & C Ltd in cash	20,000
"	31	Sold meals for cash	4,000

Required:
(a) Enter A Caterer's transactions into his ledger.
(b) Check the accuracy of the ledger entries as at 31st March 19....

Part (b) relates to the accuracy of the ledger entries which must be checked as at 31st March. This will be achieved by drawing up a trial balance.

Before we begin this task we need to introduce the capital account and the purchases account each of which has a distinct meaning in accounting:

1. The capital account represents the owners of the business. We should always think of the business as a distinct being in its own right, completely separate from the owner. And so when A Caterer invests money in the business the latter receives cash (and the Cash A/c must be debited); and the business gives a promise of repayment (which requires a credit entry in the owner's Capital A/c).
2. All goods purchased for resale must be entered in the purchases account. 'Goods' in the hospitality industry means, principally, food and drink. Any other purchases such as furniture and equipment (bought with the intention of retaining them in the business), would not be entered in the

Purchases A/c but in some other account, e.g. Furniture A/c.

Dr			Cash A/c			Cr
19...		£		19...		£
Mar 1	Capital	150,000		Mar 2	Rent	15,000
" 14	Sales	7,500		" 4	Furniture	50,000
" 22	"	5,500		" 8	Wages	6,000
" 31	"	4,000		" 18	"	6,500
				" 26	"	6,000
				" 29	H & C Ltd	20,000

Dr		Capital A/c			Cr
19...		£	19...		£
			Mar 1	Cash	150,000

Dr			Rent A/c		Cr
19...		£	19...		£
Mar 2	Cash	15,000			

Dr			Furniture A/c		Cr
19...		£	19...		£
Mar 4	Cash	50,000			

Dr			Equipment A/c		Cr
19...		£	19...		£
Mar 6	H&C Ltd	30,000			

Dr			H & C Ltd		Cr
19...		£	19...		£
Mar 29	Cash	20,000	Mar 6	Equipment	30,000

Dr			Wages A/c		Cr
19...		£	19...		£
Mar 8	Cash	6,000			
" 18	"	6,500			
" 26	"	6,000			

Dr			Purchases A/c		Cr
19...		£	19...		£
Mar 11	Blake & Son	12,000			

Dr			B Blake & Son A/c		Cr
19...		£	19...		£
			Mar 11	Purchases	12,000

Dr			Sales A/c		Cr
19...		£	19...		£
			Mar 14	Cash	7,500
			" 22	"	5,500
			" 31	"	4,000

THE TRIAL BALANCE

The most important check of the accuracy of the entries in the ledger is the agreement of the total of debit entries with the total of credit entries. In order to find out whether or not there is this agreement it is necessary to extract what is known as the **trial balance**. This is done by extracting a list of ledger accounts showing the total of the debit entries and the total of the credit entries in each account, as follows:

Trial balance
of A Caterer at 31st March 19...

	Dr £	Cr £
Cash account	167,000	103,500
Capital account		150,000
Rent account	15,000	
Furniture account	50,000	
Equipment account	30,000	
H & C account	20,000	30,000
Wages account	18,500	
Purchases account	12,000	
B Blake & Son account		12,000
Sales account		17,000
	312,500	312,500

Note how we have listed above every account we opened for A Caterer.

In practice, instead of showing the total of the debit side and the total of the credit side of an account, only the difference between the two sides is shown. Thus, whether we show that the H & C Ltd account has a debit total of £20,000 and a credit total of £30,000 or show the difference, i.e. £10,000, in the credit column has no effect on the agreement of the trial balance. We will apply the same principle to the Cash A/c balance. We would thus rewrite our trial balance as follows:

Trial balance as at 31st March 19...

	Dr £	Cr £
Cash account	63,500	
Capital account		150,000
Rent account	15,000	
Furniture account	50,000	
Equipment account	30,000	
H & C account		10,000
Wages account	18,500	
Purchases account	12,000	
B Blake & Son account		12,000
Sales account		17,000
	189,000	189,000

Balancing: Nature of ledger balances

The difference between the two sides of an account is known as the balance. A debit balance arises when the total of debit entries exceeds the total of credit entries. A credit balance arises when the total of credit entries exceeds the total of debit entries.

Closing off an account at the end of an accounting period

In practice all accounts should be 'closed off' at the end of an accounting period.

Using the following cash account as an example, we will demonstrate how to close the account at the end of the month. The closing balance in January is carried down to be the opening balance in February.

Use the following steps to close off the cash account:

1. Add up debit side – this represents the cash received in January.
2. Add up credit side – this represents the cash paid out in January.
3. The difference represents the amount of cash remaining and in this case is a debit balance, because the debit side is greater than the credit side.
4. This balance is now transferred out of the January cash account into the February account using double entry, i.e. we credit the January account and debit the February account.

Dr				Cash A/c			Cr
19...			£	19...			£
Jan 1	Capital		20,000	Jan 4	Rent		3,000
" 16	Sales		1,500	" 9	China		2,000
" 29	"		3,500	" 14	Wages		2,000
				" 31	Furniture		10,000
				" 31	Balance c/d		8,000
			25,000				25,000
Feb 1	Balance b/d		8,000				

Notes:
It will be observed that

(a) The total of the debit entries in the cash account is £25,000 and the total of the credit entries £17,000, giving a debit balance of £8,000.
(b) In order to balance the cash account (i.e. make both sides of the account equal) it is necessary to place the balance on the credit side of the account.
(c) Both money columns are then totalled and the balance is entered as the figure brought down on the debit side of the February cash account.

The abbreviations c/d and b/d stand for 'carried down' and 'brought down', respectively. When a balance is carried from one page of ledger to another or from one accounting period to another it is said to be 'carried forward', hence the abbreviations c/f and b/f are then used.

Errors in the trial balance

The trial balance may be defined as a list (or schedule) of balances, both debit and credit, extracted from ledger accounts including the cash book and the petty cash book.

When a system of double entry is used, the total of the debit entries must be equal to the total of the credit entries in the ledger. As a result, provided that double entry has been properly completed in respect of each transaction, the two sides of the trial balance must necessarily be equal.

It must be remembered, however, that the trial balance is proof only of the arithmetical accuracy of the ledger entries. There are certain types of error that a trial balance will not disclose.

Omission of entries

If both the debit and the credit entry of a transaction are omitted, the trial balance will not be affected and the failure to enter the transaction will not be revealed.

Compensating errors

These are two or more errors which cancel out. When one account is, say, overdebited with £50 and another overcredited with the same amount, the agreement of the trial balance will not be affected though there are two errors in the books.

Misposting of accounts

This error occurs when one of the entries is posted on the right side of the ledger but in the wrong account, e.g. when a cheque is paid to W M Brown & Co. and is debited in error to the account of Wm Brown & Co. Ltd.

Errors of principle

This error occurs when, though double entry is completed, the posting is not in accordance with some accounting principle, e.g. when china is purchased by a hotel and this is debited in the purchases account. China is not deemed 'purchases' in hospitality accounting since it is not purchased for resale to customers.

SUMMARY

- Good book-keeping systems based on double entry are essential to order, accuracy and profitability of a business.
- The ledger consists of a number of accounts grouped together under various headings.
- Every business transaction (e.g. any buying or selling of goods, payment of wages, disposal of fixed assets etc.) must be entered twice in the ledger.
- Double entry is based on the following principle: for every debit entry in the ledger accounts there must be a corresponding credit entry.
- As a general rule, what the business receives is debited. What it gives out is credited.
- All accounts should be 'closed off' at the end of an accounting period and the balances carried down to the next accounting period.
- The trial balance is a check on the accuracy of the entries. It confirms that the debit/credit rule has been adhered to and little more.

PROBLEMS

1. Explain what is meant by the principle of double entry.

2. What do you understand by the ledger; debit balance; credit balance?

3. From the following information write up V Goodfellow's cash account and balance it as at 7th March 19...

			£
March 1	Balance on cash account b/d	Dr	63,040
" 1	Received from B Smythe		520
" 2	Paid rent		11,000
" 3	Paid for stationery		260
" 4	Sold meals for cash		6,240
" 4	Paid wages		3,340
" 5	Paid Hotel Supplies Ltd		4,000
" 6	Paid electricity account		1,950
" 7	Paid Wm Grocer & Sons		1,100
" 7	Paid for advertising		440

4. Alice Vunderlant started business on 1st July with £2,500 in cash. She rented a small café next door to a supermarket. The following transactions took place during the first week of July:

(Hint: Start by opening a cash account and a capital account.)

			£
July	1	Paid rent for week in cash	350
"	2	Bought food for cash	450
"	3	Paid weekly wages in cash	550
"	5	Bought furniture for cash	1,000
"	6	Bought food on credit from Besco Ltd	600
"	7	Cash sales for the week amounted to	2,200

Enter the above transactions in the books of account of Alice and take out a trial balance at 7th July 19...

5. On 1st of September Mary Popkins started in business with a capital in cash of £15,000, during September her transactions were as follows:

			£
Sept	2	Paid rent in cash	2,500
"	4	Bought equipment on credit from REFS Ltd	3,000
"	6	Purchased furniture for cash	5,000
"	8	Paid wages in cash	500
"	11	Bought food on credit from Sainsbees	1,000
"	14	Sold meals for cash	1,750
"	18	Paid wages in cash	600
"	19	Purchased food for cash	750
"	22	Sold meals for cash	1,450
"	26	Paid wages in cash	650
"	29	Paid REFS Ltd by cash	1,500
"	30	Sold meals for cash	1,300

You are required to enter the above transactions in Mary Popkins' ledger and extract a trial balance as at 30th Sept.

6. On 1st January John Robinson started as a café proprietor with a capital in cash of £150,000. His transactions in January were:

			£
Jan	1	Purchased premises for cash	90,000
"	3	Paid for kitchen utensils and equipment	7,500
"	5	Paid for furniture	11,250
"	10	Paid wages	1,110
"	12	Purchased food for cash	3,750
"	14	Sold meals etc. for cash	1,680
"	16	Paid insurance	600
"	18	Paid wages	1,170
"	19	Sold meals etc. for cash	1,890
"	21	Bought food on credit from M Mann & Co.	1,050
"	23	Paid for cleaning materials	360

Jan	25	Paid wages in cash	1,140
"	27	Sold meals etc. for cash	1,350
"	29	Purchased food for cash	810
"	31	Purchased additional equipment for cash	3,000

Required:
(a) Enter the above transactions in Robinson's ledger.
(b) Extract a trial balance as at 31st January 19...
(c) Balance his cash book.

7. On 1st July 19..., William Gravett started in business as a snack bar proprietor with a capital in cash of £6,000.

His transactions in July were as follows:

July	1	Borrowed £50,000 from City Finance Co.
"	5	Bought premises for £120,000 and settled the purchase price as follows: paid a deposit of £10,000 and obtained a mortgage for the balance due (£110,000) from the Stable Building Society.
"	9	Purchased furniture on credit for £20,000 from Oak Furnishing Co.
"	13	Paid in cash £12,000 for equipment and china.
"	18	Bought food on credit from B Baker & Sons for £1,600 and from S Fish & Co. for £1,900.
"	24	Sold meals for cash £2,100.
"	28	Paid wages. £1,000
"	29	Sold meals on credit to Midland Motors Ltd £1,500 and BM Dining Club £1,700.
"	30	Borrowed from A Lender £5,000.
"	31	Paid Oak Furnishing Co. £1,000 on account.

Required:
(a) Enter Gravett's transactions in his ledger.
(b) Extract a trial balance as at 31st July 19...
(c) Balance the cash account.

8. The following balances were extracted from the books of a restaurant at 31st December 19...:

	£
Purchases	118,650
Sales	331,620
Stock of food	12,150
Debtors	29,820
Rent and rates	18,000
Wages and salaries	78,450
Light and heat	9,150
Repairs and renewals	6,030
Furniture	36,000
Creditors	15,000
Kitchen equipment	18,000

Plate and china	14,490
Cash at bank	59,010
Cash in hand	6,870
Leasehold premises	240,000
Capital	?

Required:

(a) Arrange the above balances in trial balance form.

(b) Calculate the capital of the restaurant.

Accounting for cash | 3

INTRODUCTION

Accounting for cash is an important task in any business but especially in a hospitality establishment where, due to the nature of the business, a large amount of the sales are on a cash basis.

Due to the varying circumstances of each business it will be found that the actual arrangement and layout of books of account vary somewhat from one business to another. We thus find many kinds of cash accounts (cash books, as they are usually called).

OBJECTIVES

On completion of this chapter you should be able to:
* recognize and construct single column and double column cash books;
* enter transactions into a double column cash book;
* understand and apply a 'contra entry' in the cash book;
* explain the need for a petty cash book and how the imprest system works;
* construct and enter items into the petty cash book;
* demonstrate the imprest system in use;
* understand the treatment of discount received in the accounts;
* recognize and construct a cash received book;
* understand the different kinds of bank accounts and credit cards;
* understand and construct a bank reconciliation statement.

SINGLE COLUMN CASH BOOK

This is the simplest form of cash book and has already been illustrated in Chapter 1. It takes the form of a ledger account. The debit side is used for the recording of money received (coin, notes, cheques, postal orders, travellers' cheques, etc.); the credit side is used for money paid.

EXAMPLE 3.1

The following cash transactions are to be recorded in the cash book of the Milano Restaurant and the cash book balance brought down as at 31st January:

19...			£
Jan	1	Debit balance b/d	10,000
"	2	Paid wages	1,250
"	7	Cash sales	4,200
"	11	Paid to A Supplier	450
"	16	Received from B Brown	800
"	21	Paid wages	1,250
"	26	Cash sales	4,300
"	31	Paid for linen in cash	300

Cash Book

19...			£	19...			£
Jan	1	Balance b/d	10,000	Jan	2	Wages	1,250
"	7	Cash Sales	4,200	"	11	A Supplier	450
"	16	B Brown	800	"	21	Wages	1,250
"	26	Cash Sales	4,300	"	31	Linen	300
				"	31	Balance c/d	16,050
			19,300				19,300
Feb	1	Balance b/d	16,050				

DOUBLE COLUMN CASH BOOK

Consideration of the single column cash book will indicate that it is inadequate in some respects. First, the majority of businesses keep most of their cash in a bank account and some 'office cash' on the premises. Second, though some payments are made by cheque others are in cash. Hence it is necessary to have a cash book which will distinguish between the two separate funds of cash (i.e. bank account and office cash) and thus differentiate between payments made by cheque and those in actual cash.

The double column cash book has two money columns, headed 'cash' and 'bank' on the debit side and two money columns, also headed 'cash' and 'bank', on the credit side. The cash and bank columns are used as follows:

Debit Side: All amounts paid into office cash are entered in the 'cash' column and all amounts banked in the 'bank' column.

Credit Side: All amounts paid out of office cash are entered in the 'cash' column and all payments by cheque in the 'bank' column.

Contra entry

Any amounts of cash transferred from the bank to the office cash should be credited in the bank column and debited in the cash column; any transfers of cash from office cash to the bank should be credited in the cash column and debited in the bank column. Any transfer of cash from the bank to the office, or *vice versa*, is shown in the cash book by means of a 'contra entry'. The term contra entry means that both the debit and the credit entry are to be found in the same account; contra entries are denoted by the sign '¢'. There is an example below.

EXAMPLE 3.2

The following transactions are to be entered in the cash book of the Chelsea Luncheon Club, and the cash book balanced as at 28th February 19...

				£
Feb	1	Bank balance b/d	Dr	60,000
"	1	Balance of office cash b/d		600
"	2	Paid by cheque for furniture		7,500
"	4	Paid by cheque to A B Manning		1,350
"	5	Paid for stamps – cash		90
"	7	Banked cash sales		6,450
"	9	Paid wages by cheque		2,460
"	11	Paid by cheque HCI Supplies Ltd		3,450
"	13	Received from B Naylor and banked		750
"	15	Paid manager's travel expenses – cash		180
"	18	Banked cash sales		7,350
"	20	Paid wages by cheque		2,760
"	22	Paid for stationery – cash		150
"	23	Paid for flowers – cash		60
"	24	Withdrew from bank for office use		600
"	25	Banked cash sales		5,700
"	26	Paid by cheque to M Cooper & Sons		1,950
"	27	Paid for stamps – cash		90
"	27	Paid cleaner's wages – cash		150
"	28	Paid wages by cheque		2,580

Cash Book

Date		F	Cash	Bank	Date		F	Cash	Bank
19 . . .			£	£	19 . . .			£	£
Feb 1	Balances b/d		600	60,000	Feb 2	Furniture			7,500
" 7	Cash Sales			6,450	" 4	A B Manning			1,350
" 13	B Naylor			750	" 5	Stamps		90	
" 18	Cash Sales			7,350	" 9	Wages			2,460
" 24	Bank	¢	600		" 11	HCI Supplies Ltd			3,450
" 25	Cash Sales			5,700	" 15	Manager's travel expenses		180	
					" 20	Wages			2,760
					" 22	Stationery		150	
					" 23	Flowers		60	
					" 24	Cash	¢		600
					" 26	M Cooper & Sons			1,950
					" 27	Stamps		90	
					" 27	Cleaner's wages		150	
					" 28	Wages			2,580
					" 28	Balances c/d		480	57,600
			1,200	80,250				1,200	80,250
19 . . .									
Mar 1	Balances b/d		480	57,600					

Petty cash book

In hospitality establishments it is often necessary to make numerous payments of small amounts for various expenses. Where this is so, it may be convenient to have a main cash book and a separate petty cash book. The main cash book would be in the charge of a senior clerk or the head cashier, whereas the responsibility for maintaining the petty cash book would be delegated to a relatively junior clerk.

Using the imprest system

Petty cash books are usually analysed and kept on what is known as the **imprest system**. This operates as follows. At the beginning of a period a fixed amount of cash, say £400, is advanced to the petty cashier. At the end of the period the petty cashier balances his petty cash book, and the total amount expended by him (and represented by appropriate vouchers) is refunded to him by the person in charge of the main cash book. Thus, at the beginning of each period, the petty cashier will start with the same fixed float of cash.

For example:

	£
Petty cashier's cash float on 1st January 19...	400
Petty cashier's weekly expenditure (total vouchers)	<u>320</u>
Petty cashier's balance of cash on 7th January 19...	80
Therefore (i) cash refunded to him on 7th January 19...	<u>320</u>
(ii) his cash float on 8th January 19...	<u>£400</u>

It will be observed that every petty cash payment is recorded twice: once in the total column and once in one of the analysis columns: consequently, the sum of the analysed totals should be equal to that of the total column.

In the folio column are recorded the numbers of the petty cash vouchers. These would be numbered consecutively and presented to the head cashier when requesting a refund in respect of payments made.

VPO stands for 'visitors' paid-outs'. This is a column often added in the petty cash book of a hotel. Payments made on behalf of guests staying in the hotel are recorded in this column. As soon as a payment of this kind is made, a copy of the appropriate voucher should be passed on to the reception office (bill office, in a larger hotel) to ensure that the charge is debited to the guest's account in the visitors' ledger. In many hotels the total of VPO from the petty cash book is checked against the total of debits in the VPO column of the visitors' ledger to ensure that all charges have been posted.

The petty cash book, though physically separated from the ledger, is a ledger account: as a result, every entry made in it counts for double entry purposes. It is also a **subsidiary book** in that it collects and analyses detailed transactions and enables totals to be posted to the ledger.

EXAMPLE 3.3

The petty cash book of the Wessex Hotel is kept on the imprest system. On 1st July 19..., the petty cashier's balance is £500. His expenditure during the first week of July was:

	£
July 1 Paid for postage stamps	67.50
" 2 Paid for guest's taxi fare (Room 64) – Jones	22.50
" 3 Paid manager's travel expenses	82.50
" 3 Bought flowers for guest (room 87) – Brown	45.00
" 3 Paid for postage stamps	52.50
" 5 Gave tip to delivery man	7.50
" 5 Bought bill pads for restaurant	75.00
" 6 Paid chef's fares	16.50
" 6 Paid donation to local charity	45.00
" 7 Bought pencils, pens etc.	12.50
" 7 Bought magazines for lounge	9.50

The above payments should be recorded and, assuming that the total of expenditure is refunded, the petty cash book balanced as at 7th January 19...

Petty Cash Book   16

Dr	date		F	Total	Postage	Stationery	Travel Expenses	VPO	Sundry Expenses
£	19 . . .			£	£	£	£	£	£
500.00	July 1	Balance	b/d						
	" 1	Postage stamps	1	67.50	67.50				
	" 2	Guest taxi room 64 – Jones	2	22.50				22.50	
	" 3	Manager travel	3	82.50			82.50		
	" 3	Guest's flowers room 87 – Brown	4	45.00				45.00	
	" 4	Postage stamps	5	52.50	52.50				
	" 5	Tips to Delivery man	6	7.50					7.50
	" 5	Bill pads	7	75.00		75.00			
	" 6	Chef's fares	8	16.50			16.50		
	" 7	Don. to charity	9	45.00					45.00
	" 7	Pencils, pens	10	12.50		12.50			
	" 7	Magazines	11	9.50					9.50
				436.00	120.00	87.50	99.00	67.50	62.00
500.00	" 7	Balance	c/d	64.00	L/29	L/31	L/45		L/47
				500.00					
64.00	July 8	Balance	b/d						
436.00	July 8	Cash Received							

Double entry in respect of petty cash items is completed as follows:

(a) Any amounts drawn by the petty cashier are credited in the main cash book and debited in the petty cash book.

(b) Petty cash payments are credited (individually) in the petty cash book and debited in total in the appropriate account in the ledger. Thus the total of the postage column, £120.00, would be debited in the postage account as shown below:

Postage A/c   29

19...		PC	£	
July 7	Petty Cash	16	120.00	

Note that the totals posted to the ledger are cross-referenced as follows:

(a) Under the analysis totals of the petty cash book the page number of the relevant ledger account is given. In the illustration, L/29 means that the corresponding double entry is in the postage account which is on page 29 in the ledger. The ledger folio column shows the relevant page number of the petty cash book.

(b) The VPO items, as already explained, are debited individually in the visitors' ledger. Hence the total of the VPO column is left in the petty cash book.

Treatment of discounts received

Many suppliers of hospitality establishments offer cash discounts. A cash discount is a deduction allowed from the amount due to the supplier, provided that payment is made within a specified time. Thus, if a hotel owes A Supplier £1,000 and the latter allows a discount of five per cent, provided that the payment is made within the specified time, £50 may be deducted from the amount due, and only £950 need be paid. It may be seen, therefore, that the main object of cash discounts is to encourage prompt payment.

In order to facilitate the recording of cash discounts received, many hospitality establishments add a discount received column on the credit side of their cash book. The layout of a cash book with a discount received column is illustrated below.

Cash Book   22

Date		F	Details	Bank	Date		F	Disc Recd	Bank
19...			£	£	19 . . .			£	£
Jan 1	Balance b/d			12,000	Jan 3	Wages			2,200
" 2	Sales:				" 4	A Supplier	L45	50	950
	Restaurant		2,000		" 4	X Tobacco Co.		100	2,200
	Bar		1,200		" 5	Rent			3,500
	Sundries		200	3,400	" 6	Insurance			300

The discount received column is described as a memorandum column. It is there for convenience and does not count for double entry purposes. Double entry in respect of discounts received is completed as follows. Debit both the cash paid and the discount received in the account of the supplier. Credit the periodical (usually monthly) total of the discount received column in the discount received account in the ledger.

Assuming that the total of discounts received from suppliers by the end of January 19..., is £500, the entry in the discount received account would be:

Discounts Received A/c

		19...		CB	£
		Jan 31	Cash	22	500.00

The amount paid to A Supplier would be posted to his account as shown below.

A Supplier A/c   45

19...		CB	£			£
Jan 4	Cash	22	950.00	Jan 1	Balance b/d	1,000.00
" 4	Discount	22	50.00			
			1,000.00			1,000.00

The purpose of the detail column on the debit side of the cash book is twofold: to indicate the sources of any cash banked and to facilitate an easy cross reference to the ledger account concerned.

Cash received book

Many hotels maintain, in addition to the main cash book, a cash received book. This is kept in the reception office and usually acts as a subsidiary book to the main cash book. A typical cash received book is illustrated below.

Cash Received Book

Date	Name	Room no or Fol.	Visitors' ledger Receipts	Sales Ledger Receipts	Deposits on Arrival	Total
			£	£	£	£
May 1	R W Brown, Mr	Rm 106	226.00			226.00
" 1	Midland Motors	SL 56		185.00		185.00
" 1	A Ewing, Mr & Mrs	Rm 117	85.00			85.00
" 1	S P Brown, Miss	Rm 36			100.00	100.00
	etc.					
" 1	Total – trans to Cash Book	CB/46	2,205.00	1,002.50	200.00	3,407.50

At the end of each day the cash received book would be balanced and the total of cash received debited in the main cash book:

Cash Book   46

Date		F	Detail £	Bank £	Date		F	Disc. Rec'd	Bank £
19...									
May 1	Cash Received Visitors' Ledger	CRB/21	2,205.00						
	Sales Ledger	CRB/21	1,002.50						
	Deposits on Arrival	CRB/21	200.00	3,407.50					

The corresponding credit entries would be made as indicated below:

Visitors' ledger receipts – the individual amounts received form visitors would be credited in their accounts in the visitors' ledger.

Sales ledger receipts – these, again, would be credited individually in the relevant customers' accounts in the sales ledger.

Deposits on arrival – any such deposits received would be credited in the guests' accounts in the visitors' ledger on their departure.

BANKING FOR BUSINESSES

Over the past twenty years we have seen major changes in the way we pay for goods and services provided. Nowadays larger accounts (£25 or more) tend to be settled by 'non-cash' means, for example payment by the traditional bank cheque. In addition an increasing number of settlements are made by credit cards. The banking system plays an important role in converting these non-cash payments into real money in the business's bank account.

KINDS OF BANK ACCOUNTS

Reference has already been made to the bank account. In fact, there are two kinds of bank account that may be opened by a business: a current account and a deposit account.

A current account is an account into which payments are made and on which cheques are drawn. The balance of a current account will, therefore, vary continually.

A deposit account is an account into which money is paid with the intention of leaving it in the bank for a period of time with a view to earning interest.

The main differences between a current account and a deposit account are:

1. Withdrawals from a current account may be made at any time but as a general rule notice of intention to withdraw from a deposit account must be given to the bank.
2. Interest is paid by the bank on the balance standing to the credit of a deposit account; usually no interest is allowed in the case of a standard business current account, However, this is changing and some banks will pay interest on positive balances subject to certain conditions being met.
3. Unlike a current account, a deposit account cannot be drawn upon by means of a cheque. The usual procedure is to write a letter (signed by the persons authorized to withdraw funds) to the bank informing the bank of the intention to withdraw funds from a deposit account.

Transactions affecting the current account are recorded in the bank columns of the main cash book. Any amounts lodged with the bank will be

Figure 3.1 Specimen paying-in slip

debited in the bank column; any payments by cheque will, of course, be credited in the bank column.

Before any amount is paid into a current account particulars of the cash to be banked must be entered in a **paying-in-book** supplied by the bank. This usually consists of a number of paying-in slips bound together in book form. The bank cashier detaches one copy and keeps it; the other copy of the paying-in slip, having been stamped and initialled by the cashier, remains in the book for reference. A specimen paying-in slip is shown in Figure 3.1.

Any amounts transferred from a current account to a deposit account will be credited in the main cash book and debited in a deposit account opened in the ledger. Any amounts withdrawn from the deposit account will be credited in that account and debited in some other account.

EXAMPLE 3.4

On 1st February 19..., the main cash book of the Bryton Hotel shows a debit balance of £37,520. On that day the amount of £15,000 is transferred to a deposit account opened by the hotel. This will be recorded as:

			Cash Book				37
19...			£	19...		L	£
Feb 1	Balance b/d		37,520	Feb 1	Deposit A/c	59	15,000

			Deposit A/c		59
19...		CB	£		
Feb 1	Cash	37	15,000		

On 15th November 19..., £14,000 is withdrawn from the deposit account to pay for new kitchen plant. The necessary entries will then be: Cr deposit account and Dr kitchen plant account as shown below:

			Deposit A/c					59
19...		CB	£	19...		L	£	
Feb 1	Cash	37	15,000	Nov 15	Kitchen plant	26	14,000	

			Kitchen Plant A/c		26
19...		CB	£		
Nov 15	Deposit a/c	59	14,000		

Cheques

Cheques remain a popular form for settlement of all business transactions and the only alternative to cash if the establishment will not accept credit cards.

Types of cheque.

Bankers supply two forms of cheque:

1. Bearer cheque – a bearer cheque is worded: 'pay .... or bearer' and would be paid to the person presenting the cheque. Bearer cheques are not as safe as order cheques and are, therefore, used infrequently.
2. Order cheques – an order cheque is worded: 'pay .... or Order' and is payable to a specified person or to such person as the payee may order to receive the money. A specimen of an order cheque is shown in Figure 3.2.

The parties to the cheque are:

Drawer – the person who signs the cheque (John Brown)
Drawee – the banker on whom the cheque is drawn (Eastminster Bank plc)
Payee – the person to whom the cheque is payable (Catering Supplies Ltd)

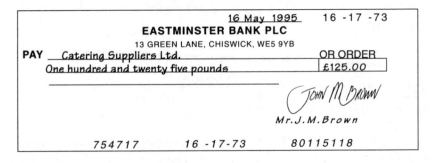

Figure 3.2 Specimen order cheque

A cheque which is not crossed is known as an **open cheque**, and cash may be obtained for it from the banker on whom it is drawn. In practice, in order to secure a measure of protection against fraud, nearly all cheques are **crossed cheques**. A crossed cheque has two parallel lines drawn across the face of it. Sometimes the words '& Co.' are written between the lines, but they are not essential to the crossing. When a cheque is crossed the banker will not pay cash over the counter. The payee must hand the cheque to his own banker who will collect it for him and credit his account.

A general crossing consists of two parallel lines with or without (a) the words '& Co.', (b) 'not negotiable'.

A special crossing consists of the name of the banker written across the face of the cheque with or without (a) the parallel lines, (b) the words 'not negotiable'. The effect of a special crossing is to instruct the paying banker to pay only the banker named in the crossing. If a banker disobeys a crossing, he becomes liable to the true owner of the cheque for any loss caused thereby.

We must now explain what is meant by the negotiability of a cheque. A cheque is, in legal language, a 'negotiable instrument'. Therefore, if it is accepted by a person in exchange for value given and in good faith, it becomes his property; his title to it cannot be disputed, provided that there is no previous forgery on it.

When a cheque is crossed 'not negotiable', it ceases to be a negotiable instrument. A person who takes a cheque so marked, takes it subject to all defects of the title of the person who gave it to him. If there is any irregularity of title, the drawer may refuse to honour the cheque and the holder of it will lose the money.

Sometimes cheques have to be **endorsed.** To endorse a cheque is to sign one's name on the back of it. Students should know when endorsement is or is not necessary. The present position is as follows:

Endorsement is necessary in the following cases:

1. Cheques cashed or exchanged across the counter.
2. Cheques tendered for the credit of an account other than that of the ostensible payee.
3. Cheques payable to joint payees; these will require endorsement if tendered for the credit of an account to which all are not parties.

Endorsement is not necessary in the following cases:

1. Cheques paid in for the credit of the account of the payee.
2. Cheques paid in for the credit of a joint or partnership account.

Cheques are sometimes 'dishonoured' (returned by the banker unpaid) for various reasons, e.g. in the event of the drawer's death or bankruptcy, or where there are insufficient funds to meet the cheque. The bank will attach a slip to a cheque so returned. This is usually marked R/D (refer to drawer) and really means that there are insufficient funds to pay the cheque. When a cheque is returned for some technical reason the bank will usually indicate this by means of an appropriate wording, e.g. 'words and figures differ', 'another signature required', 'signature differs', 'endorsement irregular'.

Credit Cards

Credit cards are widely used by private individuals and companies to settle accounts due. These cards are usually issued by well-known organizations such as Barclays Bank, Access, American Express and Diners Club although in recent times most banks and building societies have been issuing their own credit card to their customers.

The banks and other providers of these cards will have investigated the credit worthiness of the holders and, providing certain rules are followed, they will always honour the credit card debts of their customers. However, the banks do charge a commission to the hotelier and other businesses accepting their cards (usually between 1.5 and 3 per cent of total amount spent) on the grounds of security of payment, risk taken and increased usage by their customers.

Credit cards tend to be made of plastic and always bear the name and logo of the bank or other provider. In addition each card will have an individual number and show the holder's name and signature plus a latest validity date (see Figure 3.3).

Procedure for accepting a credit card

Where it is the policy of the hotel or restaurant to accept such cards it is extremely important that the establishment staff are well briefed and trained on the procedures for accepting the card as payment.

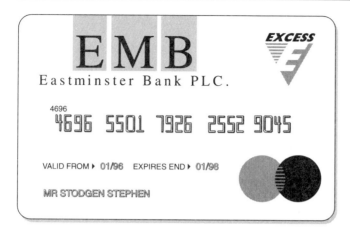

Figure 3.3 Specimen credit card

The following procedure must be observed before acceptance of the card:

1. Check that card is not out of date.
2. Check that card number is not on any blacklist of cards provided by the banks from time to time.
3. Customers should be requested to sign the bill and this signature should be checked against that on the card.
4. Ensure that the card number is clearly imprinted on the receipt form and other relevant documentation.
5. Each bank will have a pre-set 'ceiling' amount and any bill exceeding this amount must be cleared with the bank by telephone before acceptance. These 'ceilings' can be as low as £50.

At the end of each month any business that accepts credit cards will send a list to the credit card companies of the amounts spent with them by the holders together with the necessary back up documentation showing imprints of cards, signatures and amounts due. The card companies will pay out to the relevant businesses the outstanding amounts less commission and they in turn will collect the amounts due from the card holders.

Commissions paid to the credit card companies are dealt with in the books of account as follows:

Assume that during the month of May twenty five guests of the Ace Hotel settled their bills which totalled £1,200 using the 'Excess Credit Card'.

On 31st May each of the guests' accounts will be credited and the total debited to the Excess Credit Company account. Once the credit card company pays the hotel net of commission of 2 per cent, say at the end of June, its account will be credited and the cash book and commission paid account of the Ace Hotel will be debited as shown below:

Sundry Debtors A/c

19...		£	19...		£
May	Debtors (various)	1,200	May 31	Debtors (various)	1,200

Excess Credit Card Company A/c

19...	£	19...	£
May 31 Debtors (Various)	1,200	Jun 30 Cash book	1,176
		" 30 Commission paid	24
	1,200		1,200

Cash Book

19...	£	19...	
Jun 30 Excess Credit Co.	1,176		

Commissions Paid A/c

19...	£	
Mar 31 Excess Credit Co.	24	

Many large hotel groups now issue their own credit cards,which function in a similiar way to those described above except that the group head office will arrange the collection of the debt.

Bank Reconciliation Statements

Periodically, usually once a month, a business will receive a loose-leaf statement from its bank.This will show the balance of cash at the beginning of the period, any amounts paid in or withdrawn and the balance of cash at the end of the period. The bank statement is a copy of the customer's account in the books of the bank and, in theory, should contain entries identical with those in the cash book of the business. In practice, it will be found that the balance shown by the bank statement and that in the cash book rarely agree, since:

- cheques sent to suppliers and credited in the cash book may not have been presented for payment and will therefore not appear on the bank statement;
- cheques, etc received by the business, debited in the cash book and paid into the bank may not yet have been credited by the bank to the account of that business;
- the bank statement may contain items which do not appear in the cash book, e.g. bank charges, interest, or standing orders;
- errors may have arisen in either the cash book or (which is less likely) in the bank statement.

As the two balances rarely agree, it is usual to reconcile them by drawing up what is known as a bank reconciliation statement. Before this is done, it is usual to examine the bank statement and enter in the cash book all items of bank charges, interest or standing orders. The bank reconciliation is then prepared and the cash book balanced.

EXAMPLE 3.5

The cash book of the Crown Hotel Ltd is shown below:

Dr				Cash Book			Cr
Date			Bank	Date		Chq. No.	Bank
19...			£	19...			£
Jan	1	Balance b/d	10,000	Jan	2	Properties Ltd 501	2,200
"	6	Sales	1,500	"	8	H & C Ltd 502	500
"	11	Sales	2,000	"	9	B Brown & Co 503	800
"	24	Sales	1,800	"	4	H H Smith 504	1,100
				"	19	V May & Co 505	300
				"	27	A S Foods Ltd 506	400
				"	29	W Cramer 507	600
				"	30	A Grocer & Co 508	500

At the end of the period the bank statement in Figure 3.4 is received.

The bank reconciliation statement of the hotel would be prepared on the following lines:

The cash book shows a debit balance of £8,900 (the difference between the Dr and Cr totals of the cash book). An examination of the bank statement shows bank charges of £50. This would have to be credited in the cash book and debited in the bank charges account in the ledger. The cash book balance would thus be reduced to £8,850.

The next step is to reconcile the two balances, £8,850 and £10,450, i.e. to explain how the difference has arisen. This may be done by starting with the cash book balance and arriving at the balance per bank statement or vice versa. The second alternative will now be used.

BANK STATEMENT

Crown Hotel Ltd 17 Hill Lane WS7 4ES		In account with EASTMINSTER BANK PLC 13 Uphill Drive WS5 4XC		
Date	For customers use	Debit	Credit	Balance
19 . . .		£	£	£
Jan 1	Balance c/f			10,000
" 4	501	2,200		7,800
" 6	Cash		1,500	9,300
" 11	502	500		8,800
" 11	Cash		2,000	10,800
" 17	504	1,100		9,700
" 24	Cash		1,800	11,500
" 29	506	400		11,100
" 31	CH	50		11,050
" 31	507	600		10,450
ABBREVIATIONS BGC – Bank Giro Credit IN – Interest DDR – Direct Debit CH – Charges/Commissions SO – Standing Orders ATM – Cash Machine withdrawal				

Figure 3.4 Crown Hotel's bank statement

Bank reconciliation statement as at 31st January 19...

Balance per bank statement dated 31 Jan 19...				£10,450
<u>Add</u> bank charges				<u>50</u>
				10,500
<u>Less</u> Unpresented cheques				
B Brown & Co.	503		£800	
V May & Co.	505		300	
A Grocer & Co.	508		<u>500</u>	<u>1,600</u>
Cash book balance as at above date				<u>£8,900</u>

Had the bank charges been deducted from the cash book balance before drawing up the bank reconciliation statement the latter would have been done as follows:

Bank reconciliation statement as at 31st January 19...

Balance per statement dated 31 Jan 19...				£10,450
<u>Less</u> Unpresented Cheques				
B Brown & Co.	503		£800	
V May & Co.	505		300	
A Grocer & Co.	508		<u>500</u>	<u>1,600</u>
Cash book balance as at above date				<u>£8,850</u>

SUMMARY

- The simplest form of cash book is the single column cash book which is not widely used. The double column cash book is the more popular account.
- The petty cash book records the payment of small items of expenditure and normally operates on the imprest system. This means the cashier starts with a fixed sum of money which is replenished at the end of each week or month.
- Discount received: suppliers often offer a discount for prompt payment of bills. This serves to reduce the amount due and is clearly recorded in the accounts.
- The cash received book is purely a subsidiary book, used for convenience, and does not form part of the double entry system.
- Many smaller establishments use a multi-column cash book which makes the best use of a limited book-keeping system.
- There are two main types of business bank account – (a) current account (b) deposit account.
- Credit cards are widely used for payment of accounts and a strict acceptance procedure must be followed.
- Bank reconciliation statements are necessary because the cash book (situated in the business itself) and its bank account at the bank will rarely balance without adjustment.

PROBLEMS

1. Explain what you understand by the 'imprest system' as applied to the petty cash book. Give a specimen ruling of a petty cash book with five analysis columns.

2. Lisa Hoffmann runs a busy guest house and has always kept a double column cash book.

She had the following balances on 1st June 19...
Cash balance   DM430   Bank balance   DM5,770
The following transactions took place in the month of June:

			DM
June	1	Purchased food, paid by cheque	650
"	2	Paid printer's bill in cash	130
"	7	Banked cash sales	750
"	9	Paid gas bill by cheque	160
"	11	Paid casual wages in cash	195
"	15	Withdrew cash from bank for office use	400
"	19	Paid rates for month by cheque	250
"	22	Banked cash sales	815
"	24	Paid for local advertising by cheque	210
"	25	Paid chef's travel expenses in cash	85
"	28	Purchased food paid by cheque	500
"	29	Paid staff taxis by cash	65
"	30	Paid wages for month by cheque	940
"	30	Banked cash sales	1,050

Required:
(a) Draw up a two column cash book and enter all transactions for the month of June.
(b) Close off the cash book and carry the balance down to July.

3. Explain how double entry is completed in respect of discounts received from suppliers.

4. Explain the difference between a current account and a deposit account.

5. Write short explanatory notes on each of the following: bearer cheques; open cheques; crossed cheques; general crossing; special crossing.

6. Explain the position with regard to the endorsement of cheques.

7. B A Branson commenced business as a snack bar proprietor. His capital on 1st January 19... consisted of:

	£
Cash at bank	79,600
Cash in hand	400
Total	80,000

The following were Branson's transactions in January:

				£
Jan	1	Paid by cheque for food		800
"	2	Paid by cheque for:	cash register	2,400
			furniture	7,200
			kitchen utensils	5,200
"	4	Bought food paid by cheque		1,000
"	6	Banked cash sales		1,500
"	8	Cash payments:	cleaning materials	80
			stationery	10
			travelling expenses	20
"	14	Banked cash sales		600
"	16	Paid wages by cheque		900
"	18	Paid by cheque for food		2,200
"	21	Cash payments:	stationery	40
			food	60
			postage stamps	40
"	23	Banked cash sales		1,700
"	24	Withdrew from bank for office use		400
"	26	Paid water rates by cheque		600
"	27	Paid wages by cheque		840
"	28	Banked cash sales		700
"	30	Paid for advertising by cheque		1,120
"	31	Paid window cleaner in cash		80

Required:

(a) Enter the above transactions in Branson's double column cash book.

(b) Post to the ledger.

(c) Extract his trial balance as at 31st January 19...

8. Design a petty cash book to show expenditure under the headings of: postage and stationery; travelling expenses; food; miscellaneous expenses. Enter the following in your petty cash book and balance it as at 6th June 19...

			$
June	1	Balance b/d	300.00
"	1	Bought postage stamps	31.50
"	2	Paid messenger's fares	7.35
"	2	Bought envelopes	9.30
"	3	Paid for flowers	24.60
"	3	Paid chef's fares for week	43.80
"	4	Paid tip to delivery man	2.70
"	4	Paid for coffee	13.35
"	5	Paid for recorded delivery parcels	16.35
"	5	Paid for strawberries	24.90
"	6	Paid for stationery	3.60
"	6	Bought cleaning materials	32.25

9. Describe the procedure to be followed before accepting a credit card as payment of an account.

10. What is the object of a bank reconciliation statement? Draw up a bank reconciliation statement from the following information

	£
Cash book balance as at 31st March 19...	4,410
Bank statement as at 31st March 19...	4,810
Unpresented cheques	1,170
Loan interest paid to bank, not entered in cash book	700
Amounts paid in to bank, but not credited by bank until 3rd April 19...	1,470

11. From the cash book and bank statement given below prepare a bank reconciliation statement as at 31st January 19...

Cash Book

19...			£	19...				£
Jan	1	Balance	20,000	Jan	1	H & C Ltd	001	3,000
"	3	Sales	4,000	"	4	Wages	002	2,000
"	7	B Brown	2,000	"	6	H M & Co.	003	1,000
"	11	Sales	6,000	"	10	Equipe Ltd	004	4,000
"	16	G Gray	3,000	"	14	Wages	005	1,000
"	21	Sales	8,000	"	18	H M & Co.	006	2,500
"	27	Sales	4,000	"	22	Wages	007	2,000
"	31	W Green	3,000	"	29	Cater Co.	008	500
				"	31	H & C Ltd	009	2,000

Bank Statement

19...			Dr £	Cr £	Balance £
Jan	1	Balance			20,000
"	3	001	3,000		17,000
"	4	Cash		4,000	21,000
"	5	002	2,000		19,000
"	8	Cash		2,000	21,000
"	10	003	1,000		20,000
"	12	Cash		6,000	26,000
"	15	005	1,000		25,000
"	17	Cash		3,000	28,000
"	20	006	2,500		25,500
"	22	Cash		8,000	33,500
"	23	007	2,000		31,500
"	28	Cash		4,000	35,500
"	31	Chgs	100		35,400

12. Set out below are the cash book and bank statement for the Addams Hotel for the month ending 30th April 19...

You are required to prepare a bank reconciliation statement as at 30th April 19... .

Cash Book

19...		£	19...		£
Apr 1	Balance	15,200	Apr 1	Brooks & Co.	1,100
" 4	Sales	4,500	" 3	F & D Co. Ltd	2,850
" 6	H Clinton	1,150	" 7	Wages	1,800
" 10	R Reeves	950	" 12	Hotel Equipe Ltd	5,800
" 14	Sales	3,700	" 15	Smith & West	2,950
" 19	B Black	1,450	" 18	Euro Wines Ltd	1,450
" 24	Sales	4,800	" 20	Wages	1,850
" 28	S Shivers	850	" 25	Euro Wines Ltd	2,100
			" 26	In-Food Ltd	2,300
			" 29	Wages	1,940

Bank Statement

19...			Dr	Cr	Balance
			£	£	£
Apr	1	Balance			15,200
"	3	950001	1,100		14,100
"	5	Cash		4,500	18,600
"	8	950003	1,800		16,800
"	9	Credit		1,150	17,950
"	10	950002	2,850		15,100
"	14	Credit		950	16,050
"	15	Cash		3,700	19,750
"	17	950004	5,800		13,950
"	19	SO	500		13,450
"	20	Credit		1,450	14,900
"	20	950005	1,450		13,450
"	21	950006	1,850		11,600
"	23	SO	1,000		10,600
"	25	Cash		4,800	15,400
"	27	950007	2,300		13,100
"	30	950008	1,940		11,160
"	30	CH	120		11,040

Accounting for purchases

4

INTRODUCTION

From an accounting point of view 'purchases' is the name we give to the goods that we buy with the clear intention of reselling them. Only such goods will be entered in the purchases account. For catering businesses this will usually mean only food and beverages. All other acquisitions such as equipment or furniture will be entered into their own individual account and not treated as 'purchases'.

The purchases of a business fall into two categories: cash purchases and credit purchases. When food, beverages, etc. are purchased for cash, there is an immediate exchange of cash for the commodities purchased: all that needs to be recorded in the books of a business is, therefore, the payment of the purchase price and the acquisition of the goods purchased.

When food, beverages, etc. are purchased on credit, the business acquires the commodities concerned but the settlement of the purchase price (i.e. payment of the amount due) is delayed until several weeks (or sometimes months) later. In the meantime a debt exists from the business to the supplier of the goods (creditor) and this must be reflected in the supplier's account in the ledger.

OBJECTIVES

On completion of this chapter you should be able to:

- understand the meaning of cash and credit purchases;
- enter cash and credit purchase transactions into the accounts;
- differentiate between cash discount and trade discount;
- understand the purpose of and be able to draw up a Purchases Day Book;
- understand the purpose of and be able to draw up a Purchases Returns Book;
- recognize and know the purpose of an invoice, credit note and supplier's statement.

CASH PURCHASES

The treatment of cash purchases is simple. All payments made in respect of food, beverages, tobaccos, etc. purchased for cash are credited in the cash book and debited in the purchases account. For example, if a hotel buys food worth £50 for cash, the double entry will be made as follows:

		Cash Book			
19...		£	19...		£
			Apr 23	Purchases	50.00

		Purchases A/c		
19...		£		
Apr 23	Cash	£50.00		

It will be observed that no entry is made in the personal account of the supplier. The transaction is fully settled and, thus, the identity of the supplier is of no consequence.

CREDIT PURCHASES

When goods are purchased on credit, the payment of the amount due to the supplier does not take place until some time after the delivery of such goods. In the meantime, the supplier of the goods is a creditor to the business in that money is owing to him in respect of the goods with which he has parted. The debt due to the supplier is represented by a credit entry in his personal account. Double entry in respect of credit purchases is given below:

		Food Suppliers Ltd			
19...		£	19...		£
			Apr 23	Purchases	50.00

		Purchases A/c		
19...		£	19...	£
Apr 23	Food Suppliers Ltd	50.00		

Whenever goods are purchased on credit the buyer receives, either together with the goods or a few days later, an **invoice.** This shows particulars of the goods, such as the quantity, price per unit, description, and the total amount due.

Hospitality establishments which are sufficiently large in size purchase

HOTEL AND CATERING SUPPLIERS LTD
5 WEST END LANE, LONDON WE5 7QR

TO: Imperial Hotel Ltd,
Leicester Square,
London WE4 9SE

INVOICE NO. 7361
16th June 1997

	Size	Quantity	Price per Unit	£
XL Cafe Blend Coffee	0.5 Kg	20 Kg	£14.00	280.00
Olive Oil	5 L	50 L	£8.00	400.00
SMF Beans	1 Kg	10 Kg	£6.00	60.00
				740.00
Less Trade Discount 10%				74.00
			Net Due	666.00

Figure 4.1 Specimen invoice

from wholesalers rather than retailers. In such circumstances a **trade discount** is often allowed by the supplier. This is a deduction from the amount due and would only be extended to establishments buying sufficiently large quantities. Trade discount is **not** recorded in the books: all goods purchased are entered net, after deduction of trade discount.

A specimen invoice is given in Figure 4.1.

PURCHASES DAY BOOK

As already mentioned, double entry in respect of credit purchases is completed by debiting the purchases account and crediting the account of the supplier. It will be appreciated, however, that the number of invoices received is usually very large; many hospitality establishments receive hundreds of invoices each month. It would, therefore, be inconvenient to debit each separate invoice in the purchases account and, also, unusual to show this amount of detail in the ledger.

Consequently, purchase invoices are recorded as follows:

1. All invoices, having been numbered consecutively, are entered individually in a subsidiary book known as the **purchases day book.**
2. Double entry is completed by:
   (a) crediting the invoices in the accounts of suppliers individually;
   (b) debiting the periodical (weekly, monthly) total of the purchases day book in the purchases account.

In this way the number of debit entries in the purchases account is reduced considerably. As double entry is completed in the ledger, the entering of invoices in the purchases day book does not count for double entry purposes.

EXAMPLE 4.1

The following invoices are received by the Kensington Restaurant:

			£
Jan	1	B Baker & Sons	550
"	3	A G Grocer & Co.	250
"	5	H & C Suppliers Ltd	200
"	8	B Baker & Sons	450
"	11	A G Grocer & Co.	350
"	14	Food Sellers Ltd	50
"	17	H & C Suppliers Ltd	100
"	20	B Baker & Sons	150
"	24	H & C Suppliers Ltd	500
"	27	Food Sellers Ltd	300
"	29	A G Grocer & Co	200
"	31	Food Sellers Ltd	250

The invoices are entered in the purchases day book of the restaurant and posted to appropriate accounts in the ledger.

When posting, the folio number of the purchases day book is entered in the account concerned and the folio number of the purchases account is entered in the purchases day book.

Purchases Day Book 27

Date			Invoice Number	Ledger Folio	£
Jan	1	B Baker & Sons	1	L/51	550.00
"	3	A G Grocer & Co.	2	L/53	250.00
"	5	H & C Suppliers Ltd	3	L/55	200.00
"	8	B Baker & Sons	4	L/51	450.00
"	11	A G Grocer & Co.	5	L/53	350.00
"	14	Food Sellers Ltd	6	L/57	50.00
"	17	H & C Suppliers Ltd	7	L/55	100.00
"	20	B Baker & Sons	8	L/51	150.00
"	24	H & C Suppliers Ltd	9	L/55	500.00
"	27	Food Sellers Ltd	10	L/57	300.00
"	29	A G Grocer & Co.	11	L/53	200.00
"	31	Food Sellers Ltd	12	L/57	250.00
"	31	Trans. to Purchases A/c		L/106	3,350.00

B Baker & Sons

19...			PB	£
Jan	1	Purchases	27	550.00
"	8	"	27	450.00
"	20	"	27	150.00

A G Grocer & Co.

19...			PB	£
Jan	3	Purchases	27	250.00
"	11	"	27	350.00
"	29	"	27	200.00

H & C Suppliers Ltd

19...			PB	£
Jan	5	Purchases	27	200.00
"	17	"	27	100.00
"	24	"	27	500.00

Food Sellers Ltd

19...			PB	£
Jan	14	Purchases	27	50.00
"	27	"	27	300.00
"	31	"	27	250.00

Purchases A/c   106

19...		PB	£
Jan 31	Sundries	27	3,350.00

PURCHASES RETURNS

Sometimes goods which have previously been purchased have to be returned to the seller. This may be necessary when they are found to be defective in quality or damaged. Again, sometimes the seller overcharges for the goods. As a result, it often becomes necessary for a supplier to reduce the amount charged on an invoice already sent to a customer. This is done by means of a **credit note**.

A specimen credit note is shown in Figure 4.2.

Note: It is assumed that the invoice dated 1st September 1995 was not subject to a trade discount. Otherwise the percentage of trade discount would have to be deducted from the amount of the above credit note.

The accounting treatment of credit notes is as follows:

1. All credit notes, having been numbered consecutively, are entered individually in a subsidiary book, called the **purchases returns book.**
2. Double entry is completed by:
   (a) debiting the credit notes in the accounts of suppliers individually;

HOTEL AND CATERING SUPPLIERS LTD
5, WEST END LANE, LONDON WE5 7QR

To: Imperial Hotel Ltd,　　　　　　　　　CREDIT NOTE
　　Leicester Square,
　　London WE4 9SE　　　　　　　　　29th December 1996

		£
By Overcharge per invoice dated 1 September 1996		
Amount Charged –	£20.00	
Less Correct Charge –	£15.00	
		5.00

Figure 4.2 Specimen credit note

(b) crediting the periodical (weekly, monthly) total of the purchases returns account in the ledger.

At the end of the accounting period the balance of the purchases returns account is transferred to the purchases account. The latter will thus show the net purchases for the period concerned.

EXAMPLE 4.2

A hotel receives the following credit notes during the month of January 19...

			£
Jan	6	Brompton Food Market	90.00
"	13	XYZ Wines Co	80.00
"	25	Brompton Food Market	60.00
"	31	BSL Grocers	85.00

The above credit notes are entered in the purchases returns book of the hotel and posted to the appropriate ledger accounts.

Purchases Returns Book　　　　　　　　　　　　　　32

Date			C/N. No	Ledg.F.	£
Jan	6	Brompton Food Market	1	L/77	90.00
"	13	XYZ Wine Co	2	L/79	80.00
"	25	Brompton Food Market	3	L/77	60.00
"	31	BSL Grocers	4	L/81	85.00
"	31	Trans. to Purchases Returns A/c		L/109	315.00

Brompton Food Market				77
19...		PR	£	
Jan 6	Returns	32	90.00	
" 25	"	32	60.00	

XYZ Wines Co.				79
19. . .		PR	£	
Jan 13	Returns	32	80.00	

BSL Grocers				81
19. . .		PR	£	
Jan 31	Returns	32	85.00	

Purchases Returns A/c				109
	19. . .		PR	£
	Jan 31 Sundries		32	315.00

SUPPLIERS' STATEMENTS

Most suppliers who sell goods on credit send their customers a statement of account (usually monthly). This is a copy of the buyer's account in the books of the supplier and shows particulars of invoices and any credit notes sent to the customer, any cash received and, of course, the balance due to the supplier at the end of the period.

It is usual to check all suppliers' statements against their accounts in the ledger. Any cash discount offered should then be deducted before payment is made. The treatment of cash discounts was explained in Chapter 3. A specimen statement of account is shown in Figure 4.3.

HOTEL AND CATERING SUPPLIERS LTD 5, WEST END LANE, LONDON WE5 7QR		
To: Imperial Hotel Ltd, Leicester Square, London WE4 9SE	Statement 30th June 1997	
Terms: 5% Monthly		
Date		£
June 1	Goods	160.00
" 6	"	96.00
" 16	"	144.00
" 28	"	80.00
		480.00
" 12	Returns	40.00
	Balance due	440.00

Figure 4.3 Specimen statement of account

Assuming that this statement is paid within one month (i.e. before the end of July), a cash discount of £22.00 would be deducted from the amount due and a cheque for £418.00 drawn in favour of the supplier.

EXAMPLE 4.3

The following transactions took place between a hotel and Hotel Supplies Co.

			£
Jan	1	Goods purchased	400
"	4	"	300
"	13	"	400
"	21	"	500
"	27	Goods returned	100
"	31	Goods purchased	500
Feb	2	"	400
"	10	Cash paid to supplier	1,900
"	10	Discount received from supplier	100

The account of Hotel Supplies Co. is written up in the ledger of the hotel; and the account balanced as at the end of January.

Hotel Supplies Co.

19. . .			£	19. . .			£
Jan	27	Returns	100	Jan	1	Purchases	400
"	31	Balance c/d	2,000	"	4	"	300
				"	13	"	400
				"	21	"	500
				"	31	"	500
			2,100				2,100
19. . .				19. . .			
Feb	10	Cash	1,900	Feb	1	Balance b/d	2,000
"	10	Disc.Recd	100	"	2	Purchases	400

THE JOURNAL

An important rule of book-keeping is that all entries relating to transactions should be recorded in subsidiary books prior to being posted to the ledger. Thus purchase invoices are entered in the purchases day book and then posted to the ledger. Similarly, copies of restaurant bills signed by customers are entered in the restaurant sales book and then posted to the sales account and the accounts of the customers concerned.

There are, however, several classes of transaction which cannot be entered in any of the subsidiary books already dealt with; all such transactions are entered in what is variously described as the journal, the general journal or the journal proper.

Let us assume that a hotel buys kitchen equipment on credit for £10,000. This, not being intended for resale, does not constitute the hotel's 'purchases' and cannot, therefore, be entered in the hotel's purchases day book. Consequently, a journal entry must be made. This is shown below:

Journal   26

19...		Ledger	£	£
May 1	Kitchen Equipment A/c	94	10,000	
	XYZ Co. Ltd	23		10,000
	Being sundry items of			
	equipment purchased			
	per invoice K.S.6794.			

Notes:
(a) The account to be debited is entered first.
(b) Every entry in the journal is followed by a brief explanation of the transaction. This is known as the **narration** and usually starts with the word being.

When the entry in the journal has been made, it is possible to post the transaction to the ledger. Following the example, double entry in the ledger would be completed as shown:

Kitchen Equipment A/c   94

19. . .		J	£
May 1	XYZ Co. Ltd	26	10,000

XYZ Co. Ltd   23

19. . .		J	£
May 1	Kit. Equipment	26	10,000

As already mentioned, the journal is used for several types of transaction. Let us, therefore, now examine the main uses of the journal.

Journal opening entries

When, for one reason or another, a new set of books is being opened, the opening balances are journalized prior to being posted to the ledger.

Naturally, the occasions when journal opening entries are required are very infrequent. They are **not** necessary at the beginning of each accounting period, because the balances from the previous period are brought down.

Sometimes a business is purchased as a 'going concern' when, at the commencement of the new business, there are already in existence numerous assets and liabilities. A journal opening entry is then useful in that it enables one to calculate the capital of the new business easily and accurately before any ledger entries are made.

EXAMPLE 4.4

On 1st January 19..., Vera Bright commenced in business as a guest house proprietor with the following assets and liabilities:

	£
Freehold premises	100,000
Furniture and equipment	20,000
China and cutlery	2,500
Food stocks	500
Cash at bank	3,000
Creditors: ABC Ltd	500
DEF Ltd	500

The necessary journal opening entries are made and Miss Bright's capital ascertained as follows:

Journal

19...			L	£	£
Jan 1	Freehold Property	Dr		100,000	
	Furniture and Equipment	Dr		20,000	
	China and Cutlery	Dr		2,500	
	Food Stocks	Dr		500	
	Cash at Bank	Dr		3,000	
	Creditors: A.B.C Ltd				500
	D.E.F. Ltd				500
	Capital				125,000
				126,000	126,000
	Being assets and liabilities as at this date.				

Credit purchase/sale of assets

The credit purchase of an asset has already been illustrated and a further example need not, therefore, be given. Sometimes circumstances arise which necessitate the sale of an asset, e.g. when the asset is being replaced by a new one.

EXAMPLE 4.5

On 19th March 19... a hotel's restaurant furniture, standing in the books at £5,000 is sold on credit to Popular Catering Ltd. The entry necessary in the journal is shown below:

Journal

19...			L	£	£
Mar 19	Popular Catering Ltd	Dr		5,000	
	Restaurant Furniture				5,000
	Being sale of restaurant furniture per agreement dated				

SUMMARY

- There are two kinds of business purchases: cash purchases and credit purchases.
- Only goods purchased for resale should be recorded in the purchases account. i.e. food, beverages and tobaccos.
- Trade discount is never recorded in the books of account. Only the net amount is shown.
- Because of the large number of invoices received each accounting period it would not be practical to enter each one individually into the purchases account. Therefore a purchases day book is used for initial entry.
- The purchases day book does not form part of the double entry book-keeping system.
- Occasionally it is necessary to return goods to the suppliers. They will forward a credit note which, in the first instance, is entered in the purchases returns book. At the end of period the total of returns is entered in the ledger.
- Every entry relating to a transaction must be entered in a subsidiary book before being entered in the accounts.
- Unusual transactions which clearly cannot be entered in other subsidiary books should be entered in the journal.
- Opening entries, sales of fixed assets and rectification of errors are good examples of entries to be journalized.

PROBLEMS

1. Distinguish clearly between cash discount and trade discount.

2. Write short notes on the purpose of: invoice, credit note and statement of account.

3. The following invoices and credit notes are received in the month of April by the Appleby Manor Hotel:

				£
Apr	1	Food Wholesalers	Invoice	750
"	3	Smith & West (Foods) Ltd	Invoice	480
"	6	Euro Wines Ltd	Invoice	870
"	9	Food Wholesalers	Credit note	110
"	11	Food Wholesalers	Invoice	690
"	13	Smith & West (Foods) Ltd	Credit note	100
"	15	Smith & West (Foods) Ltd	Invoice	520
"	18	Euro Wines Ltd	Invoice	550
"	22	Food Wholesalers	Invoice	580
"	25	Euro Wines Ltd	Credit note	130
"	28	Smith & West (Foods) Ltd	Invoice	220
"	30	Euro Wines Ltd	Invoice	360

Required:
(a) Enter the above invoices and credit notes into the correct day books.
(b) At the end of the month post them to the appropriate ledger accounts.

4. On 1st December 19... after eleven months' trading, Jack Mason had the following balances in his books:

	£
Capital	44,000
Sales	35,000
Purchases	12,400
Cash at bank	16,800
Premises	34,500
Wages	7,400
China and cutlery	1,600
Furniture	2,500
Insurance	300
Kitchen equipment	5,000
Gas and electricity	1,500
Creditors: V A Rigby	1,000
O Kay	2,000

Arrange these in the form of a trial balance and enter balances in accounts. Mason's transactions in December were:

			£
Dec	6	Purchased food by cheque	3,000
"	10	Paid for kitchen equipment by cheque	1,000
"	14	Paid amount due to O Kay	2,000
"	16	Banked sales to date	1,700
"	19	Paid wages by cheque	1,200
"	23	Paid rates by cheque	1,540
		Bought food on credit: V A Rigby	2,400
		A M Williams	1,200
"	27	Paid by cheque for insurance to 31.3.19...	300
"	31	Banked sales to date	2,820

Enter these transactions in Mason's books and extract a trial balance as at 31st December 19...

5. On 1st January 19..., Luigi Monteforte started in business with a capital at the bank of £150,000. In January, his transactions were:

			£
Jan	1	Paid by cheque rent for premises	33,000
"	2	Paid by cheque for furniture	6,000
"	4	Paid by cheque for kitchen equipment	12,000
"	6	Paid wages by cheque	1,950
"	8	Credit purchases: F W Young & Co	990
		V Fatt & Son	660
		Jack Player & Son	480
"	10	Banked cash sales	1,710
"	14	Paid by cheque for food	1,080
"	19	Paid wages by cheque	1,980
"	22	Credit purchases: Jack Player & Son	390
		V Fatt & Son	810
		F W Young & Co	1,380
"	23	Paid by cheque for stationery	360
"	25	Credit purchases: F W Young & Co.	780
		Five Squares Ltd	450
		V Fatt & Son	570
"	26	Banked cash sales	6,570
"	28	Paid wages by cheque	2,160
"	29	Paid for advertising by cheque	1,500
"	30	Received credit notes from: V Fatt & Son	150
		F W Young & Co	90
		Jack Player & Son	120
"	31	Banked cash sales	3,480
"	31	Paid by cheque for food	990

Required:

(a) Enter the above transactions in appropriate day books.

(b) Post to ledger and extract Monteforte's trial balance as at 31st January 19...

6. On 1st July 19..., J Jones started in business as a restaurateur. His assets and liabilities were:

	£
Premises	349,500
Kitchen plant	73,500
Restaurant furniture	36,900
Glass and china	9,600
Stock of food	3,300
Cash at bank	30,600
Cash in hand	600
Creditors	12,900

You are required to make the necessary journal opening entry and ascertain his capital.

7. Jack Lane commenced business on 1st January 19... as a café proprietor with £120,000 in the bank.

His transactions in January were as follows:

			£
Jan	1	Purchased leasehold premises by cheque	81,000
"	2	Purchased furniture paid by cheque	3,000
"	3	Withdrew for petty cash	1,200
"	3	Paid by cheque for fruit and veg	2,220
"	4	Received invoices from:	
		A N B Grocers Ltd	2,100
		O K Provisions Ltd	2,520
		B S Fish & Sons	960
"	7	Paid wages by cheque	2,340
"	8	Paid by cheque for kitchen equipment	12,600
"	9	Paid out of petty cash:	
		stationery	180
		postage	120
		cleaning materials	120
"	10	Banked sales	7,500
"	11	Invoices received from:	
		O K Provisions Ltd	720
		B S Fish & Sons	1,140
		Battersea Fruiterers	1,080
"	14	Banked sales	8,160
"	15	Paid wages by cheque	2,760
"	17	Paid by cheque for food	1,260
"	19	Invoices received from:	
		A N B Grocers Ltd	1,560
		Battersea Fruiterers	780
		B S Fish & Sons	1,320

			£
Jan	21	Banked sales	10,560
"	23	Paid out of petty cash:	
		cleaning materials	180
		postage	180
		travelling expenses	60
"	24	Credit notes received from:	
		O K Provisions Ltd	180
		A N B Grocers Ltd	240
"	25	Paid wages by cheque	2,820
"	27	Banked sales	2,520
"	28	Paid by cheque for electricity	5,160
"	29	Petty cash payments:	
		stationery	120
		travelling expenses	60
"	30	Credit notes received from:	
		Battersea Fruiterers	300
		B S Fish & Sons	240
"	31	Paid wages by cheque	2,340

Required:
(a) Write up Lane's books in respect of the month of January 19...
(b) Extract his trial balance as at the end of that period

8. George Bacon is in business as a restaurateur. On 1st January 19... he decided to put his books on a double entry basis. His position then was:

	£
Leasehold premises	162,500
Stock of food	6,000
Loan from A Penny	50,000
China and cutlery	5,750
Restaurant furniture	20,750
Debtors: A G Jones	1,000
G M Browne	750
Creditors: ABC Co. Ltd	1,500
Wholesalers Ltd	4,000
Cash at bank	34,000
Cash in hand	1,000

You are required to set out the journal entry required for the opening of the books.

9. Jack Parker is in business as a café proprietor. On 1st January 19... he decided to put his books on a double entry basis. His assets and liabilities then were:

	£
	£
Freehold premises	£268,200
Furniture	15,900
Kitchen equipment	24,300
Cutlery and utensils	5,700
Creditors: XYZ Co. Ltd	1,500
J B Brown & Co.	600
Cash at bank	12,900
Stock of food	2,700

Set out the journal entry required to open Parker's books; open the necessary accounts and enter balances.

His transactions in January were:

			£
Jan	1	Purchased food, paid by cheque	3,000
"	5	Purchased additional kitchen equipment on credit from Equipment Suppliers Ltd	6,000
"	9	Banked cash sales	4,200
"	12	Paid wages by cheque	1,350
"	16	Paid XYZ Co. Ltd by cheque	1,500
"	18	Paid amount due to J B Brown & Co.	
"	20	Purchased food on credit from:	
		XYZ Co. Ltd	900
		J B Brown & Co.	1,200
"	22	Banked cash sales	4,500
"	24	Sold old furniture worth £1,500 on credit to the New Catering Co.	
"	24	Purchased new furniture on credit from Furniture Dealers Ltd	12,000
"	27	Purchased food on credit from:	
		J B Brown & Co.	600
		XYZ Co. Ltd	1,500
"	29	Paid wages by cheque	1,350
"	31	Banked cash sales	4,800

Required:

(a) Write up Parker's books (including the appropriate subsidiary books) in respect of January.

(b) Extract his trial balance as at the end of the month.

Accounting for sales $\boxed{5}$

INTRODUCTION

Accounting for sales is an important task for any business. This means making sure that the money you receive from your customers for goods and services rendered is properly accounted for and ends up safely in the establishment's bank account. From an accounting point of view it is important that all sales are recorded in some form. In larger hotels this is often achieved using a computer linked electronic billing system. This usually consists of a large number of 'point of sales' terminals situated throughout the hotel, e.g. in the bar, restaurant, kiosk etc. and connected to a central unit in the reception/accounts office. This allows a floor service waiter, for example, to 'type in' a customer charge from his station on the fifth floor and this is immediately and automatically charged to the customer's account in reception. If a manual system is in operation then the customer charge must be recorded by hand in duplicate with one copy going to the customer and one retained in the business for control purposes.

Computerized billing systems versus manual system

Recent research shows that the hospitality industry has been slow to move to any form of automated electronic billing although in very recent years, with the increased variety of equipment/software available, some inroads hav been made. Having said that, for the purposes of this textbook we will continue to concentrate on the manual system. All computer based systems are merely a mirror image of the tried and tested manual system and it is the authors' view that in order to effectively operate the automated system it is necessary to understand the original manual system, in particular the double entry relevant to the inflows of hotel revenue.

OBJECTIVES

On completion of this chapter you should be able to:

- enter a cash sale correctly into the books of account;
- enter a credit transaction correctly into the books of account;
- deal with transactions involving banqueting debtors;

- draw up a hotel visitors' ledger (tabular ledger);
- enter transactions correctly into the tabular ledger;
- carry out double entry from tabular ledger;
- understand the significance and uses of Monthly Summary Sheets;
- deal with advance deposits in the accounts;
- understand the meaning of inclusive terms, function sales and chance trade.

CASH SALES

The sales of a business may be of two kinds: cash sales and credit sales. A cash sale takes place when food, beverages, etc., are sold and the price is paid immediately. As soon as the price is paid by the customer, the transaction is fully settled. From the book-keeping point of view all that is needed is an entry in the cash book (to show that cash has been received) and an entry in the sales account (to show that something has been sold).

Hence, the double entry in respect of cash sales is:

Dr cash book

Cr sales account

EXAMPLE 5.1

On 1st April 19..., the cash sales of a restaurant amounted to £1,065 and were paid into the bank the same day. This is recorded in the books of the restaurant as shown:

				Cash Book			12
19. . . .		L.	£				
Apr 1	Sales	47	1,065				

				Sales A/c			47
				19. . .		CB	£
				Apr 1	Cash	12	1,065

CREDIT SALES

The treatment of credit sales is different and may vary from one type of hospitality establishment to another. Within a particular business, e.g. a hotel, there may be several distinct methods of recording credit sales. In general, however, credit sales in hospitality establishments fall into three main categories.

First, there are **restaurant sales.** These include all food, beverages, etc. sold on credit to non-residents, paying their accounts periodically (usually monthly). Next there are **banqueting sales.** These include all the banqueting sales in respect of which there is no immediate settlement. Finally, there are short-term credit sales to the guests of a hotel recorded in the **tabular** or **visitors' ledger.**

Restaurant sales

The general method of recording the credit sales of a restaurant is the same whether these are sales to non-residents dining in a hotel or expense account customers dining in a restaurant. Briefly, the procedure may be described as follows.

When the customer has been served, the waiter prepares a bill, usually in duplicate. This is signed by the customer, who takes the top copy of the bill. An example of a restaurant bill is shown in Figure 5.1.

	No. 116
BLUEBELL RESTAURANT 16 Second Ave, London WX 12	
Table No. 9	Date: 16th May 1997
Waiter No. 12	No. of covers: 2

		£
2 × Crème de Champignons		3.00
1 × Mixed Grill		9.00
1 × Escalope de Veau		11.75
2 × Pommes Sautées		2.00
2 × Haricots Verts		2.00
2 × Fruit Salad		3.00
	Total Meals	30.75
1 Bot. Nuits St. Georges 1990		14.50
1 Tia Maria		2.65
	Total Beverages	17.15
	Total	47.90
All figures are inclusive of VAT.		

Figure 5.1 Specimen restaurant bill

The second copy of the bill is sent to the accounts department. Here, all such bills in respect of credit sales are numbered consecutively and entered in a subsidiary book, the **restaurant sales book.**

Double entry is completed by debiting each individual bill in a customer's personal account and crediting the periodical (weekly or monthly) total of such sales in the sales account in the ledger.

EXAMPLE 5.2

The following are the credit sales of the Bluebell Restaurant:

			£
Jan	1	Midland Motors Ltd	75
"	2	Business Promotions Ltd	100
"	3	B M Blake Esq.	125
"	4	Midland Motors Ltd	300
"	4	Business Promotions Ltd	150
"	5	B M Blake Esq.	50
"	6	Midland Motors Ltd	200
"	7	Business Promotions Ltd	250

The above transactions are entered in the restaurant sales book and posted to ledger accounts.

Restaurant Sales Book   36

Date 19...		Bill No.	Ledg Fol.	£
Jan 1	Midland Motors Ltd	1	L.101	75.00
" 2	Business Promotions Ltd	2	L.103	100.00
" 3	B M Blake Esq.	3	L.104	125.00
" 4	Midland Motors Ltd	4	L.101	300.00
" 4	Business Promotions Ltd	5	L.105	150.00
" 5	B M Blake Esq.	6	L.104	50.00
" 6	Midland Motors Ltd	7	L.101	200.00
" 7	Business Promotions Ltd	8	L.103	250.00
" 7	Transferred to Sales A/c		L.201	1,250.00

Midland Motors Ltd   101

19...		SB	£	
Jan 1	Sales	36	75.00	
" 4	"	36	300.00	
" 6	"	36	200.00	

Business Promotions Ltd   103

19...		SB	£	
Jan 2	Sales	36	100.00	
" 4	"	36	150.00	
" 7	"	36	250.00	

B M Blake Esq.   104

19...		SB	£	
Jan 3	Sales	36	125.00	
" 5	"	36	50.00	

```
                    Sales A/c                           201
                         │ 19...              SB      £
                         │ Jan 7   Sundries   36    1,250.00
```

On receipt of the amount due from a customer, the cash book is debited and the account of the customer is credited. Thus, if Midland Motors paid the amount due on 31st January 19..., their account would appear as shown below:

```
                    Midland Motors Ltd                      101
19...              SB      £         │
Jan  1   Sales     36     75.00     │ Jan 31  Cash        575.00
 "   4    "         36    300.00     │
 "   6    "         36    200.00     │                    ───────
                         575.00      │                    575.00
```

Banqueting sales

From the point of view of the book-keeping involved, the treatment of banqueting sales proper is similar to that of the various functions such as wedding receptions, dinner parties, conferences, etc. We will, therefore, refer to all such sales as banqueting sales.

The arrangements with the client organizing the banquet may vary quite considerably. The organizer may agree to pay so much per cover for the meals only, in which event all drinks ordered by those taking part in the banquet would have to be paid for in cash. Any such drinks would be treated as bar cash sales or dispense bar sales.

Another common arrangement is for the organizer to agree to pay a given charge per cover for the meals and, additionally, request that a given number of bottles of wine be made available to members of the party. Then, both the meals and the wines are sold on credit.

Whatever the arrangements made, it is clear that a distinction should be made between what the organizer has agreed to pay for (credit sales) and any additional drinks, cigars and cigarettes required by particular members of the party and supplied on a cash basis.

The nature of the book-keeping records kept in respect of banqueting sales depends on the volume of banqueting business done and on the frequency of banquets undertaken for particular clients.

Where the volume of banqueting is small, it is sometimes the practice to treat all banqueting sales as if they were cash sales. No entries would then be made until such time as the client settled his account. The cash book would then be debited and the sales account credited with the amount received.

It must be pointed out that this procedure is not in accordance with the best accounting practice, as the books of the business do not reflect the true financial state of affairs.

Where the volume of banqueting business is substantial, it is usual to open a separate **banqueting sales book.** Particulars of banqueting credit sales are recorded in the same manner as are restaurant credit sales in the restaurant sales book.

Clients making frequent use of the banqueting facilities of the hotel/restaurant would have a proper ledger account opened for them. All such accounts would be posted in the same way as those illustrated in Example 5.2. Clients using the banqueting facilities infrequently (e.g. wedding receptions, twenty-first dinner parties, association annual dinners) may have a composite account opened for them, illustrated below:

Dr   Banqueting Debtors' A/c   Cr

Date		F	No. of covers	@	£	Extras £	Total £	Date		F	£
May 1	Mr & Mrs T Wedlock	61	20	30	600	200	800	May 6	Cash	CB	800
" 4	Miss D F Age	62	10	20	200	100	300	" 10	"	CB	300
" 9	XYZ Association	63	100	20	2,000	1,000	3,000	" 16	"	CB	3,000
" 18	Mr & Mrs A Wedmore	64	30	30	900		900				
" 22	Miss B Boner	65	50	30	1,500	100	1,600	" 29	"	CB	1,600
" 31	The '61 Society	66	50	30	1,500		1,500				

Whenever banqueting debtors settle their accounts a debit entry is made in the cash book and a corresponding credit entry in the banqueting debtors account. The total amount of outstanding debts may easily be determined by reference to the banqueting debtors account. In the above specimen account this amounts to £2,400.

Hotel visitors' ledger

The most convenient way of keeping the accounts of hotel guests is to maintain a hotel visitors' ledger, also known as the tabular ledger.

Of all the accounting records kept by hotels this is certainly the one in most common use either through a computer program or on a manual system and, therefore, deserves a more detailed description. Because of its layout, many students find difficulty in understanding how it is compiled and how it fits into the general scheme of double entry. These two aspects of the hotel visitors' ledger will, therefore, be dealt with first.

Figure 5.2 is a specimen of a typical hotel visitors' ledger:

Layout

The specimen visitors' ledger shown in Figure 5.2 may be divided horizontally into two sections: the upper section, including the totals and the lower section, including the second line of totals.

The upper section contains the debit side of visitors' accounts and is used to record the balances owing from visitors, brought forward from the previous day, and the charges made to visitors during the day concerned.

ROOM	1	2	3	4	5	6	7	8	9	10	
NAME	Fenton	Black	James	Stein	Dewey	Saxton	Turner	Weston	Bentley		DAILY SUMMARY
NO. OF VISITORS	1	1	2	2	1	2	2	1	1		
	£	£	£	£	£	£	£	£	£	£	£
Balance b/f	70.00	134.00	152.00	39.00	46.00	178.00	196.00	286.00			Balance b/f 1101.00
Apartments	30.00	30.00	50.00	50.00	30.00	50.00			30.00		Apartments 270.00
Breakfast	5.00	5.00	10.00	10.00	5.00	10.00	10.00	5.00			Breakfasts 60.00
E M Teas	2.00			4.00	2.00						E M Teas 8.00
Luncheons		12.00	31.00	34.00	15.00	36.00			14.00		Luncheons 142.00
Afternoon Teas	3.00		6.00		3.00	6.00			3.00		Afternoon Teas 21.00
Dinners	17.00	19.00		42.00		45.00			17.00		Dinners 140.00
Liquors		12.00		16.00		24.00			4.00		Liquors 56.00
Telephone	1.00		10.00		1.00						Telephone 12.00
Miscellaneous	8.00				10.00				25.00		Miscellaneous 43.00
Paid out		3.00		8.00		36.00					Paid Out 47.00
TOTAL	136.00	215.00	259.00	203.00	112.00	385.00	206.00	291.00	93.00		TOTAL 1900.00
Cash								291.00			Cash 291.00
Ledger							206.00				Ledger 206.00
Allowances					10.00						Allowances 10.00
Balance c/f	136.00	215.00	259.00	203.00	102.00	385.00		93.00	93.00		Balance c/f 1393.00
TOTAL	136.00	215.00	259.00	203.00	112.00	385.00	206.00	291.00	93.00		TOTAL 1900.00

Figure 5.2 Hotel visitors' ledger

The lower section contains the credit side of visitors' accounts and is used to record any cash paid by visitors in settling their accounts; any transfers from the visitors' ledger to a personal account in the sales ledger; allowances, if any, made to visitors; and the balances owing from visitors at the end of the current day carried forward to the following day.

Vertically, the visitors' ledger may also be divided into two sections: the personal accounts of visitors on the left-hand side and the somewhat smaller 'daily summary section' on the right-hand side. The latter shows the daily totals of entries made in the individual accounts of the guests.

Double entry

Although different from a conventional ledger, the visitors' ledger is a proper ledger, consisting of the personal accounts of the visitors. In fact, each of the visitors' accounts could be rewritten and presented as a conventional, double-sided account. Thus, Fenton's account could be rewritten as follows:

Fenton – Room 1

19...		£	19...		£
May 3	Balance b/d	70.00	May 3	Balance c/d	136.00
" 3	Sales	30.00			
" 3	"	5.00			
" 3	"	2.00			
" 3	"	3.00			
" 3	"	17.00			
" 3	"	1.00			
" 3	"	8.00			
		136.00			136.00
May 4	Balance b/d	136.00			

Charges debited to visitors are totalled in the last column of the visitors' ledger and, daily, transferred to the monthly summary sheet. This is totalled monthly and the individual totals posted to the appropriate accounts in the ledger. A specimen monthly summary sheet is given in Figure 5.3.

Monthly Summary Sheet   May 19...

Date	Apart-ments	Break-fasts	E.M. Teas	Lunches	A/noon teas	Dinners	Liqs	Tele-phone	Misc	Daily Total	Allow-ances
	£	£	£	£	£	£	£	£	£	£	£
May 1	300.00	65.00	12.00	226.00	42.00	192.00	99.00	33.00	19.00	988.00	15.00
" 2	260.00	70.00	7.00	172.00	34.00	162.00	63.00	6.00	32.00	806.00	
" 3	270.00	60.00	8.00	142.00	21.00	140.00	56.00	12.00	43.00	752.00	10.00
etc.											
May 31	8,800.00	960.00	400.00	6,000.00	800.00	7,600.00	900.00	900.00	950.00	27,310.00	200.00

Figure 5.3 Specimen monthly summary sheet

Notes:

(a) Column headings in the monthly summary sheet correspond with the sequence of charges in the hotel visitors' ledger.

(b) No column is provided for the paid-outs because (i) monthly summary sheet is a summary of sales, (ii) double entry in respect of paid-outs is completed by crediting the petty cash book and debiting visitors' accounts in the visitors' ledger.

Assuming that by the end of May the total of apartments sales is £8,800, this would be posted in the ledger as follows:

<table>
<thead>
<tr><th colspan="4" align="center">Sales A/c – Apartments</th></tr>
</thead>
<tbody>
<tr><td></td><td>19...</td><td></td><td align="right">£</td></tr>
<tr><td></td><td>Jan   31</td><td>MSS</td><td align="right">5,800.00</td></tr>
<tr><td></td><td>Feb 28</td><td>"</td><td align="right">6,800.00</td></tr>
<tr><td></td><td>Mar 31</td><td>"</td><td align="right">8,300.00</td></tr>
<tr><td></td><td>Apr 30</td><td>"</td><td align="right">8,600.00</td></tr>
<tr><td></td><td>May 31</td><td>"</td><td align="right">8,800.00</td></tr>
</tbody>
</table>

To sum up, double entry in respect of sales (charges) to visitors is completed by debiting the individual charges in the visitors' accounts in the visitors' ledger and crediting the monthly totals from the monthly summary sheet in the appropriate accounts in the ledger.

Any allowances made to guests should be properly authorized by the management. As may be seen from the specimen visitors' ledger (see Figure 5.2), these are credited in visitors' accounts (see Dewey, Room 5), entered in the allowances column of the monthly summary sheet and, at the end of each month, debited in the allowances account in the ledger.

The treatment of cash received from visitors is simple: the cash book is debited and the account of the visitor credited (see Weston, Room 8).

Sometimes a guest leaves the hotel without, for one reason or another, paying his account. When that happens there is, clearly, no point in keeping the guest's account in the visitors' ledger. The balance owing on the guest's departure is, therefore, transferred from the visitors' ledger to a personal account in the sales ledger.

In the specimen visitors' ledger given above, Turner left the hotel on 3rd May 19..., without settling his account. Consequently, his account in the visitors' ledger is credited with £206.00. The corresponding debit entry in his account in the sales ledger would appear as:

<table>
<thead>
<tr><th colspan="4" align="center">Turner</th></tr>
</thead>
<tbody>
<tr><td>19...</td><td></td><td align="right">£</td><td></td></tr>
<tr><td>May 3</td><td>Visitors' Ledger</td><td align="right">206.00</td><td></td></tr>
</tbody>
</table>

Assuming that a few weeks later Turner sends the hotel a cheque for £206.00 in settlement, this would be debited in the cash book and credited in his account, thus balancing the latter.

The monthly summary sheet (see Figure 5.3) is fairly typical of those used in hotels. It has, however, one serious deficiency: the allowances to customers are not analysed and, as a result, at the end of each month it is impossible to post figures of **net sales** to the ledger. **Gross sales** are posted to the credit of the various ledger accounts, and the total of monthly allowances to the debit of allowances account. In consequence, at the end of a trading period, it is impossible under this method to ascertain the exact amount of profit from any one department.

In order to remedy this, it is possible to maintain a monthly allowances sheet in conjunction with the monthly summary sheet. Under this method, allowances to visitors are analysed daily and totalled at the end of each month. They are then deducted from the gross sales in the monthly sheet. The resulting net sales are then posted to the ledger.

A specimen monthly allowances sheet is given in Figure 5.4.

Monthly Allowances Sheet   May 19...

Date	Apart-ments	Break-fast	EM Teas	Lunches	A/Noon Teas	Dinners	Liquors	Tele-phone	Misc.	Total
	£	£	£	£	£	£	£	£	£	£
May 1						8.00	7.00			15.00
" 3				5.00					5.00	10.00
etc.										
Monthly Total	40.00	20.00	30.00	10.00	10.00	40.00	30.00	10.00	10.00	200.00

Figure 5.4 Specimen monthly allowances sheet.

Monthly summary sheet   May 19...

Date	Apart-ments	Break-fast	EM Teas	Lunches	A/noon Teas	Dinners	Liqs	Tele-phone	Misc	Daily Total	Less Allow/s	Net Total
	£	£	£	£	£	£	£	£	£	£	£	£
May 1	300.00	65.00	12.00	226.00	42.00	192.00	99.00	33.00	19.00	988.00	15.00	973.00
" 2	260.00	70.00	7.00	172.00	34.00	162.00	63.00	6.00	32.00	806.00		806.00
" 3	270.00	60.00	8.00	142.00	21.00	140.00	56.00	12.00	43.00	752.00	10.00	742.00
	Etc											
Monthly Total	8,800.00	960.00	400.00	6,000.00	800.00	7,600.00	900.00	900.00	950.00	27,310.00	200.00	27,110.00
Less Allow-ances	40.00	20.00	30.00	10.00	10.00	40.00	30.00	10.00	10.00	200.00		
Net Total	8,760.00	940.00	370.00	5,990.00	790.00	7,560.00	870.00	890.00	940.00	27,110.00		

Figure 5.5 Monthly summary sheet

The monthly summary sheet shown in Figure 5.5 is a variant of the conventional type. Its main advantage is that it shows a figure of net sales for each section of the turnover.

It will be appreciated that when this type of monthly summary sheet is used there is no necessity for an allowances account in the ledger.

Sources of charges

The charges incurred by visitors may be numerous and arise in various parts of the hotel. The purpose of the present section is to explain where they originate and how they find their way to the visitors' accounts.

Apartments

This basic charge is incurred by all guests who stay at least one night. The charge originates in the reception office and is determined by reference to the room list or room index or the terms book. The charge is debited to the visitors' account as soon as such an account is opened. On subsequent days the charge is usually debited to the visitor each evening for the coming night's stay. In the specimen visitors' ledger (Figure 5.2) Turner (Room 7) and Weston (Room 8) left the hotel after breakfast. No charge for apartments is, therefore, debited to them. Bentley (Room 9) arrives before luncheon and is debited £30.00 in respect of the coming night's stay (3rd/4th May).

Clearly where a computer software package is used all the above stages are carried out automatically.

Meals

This heading, for the purpose of the visitors' ledger, includes all meals and non-alcoholic drinks, such as teas and coffees. In respect of each such meal if there is an automatic electronic billing system in operation, the waiter simply types in the customer's room number and charge which is automatically charged to the bill. In all other cases it is usual to raise a duplicate voucher, a copy of which is passed to the book-keeper for debiting a visitor's account. It is important, particularly in the case of short stay guests, that this is done as soon as possible. Otherwise a guest may leave the hotel before certain charges are debited. The second copy of such a voucher is usually passed on to the control office for checking purposes.

Drinks

This heading includes all alcoholic beverages and usually minerals. A charge in respect of drinks may originate in a dispense bar, a cocktail bar, or the lounge. The procedure adopted is the same as in the case of meals. It is usual for the person dispensing the drinks to price the voucher, though in some hotels this may be left to the book-keeper responsible for the visitors' ledger.

Sundry sales

In addition to the three basic charges – apartments, meals, and drinks – there are numerous other charges (e.g. telephone, laundry, valeting, garage, etc.) that may be incurred by a visitor. Here again, the general rule is that a voucher in duplicate must be made out and a copy thereof sent to the book-keeper for debiting the visitor's account.

Visitors' paid-outs

This heading includes various amounts paid out by the employees of the hotel on behalf of visitors. Examples of such paid-outs are theatre tickets, flowers and payments for COD mail addressed to the visitors. Any such payments would be credited to the petty cash book. A duplicate voucher would then be made out and a copy of it passed to the book-keeper for debiting the visitors' accounts.

It is important that a distinction be drawn between visitors' paid-outs and sundry sales. The former is a recovery of the hotel's payments and is not a part of current revenue; the latter is, of course, as much a part of the hotel's revenue as meals, drinks and other similar charges. It will be appreciated that what is a visitors' paid-out (VPO) in one hotel may well be regarded as a sundry sale in another. Thus where visitors' laundry is sent out, any charges made to them would normally be regarded as VPO. Where a hotel has a laundry of its own, any charges made to visitors would contain an element of profit and would, therefore, be regarded as sundry sales.

Guests' bills

In addition to opening an account in the visitors' ledger, the book-keeper will open a bill for each guest on arrival. Where a manual system operates, guests' bills are written up daily from the duplicate vouchers which are debited in the visitors' ledger.

It will be appreciated that, as identical charges are entered in the visitors' ledger and in the guests' bills, when all vouchers have been posted all balances in the visitors' ledger will correspond with the balances shown by guests' bills. In fact, as soon as all charges have been posted it is usual to compare the two sets of balances. Any differences should be investigated and put right before carrying the balances to the following day.

A specimen guest's bill is shown in Figure 5.6 – please note that for the sake of simplicity VAT has been excluded from the figures.

	2nd May	3rd May	4th May	
GRAND HOTEL LTD To: M A Jones Esq.			Room: 126	
	£	£	£	£
Balance b/f		76.00	129.50	
Apartments	25.00	25.00		
Breakfasts		5.00	5.00	
E M Teas				
Luncheons	37.50	15.50		
A/Noon Teas	3.50	3.00		
Dinners				
Liquors	6.50			
Telephone		5.00		
Miscellaneous				
Paid-outs	3.50			
Balance c/f	76.00	129.50	134.50	
Deposit				
Amount due			134.50	

Figure 5.6 Specimen guest's bill

Treatment of deposits

It is customary in many hotels to require deposits in respect of any advance bookings made by guests. Even where that is not so, some customers will send a deposit to ensure that a room is properly booked for them.

It must be realized that advance deposits do not represent current revenue (sales) but must be regarded as amounts owing to guests. It is not until such time as the guest arrives and incurs charges in excess of the deposit that the latter may be treated as current revenue.

There are several different methods of recording such deposits in the books of a hotel. One of the most popular methods is outlined as follows.

The deposit received is debited in the cash book and credited in a personal account opened for the intending visitor in the sales ledger. On the visitor's departure, the balance from the personal account (i.e. the deposit) must be transferred to the credit side of the account in the visitors' ledger.

Inclusive terms

Many hotels, particularly resort hotels, offer **inclusive** terms, that is inclusive of certain specified meals. There are two main methods of dealing with **inclusive** terms in the visitors' ledger.

Under the first method, the procedure is as follows:

1. The weekly inclusive charge is divided by seven to arrive at the daily charge.

2. The daily charge is debited in the visitors' ledger in an **inclusive terms** column (line). This additional column is usually placed between the 'balances b/f' column and the 'apartments' column.

From the visitors' ledgers the daily total of the inclusive charges would be transferred to an **inclusive terms** column of the monthly summary sheet, in the same manner as all other charges to visitors. Similarly, at the end of each month the total of inclusive charges in the monthly summary sheet would be posted to the credit of the **inclusive terms** sales account in the ledger.

Under the second method, the procedure is as follows:

1. The weekly inclusive charge is divided by seven to arrive at the daily charge.
2. The daily charge is divided into a number of component parts (e.g. apartments, breakfast, luncheon, dinner) according to what is included in the terms.
3. Each separate component part of the inclusive charge is debited in the visitors' ledger in the usual manner.

EXAMPLE 5.3

The **inclusive** terms of a hotel are £315.00 per week. On the basis of past experience the apportionment is: food – 66.67 per cent; apartments – 33.33 per cent.

Following the second method above:

the daily charge is $\dfrac{£315.00}{7}$ = £45.00

Of the daily charge:	the charge for apartments	= £15.00
	the charge for food	= £30.00

Assuming that the **inclusive** terms include breakfast, lunch and dinner, the £30.00 charged for food might then be apportioned as follows:

	£
Breakfast	5.00
Lunch	11.00
Dinner	14.00
Total	30.00

This second method is preferable to the first as, due to the analysis of the inclusive charge, all sales to visitors are recorded in a uniform manner. On the other hand, it is clear that the analysis of the inclusive charge is to an extent a matter of judgement, as there is no precise method of determining how much of the total should be credited to food and how much to apartments. It may be added that most hotels credit about one-third of the **inclusive terms** charge to apartments and about two-thirds to food.

Where **bed and breakfast terms** are offered, either of the methods outlined above may be used.

Functions

Most smaller hotels record functions sales in the visitors' ledger. The procedure is as follows:

1. All particulars of functions sales are entered in a vertical column, headed 'functions', specially provided for that purpose. Thus, if a function were sold, consisting of 20 dinners at £20.00 each and drinks to the value of £200.00, in the 'functions' column we would enter £400.00 against 'dinners' and £200.00 against 'liquors'.
2. All such functions sales will be totalled in the daily summary column and included in the daily transfers to the monthly summary sheet.

Any amounts remaining unpaid by the organizers of such functions would have to be noted. Often a special 'functions diary' is kept and any unpaid accounts noted down in it. The treatment of functions in the visitors' ledger is illustrated in the specimen in Figure 5.7.

Chance trade

Chance trade is a term applied to cash sales to non-residents. It follows, therefore, that the total of chance sales must be equal to the total of cash received. The treatment of chance trade is similar to that of functions and may be described as follows:

1. Particulars of all meals, etc. sold to chance customers are summarized, meal by meal, in what is known as the 'chance book'. This requires no special ruling and is kept for the sole purpose of summarizing all such sales prior to their entry in the visitors' ledger.
2. The totals of chance luncheons, dinners, etc. from the chance book are then debited in the 'chance' column of the visitors' ledger.
3. From the visitors' ledger the daily chance sales are transferred to the monthly summary sheet in the usual manner.

The 'chance' column should be balanced each day to ensure that the total of cash received and credited in the 'chance' column is equal to the sales debited therein. The treatment of chance sales is illustrated in the specimen given in Figure 5.7.

Vertical visitors' ledger

This is the type already described and illustrated in Example 5.2. It is known as the vertical type because all charges to visitors are recorded vertically; also each visitor's account appears vertically – the upper portion being the debit and the lower portion the credit side of the visitor's account.

There is a variant of the vertical type already described. The layout of this ledger is the same as that of the vertical type except that the daily sales are (a) accumulated monthly in the visitors' ledger and (b) posted to appropriate ledger accounts at the end of each month.

It will be appreciated that, as a result, no monthly summary sheet is

Tabular Ledger

ROOM No.	1	2	3	4	5	6	7	8	9	10					
NAME	Coles	Mills	Gordon	Bingley	Gallagher	French	Davison	Hagen	Brown	Beeson	Chance trade	Functions	Daily total	Brought Forward	Carried Forward
NO. OF VISITORS	2	1	2	1	2	2	1	1	2	1					
	£	£	£	£	£	£	£	£	£	£	£	£	£	£	£
Balance b/f	208.00	90.00	334.00	55.00	194.00	238.00	110.00	117.00					1,346.00	1,224.00	2,570.00
Apartments		40.00		40.00	70.00	70.00	40.00	40.00	70.00	40.00			410.00	390.00	800.00
Breakfast	10.00	5.00	10.00	5.00	10.00	10.00	5.00	5.00					60.00	55.00	115.00
E M Teas	6.00		6.00	3.00				3.00					18.00	21.00	39.00
Luncheons	40.00	15.00			35.00			25.00			200.00	360.00	675.00	725.00	1,400.00
Drinks	17.00		42.00	6.00		35.00			20.00		80.00	140.00	340.00	315.00	655.00
Afternoon teas		5.00		5.00			5.00	5.00			100.00		120.00	90.00	210.00
Dinners			39.00				19.00		70.00	24.00	320.00	500.00	972.00	829.00	1,801.00
Telephone	2.00				2.00					6.00			10.00	31.00	41.00
Miscellaneous						20.00							20.00	10.00	30.00
Paid-outs		10.00	10.00				5.00		5.00				30.00	50.00	80.00
Total Debits	283.00	165.00	441.00	114.00	311.00	373.00	184.00	195.00	165.00	70.00	700.00	1,000.00	4,001.00	3,740.00	7,741.00
Cash	283.00										700.00	1,000.00	1,983.00	1,574.00	3,557.00
Ledger			441.00										441.00	800.00	1,241.00
Allowances					6.00								6.00	20.00	26.00
Balance c/f		165.00		114.00	305.00	373.00	184.00	195.00	165.00	70.00			1,571.00	1,346.00	2,917.00
Total Credits	283.00	165.00	441.00	114.00	311.00	373.00	184.00	195.00	165.00	70.00	700.00	1,000.00	4,001.00	3,740.00	7,741.00

Figure 5.7 Hotel Visitors' Ledger

required with this type of visitors' ledger. A specimen is given in Figure 5.7. Two additional columns, 'functions' and 'chance trade', are inserted to illustrate the treatment of these sales in the visitors' ledger.

SOME BASIC CONSIDERATIONS

A review of the various methods of accounting for sales outlined in this chapter suggests that in each hotel there are several ways in which it is possible to record sales. It will not be out of place, therefore, to conclude this chapter with a few basic considerations that influence the actual sales accounting records kept.

An important decision that must be made in each hotel is whether the hotel visitors' ledger should be used:

- to record all the sales of the hotel, or
- to record sales to guests only.

Most smaller hotels use the visitors' ledger as a record of all the sales. Large hotels, on the other hand, tend to use it as a record of sales to guests only. Other sales (banqueting, bars, dinner parties, etc.) are then recorded in separate books of account.

Finally, the degree of analysis of charges and the degree of detail necessary should be considered. Thus, where there are numerous minor selling departments it is necessary to decide whether the sales of each department should be recorded separately, or whether some of them may be lumped together and, for accounting purposes, treated as 'sundry sales'. A similar problem arises in the treatment of functions. The treatment of functions, as described in this chapter, is rather simplified and many hotels prefer to record these in greater detail. A common arrangement is not to have just one 'functions' column in the visitors' ledger but to make several columns available for this purpose. The sales in respect of each function would thus be recorded separately.

SUMMARY

- In hospitality establishments a large proportion of sales are likely to be on a cash basis. These are straightforward double entry transactions, where we debit the cash account and credit the sales account.
- Credit sales: this is where credit is allowed to regular customers or firms with business accounts.
- The period of credit allowed will vary from a few weeks/months (in the case of banquets and expense account customers) to a few days (in the case of resident guests).
- The hotel visitors' ledger was designed to deal with short term credit given to the hotel guest and the need to record all sales made to him during his stay normally between 1 and 4 days in city hotels and longer at resort hotels.

- The hotel visitors' ledger, also called the tabular ledger, is part of the double entry book-keeping system.
- Many establishments now operate a computerized system in place of the tabular ledger. This system, however, is largely based on the manual method demonstrated in this chapter. A detailed understanding of this key area of sales accounting is very important not only from a good management point of view but also because computer systems will and do break down and need to be backed up by a detailed knowledge of the manual system.

PROBLEMS

1. Describe the two main types of the visitors' ledger.

2. Explain how double entry is completed in respect of the following:
   (a) charges to visitors;
   (b) allowances;
   (c) cash received from visitors;
   (d) visitors' paid-outs.

3. Write short explanatory notes on the book-keeping treatment of:
   (a) inclusive terms;
   (b) advance deposits.

4. Explain how the following charges to visitors originate and how they are debited in their accounts in the visitors' ledger:
   (a) apartments;
   (b) meals;
   (c) drinks; and
   (d) sundry sales.

5. Peter Fraine is a proprietor of a restaurant. The following balances appeared in his ledger on 1st January 19...

	Dr £	Cr £
Capital		300,000
Cash at bank	50,000	
Premises	150,000	
Furniture	37,500	
Equipment	50,000	
Food stocks	12,500	
	£300,000	£300,000

Open the necessary accounts and enter the above balances. Fraine's transactions in January were:

				£
Jan	1	Food purchases by cheque		2,400
"	2	Paid by cheque for advertising		1,250
"	4	Cash sales – banked		2,175
"	5	Credit sales:	E X Dining Club	550
			Midland Cars Ltd	300
			City Banking Co.	650
"	6	Paid wages by cheque		1,725
"	9	Paid by cheque for new furniture		3,750
"	10	Cash sales – banked		2,325
"	13	Paid by cheque for fruit		250
"	16	Credit sales:	City Banking Co.	425
			E X Dining Club	300
			Midland Cars Ltd	975
"	19	Paid wages by cheque		1,800
"	22	Paid by cheque for fish and poultry		475
"	26	Cash sales banked		2,500
"	27	Credit sales:	Midland Cars Ltd	400
			E X Dining Club	475
"	29	Paid for travelling expenses by cheque		300
"	31	Paid wages by cheque		1,650

Write up Fraine's books in respect of January and extract his trial balance as at 31st January 19...

6. Before business is commenced in the Hyview Hotel on 4th May 19..., the cash book balance is £197.50 and the following balances are brought forward on the visitors' ledger from the previous day:

Room No.	1	2	3	4	5	Total
No of visitors	one	one	two	two	–	six
Balance b/f	£62.50	£118.75	£98.75	£272.50	–	£552.50

During the day the business is as follows:

Breakfast:	all residents
Lunch	all residents in rooms 2, 3 and 4
Sherry:	Room 1 – £2.75
Departure:	Room 2 – account paid in cash
Dinner:	Room 1; 1 only in Room 3; 1 only in Room 4
Wine:	one bottle @ £23.50 served in Room 3
Apartments:	charged to all residents

Hotel Tariff

Apartments	–	£37.50 per person per day
Breakfast	–	£5.00
Lunch	–	£12.50
Dinner	–	£15.00

Date	Apartments	Breakfast	Luncheons	Dinner	Misc.	Total
	£	£	£	£	£	£
May 1	112.50	20.00	42.50	52.50	22.50	250.00
" 2	150.00	15.00	21.50	52.50	5.00	244.00
" 3	150.00	25.00	21.50	26.00	33.50	256.00

Monthly summary sheet   May 19...

Required:
(a) Write up the visitors' ledger for 4th May 19..., in conjunction with a simple cash book.
(b) Balance the visitors' ledger and the cash book.
(c) Enter the day's business in the monthly summary sheet.
(d) Construct a trial balance as on 4th May 19...

7. The following exercise on the visitors' ledger extends over three days. The following is the tariff of the hotel.

Bed and breakfast				Rooms
Single	– A	£37.50		1 – 6
Single	– B	£31.25		7 – 12
Double	– A	£68.75		13 – 18
Double	– B	£56.25		19 – 24

Extra child's bed in the room and breakfast	– £18.75
Early morning tea	– £ 1.25
Luncheon	– £10.00
Afternoon tea	– £ 5.00
Dinner	– £15.00
Coffee	– £ 2.50

Note: Breakfast is charged for whether taken or not.

First day

Arrivals a.m.	Room 1	– Mr J Derbyshire
	2	– Miss L Smith
	3	– Miss R Fletcher
	7	– Mr F Betts
	8	– Mr S Stanford
	14	– Capt. & Mrs J Wright
	16	– Mr & Mrs K Booth

Luncheons   All arrivals

Arrivals p.m.	Room 4	– Rev. J Smart
	10	– Miss S Lake
	17	– Mr & Mrs Spencer
	21	– Mr & Mrs F Donaldson
	22	– F/Lt. & Mrs Phipps

Afternoon teas Rooms 14, 16, 4, 10, 17, 21, 22
Dinners   Rooms 2, 3, 7, 8, 16, 17, 21, 22
Coffees   Rooms 14, 16, 4, 10

Telephones,   Rooms 2 (£1.25),7 (£2.50), 21 (£1.25)
Chance dinners 12 @ £15.00

Write up the visitors' ledger and the monthly summary sheet and carry
balances forward to the second day.

Second day
Bring forward balances from previous day.

Early morning teas	Rooms 3, 7, 16, 21, 22
Newspapers	Rooms 1 (£2.50), 7 (£1.25), 8 (£1.25), 16 (£2.50), 17 (£1.25), 21 (£2.50)
Breakfast	All visitors
Departures a.m.	Room 1 – Mr J Derbyshire, account paid in cash and closed
	Room 14 – Capt & Mrs J Wright, account paid in cash and closed
Morning coffees	Rooms 2, 3, 7, 16, 17, 21, 22
Arrivals a.m.	Room 5 – Mr F Sandringham
	Room 6 – Mr D Chalk
	Room 13 – Mjr & Mrs K Jones and son
11 a.m. Taxi	Mrs Spencer – £10.00
Flowers	Room 7 – £18.75
Luncheons	Rooms 2, 3, 7, 8, 16, 22
Chance luncheons	18 @ £10.00
Arrivals p. m.	Room 9 – Miss Thompson
	Room 11 – Col. L S Ward
	Room 18 – Mr & Mrs L Hopkins
3 p.m. Theatre tickets	Room 21 – £20.00
Afternoon teas	Rooms 8, 10, 17, 18
Chance afternoon teas	12 @ £5.00
Dinners	Rooms 2, 3, 7, 10, 17, 18, 21 (1 only)
Faxes	Rooms 17 (£8.75), 21 (£16.25)
Cigarettes	Rooms 3 (£5.00), 16 (£7.50)
Coffees	Rooms 8, 16, 17

Write up visitors' ledger and the monthly summary sheet and carry the
balances forward to the third day.

Third day
Bring forward balances from previous day.

Early morning teas	Rooms 3, 5, 7, 13 (2 only), 16, 21, 22
Newspapers	Rooms 4 (£1.25), 7 (£1.25), 8 (£1.25), 11 (£2.50), 21(£2.50).
Morning coffees	Rooms 2, 3, 13, 17, 21, 22
Departures a.m.	– Miss L Smith, account paid in cash and closed
	– Miss Thompson, account paid in cash and closed
	– Rev. J Smart, account closed and balance transferred to ledger

	– Mr S Stanford, account closed and balance transferred to ledger.
Arrivals a.m.	Room 15 – Mr & Mrs Jennings
Luncheons	Rooms 15 (plus £18.75 wine), 3 (plus £7.50 sherry), 21(plus £21.25 cigars), 13 (2 only)
Chance luncheons	12 @ £10.00, also wines £56.25, spirits £27.50, cigarettes £12.50
Afternoon teas	Rooms 6, 17
Chance afternoon teas	18 @ £5.00
Departures p. m.	Room 3 vacated, account paid in cash
Telephones	Mr Jennings £1.25, Col. L S Ward £6.25
C.O.D. parcel	Mjr Jones £5.00
Dinners	Rooms 5, 13, 18 (plus £15.00 wine)
Chance dinners	12 @ £15.00, also spirits £17.50
Private party	Mr Samuel Johnson: 10 dinners @ £15.00, liquors £60.00, cigarettes £22.50, account transferred to ledger

Write up the visitors' ledger and the monthly summary sheet.

8 The Lowcliffe Hotel maintains personal accounts for certain non-residents frequenting its restaurant.

   The following were the balances owing from non-residents on 1st January 19...

	£
Col. S Merrick	250
V S May & Co.	550
E M Browne Esq.	325
Essex Plastics Ltd	800
Winter Sports Ltd	375

The following transactions took place with the above customers during the month of January.

			£
Jan 1	Credit sales:	V S May & Co.	75
		Essex Plastics Ltd	100
		Col. S Merrick	200
		Winter Sports Ltd	325
" 8	Credit sales:	E M Browne Esq.	100
		Winter Sports Ltd	225
		V S May & Co.	125
" 13	Cheques received from:	Essex Plastics Ltd	800
		Col. S Merrick	250
		E M Browne Esq.	325
" 19	Credit sales:	V S May & Co.	350
		Col. S Merrick	50

			Essex Plastics Ltd	250
"	21	Cheque from E M Browne Esq. returned by bank, marked R/D		
"	22	Credit sales:	V S May & Co.	100
			Col. S Merrick	125
			Essex Plastics Ltd	150
"	28	Received cheque from V S May & Co.		550
"	31	E M Browne Esq. paid cash		325
"	31	Credit sales: Winter Sports Ltd		225
		Essex Plastics Ltd		275
		V S May & Co.		200

Required:

(a) Write up the restaurant sales book and the cash book of the hotel.

(b) Post to ledger.

(c) Balance all customers' accounts as at 31st January 19...

Accounting for value added tax | 6

INTRODUCTION

This chapter covers the basic rules governing VAT and illustrates how this important tax is dealt with in the books of account. We will also examine the basic rules of VAT and how it is dealt with in the subsidiary books and the ledger.

OBJECTIVES

On completion of this chapter you should be able to:

- understand the nature and meaning of VAT;
- differentiate between zero-rating and exemptions as it relates to VAT;
- calculate the value of VAT for inclusive and exclusive amounts;
- enter VAT into the basic records and show how VAT is double entered in the books of account;
- calculate and enter VAT in the cash book;
- calculate and enter VAT in the relevant day books;
- transfer all VAT amounts to the Customs and Excise account;
- understand how VAT applies to long-stay residents in hotels and similiar types of establishment.

VALUE ADDED TAX (VAT)

Value added tax was introduced in the UK on 1st April 1973. The initial rate of VAT was, apart from the zero rate, 10 per cent, but this has changed several times in recent years. VAT is payable to Customs and Excise by taxable persons, which includes individuals, partnerships and limited companies. 'Taxable persons' usually means the same as 'registered persons', but it also includes any person who ought to be registered but has not taken the necessary steps to secure registration.

The final burden of the tax is borne by the customer and, consequently, VAT is not an operating cost. In reality, this means that the business is merely acting as a tax collector for the government of the day.

Every VAT registered business must pay 'surplus' VAT to the revelant government department, usually at three-monthly intervals. By 'surplus' we mean the difference between the VAT received from customers and the VAT paid to suppliers. These are known as output tax and input tax respectively.

Output tax and input tax

From the tax that a business collects from its customers (output tax) It will deduct the tax it has paid on its own purchases (input tax) and remit the difference to Customs and Excise.

Zero rating and exemptions

Both zero rating and exemption mean that no output tax is chargeable on sales. There are, however, two important differences:

1. Zero-rated supplies are technically taxable (though the rate of tax is nil) and the VAT charged on inputs relating to them can be reclaimed like other input tax. Exempt supplies, on the other hand, are outside VAT and the input cannot be deducted or reclaimed.
2. A person who makes zero-rated supplies will generally be registered with Customs and Excise and make VAT returns. A person who makes only exempt supplies does not have to register or make returns.

AN ASSUMED RATE

The VAT rate is subject to change and indeed has been altered many times over the years. For this reason and for simplicity **an assumed rate of 20 per cent for VAT** will be used for all examples in this textbook. The student should note that the current rate of VAT is likely to be different.

VAT INCLUSIVE AMOUNTS

Calculating VAT is relatively easy where we are given the value of the goods and asked to add on VAT. Thus if we buy goods for £200 + VAT @ 20 per cent:

	£
Cost of goods	200
Add VAT @ 20%	40
Total cost inclusive of VAT	240

However, there are many cases when we will only be given the VAT inclusive figure and where we will be expected to work out the value of the VAT element included therein. Take the following example:

Sold goods for £240 inclusive of VAT @ 20 per cent. You are required to work out the value of the VAT included in the figure of £240.

A common student mistake is to attempt to work out 20 per cent of £240, which will give a figure of £48 for VAT. We need only look at the example above to know this is incorrect.

The £240 includes 20 per cent VAT, it therefore represents 120 per cent.

	£	%
Basic selling price	?	100%
Add VAT @ 20 per cent	?	20%
Selling price inclusive of VAT	240	120%

To calculate the VAT figure one simply divides £240 by 120 to find one per cent and multiply by 20 to find twenty per cent as shown below:

$$£240 \times \frac{20}{120} = £40$$

Students should remember that the 'basic price' (price before the addition of VAT) is always to be taken as 100 per cent, this is illustrated below:

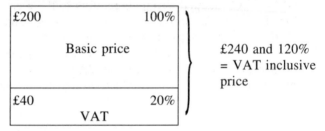

VAT: BASIC RECORDS

Every time a business buys goods or services (other than those zero-rated or exempted) it is charged VAT. When, in turn, the business sells its goods or services to its customers, it also charges VAT.

At intervals – normally every three months – the business will add up all its input tax (i.e. tax paid to its suppliers) and all the output tax (charged to its customers). The difference is then remitted to Customs and Excise. If a situation arises where the total of the output tax is less than the total of the input tax, the difference is the amount owing to the business from Customs and Excise.

It will be appreciated that the introduction of VAT must have some effect on the basic accounting records. In order to be able to calculate the totals of input and output it is necessary to design accounting records which make this information readily available. The illustrations which follow assume that VAT is charged at the rate of 20 per cent.

Accounting records will be required to deal with the two key types of transaction:

1. Cash transactions – where receipt or payment is by cash or cheque etc.
2. Credit transactions – entered via the day books and paid later.

CASH TRANSACTIONS

The standard two column cash book will need to be altered to accommodate VAT. This is achieved by adding an extra column on each side of the cash book as shown below:

Dr   Cash book   Cr

Date		VAT	Cash	Bank	Date		VAT	Cash	Bank

The total amount of cash received (i.e. including the VAT) is always placed in either the cash or bank column and the VAT shown in the VAT column.

These VAT columns are purely **memorandum columns** and do not form part of the double entry book-keeping system. They are a convenient way of collecting together VAT amounts from cash transactions At the end of the accounting period the total of each column is transferred to the Customs and Excise A/c (VAT A/c) on the opposite sides to its placement in the cash book.

EXAMPLE 6.1

To demonstrate the procedure we will now enter the following transactions into the cash book, close it off and transfer the VAT totals to the Customs and Excise account.

Assume an opening balance of £500 cash, £12,000 in the bank and a VAT rate of 20 per cent.

1. Purchased food for £450, paid by cheque.
2. Cash sales £840 inclusive of VAT.
3. Bought stationery for £220 + VAT, paid in cash.
4. Bought food for cash £600.
5. Purchased Beverages for £560 + VAT paid by cheque.
6. Cash sales £1,440 inclusive of VAT.

Note: in the UK the purchase of food as a raw material is zero-rated whereas alcoholic beverages, minerals etc. are always subject to VAT. However the resale of this food in the form of meals **is subject to VAT.**

Cash Book

Date		VAT	Cash	Bank	Date		VAT	Cash	Bank
		£	£	£			£	£	£
	Balance b/d		500	12,000		Purchases			450
	Sales	140	840			Stationery	44	264	
	Sales	240	1,440			Purchases		600	
						Purchases	112		672
						Balance c/d		1,916	10,878
		380	2,780	12,000			156	2,780	12,000
	Balance b/d		1,916	10,878					

Customs & Excise A/c

		£			£
Jan 31	Cash book	156	Jan 31	Cash book	380

CREDIT TRANSACTIONS

Credit transactions will be entered in the day books if trading items or in the journal for other items (e.g. purchase of a fixed asset).

EXAMPLE 6.2

Enter the following credit transactions into the books of account.
 Sold meals and beverages to the following on credit:

J Manning	£180 + VAT
Mrs B Grace	£210 + VAT
Capt. R J Elme	£145 + VAT

Purchased goods from the following on credit:

Vintners Spirits Co.	£270 + VAT
Surrey Foods Ltd	£380
Spanish Wine Co.	£440 + VAT

The following is an example of the type of record that may be used to record particulars of VAT output.

Restaurant Sales Day Book

Date	Customer	F	Total	Food	Bev.	VAT
		SL	£	£	£	£
May 1	Mr J Manning	10	216	120	60	36
" 2	Mrs B Grace	16	252	135	75	42
" 3	Capt. R J Elme	24	174	100	45	29
	Etc.					
" 31	Totals		5,280	3,000	1,900	380

Double entry at the end of May would be completed as follows:

(a) All food and beverages sold plus the output tax would be debited in the accounts of the guests.
(b) The totals of food sales and beverage sales exclusive of VAT would be credited in the appropriate accounts in the ledger.
(c) The monthly total of VAT collected from the customers would be credited to the Customs and Excise account.

Similiar procedures would have to be applied in respect of any supplies purchased by the business which are chargeable to VAT. Any food purchased is zero-rated but alcoholic beverages are subject to VAT. The purchases day book will, therefore, have to provide for the easy recording of all the relevant VAT inputs. An example, based on VAT at 20 per cent, is shown below:

Purchases Day Book

Date	Suppliers	F	Total	Food	Bev.	VAT
		BL	£	£	£	£
May 1	Vintners Spirit Ltd	44	324		270	54
" 2	Surrey Food Co.	76	380	380		
" 3	Spanish Wine Co.	82	528		440	88
	Etc.					
" 31			4,420	2,500	1,600	320

From the purchases day book, the totals would be posted as follows.

(a) The total of food and beverages plus the VAT input would be credited to the accounts of the suppliers.
(b) The totals of food and beverage purchases would be debited in the appropriate accounts in the ledger.
(c) The monthly total of VAT paid to the suppliers would be debited to the Customs and Excise account.

The monthly totals of VAT would be transferred to the Customs and Excise account as shown below:

Customs & Excise A/c					
19...		£	19...		£
May 31	Purchases Day Book	320.00	May 31	Rest Sales Book	380.00

Students should remember that, in addition to any VAT paid on alcoholic beverages, input tax will be paid on other supplies such as china, cutlery, stationery, telephone, repairs to furniture and equipment, etc. All such VAT input payments should be recorded in an appropriately designed subsidiary book to enable a monthly transfer to the Customs and Excise account.

HOTELS AND SIMILAR ESTABLISHMENTS

Hotels, boarding houses, motels, youth hostels and bed and breakfast establishments are, for VAT purposes, in the same category. VAT is chargeable at the full current rate on the full amount payable for the provision of accommodation, meals and services.

For any period which follows the first four weeks of a stay the value of the supply of accommodation and facilities is reduced for VAT purposes. The reduction takes the form of calculating VAT only on that part of the total charge (exclusive of VAT) which represents the provision of facilities other than the right to occupy the room; and that part is taken to be not less than 20 per cent of the amount payable for the accommodation and facilities. 'Facilities' for this purpose include cleaning, bed-making, entertainment, floral decorations, room service, television, radio and non-personal laundry.

CATERING ESTABLISHMENTS

VAT is chargeable at the current standard rate on the full amount payable for the food and beverages supplied in the course of catering. This applies to all establishments whose turnover exceeds a given threshold value which is set annually by the Customs and Excise department (the 1995/96 threshold is for turnovers in excess of £46,000). For this purpose 'catering' includes restaurants, cafés, industrial canteens, office canteens, etc., whether operated by the business itself or by an outside catering contractor. Also included for this purpose are catering establishments at railway stations, street stalls, beach cafés, etc. Excluded for this purpose – and hence zero-rated – are 'take-away' operations, e.g. the supply of fish and chips, Chinese food, etc.

WORKED EXAMPLE

Anastasia Brown started business on 1st February 19... with £100,000 in the bank. The following transactions took place in February:

Feb 1 Transferred £5,000 from the bank account to the cash account.
" 2 Leased premises, paid by cheque, £36,000 + VAT.
" 3 Purchased food on credit from the following: L Ferrone £1,600, R Allen £1,100 and L Randell £2,300.
" 4 Bought office equipment, paid by cheque £2,850 + VAT.
" 5 Cash sales to date £1,800 inclusive of VAT.
" 5 Purchased whisky, spirits etc. on credit from MacKay & Co. £1,300 +VAT.
" 6 Paid wages in cash £490.
" 6 Bought food, paid by cash £360.
" 7 Sold meals on credit to: B Braham Ltd £450 + VAT, J Gush & Co. £600 + VAT, J MacSavage £350 + VAT.
" 9 Bought motor van, paid by cheque, £12,800 + VAT.
" 10 Bought alcoholic beverages for cash £960 inclusive of VAT.
" 12 Cash sales to date £3,600 inclusive of VAT.
" 14 Sold meals on credit to: B Braham Ltd £280 + VAT, P Creed £425 + VAT.
" 16 Bought stationery for cash £240 inclusive of VAT.
" 20 Bought kitchen equipment, paid by cheque £7,500 + VAT.
" 21 Paid wages in cash £1,900.
" 25 Purchased draft & bottled beers on credit from Brit. Brewers Ltd £1,450 + VAT.
" 26 Cash sales to date £8,400 inclusive of VAT.
" 27 Transferred cash to the value of £10,000 from cash account to bank account.
" 28 Paid L Ferrone by cheque £1,600.

You are required to enter Miss Brown's transactions into her ledger using a three column cash book. Open all relevant day books and take out a trial balance at 28th February 19...

Suggested Solution

Restaurant Sales Day Book

Date	Customer	Total	Food	Bev.	VAT
		£	£	£	£
Feb 7	B Braham Ltd	540	200	250	90
" 7	J Gush & Co.	720	400	200	120
" 7	J MacSavage	420	230	120	70
" 14	B Braham Ltd	336	150	130	56
" 14	P Creed	510	325	100	85
	Totals	2,526	1,305	800	421

Purchases Day Book

Date	Suppliers	F	Total	Food	Drink	VAT
		BL	£	£	£	£
Feb 3	L Ferrone		1,600	1,600		
" 3	R Allen		1,100	1,100		
" 3	L Randell		2,300	2,300		
" 5	MacKay & Co.		1,560		1,300	260
" 25	Brit. Brewers Ltd		1,740		1,450	290
" 28	Totals		8,300	5,000	2,750	550

Cash Book

Date		VAT	Cash	Bank	Date		VAT	Cash	Bank
Feb 1	Capital			100,000	Feb 2	Cash			5,000
" 2	Bank		5,000		" 2	Lease	7,200		43,200
" 5	Sales	300	1,800		" 4	Office Equip	570		3,420
" 12	Sales	600	3,600		" 6	Wages		490	
" 26	Sales	1,400	8,400		" 6	Purchases		360	
" 27	Cash ¢			10,000	" 7	Motor	2,560		15,360
					" 10	Purchases	160	960	
					" 16	Stationery	40	240	
					" 20	Equipment	1,500		9,000
					" 21	Wages		1,900	
					" 27	Bank ¢		10,000	
					" 28	Ferrone			1,600
					" 28	Balance c/d		4,850	32,420
		2,300	18,800	110,000			12,030	18,800	110,000
Mar 1	Bal b/d		4,850	32,420					

Capital A/c

			Feb 1	Cash Book	100,000

Leasehold Premises A/c

Feb 2	Cash Book	36,000		

Sales A/c

			Feb 5	Cash book	1,500
			12	"	3,000
			26	"	7,000
			28	SDB	2,105

Purchases A/c

Feb 6	Cash book	360				
" 10	Cash book	800				
" 28	PDB (food)	5,000				
" 28	PDB (bev.)	2,750				

Motor Van A/c

Feb 7	Cash book	12,800	

Stationery A/c

Feb 16	Cash book	200	

Wages A/c

Feb 6	Cash book	490	
" 21	Cash book	1,900	

Office Equipment A/c

Feb 4	Cash book	2,850	

Kitchen Equipment A/c

Feb 20	Cash book	7,500	

Customs & Excise A/c

Feb 28	PDB	550	Feb 28	SDB	421
" 28	Cash book	12,030	" 28	Cash book	2,300
			" 28	Balance c/d	9,859
		12,580			12,580
Mar 1	Balance b/d	9,859			

L Ferrone

Feb 28	Cash book	1,600	Feb 3	PDB	1,600

R Allen & Son

			Feb 3	PDB	1,100

L Randell

			Feb 3	PDB	2,300

Brit Brewers Ltd

			Feb 25	PDB	1,740

MacKay & Co.

			Feb 5	PDB	1,560

B Braham Ltd

Feb 6	SDB	540	
" 16	SDB	336	

J Gush & Co.

Feb 6	SDB	720	

J MacSavage & Sons Ltd

Feb 6	SDB	420	

P Creed

Feb 16	SDB	510	

Trial balance of A Brown
at 28th February 19...

		£	£
Cash Book:	Cash	4,850	
	Bank	32,420	
Capital A/c			100,000
Lease A/c		36,000	
Sales A/c			13,605
Purchases A/c		8,910	
Motor Van A/c		12,800	
Stationery A/c		200	
Wages A/c		2,390	
Office Equipment A/c		2,850	
Kitchen Equipment A/c		7,500	
Customs & Excise A/c		9,859	
R Allen & Son A/c			1,100
L Randell A/c			2,300
Brit Brewers Ltd A/c			1,740
MacKay & Co. A/c			1,560
B Braham Ltd A/c		876	
J Gush & Co. A/c		720	
J MacSavage & Sons Ltd A/c		420	
P Creed A/c		510	
		120,305	120,305

THE FOUR COLUMN CASH BOOK

In the interest of clarity, discounts allowed and discounts received columns were excluded from the cash book. In reality, however, many cash books dealing with VAT will be four-column accounts as illustrated below. This should not cause the student any major difficulty. The important point to remember is that the VAT columns are not part of the double entry system. They are merely memorandum columns placed there for convenience. The same is true of discount columns, see Chapter 3 for further details.

Dr						Cash Book					Cr
Date		Disc.	VAT	Cash	Bank	Date		Disc.	VAT	Cash	Bank

SUMMARY

- VAT is an indirect tax levied on the majority of goods sold to the public in the UK.
- Certain goods are excluded from VAT being either zero rated or exempt. The most important of these from a hospitality point of view is food-stuffs.
- Food bought in as a raw material is zero rated whereas food sold to the customer in the form of meals, etc. is fully subject to VAT.
- Zero rated means that it is possible to tax it, but at present it is set at a 'zero' rate.
- Exempt means, in general, that it cannot be taxed without an official change in the law of the land.
- VAT is a tax on the final consumer. It should be clear that the business is merely acting as a tax collector for the government of the day.
- The VAT element of each business transaction is recorded separately in the relevant subsidiary books in such a way that the items in the profit and loss account are exclusive of VAT.
- Businesses charge VAT on their outputs and pay VAT on their inputs, the excess being paid to or received from the Customs & Excise.
- VAT is recorded in the Customs & Excise account in the ledger.
- Small businesses are not always subject to VAT. The turnover of a business must exceed a given level before a business must charge VAT. This level is set by the Chancellor each year in his budget speech.
- Businesses which exceed the given level of turnover are legally bound to register with Customs & Excise to pay VAT.
- Special VAT rules apply to long stay guests in hotels and similiar establishments.

PROBLEMS

1. Write short notes on the meaning of input and output tax.

2. Give an outline of the accounting records necessary for the recording of VAT.

3. Harry Hardy received a cash prize of £75,000 and decided to buy his local bistro. He took it over on 1st February and the following are his transactions during that month.

Feb 1   Paid £72,000 of opening cash into the business's bank account.
" 1   Withdrew from bank for office cash £10,000.
" 2   Borrowed £100,000 from Risk Finance Ltd and received a cheque for this amount.
" 3   Bought food on credit from Mills & Co. £880 and from Thomas & Creed Ltd £1,030.
" 4   Bought wines on credit from Waterloo Wines Ltd £2,200 +VAT, beers from Bitter Casks & Co. £600 +VAT and spirits from Alcohol Prods Ltd £740 +VAT.
" 6   Sold meals on credit to W Reeves £600 +VAT.
" 7   Banked cash sales to date £1,600 inclusive of VAT.
" 8   Bought furniture, paid by cheque, £5,000 + VAT.
" 10 Paid wages in cash £2,100.
" 12 Sold meals etc. on credit to the following: H Alder £480+VAT, S Calver £330+VAT.
" 14 Bought food, paid in cash £280.
" 16 Banked cash sales £3,700 inclusive of VAT.
" 19 Paid Waterloo Wines Ltd by cheque total amount owing.
" 22 Paid wages in cash £2,700.
" 25 Bought kitchen equipment on credit from B Knight & Son Ltd £1,900 + VAT.
" 27 Paid Mills & Co. by cheque total amount owing.
" 28 Received from W Reeves a cheque for total amount owing.
" 28 Banked cash sales £3,900 inclusive of VAT.

Required:
   (a) Enter the above transactions into the account of the business.
   (b) Take out a trial balance at 28th of February 19...

4. Lisa Long and John Johnson invested £12,000 each in a small licensed restaurant in their local village. They started business on 1st June and the following transactions took place during June:

June 1 Paid £18,000 of the opening capital into the bank, the remainder they kept as office cash.
" 2   Bought furniture on credit from Fine Furniture Ltd £6,000 + VAT.
" 3   Bought food £2,400, paid by cheque.
" 3   Bought wines etc., paid by cheque £2,200 inclusive of VAT.
" 5   Bought food on credit from Salisbury Foods Ltd £1,200.

" 6 Paid wages in cash £700.

" 7 Banked cash sales £1,900 inclusive of VAT.

" 9 Sold meals etc. on credit to A Grant £780 + VAT and H Hanover £240 + VAT.

" 11 Bought equipment on credit from Catman Supplies Ltd £1,400 + VAT.

" 12 Bought wines on credit from Euston Wines Ltd £1,050 + VAT. and beers from Best Brewers Ltd £980 + VAT.

" 13 Bought food on credit from Hospide Foods Ltd £530 and Total Supplies Company £480.

" 15 Banked cash sales £4,950 inclusive of VAT.

" 18 Paid Fine Furniture Ltd £3,600 on account – by cheque.

" 19 Sold meals on credit to J Lloyd £550 +VAT.

" 22 Paid wages in cash £1,800.

" 23 Purchased food for cash £500.

" 25 Transferred £300 from bank to cash.

" 27 Paid Catman Supplies Ltd amount owing – by cheque.

" 29 Paid in cash electricity for month £140 inclusive of VAT and telephone £280 inclusive of VAT.

" 30 Banked cash sales £3,600 VAT inclusive.

Note: You may assume a uniform rate of VAT at 20 per cent

You are required to enter the above transactions in the appropriate books and extract a trial balance as at 30th June.

5. Annette Logan sold her luxury flat with a view to starting her own business. She leased a suitable restaurant on 1st July 19.... The following represents her transactions for the month of July:

July 1 Started business with £100,000 in the bank.

" 1 Leased fully equipped restaurant on 10 year renewable lease, paid 'one off' premium of £30,000 – by cheque.

" 2 Transferred from the bank to office cash £10,000.

" 2 Paid monthly rent by cheque £1,800.

" 4 R Renolds lent the business £25,000 by cheque.

" 6 Bought wines and spirits on credit from Eurowine Ltd £6,000 + VAT.

" 7 Bought food on credit from 5 Star Cash & Carry £740 and from Meat Eaters Ltd £460.

" 10 Banked cash sales £2,800 VAT inclusive.

" 11 Paid wages in cash £2,300.

" 13 Purchased new furnishings £2,500 + VAT, paid by cheque.

" 15 Sold meals etc. on credit to D Kilburn £410 + VAT.

" 18 Bought additional crockery, glasses etc. on credit from P Plate and Son for £1,600 + VAT.

" 19 Banked cash sales for meals etc. £5,900 VAT inclusive.

" 22 Paid wages in cash £1,800.

" 23 Bought food for cash £280.

" 24 Purchased beers etc. on credit from New Haven Brewers Ltd £680 + VAT.

" 25 Sold meals etc. on credit to M Hughes £270 + VAT, S Sands £310 + VAT.

" 27 Paid Eurowine Ltd by cheque total amount owing.

" 29 Bought spirits, beers etc. on credit from Westbury Brewing Ltd £980 + VAT.

" 29 Purchased food on credit from 5 Star Cash & Carry £860.

" 30 Paid wages in cash £2,500.

" 30 Received cheque from D Kilburn in payment of account.

" 31 Banked cash sales £9,400 VAT inclusive.

Required:

(a) Enter the above transactions in the books of the business. Assume that VAT is chargeable at 20 per cent.

(b) Take out a trial balance as at 31st July.

6. Describe the operation of value added tax and explain why it is not a business expense.

7. Explain how zero rating differs from exemption.

Organization of accounts 7

INTRODUCTION

Having considered all the basic accounting records, it is now proposed to examine what may be described as the organization of accounts. The first considerations are the component parts of a full set of books, the relationships that exist between the component parts, and some related practical problems.

OBJECTIVES

On completion of this chapter you should be able to:

- identify the separate components of a ledger system, known as the divisions of the ledger;
- list all subsidiary books in a hotel or catering book-keeping system;
- describe a source document;
- understand the need for and importance of source documents;
- know what is meant by a control account;
- operate a book-keeping system where control accounts are in use;
- explain the use of ledger folios.

DIVISIONS OF THE LEDGER

Though we often speak of the ledger, in practice this important book of account is divided into a number of separate sections. The most important object of the division of the ledger into sections is to enable a number of clerks to work on the books simultaneously.

The precise division of the ledger is primarily a matter of convenience, and in practice the number of the divisions will vary from two (in smaller businesses) to possibly as many as ten, fifteen, or even more (in large businesses). Most medium-sized businesses tend to divide their ledger into three sections, as shown below.

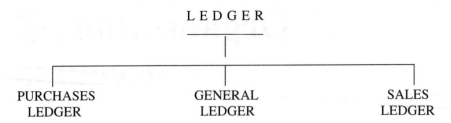

Purchases ledger

This ledger is also known as the bought ledger or the creditors' ledger, and contains the personal accounts of the suppliers (or creditors) of the business. It should be pointed out that the purchases account, though closely linked with this ledger, is kept in the general ledger dealt with below.

Whilst in the majority of hospitality establishments only one purchases ledger is kept, there are some which divide it into several subsections. Thus a very large hotel could divide its purchases ledger into the following subsections: food, beverage, tobaccos and sundries, and non-consumable supplies.

Each subsection would then contain a distinct group of suppliers' accounts and might be in the charge of a separate clerk.

Sales ledger

This is also known as the sold ledger or the debtors' ledger and contains the personal accounts of the customers (or debtors) of the business. Again, it is pointed out that the sales account is not kept in this ledger but in the general ledger.

The meaning and nature of the 'sales ledger' must now be explained in relation to hospitality establishments. In such establishments the term 'sales ledger' could be applied to two different sets of personal accounts.

It could be applied to the hotel visitors' ledger. This is strictly a sales ledger, in that it contains the personal accounts of the visitors. In practice, however, the visitors' ledger is not usually referred to as a sales ledger but as the visitors' ledger or the tabular ledger.

It could also be applied to the ledger containing the personal accounts of non-residents, any unpaid accounts transferred from the visitors' ledger and, possibly, advance deposits received from intending visitors. This ledger is usually referred to as the sales ledger, though there are many who describe it as the personal ledger. The latter is not an accurate description of this ledger, but is mentioned here in order to clarify the terminology in current use.

Most large hotels keep the two ledgers mentioned above. Some of the largest hotels might well sub-divide their sales ledger into two or three appropriate sections, such as non-residents, banqueting, transfers from HVL, etc., though it is not suggested that each such section would necessarily be looked after by a separate clerk.

Although many non-residential catering establishments maintain a sales ledger, it seems that the majority of them sell on a cash basis only and, in consequence, do not need personal accounts for their customers.

General ledger

Whilst the purchases and sales ledgers contain personal accounts, the general ledger contains impersonal accounts, i.e. accounts other than those of suppliers and customers. Impersonal accounts are of two kinds:

(a) Nominal accounts – those recording gains and losses (or income and expenditure), e.g. wages account, rent account, purchases account, discount received account.

(b) Real accounts – these may also be described as property accounts, e.g. premises account, kitchen plant account, restaurant furniture account.

In many businesses the general ledger is sub-divided into two sections:

The **nominal ledger** contains all the nominal accounts of the business.
The **private ledger** contains all property (real) accounts as well as accounts of a confidential nature, such as capital account, proprietor's salary account, profit and loss account.

SUBSIDIARY BOOKS

In addition to the ledger or ledgers, a business will keep a number of subsidiary books. These are also described as day books, journals, books of prime entry and books of original entry. The most important objects of subsidiary books are:

1. To relieve the ledger of unnecessary detail. Thus, the periodical totals from the purchases day book are posted to the purchases account, which considerably reduces the number of entries in that account. Similarly, the periodical analysed totals from the petty cash book are posted to the respective accounts in the ledger, which, again, results in a considerable reduction of entries in the accounts concerned.

2. To classify transactions and enable periodical totals to be posted to appropriate accounts in the ledger. To this end separate subsidiary books are kept for different kinds of transaction. There are the purchases day book for credit purchases and the purchases returns book for purchases returns. Also, there are analysis columns in the petty cash book for the different kinds of petty cash expenditure. As a result, it is possible to record different kinds of transactions in separate books. Once the subsidiary books have been written up, their totals (weekly, monthly) are available for posting to ledger accounts.

The most important subsidiary books in common use are listed below:

- Purchases day book
- Purchases returns book
- Sales day book
- Sales returns book
- Wages book
- Journal
- Cash book
- Petty cash book

Whilst the distinction between ledger accounts and subsidiary books is quite clear, there are several accounting records which need a more detailed explanation.

The cash book, as indicated above, is a subsidiary book. Yet, at the same time, it is also part of the ledger – though usually kept as a separate book. As a result, any transaction entered in the cash book (i.e. cash transaction) must not be entered in any other subsidiary book. Thus cash purchases are not entered in the purchases day book, nor is the purchase of assets for cash journalized. All entries made in the cash book count for double entry purposes.

The petty cash book is in the same category. It is both a subsidiary book and a ledger account.

The hotel visitors' ledger is, again, a ledger and a subsidiary book. It is a ledger because it contains the personal accounts of hotel visitors; it is a subsidiary book because it collects similar transactions (apartments, breakfasts, luncheons, dinners, telephone and other charges) together and enables a daily total of each such group of transactions to be posted, via the monthly summary sheet, to the appropriate nominal accounts in the ledger. In the case of the vertical type of hotel visitors' ledger, the vertical columns are the ledger accounts whilst the horizontal columns are in the nature of subsidiary books.

Finally, the nature of the monthly summary sheet is another accounting record which is rather difficult to define. It is not a subsidiary book, in that it is not a record of individual transactions but one of daily totals, nor is it a set of ledger accounts. It is a statistical summary of sales, half-way between a subsidiary book and a ledger.

Subsidiary books and double entry

At this point, it is necessary to state briefly the following important book-keeping rule:

Every transaction must be entered in a subsidiary book before being posted to the ledger.

The above rule will have already been observed from the illustrations given in the previous chapters. Thus purchase invoices are entered in a purchases day book before being posted to the purchases account and the accounts of suppliers in the bought ledger.

Hence the book-keeping process is a two-stage process: stage one comprises the entries in a subsidiary book; stage two comprises the ledger postings. Double entry in respect of all transactions is completed in the ledger and no entries in subsidiary books count for double entry purposes. The student's attention is, however, drawn to the exceptional position of the cash book and the petty cash book as explained above.

SOURCES OF ENTRIES

In practice it will be found that every entry made in the books of a business is supported by a document, e.g. an invoice, credit note, or petty cash voucher. All such documents are referred to as 'sources of entries' or 'documentary evidence', and are necessary for two reasons:

1. To provide the book-keeper with detailed information regarding the transactions of the business. Clearly, in the absence of such information it would be extremely difficult to maintain the books.
2. To provide the necessary evidence that the books constitute a true record of the transactions that have taken place. As a result, it is possible to support each entry in the books by some document and, in this way, prove that the books are a true expression of the transactions of the business.

It may so happen that no actual documentary evidence is available, in which case a substitute document must be provided. For instance, when a purchase invoice is mislaid and cannot be found, it is possible to ask the supplier concerned to issue a duplicate invoice. When an amount is paid out of petty cash and no voucher can practicably be obtained for it (e.g. in respect of gratuities to delivery men, taxi fares, etc.) an internal petty cash voucher must be raised and signed by some responsible person .

The following is a list of the main source of entries used for books of account:

Purchase day book:		suppliers' invoices
Purchases returns book:		suppliers' credit notes
Sales day book:		copies of bills signed by customers and copies of accounts sent to banqueting debtors
Sales returns book:		copies of credit notes sent to customers; this book is not often used in hospitality establishments
Wages book:		time sheets, clock cards and similar records
Journal:		various documents according to the nature of transaction, e.g. invoices in respect of assets purchased on credit
Cash book:	**Dr**	in respect of cheques received, copies of receipts issued to customers; in respect of cash sales, till rolls; in respect of all amounts banked, the paying-in book; also bank statement in respect of amounts credited by the bank
	Cr	cheque counterfoils or copies of cheques; suppliers' accounts and statements in respect of all payments made; also the bank statement in respect of amounts debited by the bank such as bank charges, bank interest
Petty cash book:	**Dr**	cheque counterfoils in respect of any floats received by petty cashier
	Cr	petty cash vouchers, external and internal

Visitors' ledger:
    Dr departmental vouchers (see Chapter 4 'sources of charges')

    Cr copies of receipts issued in respect of accounts settled; also monthly allowances sheet or allowances book in respect of allowances to guests

It will be appreciated that, as there is some documentary evidence in respect of each entry in the books, it is possible to trace each transaction from the ledger posting to the original documentary evidence and vice versa. The following illustration shows the path of a transaction in respect of a credit purchase:

Order placed to supplier	*Order form*
Goods received by hotel	*Delivery note*
Charge made by supplier	*Invoice*
Purchase recorded by hotel – stage I	*Purchases day book*
– stage 2	Dr purchases account
	Cr supplier's account

LEDGER FOLIOS

Reference has already been made to what are known as ledger folios. A folio is a page of a ledger or subsidiary book. Folio numbers are the page numbers of the ledger or subsidiary books.

In practical book-keeping, every time an entry is made a cross-reference is provided in the folio column to the corresponding entry in some other book. This method of cross-referencing has two advantages. First, in respect of each entry there is an immediate cross-reference to a corresponding entry in some other book and secondly, the insertion of ledger folios provides proof that double entry has been completed.

Two illustrations are now given to make this clear.

Cash transactions

A cash transaction is entered on one side of the cash book and on the opposite side of a ledger account. The page number of the ledger account concerned is shown in the folio column of the cash book; the page number of the cash book is shown in the folio column of the ledger account.

Cash book   46

19...		Folio	£	19...		Folio	£
Jan 1	Sales	GL37	6,000	Jan 2	Wages	GL16	2,000

Wages A/c 16

19...		Folio	£	19...		Folio	£
Jan 2	Cash	CB46	2,000				

Sales A/c 37

19...		Folio	£	19...		Folio	£
				Jan 1	Cash	CB46	6,000

Credit transactions

Most credit transactions occur in respect of the purchases and sales of a business. As already explained, all such credit transactions are recorded in a subsidiary book prior to being posted to the ledger (see below).

Purchases day book 51

19...			Folio	£
Jan	1	Supplier A	BL24	4,000
"	8	" B	BL16	2,000
"	23	" A	BL24	1,000
"	29	" B	BL16	3,000
		Transfer to Purchases A/c GL21		10,000

Purchases A/c 21

19...		Folio	£	19...		Folio	
Jan 31	Sundries	PB51	10,000				

Supplier A 24

19...		Folio	£	19...		Folio	£
				Jan 1	Purchases	PB51	4,000
				" 23	"	PB51	1,000

Supplier B 16

				19...		Folio	£
				Jan 8	Purchases	PB51	2,000
				" 29	"	PB51	3,000

The page number of the ledger accounts concerned is shown in the folio columns of the subsidiary books; the page number of the appropriate subsidiary book is shown in the ledger accounts.

The abbreviations GL, BL, CB, and PB are in common use and refer to the general ledger, bought ledger, cash book and purchases day book respectively.

As explained in Chapter 4, there are certain transactions which are passed through the journal and all such transactions are folioed in the same manner.

CONTROL ACCOUNTS

Another important feature of practical book-keeping is the maintenance of what are known as 'control accounts'. A control account is a device which makes a ledger 'self-balancing' by enabling a clerk to balance a section of the accounts (usually bought ledger or sales ledger) independently of the other sections.

In most businesses, including hospitality establishments, it will be found that the largest group of accounts consists of personal accounts of suppliers and customers. It will be appreciated that, whilst the number of nominal and real accounts in a medium-sized business is not likely to exceed about fifty, the number of personal accounts may well run into hundreds.

When, at the end of an accounting period, a total trial balance is extracted and fails to balance, it is impossible in the absence of control accounts to determine immediately in which section of the ledger the errors have arisen. It is, therefore, often necessary to check all the accounts – real, nominal and personal: a process that may take several days.

A control account, by making a ledger self-balancing, enables the clerk concerned to determine at the end of each period whether or not his section of the ledger balances and, in this way, not only helps in the location of errors but reduces considerably the time spent by clerks on periodical checking of accounts and 'looking for errors'.

In order to understand the operation of control accounts, the following two points must be clearly appreciated:

1. A control account is a **total account** and shows in summary form the detailed entries made in a particular ledger.

2. A control account, though described as an account, is a **memorandum account.** Any entries made in a control account do not, therefore, count for double entry purposes. As a result, it does not really matter whether the entries are made in a control account on the same side as in the ledger controlled by it, or whether such entries are reversed. In practice, when the control account is kept in the ledger concerned, the entries in the control account are usually reversed. This enables the clerk to extract what is known as a 'sectional trial balance'. When the control account is kept in another ledger (usually the general ledger), any entries made in it are usually kept on the same side as in the ledger concerned.

The following example illustrates the compilation of a control account by reference to the accounts of suppliers.

EXAMPLE 7.1

On 1st January 19..., the following balances appeared in the bought ledger of a hotel:

Hotel Suppliers Ltd	£3,000
B Brown & Sons	£4,500
Holland Bacon Co.	£1,500
	£9,000

If the hotel's bought ledger control account was kept in the bought ledger then, on the above date, it would appear as shown below:

Bought Ledger Control A/c

19...			£	
Jan 1	Balances	b/d	9,000	

In January the hotel makes the following transactions with its suppliers:

Credit purchases

			£
Jan	2	Hotel Suppliers Ltd	750
"	4	Holland Bacon Co.	900
"	7	B Brown & Sons	1,200
"	11	Holland Bacon Co.	300
"	16	Hotel Suppliers Ltd	1,050
"	22	Brown & Sons	1,650
"	25	Hotel Suppliers Ltd	1,800
"	31	Holland Bacon Co.	750
		Total	£8,400

Purchases returns

			£
Jan	6	Hotel Suppliers Ltd	150
"	18	B Brown & Sons	300
"	30	Holland Bacon Co.	150
		Total	£600

Payments to suppliers:

			Cheque	Discount	Total
Jan	20	Hotel Suppliers Ltd	£2,850	£150	£3,000
"	20	B Brown & Sons	4,290	210	4,500
			£7,140	£360	£7,500

The credit purchases and purchases returns are entered in the purchases day book and the purchases returns book and then posted to the ledger in the usual manner. In order to have the necessary information to compile the bought ledger control account, it is necessary to insert an additional bought ledger column in the cash book. Every time a payment to a supplier is made the total of cash and discount is entered in the bought ledger column, an example of which is illustrated below:

Cash Book

		Bought Ledger	Disc. Rec'd	Bank
		£	£	£
Jan 20	Hotel Suppliers Ltd	3,000	150	2,850
" 20	B Brown & Sons	4,500	210	4,290

Assuming that, by the end of January, all the transactions given above have been recorded in the books of the hotel, the personal accounts of the suppliers would appear as follows:

Hotel Suppliers Ltd

19...			£					£
Jan	6	Returns	150	Jan	1	Balance b/d		3,000
"	20	Cash	2,850	"	2	Purchases		750
"	20	Discount	150	"	16	"		1,050
				"	25	"		1,800

B Brown & Sons

19...			£					£
Jan	18	Returns	300	Jan	1	Balance b/d		4,500
"	20	Cash	4,290	"	7	Purchases		1,200
"	20	Discount	210	"	22	"		1,650

Holland Bacon Co.

19...			£					£
Jan	30	Returns	150	Jan	1	Balance b/d		1,500
				"	4	Purchases		900
				"	11	"		300
				"	31	"		750

In order to prove the accuracy of the postings to the above personal accounts, the bought ledger clerk compiles the bought ledger control account and takes out a sectional trial balance.

He compiles the bought ledger control account by taking the totals of transactions posted to the bought ledger from the relevant subsidiary books. Thus, by referring to the purchases day book, he sees that the total of invoices credited to suppliers in January was £8,400. The total of credit notes, cash paid and discounts received is ascertained by reference to the purchases returns book and the cash book. The completed bought ledger control account is shown below:

Bought Ledger Control A/c

19...		£	19...			£
Jan 1	Balance b/d	9,000	Jan	31	Returns	600
" 31	Purchases	8,400	"	31	Cash & Disc.	7,500
			"	31	Balance c/d	9,300
		17,400				17,400
Feb 1	Balance b/d	9,300				

At this stage the clerk knows that, in the absence of any errors in the books, each and every entry in the personal accounts of suppliers is included in one of the totals entered in the control account. A sectional trial balance can therefore be extracted, as shown below:

Sectional Trial Balance. Bought Ledger 31st January 19...

	Dr £	Cr £
Hotel Suppliers Ltd		3,450
B Brown & Sons		2,550
Holland Bacon Co.		3,300
Bought ledger control account	9,300	
	9,300	9,300

As the accuracy of the postings has been proved, it is safe for the clerk to balance the accounts of suppliers and bring the balances down as at the end of the month.

The above procedure also applies to the personal accounts of the customers of a business, i.e. the sales ledger. In fact, many hotels and restaurants maintain sales ledger control accounts and prove the accuracy of the postings to such accounts before sending out monthly statements of account to the customers.

Control accounts may also be applied to accounts other than personal accounts, though in most hospitality establishments the scope for such applications is limited.

Finally, it is necessary to mention the treatment of certain non-routine transactions affecting control accounts, e.g. bad debts written off, legal expenses debited to customers, etc. It will be realized that any entries made in respect of such uncommon transactions will not be included in the totals of subsidiary books used to compile control accounts. It is important to ensure, therefore, that all such transactions are posted separately to the appropriate control account. The balance of the control account will not otherwise be equal to the sum total of the individual balances extracted from the ledger concerned.

SUMMARY

- The ledger is often divided into smaller parts for convenience of operation.
- In most cases the ledger is divided into three parts: general ledger, purchases ledger and sales ledger.
- The sales ledger contains the personal accounts of debtors while the purchases ledger contains those of creditors.
- The general ledger will normally include two control accounts which represent the sales ledger and purchases ledger. Total transactions for the period in respect of debtors and creditors will be recorded in the two single control accounts.
- Every entry made in the books should be supported by documentation, e.g. invoice or voucher.
- Every transaction must be entered in a subsidiary book before being posted to the ledger.
- The cash book and the hotel visitors' ledger are both subsidiary books and ledger accounts.
- A control account is a total account which shows in summary form the detailed entries of a particular ledger.
- It is important to note that control accounts are merely memorandum accounts and do not form part of the double entry book-keeping system.

PROBLEMS

1. Explain what is meant by general ledger; nominal ledger; private ledger; bought ledger and sales ledger.

2. A large hotel keeps its ledger accounts in five separate ledgers: private, nominal, bought, sales, and visitors' ledger. You are required to indicate in which of the above ledgers you would expect to find each of the following accounts: freehold premises; rates; discount received; sales; M W Biscuits Ltd (supplier); Col. J St John (customer, non-resident); repairs and renewals; capital; sales; W R Stillings (customer, resident); restaurant furniture; purchases returns; advertising; kitchen plant.

3. List the main subsidiary books. Enumerate their main objects. Explain the relationship between the subsidiary books and the ledger.

4. (a) What do you understand by the term 'sources of entries'?
   (b) What are the sources of entries for the following:
      (i) petty cash book;
      (ii) purchases day book;
      (iii) cash book.

5. Explain the use of ledger folios in practical book-keeping.

6. Write short notes on the objects and advantages of control accounts.

7. On 1st June 19..., the total amount owing to the suppliers of a hotel

was £9,600. During that month the hotel bought further goods from its suppliers costing £10,500. Goods found damaged, £900, were returned to suppliers. Also, the hotel paid its suppliers £7,500 and received cash discounts amounting to £450. How much did the hotel owe its suppliers on 30th June 19... ?

8. From the following information write up the sales ledger control account and the bought ledger control account of a restaurant. Assume that both accounts are kept in the general ledger.

			£
Dec	1	Total bought ledger balances	7,650
"	1	Total sales ledger balances	15,420
"	31	Credit purchases	9,480
"	31	Credit sales	18,540
"	31	Purchases returns	570
"	31	Allowances to customers	300
"	31	Cash paid to suppliers	6,030
"	31	Discounts received	300
"	31	Cash received from customers	12,420
"	31	Bad debts written off	930

9. The Pronto Catering Co. maintains a sales ledger controlled by a control account kept in that ledger. From the information given below, you are required to write up the sales ledger control account for three months, balancing it at the end of each month.

	January £	February £	March £
Opening sales ledger balances	13,500		
Credit sales	15,600	16,350	17,250
Allowances to customers	300	450	600
Cash received from customers	12,900	14,400	15,600

10. From the following information you are required to:
   (a) write up the purchases day book and the purchases returns book;
   (b) show the necessary extracts from the cash book;
   (c) post the transactions to the ledger accounts;
   (d) compile a bought ledger control account;
   (e) extract a sectional trial balance as at 31st January 19...

Bought ledger balances on 1st January 19...

	£
Wm Butcher & Sons	1,200
N O Nicotine Ltd	900
Catering Supplies Ltd	1,800
B N May Ltd	2,100

Invoices received

			£
Jan	1	B N May Ltd	900
"	3	Catering Supplies Ltd	1,380
"	6	Wm Butcher & Sons	660

			£
Jan	9	N O Nicotine Ltd	480
"	13	Catering Supplies Ltd	240
"	15	Wm Butcher & Sons	630
"	18	B N May Ltd	570
"	21	N O Nicotine Ltd	330
"	24	Catering Supplies Ltd	690
"	27	Wm Butcher & Sons	960
"	29	B N May Ltd	480
"	31	Catering Supplies Ltd	810

Credit notes received

			£
January	3	Catering Supplies Ltd	60
	12	Wm Butcher & Sons	120
	19	B N May Ltd	30
	27	N O Nicotine Ltd	90

Payments to suppliers

January	24	Wm Butcher & Sons	£1,200 less CD £30
	24	B N May Ltd	£2,100 less CD £60
	24	Catering Supplies Ltd	£1,800 less CD £90

Having agreed your sectional trial balance, balance all personal accounts and bring balances down as at the end of January.

11. On 15th May the visitors' ledger control account had a debit balance of £5,000.

Transactions for the day are summarized below:

	£
Opening balance 1st May	5,000
Sales – Apartments	3,500
Meals	1,000
Drinks	300
Telephone	50
Allowances	20
Cash received from guests	4,800
Transfers to sales ledger	200

Required:
    (a) write up the visitors' ledger control account;
    (b) balance it and carry forward balance to the following day.

Maintaining a full set of books

8

INTRODUCTION

The purpose of the present chapter is two-fold: firstly to illustrate the operation of a full set of books; secondly to give the student adequate practice in keeping a reasonably realistic set of records. Two suggestions are, therefore, made. First, students are encouraged to study carefully the example given below; in particular they should study the 'explanatory notes' given in the example. Second, they are encouraged to tackle as many as possible of the problems following this chapter. These have been designed to give students sufficient practice in book-keeping techniques and to equip them with the ability to keep a fairly complex set of accounts.

OBJECTIVES

On completion of this chapter you should be able to:

- set up a full set of accounting records;
- correctly enter transactions into the relevant day books;
- correctly carry out the appropriate double entry into the books of account;
- prove the personal accounts;
- close off all relevant accounts and take out a trial balance;
- successfully tackle a fairly complex book-keeping exercise.

TACKLING A QUESTION

The following worked example starts with a trial balance which lists all the assets, liabilities, revenues and expenses at 30th November.

Review all the items therein and bear in mind that you will have to open a separate account for each item in the trial balance and enter the appropriate opening balance.

The next section of the question covers all transactions that took place in the month of December. All these transactions will need to be double entered into the accounts you have just opened or into a new account if it is a new expense not encountered before.

Many of the transactions are credit transactions which means they must first be entered into the appropriate day book.

The student is reminded that a petty cash book is in operation and the appropriate transactions should be entered therein.

Once all transactions are entered up and the accounts closed off and proved then proceed to a new trial balance at the end of December.

WORKED EXAMPLE

On 30th November 19 . . ., after eleven months' trading, the following balances were extracted from the books of the Gatto Nero Restaurant:

		£	£
Capital			600,000
Furniture		57,000	
Rent and rates		35,400	
Postage and stationery		4,050	
Sales			778,800
Repairs and renewals		29,850	
Petty cash		450	
Kitchen equipment		58,500	
Collector of taxes			1,950
Purchases		389,550	
Gas and electricity		36,300	
Advertising		51,900	
Discounts received			8,850
Glass, cutlery and china		11,850	
Miscellaneous expenses		2,550	
Wages and salaries		176,700	
Stock of food, 1st January 19 . . .		15,150	
Creditors:	A M Grocer & Sons		4,800
	Wholesalers Ltd		1,500
	Devon Produce Co.		6,000
	Quick Foods Ltd		3,000
Debtors:	The '65 Club	1,050	
	Agrarian Society	1,800	
	S G Curtis Esq.	450	
	Wm Brown & Co. Ltd	750	
Purchases returns			2,400
Leasehold premises		450,000	
Cash at bank		84,000	
		£1,407,300	£1,407,300

Open the necessary accounts and enter the above balances. During December, the transactions of the restaurant were as follows:

				£
Dec	1	Withdrew from bank for petty cash		300
"	1	Banked cash sales		7,950
"	2	Received invoices from:	Quick Foods Ltd	2,400
			Devon Produce Co.	1,170
			Wholesalers Ltd	3,660
"	3	Paid out of petty cash:	fruit	30
			duplicating paper	90
			floor polish	30
"	4	Purchased food, paid by cheque		2,850
"	5	Restaurant credit sales:	Wm Brown & Co. Ltd	300
			Agrarian Society	750
			The '65 Club	900
"	6	Banked cash sales		6,150
"	7	Paid wages – net		3,900
"	7	Tax deducted on above		360
"	8	Paid for new china by cheque		1,950
"	9	Received cheques from customers:	The '65 Club	1,050
			Agrarian Society	1,800
			Wm Brown & Co. Ltd	750
"	10	Received invoices from:	A M Grocer & Sons	2,250
			Devon Produce Co.	1,500
			Quick Foods Ltd	2,430
"	11	Banked cash sales		6,450
"	12	Received credit notes from:	Devon Produce Co.	150
			Wholesalers Ltd	90
"	12	Paid out of petty cash:	postage stamps	90
			vegetables	60
			gratuities	30
"	13	Purchased food, paid by cheque		1,320
"	14	Restaurant credit sales:	S G Curtis Esq.	150
			Wm Brown & Co. Ltd	900
			The '65 Club	420
"	14	Paid wages – net		3,840
"	14	Tax deducted on above		330
"	15	Received invoices from:	Quick Foods Ltd	570
			Wholesalers Ltd	1,920
			A M Grocer & Sons	1,950
"	16	Banked cash sales		6,930
"	17	Paid collector of taxes in respect of tax due		1,950
"	18	Paid by cheque for stationery		1,110
"	19	Received credit notes from:	A M Grocer & Sons	60
			Devon Produce Co.	120
"	20	Paid by cheque for repairs		2,490
"	21	Restaurant credit sales:	Agrarian Society	360
			The '65 Club	390
			Wm Brown & Co. Ltd	1,020

				£
Dec	21	Paid wages – net		4,470
"	21	Tax deducted on above		390
"	22	Banked cash sales		11,850
"	22	Paid for gas by cheque		1,620
"	22	Paid out of petty cash:	flowers	60
			restaurant bills	30
			fruit	90

Dec 23 Paid the following suppliers' accounts as at 30th November 19. . .

A. M. Grocer & Sons – cash disc.	£120.00	
Wholesalers Ltd	4%	
Devon Produce Co.	3%	
Quick Foods Ltd	2%	

				£
"	24	Received credit notes from:	Wholesalers Ltd	60
			Quick Foods Ltd	90
"	25	Received cheque from	S G Curtis Esq.	450
"	25	Banked cash sales		6,150
"	26	Paid by cheque for advertising		900
"	27	Restaurant credit sales:	S G Curtis Esq.	300
			Agrarian Society	450
"	28	Paid wages – net		3,990
"	28	Tax deducted on above		330
"	29	Received invoices from:	Devon Produce Co.	1,170
			A M Grocer & Sons	1,290
"	30	Bank cash sales		8,970
"	30	Paid out of petty cash:	travelling expenses	30
			vegetables	60
"	31	Paid by cheque for kitchen equipment		6,000

Required:

(a) Write up the books of the restaurant in respect of December 19... .

(b) Compile a bought ledger control account and a sales ledger control account.

(c) Prove the accuracy of the personal accounts.

(d) Extract a total trial balance as at 31st December 19...

Suggested Solution

(a) Restaurant books

Purchases Day Book   10

19 . . .			£
Dec 2	Quick Foods Ltd	BL4	2,400
" 2	Devon Produce Co.	BL3	1,170
" 2	Wholesalers Ltd.	BL2	3,660
" 10	A M Grocers & Sons	BL1	2,250
" 10	Devon Produce Co.	BL3	1,500
" 10	Quick Foods Ltd	BL4	2,430
" 15	Quick Foods Ltd	BL4	570
" 15	Wholesalers Ltd	BL2	1,920
" 15	A M Grocers & Sons	BL1	1,950
" 29	Devon Produce Co.	BL3	1,170
" 29	A M Grocers & Sons	BL1	1,290
	Transfer to Purchases A/c.	GL16	20,310

Purchases Returns Book   16

19 . . .			£
Dec 12	Devon Produce Co.	BL3	150
" 12	Wholesalers Ltd.	BL2	90
" 19	A M Grocers & Sons	BL1	60
" 19	Devon Produce Co.	BL3	120
" 24	Wholesalers Ltd	BL2	60
" 24	Quick Foods Ltd	BL4	90
" 31	Transfer to Purchases Returns A/c.	GL17	570

Notes:
(a) The invoices and credit notes received from suppliers are entered in the subsidiary books in chronological order.
(b) In many establishments the invoices and credit notes would be numbered and after posting filed consecutively rather than alphabetically. The invoice/credit note numbers are then shown in the subsidiary books.
(c) Against each invoice and credit note there is shown a folio of the bought ledger account to which the document has been posted.
(d) Finally, note that the totals from the subsidiary books are posted to the ledger as at the end of the period concerned.

Restaurant Sales Book 25

19...				£
Dec 5	Wm Brown & Co. Ltd	SL4		300
" 5	Agrarian Society	SL2		750
" 5	The '65 Club	SL1		900
" 14	S G Curtis Esq.	SL3		150
" 14	Wm Brown & Co. Ltd	SL4		900
" 14	The '65 Club	SL1		420
" 21	Agrarian Society	SL2		360
" 21	The '65 Club	SL1		390
" 21	Wm Brown & Co. Ltd	SL4		1,020
" 27	S G Curtis Esq.	SL3		300
" 27	Agrarian Society	SL2		450
" 31	Trans. to Sales A/c	GL18		5,940

Notes:

(a) As already explained, only credit sales are entered in the restaurant sales book.

(b) The sources of entries are the copies of customers' bills.

Petty Cash Book 14

£				F.	Total	Food Purchases.	Postage & Stationery	Misc. Expenses
					£	£	£	£
450	Nov	30	Balance	b/d				
300	Dec	1	Cash Rec'd	CB				
	"	3	Fruit	1	30	30		
	"	3	Duplic. Paper	2	90		90	
	"	3	Floor. Polish	3	30			30
	"	12	Postage Stamps	4	90		90	
	"	12	Vegetables	5	60	60		
	"	12	Gratuities	6	30			30
	"	22	Flowers	7	60			60
	"	22	Restaurant Bills	8	30		30	
	"	22	Fruit	9	90	90		
	"	30	Travel Expenses	10	30			30
	"	30	Vegetables	11	60	60		
					600	240	210	150
		31	Balance	c/d	150	GL16	GL11	GL15
750	19...				750			
150	Jan	1	Balance	b/d				

Notes:

(a) The choice of headings for the analysis columns is primarily dependent on what expenses are actually paid out of petty cash.

(b) It is usual to enter each item of petty cash expenditure separately.

(c) It is important to remember to post the analysed totals to the ledger every time the petty cash book is balanced; also to show the folios of the ledger accounts debited.

(d) As may be seen from the folio column, all petty cash vouchers are numbered consecutively for filing purposes.

Cash Book 1

Date	Details	F.	Sales Ledger	Bank	Date	Details	Folio	Bought Ledger	Disc. Rec'd	Bank
19...				£	19...					£
Nov 30	Balance	b/d		84,000	Dec 1	Petty Cash	PL14			300
Dec 1	Sales	GL18		7,950	" 4	Purchases	GL16			2,850
" 6	"	GL18		6,150	" 7	Wages	GL9			3,900
" 10	The '65 Club	SL1	1,050		" 8	China	GL4			1,950
" 10	Agrarian Society	SL2	1,800		" 13	Purchases	GL16			1,320
" 10	W Brown & Co.	SL4	750	3,600	" 14	Wages	GL9			3,840
" 11	Sales	GL18		6,450	" 17	Taxes	GL8			1,950
" 16	"	GL18		6,930	" 18	Stationery	GL11			1,110
" 22	"	GL18		11,850	" 20	Repairs	GL12			2,490
" 25	S G Curtis	SL3	450	450	" 21	Wages	GL9			4,470
" 25	Sales	GL18		6,150	" 22	Gas	GL13			1,620
" 30	"	GL18		8,970	" 23	A M Grocer	BL1	4,800	120	4,680
					" 23	Wholesalers	BL2	1,500	60	1,440
					" 23	Devon Produce	BL3	6,000	180	5,820
					" 23	Quick Foods	BL4	3,000	60	2,940
					" 26	Advertising	GL14			900
					" 28	Wages	GL9			3,990
					" 31	Kitchen Equip	GL3			6,000
					" 31	Balance	c/d			90,930
			4,050	142,500				15,300	420	142,500
Jan 1	Balance	b/d		90,930						GL7

Notes:

(a) The object of the sales ledger and bought ledger columns is to accumulate totals for control accounts. Thus, by reference to the bought ledger column, it may be seen that the total of cash and discounts debited in suppliers' accounts in December was £15,720.

(b) The discount received column is in the nature of a subsidiary book; any amount entered in it does not count for double entry purposes. Whenever the cash book is balanced, the total of discounts received should be posted to the credit of the discount received account.

GENERAL LEDGER

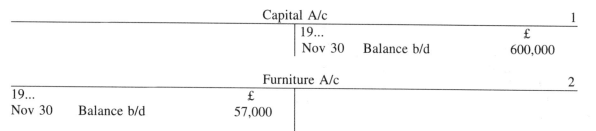

Capital A/c 1

		19...		£
		Nov 30	Balance b/d	600,000

Furniture A/c 2

19...		£		
Nov 30	Balance b/d	57,000		

Kitchen Equipment A/c   3

19...			£	
Nov 30	Balance	b/d	58,500	
Dec 1	Cash	CB1	6,000	

Glass, Cutlery & China A/c   4

19...			£	
Nov 30	Balance	b/d	11,850	
Dec 8	Cash	CB1	1,950	

Leasehold Premises A/c   5

19...			£	
Nov 30	Balance	b/d	450,000	

Stock A/c   6

19...			£	
Nov 30	Balance	b/d	15,150	

Discount Received A/c   7

							£
				19...			
				Nov 30	Balance	b/d	8,850
				Dec 31	Cash	CB1	420

Collector of Taxes A/c   8

19...			£	19...			£
Dec 17	Cash	CB1	1,950	Nov 30	Balance	b/d	1,950
				Dec 7	Wages	GL9	360
				" 14	"	GL9	330
				" 21	"	GL9	390
				" 28	"	GL9	330

Wages A/c   9

19...			£	
Nov 30	Balance	b/d	176,700	
Dec 7	Cash	CB1	3,900	
" 7	Coll. of Taxes GL8		360	
" 14	Cash	CB1	3,840	
" 14	Coll. of Taxes GL8		330	
" 21	Cash	CB1	4,470	
" 21	Coll. of Taxes GL8		390	
" 28	Cash	CB1	3,990	
" 28	Coll. of Taxes GL8		330	

Rent and Rates A/c 10

19...			£	
Nov 30	Balance	b/d	35,400	

Postage and Stationery A/c 11

19...			£	
Nov 30	Balance	b/d	4,050	
Dec 18	Cash	CB1	1,110	
" 31	Petty Cash	PC14	210	

Repairs and Renewals A/c 12

19...			£	
Nov 30	Balance	b/d	29,850	
Dec 20	Cash	CB1	2,490	

Gas and Electricity A/c 13

19...			£	
Nov 30	Balance	b/d	36,300	
Dec 22	Cash	CB1	1,620	

Advertising A/c 14

19...			£	
Nov 30	Balance	b/d	51,900	
Dec 26	Cash	CB1	900	

Miscellaneous Expenses A/c 15

19...			£	
Nov 30	Balance	b/d	2,550	
Dec 31	Petty Cash	PC14	150	

Purchases A/c 16

19...			£	
Nov 30	Balance	b/d	389,550	
Dec 4	Cash	CB1	2,850	
" 13	"	CB1	1,320	
" 31	Sundries	PB10	20,310	
" 31	Petty Cash	PC14	240	

Purchases Returns A/c   17

			£
19...			
Nov 30	Balance	b/d	2,400
Dec 31	Sundries	PR16	570

Sales A/c   18

			£
19...			
Nov 30	Balance	b/d	778,800
Dec 1	Cash	CB1	7,950
" 6	"	CB1	6,150
" 11	"	CB1	6,450
" 16	"	CB1	6,930
" 22	"	CB1	11,850
" 25	"	CB1	6,150
" 30	"	CB1	8,970
" 31	Sundries	SB25	5,940

Notes:
(a) The pages of the ledger are numbered, and it will be seen that similar accounts are grouped together: accounts 2–6 are those for assets, accounts 9–15 are those for recording expenses, and accounts 16–18 record the buying and selling of goods. In practice, one, two, or more pages of the ledger would be allotted to each account.
(b) Note how certain accounts collect totals from various subsidiary books.
(c) The balance of the purchases returns account is usually transferred to the purchases account before the preparation of the trading account.
(d) The accounts are not balanced, as some would be transferred to the trading and profit and loss accounts. Others would require certain adjustments.

BOUGHT LEDGER

A M Grocer & Sons A/c   1

19...			£	19...			£
Dec 19	Returns	PR16	60	Nov 30	Balance	b/d	4,800
" 23	Cash	CB1	4,680	Dec 10	Purchases	PB10	2,250
" 23	Discount	CB1	120	" 15	"	PB10	1,950
" 31	Balance	c/d	5,430	" 29	"	PB10	1,290
			10,290				10,290
				19...			
				Jan 1	Balance	b/d	5,430

Wholesalers Ltd A/c

2

19...			£	19...			£
Dec 12	Returns	PR16	90	Nov 30	Balance	b/d	1,500
" 23	Cash	CB1	1,440	Dec 2	Purchases	PB10	3,660
" 23	Discount	CB1	60	" 15	"	PB10	1,920
" 24	Returns	PR16	60				
" 31	Balance	c/d	5,430				
			7,080	19...			7,080
				Jan 1	Balance	b/d	5,430

Devon Produce Co. A/c

3

19...			£	19...			£
Dec 12	Returns	PR16	150	Nov 30	Balance	b/d	6,000
" 19	"	PR16	120	Dec 2	Purchases	PB10	1,170
" 23	Cash	CB1	5,820	10	-do-	PB10	1,500
" 23	Discount	CB1	180	29	-do-	PB10	1,170
" 31	Balance	c/d	3,570				9,840
			9,840	19 . . .			
				Jan 1	Balance	b/d	3,570

Quick Foods Ltd A/c

4

19...			£	19...			£
Dec 23	Cash	CB1	2,940	Nov 30	Balance	b/d	3,000
" 23	Discount	CB1	60	Dec 2	Purchases	PB10	2,400
" 24	Returns	PR16	90	" 10	"	PB10	2,430
" 31	Balance	c/d	5,310	" 15	"	PB10	570
			8,400				8,400
				19...			
				Jan 1	Balance	b/d	5,310

Notes:
(a) Personal accounts are not balanced before being agreed with the bought ledger or sales ledger control account.
(b) In practice, one or more pages would be allotted to each personal account.

SALES LEDGER

The '65 Club A/c   1

19...			£	19...			£
Nov 30	Balance	b/d	1,050	Dec 10	Cash	CB1	1,050
Dec 5	Sales	SB25	900	" 31	Balance	c/d	1,710
" 14	"	SB25	420				
" 21	"	SB25	390				
			2,760				2,760
19...							
Jan 1	Balance	b/d	1,710				

Agrarian Society A/c   2

19...			£	19...			£
Nov 30	Balance	b/d	1,800	Dec 10	Cash	CB1	1,800
Dec 5	Sales	SB25	750	" 31	Balance	c/d	1,560
" 21	"	SB25	360				
" 27	"	SB25	450				
			3,360				3,360
19...							
Jan 1	Balance	b/d	1,560				

S G Curtis Esq. A/c   3

19...			£	19...			£
Nov 30	Balance	b/d	450	Dec 25	Cash	CB1	450
Dec 14	Sales	SB25	150	" 31	Balance	c/d	450
" 27	"	SB25	300				
			900				900
19...							
Jan 1	Balance	b/d	450				

Wm. Brown & Co. Ltd A/c   4

19...			£	19..			£
Nov 30	Balance	b/d	750	Dec 10	Cash	CB1	750
Dec 5	Sales	SB25	300	" 31	Balance	c/d	2,220
" 14	"	SB25	900				
" 21	"	SB25	1,020				
			2,970				2,970
19...							
Jan 1	Balance	b/d	2,220				

Notes:

(a) See notes following bought ledger accounts.

(b) It is important to ensure that no statements are sent to customers before sales ledger accounts are proved. This is achieved by means of a sectional or total trial balance.

(b) Bought and sales ledger control accounts

Bought Ledger Control A/c

19...			£	19...			£
Dec 31	Returns		570	Nov 30	Balance	b/d	15,300
" 31	Cash & Disc		15,300	Dec 31	Purchases	PB10	20,310
" 31	Balances	c/d	19,740				
			35,610				35,610
				19...			£
				Jan 1	Balance	b/d	19,740

Sales Ledger Control A/c

19...			£	19...			£
Nov 30	Balances	b/d	4,050	Dec 31	Cash	CB1	4,050
Dec 31	Sales	SB25	5,940	" 31	Balances	c/d	5,940
			9,990				9,990
19...							
Jan 1	Balances	b/d	5,940				

Notes:

(a) In this case the control accounts are kept in the general ledger and, as explained previously, show in summary form the detailed transactions posted to the bought ledger and the sales ledger. Thus, by reference to the bought ledger control account, the total amount owing to the suppliers of the restaurant is, at the end of December, £19,740.

(b) The control accounts are compiled at the end of each period (week, month, quarter) by extracting the necessary totals from the relevant subsidiary books.

(c) As the balance of a control account is equal to the sum total of the individual balances in the ledger it controls, when extracting a total trial balance it is not necessary to list the individual personal accounts. Instead, the balance of the control account may be shown in the total trial balance.

(c) Proving personal accounts

The method of extracting a sectional trial balance has already been explained. In this case the control accounts are kept in the general ledger and the extraction of a sectional trial balance is not, therefore, possible.

The accuracy of the personal accounts may still be proved by listing all the personal accounts and their balances and agreeing the total of such balances with the balance of the appropriate control account as at that date. This method of controlling personal accounts is illustrated below.

Bought ledger control as at 31st December 19...

	£
A M Grocer & Sons	5,430
Wholesalers Ltd	5,430
Devon Produce Co.	3,570
Quick Foods Ltd	5,310
Control account balance	19,740

Sales ledger control as at 31st December 19...

	£
The '65 Club	1,710
Agrarian Society	1,560
S G Curtis Esq.	450
Wm Brown & Co. Ltd	2,220
Control account balance	5,940

It will be realized that whether one extracts a sectional trial balance or proves the personal accounts as shown above does not really matter. In both cases one is, in fact, agreeing a number of individual balances with the balance of a control account, which does not form a part of the system of double entry.

(d) Trial balance

Trial balance as at 31st December 19...

		£	£
Capital account	1		600,000
Furniture account	2	57,000	
Kitchen equipment account	3	64,500	
Glass, cutlery and china account	4	13,800	
Leasehold premises account	5	450,000	
Stock account	6	15,150	
Discount received account	7		9,270
Collector of taxes account	8		1,410
Wages and salaries account	9	194,310	
Rents and rates account	10	35,400	
Postage and stationery account	11	5,370	
Repairs and renewals account	12	32,340	
Gas and electricity account	13	37,920	
Advertising account	14	52,800	
Miscellaneous expenses account	15	2,700	
Purchases account	16	414,270	
Purchases returns account	17		2,970
Sales account	18		839,190
Cash book	1	90,930	
Petty cash book	14	150	
Bought ledger control account			19,740
Sales ledger control account		5,940	
		1,472,580	1,472,580

Notes:
(a) It is useful to show the folios of the accounts listed in the trial balance in case any of them have to be referred to or checked.
(b) Should the trial balance fail to balance, only the general ledger accounts (including the cash book and the petty cash book) would have to be checked as the accuracy of the personal accounts has already been proved by means of the control accounts.

SUMMARY

- It is important in carrying out this task to adopt a systematic approach.
- Scan the question carefully before commencing in order to decide what exactly is involved.
- Keep a close eye on the worked example and especially the explanatory notes.
- It may be useful to set up the day books, cash book and a good number of blank 'T' accounts in advance.
- Ensure that you leave plenty of space for entries in the key day books and the cash book.

PROBLEMS

1. The following trial balance was extracted from the books of a restaurant as at 1st January 19 . . .

		£	£
Capital			300,000
Premises		223,500	
China and cutlery		13,050	
Stock		6,450	
Rent and rates			750
Cash at bank		57,450	
Petty cash		300	
Gas and electricity			1,050
Creditors:	A Allen		1,500
	B Bailey		450
	C Cooper		1,350
Debtors:	M Maynard	1,050	
	B I C Ltd	1,800	
	Midland Motors Ltd	1,500	
		305,100	305,100

The following were the transactions of the restaurant in January:

Jan 1	Paid gas by cheque		£3,750
" 1	Cash sales		1,950
" 2	Petty cash payments:	fruit	60
		manager's fares	30
" 2	Cash sales		1,650
" 2	Credit sales:	BlC Ltd	150
		M Maynard	90
" 5	Paid A Allen's account less 4% cash discount		
" 5	Credit purchases:	A Allen	2,250
		C Cooper	3,630
		D Dawson	540
" 5	Cash sales		2,430
" 6	Purchased new china, paid by cheque		600
" 6	Petty cash payments:	stationery	30
		postage stamps	60
" 7	Midland Motors Ltd paid their account as at 1.1.19...		
" 7	Cash sales		2,610
" 7	Credit sales:	BlC Ltd	240
		M Maynard	60
		BSA Society	330
" 8	Cash sales		1,590
" 8	Paid wages and salaries by cheque		4,980
" 11	Purchased stationery, paid by cheque		420
" 11	Cash sales		1,950
" 11	Credit sales:	BSA Society	270
		BlC Ltd	90
" 12	Credit purchases:	A Allen	1,110
		B Bailey	2,490
" 12	Cash sales		1,650
" 13	Purchased food, paid by cheque		2,730
" 13	Cash sales		2,640
" 14	Paid C Cooper's account as at 1st January less £60 cash discount		
" 14	Cash sales		1,860
" 16	Credit purchases:	D Dawson	1,230
		C Cooper	570
		B Bailey	3,570
" 18	Cash sales		2,130
" 19	Credit sales:	Midland Motors Ltd	240
		BSA Society	210
" 19	Cash sales		2,430
" 20	Paid B Bailey's account as at 1st January		
" 20	Cash sales		1,470
" 21	Balanced petty cash – drew cheque to make up imprest to £600		
" 21	Cash sales		3,030

Jan 22	Credit purchases:	D Dawson	1,650
		A Allen	1,410
" 22	Cash sales		2,280
" 25	Paid wages and salaries by cheque		4,470
" 26	Credit sales:	BSA Society	240
" 26	Cash sales		2,430
" 27	Petty cash payments:	gratuities	30
		vegetables	60
		flowers	30
" 27	Cash sales		1,920
" 28	BIC Ltd paid their account as at 1st January		
" 28	Cash sales		2,220
" 29	Credit purchase:	B Bailey	690
" 29	Cash sales		2,070
" 30	Paid out of petty cash: manager's fares		30
" 30	Cash sales		2,640
" 30	Purchased food from D Dawson, paid by cheque		510
" 31	Credit sales:	Midland Motors Ltd	120
		BSA Society	30
" 31	Cash sales		2,640

Required:

(a) Pass the above transactions through the books of the business.

(b) Extract a trial balance as at 31st January 19...

(c) Close the cash book and the petty cash book and all personal accounts. Use separate sheets of paper for the main divisions of the ledger.

2 The following were the balances in the book of a restaurant after eleven months' trading at 30th November 19...

Trial Balance

	£	£
Capital		300,000
Stock of food, 1st January 19...	9,300	
Sales		390,600
Purchases	195,900	
Wages and salaries	88,350	
Collector of taxes		1,050
Advertising	25,650	
Fuel and light	22,200	
Cash at bank	41,700	
Petty cash	300	
Repairs and replacements	14,550	
Restaurant furniture	27,000	
China, glass and cutlery	6,450	
Miscellaneous expenses	2,250	
Rates	18,900	

	£	£
Discounts received		4,350
Leasehold premises	222,000	
Kitchen plant	28,500	
Purchases returns		1,500
Creditors: Food Sellers Ltd		750
Dutch Dairy Co.		3,000
Catering Supplies Ltd		1,500
Oriental Foods Ltd		2,400
Postage and stationery	2,100	
	£705,150	£705,150

Open the necessary accounts and enter the above balances.

During December the transactions of the restaurant were as shown below:

			£
Dec 1	Withdrew from bank for petty cash		450
" 2	Banked cash sales		1,050
" 2	Received invoices from:	Oriental Foods Ltd	450
		Catering Supplies Ltd	750
		Dutch Dairy Co.	600
		Food Sellers Ltd	540
" 3	Petty cash payments:	food	60
		stationery	90
		cleaning materials	30
" 4	Banked cash sales		3,450
" 5	Purchased cutlery on credit from Sheffield Cutlery Co.		5,250
" 6	Banked cash sales		2,550
" 6	Paid wages and salaries		2,280
" 6	Tax deducted on above		240
" 7	Received invoices from:	Dutch Dairy Co.	1,050
		Food Sellers Ltd	900
		Catering Supplies Ltd	750
" 8	Banked cash sales		2,400
" 8	Paid by cheque for food		2,160
" 8	Petty cash payments:	postage	120
		food	90
		cleaning materials	60
" 9	Paid for electricity by cheque		2,700
" 9	Received credit notes from:	Food Sellers Ltd	150
		Dutch Dairy Co	180
		Oriental Foods Ltd	120
" 10	Banked cash sales		2,550
" 10	Paid by cheque for stationery		1,110
" 11	Purchased food, paid by cheque		2,220
" 11	Received credit note from Dutch Dairy Co.		60
" 12	Banked cash sales		2,490

Dec 12	Paid wages and salaries by cheque		2,070
" 12	Tax deducted on above		210
" 13	Received invoices from: Dutch Dairy Co.		600
	Catering Supplies Ltd		900
	Oriental Foods Ltd		1,200
	Food Sellers Ltd		300
" 13	Paid by cheque for repairs		1,290
" 14	Banked cash sales		2,370
" 14	Paid the following suppliers' accounts as at the end of the previous month and deducted discounts as indicated:		
	Food Sellers Ltd	CD 4%	
	Dutch Dairy Co.	CD 3%	
	Catering Supplies Ltd	CD 4%	
	Oriental Foods Ltd	CD 5%	
" 15	Petty cash payments: stationery		30
	food		120
" 16	Banked cash sales		2,490
" 16	Drew cheque for tax deducted in respect of previous month		1,050
" 17	Received invoices from: Food Sellers Ltd		690
	Oriental Foods Ltd		390
	Dutch Dairy Co.		450
" 19	Banked cash sales		2,640
" 19	Paid for advertising by cheque		1,110
" 20	Banked cash sales		1,830
" 20	Paid wages and salaries by cheque		2,400
" 20	Tax deducted on above		240
" 21	Received credit note from Catering Supplies Ltd		90
" 22	Banked cash sales		2,490
" 23	Paid out of petty cash for stationery		30
" 24	Banked cash sales		2,670
" 24	Received invoices from: Dutch Dairy Co.		1,410
	Oriental Foods Ltd		1,230
" 25	Purchased food, paid by cheque		480
" 26	Received credit note from Dutch Dairy Co.		60
" 26	Banked cash sales		1,170
" 27	Paid by cheque for kitchen plant		2,250
" 28	Banked cash sales		1,110
" 28	Paid wages and salaries by cheque		2,280
" 28	Tax deducted on above		180
" 29	Invoices received from: Catering Supplies Ltd		480
	Food Sellers Ltd		1,170
" 30	Banked cash sales		2,490
" 30	Paid by cheque for kitchen fuel		1,350
" 30	Sold for cash old cutlery		150
" 31	Banked cash sales		2,460
" 31	Paid by cheque for stationery		330

Required:

(a) Write up the books of the restaurant in respect of December 19 . . .

(b) Extract a trial balance and balance all personal accounts, the cash book and the petty cash book.

3. J Robinson started in business on 1st January 19 . . ., with a capital in cash of £30,000, which he paid into his business bank account. His transactions in January were:

			£
Jan 1	Paid three months' rent by cheque		4,650
" 2	Purchased kitchen equipment by cheque		7,650
" 3	Paid by cheque for cutlery and utensils		1,590
" 4	Bought food by cheque		2,490
" 9	Paid wages by cheque		930
" 13	Banked sales		2,310
" 16	Bought food on credit from XYZ Supplies Ltd		2,200
" 19	Bought food on credit from A K Jones & Co.		1,380
" 22	Banked sales		2,070
" 25	Paid wages by cheque		1,110
" 27	Bought food on credit from XYZ Supplies Ltd		1,140
" 28	Withdrew from bank for private use		900
" 29	Banked sales		3,210
" 31	Bought food on credit from A K Jones & Co.		990
" 31	Bought cutlery on credit from Catering Supplies Ltd		1,800

Required:

(a) Enter the above transactions in appropriate subsidiary books.

(b) Post to ledger.

(c) Extract Robinson's trial balance as at 31st January 19 . . .

Part II
Financial accounting in the hospitality industry

Accounting conventions and concepts | 9

INTRODUCTION

Up to this point in our study we have been dealing with accounting purely from a book-keeping perspective, that is to say, collecting and classifying mainly financial data, recording it using double entry and taking out a trial balance. In the next few chapters we will be moving on to the production of financial statements such as the trading and profit and loss account and the balance sheet which are widely used by many sections of the business community and therefore need to be reliable and objective to gain the trust of society. This chapter briefly examines part of the regulatory framework which assists in making these accounts more dependable, fair and objective.

OBJECTIVES

On completion of this chapter you should be able to:

- understand the need for a regulatory framework in the production of final accounts;
- list the different types of users likely to depend on final accounts;
- know the meaning of accounting concepts and conventions;
- explain the meaning of SSAPs and FRSs;
- define capital expenditure, revenue expenditure;
- list correctly items of capital and revenue expenditure;
- comprehend the need to differentiate between capital and revenue expenditure.

FINANCIAL STATEMENTS

The final accounts of a business tell us, amongst other things, what profit was made in the past year and places a value on the assets of the business at a point in time.

These accounts are produced mainly for the operators of that business but many other people need to depend on their honesty and accuracy. For example, a prospective buyer, a bank manager who is considering giving a loan, or a supplier who intends to allow credit to the business, must be able to trust the accounts and will require to be assured about the objectivity of the accounts. The Inland Revenue in particular would need to be convinced of their validity.

It is easy to believe that accounting is an exact science. This is not always the case. In certain types of transactions there are a number of different accounting practices which can be used, each one with the potential to produce a different profit or valuation. Over the years society and accountants have developed a regulatory framework which should be applied to the preparation of final accounts for all businesses. This allows outsiders such as investors and bank managers to have a certain amount of confidence when examining the accounts of a business.

THE REGULATORY FRAMEWORK

Limited companies (which we deal with in Chapter 16) are bound by law to comply with all aspects of the regulatory framework. Much of this is laid out in the Companies Act 1985.

The regulatory framework consists of a number of rules, regulations, assumptions and statements by which all accountants must abide by when preparing final accounts for a limited company. A detailed study of the above is beyond the scope of this textbook. However, traditionally the accounts of sole traders and partnerships are produced by accountants complying with much of the above mentioned regulation. It is clearly in everyone's interest that any financial statement is seen to be honest, fair, objective and comparable from one year to another and from business to business.

Accounting conventions and concepts

These conventions and concepts have developed and evolved over the years. They represent rules and assumptions which all accountants should follow when preparing final accounts. This is established accounting custom and practice and not dependent on law.

The difference between concept and convention is not always clear. A concept tends to be 'the underlying idea' or assumption, whereas a convention is a custom or rule now embedded in the system but developed over a period of time.

ACCOUNTING CONCEPTS

The business entity concept

This relates to the separation of a business from its owner. The business is assumed to stand as an entity in its own right and completely separate from the owner. It means that the transactions recorded in the accounts of a business are recorded purely from the point of view of the business.

Although a business may be run entirely for the benefit of the owner, the business and the owner are regarded from an accounting standpoint as two separate entities.

The going concern concept

In the absence of clear evidence to the contrary it will always be assumed, from an accounting point of view, that the business will continue to operate for the foreseeable future. This is important, particularly in the valuation of the assets of a business. Clearly plant and machinery which is used daily to produce goods for the business has a different value than if it was going to be sold off on completion of the accounts.

The cost concept

This states a simple but important rule – that assets are normally shown in the final accounts at their original cost price and that this is the basis for setting depreciation and future values of the asset while in the service of the business.

The money measurement concept

This means that accounting is only concerned with facts and actions of a business which can be measured in monetary terms with a reasonable degree of objectivity. Accounting cannot show the quality of a product or service, or the level of competence or otherwise of the management etc. It therefore confines itself to expressing written values only where there is a clear known monetary value. This can lead to many good businesses being undervalued in the balance sheet.

The realization concept

This means that in accounting terms profit is normally regarded as being earned or realized at the point in time when the goods or services are passed to the customer and he becomes responsible for them. This is an important concept. Please note that it is the time when the goods change hands which is important, not when they are paid for or when contracts are signed etc. This can, of course, cause difficulties in the calculation of profits if goods are later returned or some commission or allowance is made at a later date. None the less the rule stands. Any known or suspected allowances/commissions should be taken into account at the point of sale or as soon thereafter as possible.

The dual aspect concept

We have already referred to this in Chapter 1. It is a key concept and states that from an accounting standpoint, there are two aspects to all business transactions, one represented by the assets of the business and the other by the claims against them. These two aspects are always equal to each other, as shown in the accounting equation:

$$Assets = Liabilities + Capital$$

The matching concept or accruals concept

The matching concept is based on the view that the profit of a business is the difference between all revenues (cash and credit) and the expenses 'used up' in that period, rather than the difference between cash received and cash expended in any accounting period. This means we must be careful, in any given accounting period, to include all expenditure used in that period no matter when we pay for it. In simple terms the matching concept means matching up the actual sales (both cash and credit) of a period with all those costs and only those costs which were used up in order to generate the aforementioned sales. This means excluding prepayments but including accruals (see Chapter 10 for details).

ACCOUNTING CONVENTIONS

Materiality

Simply put it means that in the production of the final accounts, the accountant should ideally validate each and every figure. This, however, would be time consuming and often cost more than it is worth. Therefore only material figures shall be validated. What represents a material value will differ from business to business.

Accounting does not serve a useful purpose if the cost of recording a transaction outweighs the value of the transaction itself.

In order for a business transaction to be material it must be above a certain value. The figure will vary from business to business.

Certainly if the cost of dealing with a transaction in the correct/proper accounting fashion is more than the value of the transaction itself then, as a general rule, the amount in question would not be regarded as material. For example, in the case of tea making facilities in the bedrooms of a small hotel, the cost of controlling tea making provisions (teabags,coffee sachets, etc.) would normally outweigh any losses expected. It is therefore not regarded as material in an accounting sense.

Prudence

This convention is a sound common sense approach to costs, valuations, etc. It states that where there are two or more possible costs for an item, the accountant should err on the side of caution and normally choose the higher cost, which will, in turn, understate rather than overstate profit. One of the best known examples of the convention of prudence is where stock on hand is always valued in the balance sheet at cost or net realizable value whichever is lower.

Consistency

This means that once a business has adapted a certain accounting practice it must, as a general rule, continue using the same practice over future years. Some of the concepts/conventions listed above are subject to a fairly broad interpretation which allows a number of different accounting practices to be used. If a business were to deal with a specific item one way this year and a different way next year it would be unlikely to give an equitable picture of events over a number of years. This is why the consistency convention is so important. It states that once an accounting practice is chosen it must be used consistently over the years unless there are strong logical reasons for change. The consistency concept allows valid comparisons to be made year on year and across companies.

OTHER REGULATIONS – SSAPs AND FRSs

The following are brief details relating to other important rules laid down by the major accounting boards and which must be followed by all qualified accountants.

Statements of standard accounting practice (SSAP)

In 1970 the accounting bodies set up a special committee to create and issue accounting rules for dealing with certain specific areas, so that all accountants might deal with these in the same way. The rules are usually referred to as SSAPs.

Financial reporting standards (FRS)

This is a new committee which replaces the one named above but with increased powers. They are still charged with issuing accounting rules and procecures laid down by the accounting bodies but new rules from this body are referred to as FRSs instead of SSAPs. We will meet FRS 1 in Chapter 20, dealing with working capital issues.

CAPITAL AND REVENUE EXPENDITURE

Capital expenditure incurred in the purchase of fixed assets e.g. buildings, fixtures and fittings, etc. or expenditure which adds value to a fixed asset, e.g improvement to the structure of a restaurant.

Revenue, on the other hand, is expenditure which does not add value to a fixed asset but is merely the cost of running the business during a specific period of time.

The prime example often used to explain the difference between capital and revenue expenditure is that of the motor van purchased for use in the business. Clearly the original purchase of the van is capital expenditure while the cost of running the van, such as petrol, road tax, maintenance, depreciation etc. is revenue expenditure.

The distinction is important because if it is revenue expenditure, it is chargeable to the trading and profit and loss account. On the other hand, capital expenditure may not be charged to this account but is simply added to the value of fixed assets in the balance sheet.

If capital expenditure is accidently treated as revenue expenditure, this will increase expenses and thus understate profit. If the reverse happens profit is overstated. The accurate calculation of net profit is therefore dependent on the correct allocation of expenditure between capital and revenue expenditure.

The student will know from the study of Chapter 2 that the balances in the trial balance fell into two categories. The debit balances were either assets or expenses and the credit balances liabilities or income. This was, in fact, an over-simplification as in practice what is an expense and what is an asset depends on what the accountant describes as the distinction between capital and revenue. A particular debit balance may be an asset, or an expense, or partly one and partly the other.

The distinction between capital and revenue expenditure is of fundamental importance in the construction of final accounts and may be summarized as follows:

- When, during an accounting period, an expenditure has taken place and at the end of that period there is **something to show for it** the expenditure is regarded as capital expenditure. Examples would be expenditure on premises, kitchen plant and furniture.
- When, on the other hand, an expenditure has taken place and at the end of the current accounting period there is **nothing to show for it** the expenditure is regarded as revenue expenditure. Examples of revenue expenditure would be rent, rates, wages, salaries, insurance, etc.

It will be appreciated, on reflection, that the distinction between capital and revenue expenditure depends on the time factor: over a sufficiently long period all expenditure is of a revenue nature as (with the exception of land) nothing will last indefinitely.

All expenditure of a business results in the accrual of benefits. Whilst some of the benefits accrue over a long period (use of furniture, kitchen equipment, premises), others are short-lived (services of employees – resulting from wages paid, insurance against risks – resulting from premiums paid). When, therefore, we consider expenditure in relation to the time factor, we may distinguish between capital and revenue expenditure as follows.

- Where the benefits of expenditure are completely exhausted within the accounting period the expenditure is of a revenue nature. It must, therefore, be debited in the profit and loss account (sometimes also referred to as the revenue account.)
- Where the benefits of expenditure are prolonged beyond the end of the accounting period, the expenditure is, to that extent, capital expenditure and must be carried to the balance sheet.

Finally, it may be added that, in general, capital expenditure consists of expenditure incurred in acquiring assets for the purpose of earning income or increasing the earning capacity of the business, whereas revenue expenditure consists of expenditure in replacing and repairing fixed assets as well as of the current expenses of the business.

Cases sometimes arise when it is rather difficult to decide whether a particular item of expenditure is of a capital or a revenue nature. Thus legal expenses are usually a revenue expense. When, however, these are incurred in connection with the purchase of premises they must be regarded as capital expenditure and debited in the premises account. Repairs are usually a revenue item. When, however, the effect of the repairs is to improve the asset in some way (rather than maintain it in its usual condition), the cost of such repairs should be capitalized, i.e. debited in the asset account rather than written off to the profit and loss account. For instance, when a new restaurant front is put in, it is quite legitimate to capitalize a part of the cost as, invariably, a new restaurant front is an improvement on an old one.

Finally, advertising is usually regarded as revenue expenditure. When, however, a newly-established hotel undertakes an advertising campaign in order to create a market for the accommodation, food and services offered, the whole cost of advertising should not be charged against the profits of the first accounting period but spread over several years.

From what has been said it will be realized that before the final accounts are prepared it is necessary to examine all items of expenditure and ensure that only revenue expenses are charged against the income of the period concerned. Otherwise the profit and loss account will not show the correct profit or loss; similarly items other than those of a capital nature might be carried to the balance sheet.

CAPITAL AND REVENUE RECEIPTS

Our consideration of the distinction between capital and revenue has, so far, been in connection with the expenditure side of the business. It will be appreciated, however, that the same considerations apply on the income side. Thus, whilst most of the receipts of a business are of a revenue nature, constituting proper income for the current accounting period, certain kinds of receipts (such as deposits on advance bookings, or any amounts received on the sale of fixed assets) may at the end of a period, be regarded as capital items.

As a result, it is also necessary to examine all items of income to ensure that the fundamental distinction between capital and revenue is observed in the preparation of final accounts This is further explained in Chapter 11.

SUMMARY

- Accounting policies and procedures followed in the preparation of the final accounts can materially alter profit and/or the valuation of assets.
- There are many different users of final accounts, for example, managers/directors/owners, creditors, bank managers, lending institutions, investors, taxation officials etc.
- In order for accounting to survive as a credible business tool, it is imperative that the accounts produced are seen by a wide number of users as true, fair and objective.
- There is in existence a regulatory framework to help ensure the validity and objectivity of the accounts; part of this framework consists of the concepts and conventions governing the preparation of accounts.
- In recent years the concepts and conventions have been backed up by SSAPs and the newer FRSs to help ensure uniformity of practice and improve consumer confidence.
- Capital expenditure is that incurred in the purchase of fixed assets.
- Revenue expenditure is that expenditure which does not add value to fixed assets, but is merely the costs incurred in running the business.
- The distinction between capital and revenue expenditure is important because only revenue expenditure is chargeable to the profit and loss account.
- Failure to differentiate between capital and revenue expenditure will result in the overstating or understating of profit.

PROBLEMS

1. 'It is imperative that the general public should have full confidence as to how financial statements are prepared.'
   You are required to explain why such a high level of confidence is required and the steps taken to achieve it.

2. Explain briefly what you understand by the terms accounting concepts and conventions.

3. List three accounting concepts and give a detailed definition of each.

4. The realization concept is central to the calculation of accurate profits. Define the aforementioned concept and say if you agree with the content of the statement.

5. Write a short note on:
   (a) capital expenditure;
   (b) revenue expenditure.

6. Explain why it is so important to distinguish between capital and revenue expenditure.

Preparation of final accounts **10**

INTRODUCTION

The most important purpose of any business is to earn a profit. It is, therefore, necessary from time to time – and in practice at least once a year – to prepare an account showing how much profit (or loss) has in fact been made. Similarly, it is essential from time to time to review the financial position of the business to ascertain what assets (property) it owns and what liabilities (debts) it owes to outsiders.

In order to achieve the foregoing it is necessary to prepare what are known as the 'final accounts' of the business. These consist of:

1. The trading, profit and loss account
This shows the income and expenditure of a particular accounting period and the resulting gross profit (or gross loss) and the net profit (or net loss).

2. The balance sheet
This, strictly speaking, is not an 'account' but a financial statement showing the assets and the liabilities at a particular point in time.

OBJECTIVES

On completion of this chapter you should be able to:

- differentiate between assets, liabilities, income and expenses as they appear in the trial balance;
- extract items properly from the trial balance and place them correctly in the final accounts;
- draw up a 'ledger style' trading and profit and loss account to show how double entry is completed;
- draw up a simple balance sheet;
- understand the meaning of a trading account and its construction;
- deal with changes in stock value, staff meals and other items affecting the trading account;
- draw up a trading, profit and loss account using the standard vertical style as well as a balance sheet.

START WITH THE TRIAL BALANCE

It is usual to prepare the final accounts from a trial balance extracted from the ledger at a particular date. The trial balance consists of debit balances and credit balances. A debit balance may be one of two things. It may be an asset, e.g. furniture, china, cash, etc. or an expense (or loss), e.g. wages, rent, purchases. Similiarly a credit balance may represent one of two things. It may be a liability, e.g. an amount owing to suppliers, or a gain (or income) such as sales, as is indicated in the chart below.

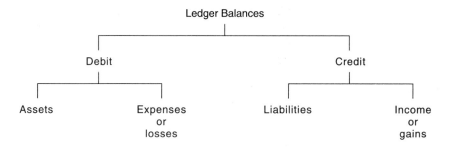

Balances which represent expenses and income are used to construct the trading, profit and loss account; balances which represent assets and liabilities are used to construct the balance sheet. Students will find it useful to remember, therefore, that the balances from the trial balance are, so to speak, channelled in two directions – some to the trading, profit and loss account, others to the balance sheet.

DRAWING UP THE FINAL ACCOUNTS

In the following example we will construct the trading and profit and loss account in the form of a ledger account to demonstrate how double entry is completed.

EXAMPLE 10.1

The following trial balance was extracted from the books of A Caterer at 31st December 19..., after a year's trading.

Trial balance as at 31st December 19...

Account	Dr	Cr	Nature of balance	Destination of item
	£	£		
Sales		400,000	Income	Trading account
Premises	300,000		Asset	Balance sheeet
Rent and rates	34,000		Expense	Profit and loss
Kitchen plant	82,000		Asset	Balance sheet
Creditors		12,000	Liability	Balance sheet
Repairs & renewals	17,000		Expense	Profit and loss
Furniture	54,000		Asset	Balance sheet
Purchases	160,000		Expense	Trading account
Cash at bank	28,000		Asset	Balance sheet
Wages & salaries	110,000		Expense	Profit and loss
Debtors	8,000		Asset	Balance sheet
Capital		300,000	Liability	Balance sheet
Light & heat	19,000		Expense	Profit and loss
X Finance Co. loan		100,000	Liability	Balance sheet
	812,000	812,000		

When we have determined the nature of each balance in the trial balance, and its destination, we may proceed to construct the final accounts. This is done by:

1. Debiting all expenses (losses) and crediting all income (gains) in the trading, profit and loss account.
2. Listing all assets and all liabilities in the the balance sheet, the structure of which is explained in detail in the following text.

To complete double entry the account is shown as follows:

Trading, profit and loss account for year ended 31st December 19...

	£		£
Purchases	160,000	Sales	400,000
Gross profit c/d	240,000		
	400,000		400,000
Wages & Salaries	110,000	Gross Profit b/d	240,000
Repairs, Renewals	17,000		
Rent & Rates	34,000		
Light & Heat	19,000		
Net profit	60,000		
	240,000		240,000

The trading, profit and loss account is rarely presented in this form today, other than for double entry purposes. It will usually take the following form:

Trading, Profit and Loss Account
for year ended 31st December 19...

		£
Sales		400,000
Less purchases*		160,000
Gross profit		240,000

Less other expenses	£	
Wages and salaries	110,000	
Repairs & renewals	17,000	
Rent & rates	34,000	
Light & heat	19,000	
		180,000
Net profit		60,000

Note:
* It will be observed that there is no opening or closing stock in this illustration. The stocks have been left out for the sake of clarity and will be dealt with later in this chapter.

BALANCE SHEET

The object of the balance sheet is to show, at a particular point in time, the financial position of a business. That means, to show what assets the business owns, what liabilities it has and how much capital there is in the business. The balance sheet is **not** an account but a list of balances remaining in the ledger (i.e. assets and liabilities), after the preparation of the trading, profit and loss account.

Balance sheet as at 31st December 19...

Fixed Assets		£		
Premises		300,000		
Kitchen plant		82,000		
Furniture		54,000		
		436,000	(a)	
Current Assets				
Debtors	8,000			
Cash at bank	28,000			— Top half
	36,000			
Less current liabilities				
Creditors	12,000			
Net current assets*		24,000	(b)	
Less long term liabilities				
X Finance Co. loan		(100,000)	(c)	
		360,000	(d)	

continued on next page

Financed by:	£		
Capital at 1st January 19...	300,000	(e)	Bottom
Add net profit for year	60,000	(f)	half
Total capital employed	360,000	(g)	

* Current assets less current liabilities equals net current assets.

Notes:

(a) The balancing figure (d) from the top half of the balance sheet must equal the balance (g) from the bottom half.

(b) Please note: a + b – c = d and e + f = g

(c) The net profit of £60,000 is, in the balance sheet, added to the capital as at the beginning of the year. As a result, the capital at the end of the year is £360,000.The student should note that the capital of a business is a debt from the business to the proprietor.

The top half of the balance sheet

Here we list all assets (debit balances in the ledger) in what is known as the order of liquidity, i.e. according to how easy or how difficult it is to turn the asset concerned into cash. It is usual to start with the least liquid assets (premises, kitchen plant, restaurant furniture) and to end with the most liquid (cash). As most hospitality establishments have a large proportion of non-liquid (fixed) assets these are usually shown first at the top of the balance sheet. Next we list the **current assets** and the **current liabilities,** (see below for details).

Current liabilities are taken away from current assets to give the **net current assets** or **working capital**.

Finally, long-term liabilities are taken away from total of fixed assets + net current assets, which gives the net worth of the business at that point in time.

The bottom half of the balance sheet

This shows the investment made in the business by the owner, usually referred to as **the capital a/c** and any accumulated profits owing to him, less any drawings (see below) which in turn gives the total capital employed.

The balance of the top half of the balance sheet (net worth) must be equal to the balance of the bottom half (total capital employed).

KINDS OF ASSETS AND LIABILITIES

In order to make the balance sheet more intelligible and meaningful, it is usual to provide suitable subheadings, and to show the different kinds of assets and liabilities separately. The subheadings commonly provided are:

Fixed assets

These are the assets of a permanent nature, intended for use in the business as distinct from resale to customers, e.g. premises, kitchen equipment, restaurant furniture, glass, china and cutlery.

Current assets

These are cash balances and other assets intended for conversion into cash, e.g. stocks of food, beverages, tobaccos, as well as debtors.

It will be appreciated that the distinction between fixed and current assets also depends on the nature of the business. Thus, furniture in a hotel is a fixed asset, whilst in the case of a dealer in furniture it is a current asset. What, then, matters is the intention of the owner of the asset, i.e. whether he has acquired it for the purpose of increasing the income-earning capacity of the business (retention of asset), or for resale to customers (conversion of asset into cash).

Current liabilities

These are liabilities of a temporary nature, usually payable within weeks or months of the date of the balance sheet. Examples of current liabilities are creditors, expenses due but unpaid and bank overdrafts, though the latter are sometimes permanent rather than temporary.

Long-term liabilities

These are liabilities of a more permanent nature such as mortgages and bank loans extending over more than one year.

Capital

The capital account of a business represents a liability from the business to its proprietor.

Drawings

Drawings represent money or money's worth (e.g. food, drink) withdrawn from the business by the owner for his own personal use and as such must be deducted from the capital owing to him at the end of the relevant accounting period.

TRADING ACCOUNT

The object of the trading account is to show how much gross profit (or gross loss) has been earned during the period under consideration. Gross profit may be defined as the excess of sales over the 'cost of sales' (also referred to as the 'cost of goods sold').

The gross profit on food sales is food sales less the cost of food consumed. Similarly, the gross profit on bar sales is the excess of bar sales over the cost of wines, spirits, beers, minerals, etc. consumed.

The gross profit on other sales – cigars, cigarettes, tobaccos and any shops or kiosks operated by the establishment – is calculated in a similar manner.

The actual treatment of room sales in the trading account is rather difficult in that the sale of hotel accommodation does not involve a cost of sales. The best method of dealing with room sales is illustrated in Chapter 20 (departmental profit method).

Working out the 'cost of sales' and the treatment of stocks

In order to arrive at the cost of sales, it is necessary to start with the opening stock and add the purchases for the period to it, thereafter deduct the closing stock to arrive at cost of sales. The basic formula is, therefore:

OPENING STOCK + PURCHASES − CLOSING STOCK = COST OF SALES.

A typical trading account of a non-residential catering establishment will therefore take the form shown below:

Specimen Trading Account for accounting period ended . . . .

	£
Sales	X
Opening stock	X
Add purchases	X
	X
Less Closing stock	X
Cost of sales	X
Gross profit c/d	X

The trading, profit and loss account forms a part of the system of double entry. As a result, for every one entry made in that account there must be a corresponding entry made in some account in the ledger. Double entry in respect of the opening and closing stocks in the trading account is completed in the stock account.

Let us assume that on 1st January 1996, a restaurant had a stock of food valued at £4,000. During the year ended 31st December 1996, the purchases of the restaurant amounted to £160,000 and the sales £400,000. At 31st December 1996, the stock of the restaurant was valued at £5,000.

On 1st January 1996, the stock account appeared as:

Stock A/c

1996		£		
Jan 1	Balance b/d	4,000		

At 31st December 1996, the stock available at the beginning of the year would be debited in the trading account and credited in the stock account. The stock account would then appear as follows:

Stock A/c

1996		£	1996		£
Jan 1	Balance b/d	4,000	Dec 31	Trading A/c	4,000

Also at 31st December 1996, it would be necessary to enter the closing stock in the trading account (to arrive at the cost of sales) as well as in the stock account (to show the value of the stock in existence at that date). This would be done by debiting the stock account and crediting the trading account.

The entry in the stock account would be dated 1st January 1997, as the closing stock for 1996 immediately becomes the opening stock for 1997.

In the trading account, the closing stock may be credited under the figure of sales, but it is usual to show it as a deduction on the debit side. Whether we do one or the other does not affect the amount of gross profit.

When the above entry has been made the stock account will appear as follows:

Stock A/c

1996		£		£
Jan 1	Balance b/d	4,000	Dec 31 Trading A/c	4,000
1997				
Jan 1	Balance b/d	5,000		

As may be seen from the above, the same procedure is adopted from one year to another and the same stock account is used over a period of years.

Finally, the trading account of the restaurant would be prepared as shown below:

Trading Account for year ended 31st December 19...

	£	£
Sales		400,000
Opening stock	4,000	
Add purchases	160,000	
	164,000	
Less Closing stock	5,000	
Cost of sales		159,000
Gross profit c/d		241,000

Staff meals

Many hospitality establishments properly regard the cost of staff meals as a labour cost. Where that is so an adjustment should be made in respect of the actual or estimated cost of such meals for the purpose of final accounts. As that portion of food purchases which is consumed by the staff is not available for sale to customers, the necessary adjustment is: Dr staff meals account and Cr purchases account.

Where an adjustment in respect of staff meals is made the formula for arriving at the cost of sales is:

OPENING STOCK + (PURCHASES − STAFF MEALS) − CLOSING STOCK = COST OF SALES

Other items affecting trading account

The book-keeping treatment of **purchases returns** was considered in Chapter 4. When the final accounts are prepared from a trial balance showing an item of purchases returns, it is usual to show the latter as a deduction from the purchases in the trading account.

Finally, the item **allowances to customers** is sometimes shown as a separate balance in the trial balance – particularly in the case of hotels. This, as explained in Chapter 5, is a reduction of sales and should, therefore, be shown as such in the trading account.

The specimen trading, profit and loss account shown in Figure 10.1 illustrates the correct layout for the various items affecting the trading account followed by a standard profit and loss account.

PROFIT AND LOSS ACCOUNT

The object of the profit and loss account is to show how much net profit (or net loss) has been earned by the business. Net profit may be defined as the difference between total income and total expenditure in respect of the period concerned. It may also be defined as the excess of gross profit, plus any other income, over the expenditure for the period covered by the accounts. Hence:

TOTAL INCOME − TOTAL EXPENDITURE = NET PROFIT
OR
GROSS PROFIT + OTHER INCOME — EXPENDITURE = NET PROFIT

Trading, Profit and Loss Account
for accounting period ended . . .

	£	£
Sales		502,000
Less Allowances		2,000
		500,000
Less Cost of sales		
Opening stock	4,000	
Add Purchases	200,000	
	204,000	
Less Returns	3,000	
	201,000	
Less Staff meals	17,000	
	184,000	
Less Closing stock	6,000	178,000
Gross profit		322,000
Add Other income		
Rent received	16,000	
Discount received	4,000	20,000
		342,000
Less other expenses		
Wages & salaries	142,000	
National insurance etc.	13,000	
Staff meals	17,000	
Repairs, renewals	23,000	
Depreciation	50,000	
Rent & rates	27,000	
Light & heat	17,000	
Postage, telephone	4,000	
Bank interest	2,000	
Accountancy fees	500	
Legal expenses	1,000	
Misc. expenses	1,500	298,000
Net profit		44,000

Notes:

(a) The gross profit together with the other income of the establishment amounts to £342,000: the expenses for the current year are £298,000 and the resulting net profit is thus £44,000.

(b) When constructing the profit and loss account care must be taken to ensure that similar items are placed together.

(c) The net profit is transferred from the profit and loss account to the credit side of the proprietor's capital account.

Figure 10.1 Specimen trading, profit and loss account

It is emphazised that in arriving at the net profit for any one accounting period, it is essential to take into account only items of income and expenditure in respect of that period. This is further explained in the next two chapters.

Items peculiar to hospitality establishments

An examination of profit and loss accounts of hospitality establishments would disclose certain items which are not usually found in the final accounts of other businesses. Some of the important items are listed below.

Hire of equipment

This is a charge paid in respect of various items of equipment (e.g. cutlery, china, furniture) hired by an establishment, usually in connection with outdoor catering activities. Any amounts so paid out must be debited in the profit and loss account.

Rentals

This is similar to the hire of equipment, explained above. Rentals paid by hospitality establishments are usually in respect of hire of television, though it is not unusual for hotel-keepers and caterers to pay such rentals in respect of kitchen equipment and furniture.

Commissions payable

This item is often found in the profit and loss account of hotels rather than non-residential establishments. Commissions are payable usually to travel agents in respect of hotel bookings secured by them.

Staff meals

As already explained, this is the cost of food consumed by the staff of an establishment and is regarded as a labour cost.

Professional charges

This usually consists of fees, etc. paid to solicitors and/or auditors. Many licensed establishments employ professional stocktakers for the stocktaking of alcoholic beverages. Where that is so the fees of the stocktakers are often debited in the same account as those of the solicitors and/or auditors, and subsequently written off to the profit and loss account.

Household supplies

These are mainly cleaning materials and other non-consumable supplies (brooms, dusters, detergents, etc.) used in the housekeeping department.

Rents received

This constitutes additional income of a hotel subletting (usually) ground floor accommodation to banks, shops and other businesses. Any such rents received may form a substantial source of income, especially in the case of hotels.

Sundry receipts

The nature of this item will vary from one business to another. In many hospitality establishments sundry may include amounts received in respect of the sale of swill, used linen and similar items.

FINAL ACCOUNTS

WORKED EXAMPLE

The following balances were to be found in the ledger of the Schifflandi Restaurant for the year ended 31st December 1996.

	SFrs	SFrs
Capital at 1st Jan 1996		7,800,000
Stock at 1st Jan 1996	150,000	
Kitchen plant	1,200,000	
Debtors	180,000	
City Finance Co. loan account		2,300,000
Cash at bank	200,000	
Furniture	1,600,000	
Creditors		510,000
Wages and salaries	1,300,000	
Staff meals	15,000	
Repairs, renewals	61,000	
Light and heat	39,000	
Misc. expenses	145,000	
Drawings	200,000	
Freehold hotel	8,000,000	
Purchases	2,350,000	
Purchases returns		190,000
China and cutlery	200,000	
Sales		5,250,000
Postage and telephone	110,000	
Rent and rates	300,000	
	16,050,000	16,050,000

Note: On the 31st December 1996 the closing stock was SFrs185,000.

Using the above trial balance you are required to draw up a trading, profit and loss account for the Schifflandi Restaurant for the year ended 31st December 1996 and a balance sheet at that date.

Final accounts would be drawn up as shown below:

Trading and Profit and Loss Account of the Schifflandi Restaurant for year ended 31st December 1996

	SFrs	SFrs	SFrs
Sales			5,250,000
Less cost of sales			
Opening stock at 1/1/96		150,000	
Add Purchases	2,350,000		
Less Purchases returns	190,000	2,160,000	
		2,310,000	
Less Closing stock		185,000	
Cost of sales			2,125,000
Gross profit			3,125,000
Less Other expenses			
Wages and salaries		1,300,000	
Staff meals		15,000	
Repairs, renewals		61,000	
Rent and rates		300,000	
Light and heat		39,000	
Postage and telephone		110,000	
Misc. expenses		145,000	1,970,000
Net profit			1,155,000

Schifflandi Restaurant
Balance sheet as at 31st December 1996

	SFrs	SFrs
Fixed Assets		
Freehold hotel		8,000,000
Kitchen plant		1,200,000
Furniture		1,600,000
China and cutlery		200,000
		11,000,000
Current Assets		
Stocks	185,000	
Debtors	180,000	
Cash in bank	200,000	
	565,000	
Less Current Liabilities		
Creditors	510,000	
Net current assets		55,000
		11,055,000
Less Long-term Liabilities		
City Finance Co. loan		2,300,000
		8,755,000

continued over page

Financed by:

	SFrs
Capital at 1st January 19...	7,800,000
Add Net profit for year	1,155,000
	8,955,000
Less Drawings	200,000
Total capital employed	8,755,000

Capital account

From the balance sheet given above it may be seen that the balance of the capital account increased from SFrs 7,800,000 to SFrs 8,755,000. The capital of a business is not static but is, in fact, changing continually, being increased by any profits made as well as by any fresh capital introduced by the proprietor and decreased by any losses incurred as well as amounts, if any, withdrawn by the proprietor.

At the end of each accounting year it is necessary, therefore, to transfer all additions, as well as all withdrawals of capital, to the capital account in order that the correct amount of capital may be shown in the balance sheet.

As already mentioned above, the net profit for the year is debited in the profit and loss account and credited in the capital account. If a net loss were made, the opposite entries would be required.

Any drawings (amounts of cash withdrawn by the proprietor for private use) are credited in the cash book and debited in the drawings account. At the end of each year the balance of the drawings account is transferred to the debit side of the capital account. Drawings in goods (food, wines, spirits and tobaccos consumed by the proprietor) should be credited in the purchases account and debited in the drawings account; these, too, are then debited in the capital account.

The capital account given in the balance sheet above would appear in the ledger as:

Capital A/c

1996		SFrs	1996		SFrs
Dec 31	Drawings	200,000	Jan 1	Balance b/d	7,800,000
" 31	Balance c/d	8,755,000	Dec 31	Net Profit	1,155,000
		8,955,000			8,955,000
			1997		
			Jan 1	Balance b/d	8,755,000

SUMMARY

- In the preparation of final accounts the starting point is the trial balance.
- A debit balance in the trial balance is either an asset or an expense. A credit balance is either a liability or a gain (income).

- The trading, profit and loss account and the balance sheet are known as the final accounts.
- The trading, profit and loss account is an integral part of the double entry book-keeping system.
- The balance sheet is not strictly speaking an 'account', but a financial statement showing the net worth of the business at a specific point in time.
- The object of the trading account is to establish how much gross profit has been made.
- Cost of sales means the cost of goods used in order to generate the sales, and is worked out as follows:

Opening stock + purchases − closing stock = Cost of sales

- The cost of sales calculation may have to be adjusted for purchases returns, staff meals and other relevant items.

PROBLEMS

1. Explain the object of each of the following: trading account; profit and loss account; balance sheet.

2. Write short, explanatory notes on the treatment of: staff meals; drawings.

3. Using the following information you are required to draw up a trading account at 31st December 1996. An allowance of £3,000 is to be made for staff feeding.

	£
Purchases	300,000
Sales	700,000
Opening stock at 1st Jan 1996	4,000
Closing stock at 31st Dec 1996	6,000

4. Explain what is meant by: fixed asset; current asset; long-term liability; current liability.

5. Arrange the following assets in the order of liquidity, starting with the least liquid asset: debtors; restaurant furniture; china and cutlery; premises; kitchen plant; cash at bank.

6. The following balances were extracted from the ledger of Acropolis Restaurant at 31st December 19... :

	£	£
Capital		100,000
Stocks, 1st January 19...	7,500	
Wages and salaries	50,000	
Rent	10,000	
Sales		200,000
Purchases	100,000	
Insurance	2,000	
Gas and electricity	5,000	
Kitchen utensils	15,000	
Restaurant furniture	40,000	
Creditors		20,000
Postage and telephone	3,000	
China and cutlery	10,000	
Kitchen equipment	50,000	
Cash at bank	27,500	
	320,000	320,000

You are required to prepare the restaurant's trading, profit and loss account for the year ended 31st December 19..., and a balance sheet as at that date. Stocks at 31st December 19... were valued at £2,500.

7. Distinguish clearly between 'fixed assets' and 'current assets'. State which of the following are fixed and which current: leasehold premises; cash at bank; glass, china and linen; restaurant furniture; banqueting debtors; liquor stock.

8. The following trial balance is from the accounts of Chico's Fast Food Operation. You are required to prepare a trading, profit and loss account for the year ended 31st December 19..., and a balance sheet as at that date.

	£	£
Capital		450,000
Gas and electricity	26,700	
Rent and rates	28,500	
Stock, 1st January	9,300	
Discounts received		2,400
Sundry receipts		750
China and cutlery	18,300	
Purchases	276,900	
Freehold premises	330,000	
Purchases returns		1,500
Printing and stationery	9,450	
Furniture	37,500	
Cash in hand	300	
Creditors		17,850
Wages and salaries	150,600	
Staff meals	18,000	

	£	£
Postage and telephone	6,300	
Drawings	25,500	
Sales		648,300
Kitchen equipment	72,000	
Miscellaneous expenses	10,500	
Professional charges	9,000	
Cash at bank	91,950	
	1,120,800	1,120,800

Note: Stock at 31st December 19... was valued at £9,900.

9. On 1st December 19..., after eleven months' trading, Nicola Weiss had the following balances in her books:

		£
Capital		165,000
Sales		142,500
Purchases		36,000
Cash at bank		42,000
Premises		106,250
Wages		78,500
China and cutlery		8,000
Furniture		26,250
Insurance		1,750
Drawings		12,500
Gas and electricity		3,750
Creditors:	N Morris		2,500
	A Austin		5,000

Arrange these in the form of a trial balance and enter balances into the accounts.

Nicola's transactions in December were:

			£
Dec	2	Purchased food by cheque	7,500
"	6	Drew cheque for private expenses	2,500
"	10	Paid amount due to N Morris	
"	14	Banked sales to date	4,250
"	16	Paid wages by cheque	2,000
"	19	Paid rates by cheque	3,850
"	23	Bought food on credit:	
		N Morris	6,000
		A Austin	3,000
"	27	Paid by cheque for insurance	750
"	31	Banked sales to date	7,800

Required:
(a) Enter these transactions in Nicola's books and extract a trial balance as at 31st December 19...

(b) Prepare Nicola's trading, profit and loss account for the year ended 31st December 19..., and a balance sheet as at that date. The stock of food at 31st December 19... was valued at £2,800.

(c) Make an allowance for staff feeding which is estimated at £2,450 for the year.

Adjustments to final accounts: accruals and prepayments

INTRODUCTION

Most of the double entry and other book-keeping work carried out so far in our studies leads directly to the trial balance. However, in most cases, it will be necessary to adjust these figures before proceeding to produce the final accounts.

These adjustments are governed by the accruals concept (also known as the matching concept) which means in simple terms that when a business draws up a trading, profit and loss account in order to work out net profit for an accounting period, it may only include revenues exclusively from that period to be matched against expenditure used up in that same period in order to achieve those revenues.

This important concept is explained in more detail later in this chapter.

The adjustments are usually dealt with at the end of the period and double entry for each one is recorded in the journal before posting to the ledger.

OBJECTIVES

On completion of this chapter you should be able to:

- understand the need for adjusting the trial balance before drawing up the final accounts;
- define the accruals concept and be clear about its relationship to final accounts adjustments;
- know the meaning of the terms 'prepayment' and 'accrual';
- deal with prepaid and accrued expenses in the ledger, profit and loss account and balance sheet;
- define and differentiate between bad debts and provision for bad debts;
- make all necessary adjustments to the ledger and final accounts for bad debts.

THE ACCRUALS CONCEPT

Adjustments to final accounts are governed by the principle enshrined in the accruals or matching concept This principle is, in many ways, simply good common sense. It means that:

in order to work out the true profit for a period, one must only take account of sales made in that period and take away from it only expenses used in that period in order to produce those sales, irrespective of when they are paid for.

Say, for example, Joe, the owner of a snack bar, wishes to work out his profit for the month of February. Clearly he will add together all the sales for February and take away all expenses incurred during February in order to generate those sales.

Now, he may well have paid his rent for the whole year (say £1,200), in advance, at the start of February; but in respect of February's profit, only the amount used up, i.e. £100 or one month's rent, may be taken away from sales as an expense in order to find February's profit.

The remaining £1,100 is held in the balance sheet as a prepayment.

Take another example. Let us assume that Joe pays for electricity used at the end of each week (say £150 per week). It could well happen that at the end of February he will have paid only the first three weeks' electricity. This means that when Joe draws up his monthly profit and loss account for February, the electricity account in his ledger will show only £450 (the amount actually paid to date), when clearly £600 has been used. The accruals concept states that Joe must 'accrue' the missing £150 and show the true cost for the month of £600 in February's profit statement.

The outstanding £150 will be carried to the balance sheet as a debt still to be paid.

ADJUSTMENTS IN NOMINAL ACCOUNTS

Many expenses, such as electricity, gas, rent and rates, insurance are posted in the ledger as they are **paid** rather than as they are **incurred**. As stated earlier, the amounts to be treated as expenses in the profit and loss account for any specific accounting period is the expenditure incurred (used up) in that period and not simply the amount which happens to have been paid.

In many cases it will be found that the expenditure incurred is different from the amount paid during the accounting period. Some expenses such as electricity and gas, are paid in arrears; others such as rent and insurance are often paid in advance.

PREPAYMENTS AND ACCRUALS

Prepayments and accruals are, in simple terms, a convenient way of making adjustments to the amounts paid so that the profit and loss account is charged with the correct expenditure incurred and therefore conforms to the accruals concept.

Pre-paid expenses

Several expenses (e.g. insurance) are payable in advance and, at the end of an accounting period, it is necessary to ensure that only that part of the expense which applies to the current accounting period is debited to the profit and loss account.

EXAMPLE 11.1

A travel agent's accounting year ends on 31st December. On 31st March 1996, the travel agency takes out an insurance policy and pays the full annual insurance premium of £1,000.

Clearly, at the end of 1996, of the £1,000 that has been paid only £750 applies to the current accounting period. The balance of £250 has been paid in respect of the following accounting period. At the end of 1996, the balance of £250 represents a benefit which is still to come and must, therefore, be shown in the travel agent's balance sheet.

The travel agent's insurance account for 1996 and 1997 as well as the relevant extracts from the corresponding profit and loss accounts and balance sheet are shown below:

Insurance A/c

1996		£	1996		£
Mar 31	Cash	1,000	Dec 31	P&L A/c	750
			" 31	Balance c/d	250
		1,000			1,000
1997		£	1997		£
Jan 1	Balance b/d	250	Dec 31	P&L A/c	1,000
Mar 31	Cash	1,000	" 31	Balance c/d	250
		1,250			1,250
1998		£			
Jan 1	Balance b/d	250			

(EXTRACT FROM)
Profit and Loss A/c for year ended 31st December 1996

Less other expenses	
Insurance	£750

Profit and Loss A/c for year ended 31st December 1997

Less other expenses	
Insurance	£1,000

(EXTRACT FROM)
Balance sheet as at 31st December 1996

Current assets	
Pre-paid insurance	£250

Balance sheet as at 31st December 1997

Current assets	
Pre-paid insurance	£250

EXAMPLE 11.2

At 31st December 19... , before the preparation of the final accounts, the stationery account of a health club appears as follows:

Stationery A/c

19...		£
Jan 17	Cash	900
May 4	"	300
Oct 31	Petty cash	150
Dec 14	Cash	750

On 31st December you ascertain that there is a stock of unused stationery valued at £300.

Clearly then, although £2,100 has been paid in respect of stationery, the amount consumed during the current accounting period is £1,800. The balance of £300 represents benefits still to come and must be shown in the balance sheet.

The stationery account would be adjusted as shown:

Stationery A/c

19...		£	19...		£
Jan 17	Cash	900	Dec 31	P&L A/c	1,800
May 4	"	300	" 31	Balance c/d	300
Oct 31	Petty cash	150			
Dec 14	Cash	750			
		2,100			2,100
19...		£			
Jan 1	Balance b/d	300			

As a result of the above adjustment, £1,800 will be debited in the health club's profit and loss account, and the unused stationery of £300 will be shown as a current asset in the balance sheet.

Accrued expenses

Some expenses are payable in advance and others are payable in arrears. Often there are, at the end of an accounting period, expenses which have been incurred but which have not been paid. Such expenses are called accrued expenses.

In order to arrive at the true net profit (or net loss) for a given period, it is necessary to show in the profit and loss account all income and all expenditure in respect of that period. Actual payment does not matter; what matters is when an expense is incurred. Consequently all expenses in respect of a particular period must be charged against the income of that period.

EXAMPLE 11.3

A restaurateur pays £1,500 rent quarterly after occupation of the premises. When he prepares his final accounts on 31st December 1996, he finds that he has not paid last quarter's rent due.

Show the entries necessary in the rent account, and the relevant extracts from the profit and loss account and the balance sheet. The entries and extracts required are given below:

Rent A/c

1996		£	1996		£
Mar 31	Cash	1,500	Dec 31	P&L A/c	6,000
Jun 30	"	1,500			
Sep 30	"	1,500			
Dec 31	Balance c/d	1,500			
		6,000			6,000
			1997		£
			Jan 1	Balance b/d	1,500

Notes:
(a) As the rent incurred in 1996 is £6,000 this amount must be debited in the profit and loss account, even though the full amount of the rent has not been paid.
(b) At the end of 1996, £1,500 is owing to the landlord and this is shown as a current liability in the balance sheet.
(c) When the accrued rent is actually paid the £1,500 will be credited in the cash book and debited in the rent account, thus closing the latter.

(EXTRACT FROM)
Profit and loss A/c for year ended 31st December 1996

Less: other expenses	
Rent	£6,000

(EXTRACT FROM)
Balance Sheet as at 31st December 1996

Less: current liabilities
Accrued Rent   £1,500

EXAMPLE 11.4

A hotel prepares its annual profit and loss account at 30th September each year. At 30th September 19... , before the preparation of the profit and loss account, the electricity account of the hotel shows a debit balance of £16,800 and you are informed that electricity consumed but not yet paid for amounts to £1,200.

You are required to make the necessary adjustment in the electricity account:

Electricity A/c

19...		£	19...		£
Sept 30	Sundries	16,800	Sept 30	P&L A/c	18,000
" 30	Balance c/d	1,200			
		18,000			18,000
			19...		£
			Oct 1	Balance b/d	1,200

As a result of the adjustment in the above electricity account the full cost of electricity consumed (£18,000) is debited in the hotel's profit and loss account. The amount of electricity accrued is shown as a current liability in the balance sheet.

ADJUSTMENT OF INCOME

Sometimes income due in respect of a particular period is not received until the following period. Similarly, certain items of income may be received before they are due. Hence, as in the case of various items of expenditure, adjustment of income items is often necessary.

EXAMPLE 11.5

On 31st March 19... , a hotel sublets ground floor accommodation to a travel agency. The full annual rent of £18,000 is payable in advance. The hotel prepares its annual accounts on 31st December each year.

You are required to show the adjustment necessary in the hotel's rent receivable account as well as the relevant extracts from the profit and loss account and the balance sheet. Proceed as shown below:

Rent Receivable A/c

19...		£	19...		£
Dec 31	P&L A/c	13,500	Mar 31	Cash	18,000
" 31	Balance c/d	4,500			
		18,000			18,000
			19...		£
			Jan 1	Balance b/d	4,500

(EXTRACT FROM)
Profit & Loss account for year ended 31st December 19...

Add other income	
Rent receivable	£13,500

(EXTRACT FROM)
Balance sheet as at 31st December 19...

Less current liabilities	
Rent received in advance	£4,500

Notes:
(a) As during 19... the premises were sublet for 9 months, only 9/12ths of the rent is transferred to the profit and loss account.
(b) The above credit balance of £4,500 represents a liability from the hotel to the travel agency and must be shown as such in the balance sheet.

EXAMPLE 11.6

A hotel company has certain investments, the income from which is receivable twice a year at 30th June and 31st December, the latter being the end of the company's accounting year.

Before the company's profit and loss account is prepared, it is ascertained that whilst the investment income in respect of the first half year, £1,800, has been duly received, the income due for the second half year has not. Show how you would deal with the above in the investment income account, profit and loss account and balance sheet.

Investment Income A/c

19...		£	19...		£
Dec 31	P&L A/c	3,600	Jun 30	Cash	1,800
			Dec 31	Balance c/d	1,800
		3,600			3,600
19...		£			
Jan 1	Balance b/d	1,800			

The debit balance of £1,800 shown above represents a debt owing to the hotel company and must, therefore, be shown as an asset in the balance sheet:

(EXTRACT FROM)
Profit & Loss account for year ended 31st December 19...

Investment income	£3,600

(EXTRACT FROM)
Balance Sheet as at 31st December 19...

Current assets	
Investment income	£1,800

ADJUSTMENTS IN PERSONAL ACCOUNTS

Quite apart from any adjustments that may have to be made in nominal accounts, there are several kinds of adjustments that often become necessary in personal accounts, i.e. adjustments in respect of debtors and creditors. Please note that some of the adjustments dealt with in this section concern accounts other than personal accounts. It is, however, convenient to deal with them in this section rather than elsewhere.

Bad debts

A debt is regarded as bad, or irrecoverable, when all reasonable efforts to secure payment have failed. Then, quite obviously, there is no point in keeping the customer's account with a debit balance; and the only solution is to close it by transfer to the bad debts account. Double entry in respect of any bad debts written off is, therefore: Dr bad debts account; Cr debtor's personal account. At the end of the accounting period, the total of any bad debts written off is transferred from the bad debts account to the debit of the profit and loss account.

EXAMPLE 11.7

The following balances appeared in the sales ledger of a hotel:

	£
V Brite Enterprises Ltd	300
N O Cash	150
S O Pennyless	75

You are informed that V Brite Enterprises Ltd are not able to pay the full amount due and that a dividend of only 25p in the £ will be received. Similarly you are informed that no payment is to be expected from either N O Cash or S O Pennyless.

Show the entries necessary in the accounts of the above customers, the bad debts account and the relevant extract from the profit and loss account.

Proceed as shown in the following accounts:

V Brite Enterprises Ltd

19...		£	19...		£
Dec 31	Balance b/d	300	Dec 31	Bad debts	225
		___	" 31	Balance c/d	75
		300			300
19...					
Jan 1	Balance b/d	75			

NO Cash

19...		£	19...		£
Dec 31	Balance b/d	150	Dec 31	Bad debts	150

SO Pennyless

19...		£	19...		£
Dec 31	Balance b/d	75	Dec 31	Bad debts	75

Bad Debts A/c

19...		£	19...		£
Dec 31	V Brite Enterprises Ltd	225	Dec 31	P&L A/c	450
" 31	NO Cash	150			
" 31	SO Pennyless	75			
		450			450

(EXTRACT FROM)
Profit & Loss account for year ended 31st December 19...

Less other expenses	
Bad debts	£450

Note: When the dividend of 25p in the £ is actually received from the customer it will be debited in the cash book and credited in the customer's personal account, thus closing the latter.

Provision for bad debts

At the end of each accounting period it is usually found that whilst certain debts are definitely bad others are doubtful, in that it is difficult to foresee whether or not they will, in fact, be paid.

As already explained, all debts which are regarded as definitely bad are treated as a loss and, therefore, written off to the profit and loss account. Clearly, however, it is prudent to make some provision for debts which may prove bad, especially if it is known from experience that a certain, more or less fixed, percentage of debtors fail to pay the amounts due from them in each accounting period. As a result, many businesses create a provision for bad debts; this is also known as a provision for doubtful debts and provision for bad and doubtful debts. The actual amount of the provision to be created may be arrived at in three different ways:

1. It may, from past experience, be expressed as a percentage of total debtors.
2. It may be based on amounts provided for specific doubtful debts, e.g. £50 in respect of the amount due from A, £20 in respect of the sum owing from B, etc.
3. Finally, the amount of the provision may be based partly on method (1.) and partly on method (2.).

EXAMPLE 11.8

On 31st December 1996, the debtors of a hotel amounted to £3,000. On the basis of past experience it was expected that 5 per cent of the debts due would prove bad.

Show how you would deal with the above in the appropriate ledger accounts, the profit and loss account and the balance sheet.

The necessary entry in the profit and loss account is shown below:

(EXTRACT FROM)
Profit & Loss account for year ended 31st December 1996

Less other expenses	£
Provision for bad debts	150

The provision for bad debts is an anticipated loss and must, therefore, be debited in the profit and loss account. Double entry is completed by crediting the provision for bad debts account:

Provision for bad debts A/c

	1996		£
	Dec 31	P&L A/c	150

In the balance sheet the provision is shown as a deduction from the debtors:

EXTRACT FROM
Balance sheet as at 31st December 1996

Current Assets	£	£
Debtors	3,000	
Less Prov. for bad debts	150	2,850

It will have been noticed that the creation of the provision does not involve any adjustments in the personal accounts of the debtors. That, in any case, would be difficult as it is not known which of them will prove bad nor how far any particular debt is to be regarded as bad. An important result of the provision is that the figure of debtors in the balance sheet is stated more realistically. Surely it would have been wrong to show the debtors as £3,000 if it is known that £3,000 is not likely to be collected from them. In the balance sheet above we say, in effect: 'Our customers owe us £3,000, but we expect that £150 will not be paid by them and, therefore, the value of this asset is £2,850.'

WORKED EXAMPLE

Adjustments to Final Accounts

The following is the trial balance of the Sole Mio Restaurant as at 31st December 1996.

	£	£
Purchases	65,900	
Sales		171,500
Stock at 1st Jan 1996	8,500	
Postage & telephone	1,800	
Motor expenses	1,200	
Wages & salaries	41,900	
Sundry expenses	8,300	
Rent & business rates	10,500	
Bad debts	200	
Light & heat	7,800	
Debtors	12,500	
Creditors		16,600
Leasehold premises	120,000	
Motor vehicles	39,000	
Fixtures & fittings	25,000	
Bank balance	11,000	
Drawings	8,900	
Capital at 1st Jan 1996		174,300
Disc. Received		100
	362,500	362,500

Notes:
(a) Closing stock on 31st December 1996 was £9,900.
(b) There were expenses owing as follows: sundry expenses £2,800; motor expenses £900.
(c) There were expenses prepaid as follows: rates £1,000; telephone £300.
(d) You are to create a provision for bad debts equal to 2% of debtors.

Proceed as indicated below:

Trading and profit and loss account of the Sole Mio Restaurant
for year ending 31st December 1996

	£	£	£
Sales			171,500
Less cost of sales:			
Opening stock at 1st Jan 96		8,500	
Add purchases		65,900	
		74,400	
Less Closing stock at 31st Dec 96		9,900	
Cost of sales			64,500
Gross profit			107,000
Add: Discount received			100
			107,100
Less other expenses:			
Wages & salaries	41,900		
Postage & telephone (£1,800 − £300)	1,500		
Motor expenses (£1,200 + £900)	2,100		
Sundry expenses (£8,300 + £2,800)	11,100		
Bad debts	200		
Rent & rates (£10,500 − £1,000)	9,500		
Light & heat	7,800		
Provision for bad debts	250		74,350
Net profit			32,750

Notes:
(a) Adjustments to prepayments and accruals are shown in brackets in the answer above. Please note that the actual prepayments and accruals will also be shown in the balance sheet.
(b) The provision for bad debts is worked out as follows:
2% of £12,500

Balance Sheet for the Sole Mio Restaurant
as at 31st December 1996

Fixed Assets	£	£	£	£
Leasehold premises				120,000
Fixtures and fittings				25,000
Motor vehicles				39,000
				184,000
Current Assets				
Stock			9,900	
Debtors	12,500			
Less Prov. for bad debts	250		12,250	
Prepayments (£1,000 + £300)			1,300	
Cash at bank			11,000	
			34,450	
Less Current Liabilities				
Creditors		16,600		
Accrued expenses (2,800 + £900)		3,700	20,300	
Net current assets				14,150
				198,150
Financed by:				
Capital at 1st Jan. 1996				174,300
Add Net profit for year				32,750
				207,050
Less Drawings				8,900
				198,150

SUMMARY

- In the normal course of events, the trial balance will need adjusting before final accounts can be drawn up.
- The accruals concept governs most period-end adjustments to the final accounts.
- The distinction between capital and revenue expenditure is of fundamental importance in the construction of final accounts.
- Adjustments to expense accounts arise because many expenses are only posted in the accounts as they are paid, rather than as they are incurred.
- When an expense is paid in one time period but not fully used up in that period, the part remaining is regarded as a prepayment.
- An accrual, on the other hand, is an expenditure which has been fully used up in this time period but has not yet been recorded or paid for.
- A prepayment reduces the value of the expense in the P & L account and is shown in the balance sheet as a current asset.
- An accrual will increase the value of the expense in the P & L account and is shown in the balance sheet as a current liability.

- A bad debt is an amount owing which is regarded as irrecoverable.
- Businesses operate a provision for bad debts account because it is prudent to do so and it shows a truer figure of outstanding debts.

PROBLEMS

1. Explain what information is conveyed to you by the following balances standing in the ledger of a restaurant at 31st December 19..., after balancing the accounts and preparing the final accounts for the year ended at that date:
   (a) a debit balance on rent account;
   (b) a credit balance on rent receivable account;
   (c) a debit balance on stationery account;
   (d) a credit balance on electricity account.

2. From the following trial balance of the Bruce Hotel at the 31st December 1996, you are required to produce a trading, profit & loss account and a balance sheet at that date.

	£	£
Capital at 1/1/96		100,000
Freehold premises	160,000	
Kitchen equipment	25,000	
Furniture & fittings	15,000	
Sales		260,000
Purchases	76,000	
Purchases returns		2,500
Wages	61,000	
Heating & light	9,500	
Business rates	12,000	
Debtors	18,500	
Creditors		17,700
Food stock at 1/1/96	14,000	
Bank (overdrawn)		6,300
Cash in hand	9,000	
Advance deposits		2,500
Value added Tax		11,000
	400,000	400,000

Notes:
(a) The closing food stock was valued at £9,500.
(b) The estimated cost of staff meals is £850.
(c) Prepaid electricity amounted to £400.
(d) Business rates for the final quarter of the year are due but not yet paid.
(e) A purchases invoice to the value of £1,200 had not been entered in the books.

3. Henri Dupont presents the following trial balance of the books of his restaurant at 31st December 19...:

	FFrs	FFrs
Capital		500,000
Provision for bad debts		1,500
Banqueting debtors	20,000	
Repairs and replacements	6,000	
Sales		600,000
Furniture	30,000	
Purchases returns		2,500
Postage and telephone	4,000	
Purchases	300,000	
Wages and salaries	147,500	
Drawings	12,500	
Creditors		30,500
Stock	10,000	
Cash at bank	108,000	
Premises	450,000	
Gas and electricity	34,000	
Bad debts	2,500	
China, cutlery and linen	10,000	
	1,134,500	1,134,500

You are asked to prepare the trading, profit and loss account for the year ended 31st December 19..., and a balance sheeet as at that date, taking the following into consideration:
(a) Stock at 31st December 19... was valued at FFrs11,000.
(b) An invoice for advertising for FFrs1,750 was due for payment but had not been included in the accounts.
(c) The estimated cost of staff meals is FFrs500 per month.
(d) Two purchase invoices amounting to FFrs5,000 had not been entered in the books.
(e) Mr Dupont estimates that FFrs5,000 included in the purchases represents private consumption by himself and his family.

4. The following trial balance was extracted from the books of a restaurant at 31st December 1996:

	DM	DM
Capital at 1st Jan 1996		300,000
China and cutlery	12,000	
Restaurant furniture	6,000	
Sales		157,500
Purchases	73,800	
Legal and professional charges	3,750	
Purchases returns		2,700
Wages and salaries	39,300	
Bank charges	600	
Cash in hand	2,250	
Creditors		13,950
Debtors	3,000	
Provision for bad debts		300
Stock at 1st Jan 1996	3,600	
Postage and stationery	4,800	
Rent and rates	9,600	
Leasehold premises	360,000	
Drawings	15,000	
Cash at bank	18,450	
Cleaning materials	1,800	
Loan from Merchant Bank PLC		100,000
Repairs and replacements	3,900	
Telephone	1,650	
Miscellaneous expenses	4,950	
Loan interest	10,000	
	574,450	574,450

Required:
Prepare the restaurant's trading, profit and loss account for the year ended 31st December 1996, and a balance sheet as at that date. The following are to be taken into account:
(a) final stock was valued at DM4,200;
(b) accrued salaries DM600;
(c) prepaid rent amounted to DM1,600;
(d) staff meals are estimated at DM3,500.

5. From the following trial balance of the Red Fox Hotel at 31st March 1997, draw up a trading, profit and loss account and a balance as at that date.

	£	£
Capital at 1st April 1996		200,000
Sales		620,000
Purchases	252,000	
Leasehold premises	300,000	
Kitchen equipment	50,000	
Furniture and fittings	30,000	
Purchases returns		5,000
Wages	122,000	
Heat and light	19,000	
Customs & excise		22,000
Cash in hand	38,000	
Stock of food & beverage	28,000	
Bank		12,600
Advance deposits		5,000
Creditors		35,400
Debtors	37,000	
Business rates	24,000	
	900,000	900,000

Notes:

(a) Stock of food and beverage on hand at 31st March 1997 is £19,000.
(b) Staff meals allowance for the year is £10,000.
(c) Accruals: wages £2,000, heat and light £600.
(d) Prepayments: business rates £400.
(e) The owner of the Red Fox Hotel estimates that £3,000 worth of food at cost, included in purchases, was taken for his private consumption.

6. The following trial balance was extracted from the books of the Carlton Hotel at the 30th June 1997:

	£	£
Leasehold premises	630,000	
Drawings	40,000	
Cash at bank	12,400	
Purchases	440,000	
Wages and salaries	348,000	
Cash at bank	92,500	
Purchases returns		4,000
Sales		1,145,000
Furniture & fittings	98,000	
Kitchen equipment	112,000	
China and cutlery	20,600	
Capital at 1st July 1996		600,000
Bank charges	3,000	
Creditors		184,000
Provision for bad debts		4,500
Debtors	120,500	
Customs and Excise		178,000
Stock at 1st July 1996	38,000	
Postage and stationery	9,000	
Rent	60,000	
Business rates	80,000	
Cleaning materials	18,000	
Loan from Jaws Ltd		100,000
Advertising	24,000	
General expenses	37,500	
Telephone	32,000	
	2,215,500	2,215,500

Required:

Prepare the trading, profit and loss account for the year ended 30th June 1997 and a balance sheet at that date, taking the following into consideration:

(a) Stock at 30th June 1997 was valued at £44,000.

(b) The estimated cost of staff feeding was £17,000.

(c) An invoice from the telephone company for £2,200 was due for payment but had not been included in the accounts.

(d) The annual charge for rent is £50,000, any payment above that level is to be treated as prepaid.

(e) There is an accrual due in respect of wages and salaries of £4,600, but not yet included in the figure above. This represents accrued holiday pay.

Adjustments to final accounts: depreciation

12

PINTRODUCTION

Depreciation can have several different meanings depending on the context. However, we are only interested in its accounting meaning. In this respect depreciation represents that part of the cost of a fixed asset used up or consumed in the service of the business. It is a legitimate cost of running the business just as much as electricity, rent or other expense. It is therefore charged to the profit and loss account before profit is worked out.

OBJECTIVES

After studying this chapter you should be able to:

- define the term depreciation from an accounting point of view;
- understand the various different causes of depreciation;
- list and explain the three main methods of depreciation;
- differentiate between straight line, reducing balance and revaluation methods;
- calculate annual depreciation using all three methods;
- understand what is meant by a provision for depreciation account;
- enter depreciation correctly into the ledger accounts, trading, profit and loss account and balance sheet;
- list other methods of depreciation.

NATURE AND CAUSES OF DEPRECIATION

Depreciation may be defined as the loss in the value of an asset. The term 'depreciation' has, however, more than one meaning. To most people depreciation denotes a physical deterioration of an asset. To the accountant, however, it means an amount of expense, arising out of the physical deterioration and other causes, that has to be charged against profits. It is with the latter meaning of depreciation that we shall be mainly concerned in this chapter.

There are several distinct factors causing assets to lose value, and these may be summarized as follows:

Wear and tear

This is the most common cause of depreciation and arises out of the actual usage of the asset in the normal course of business. Assets which lose in value as a result of this cause are: kitchen plant, furniture, bedding, linen, glass, china and similar assets. Also under the heading of wear and tear we have exceptional damage or deterioration, due to accidental happenings taking place in the course of business, resulting in breakage and destruction.

Time factor

There are several assets that lose in value simply as a result of the passage of time, e.g. Leasehold premises. Thus, when a lease of premises is purchased for £100,000, and the lease has ten years to run, the cost of the lease (loss in value) is £10,000 p. a. and thus depends on the passage of time, quite irrespective of the actual use made of the premises.

Obsolescence

An asset is said to be obsolete when it has to be scrapped before the end of its effective life because, owing to an improved version of the asset being available on the market, its continued use in the business would be uneconomical. In other words, obsolescence takes place when an asset, still in a good working condition, has to be replaced because it no longer pays to use it in the business. An example would be the replacement of an old-fashioned type of charcoal grill by an underfired gas grill.

Other causes

There are one or two other causes of depreciation. A change in consumer demand may necessitate a different type of service (e.g. self-service rather than waitress service) and result in some of the existing equipment being scrapped. Similarly, an asset may become inadequate for the purpose for which it was initially intended. For instance, as a result of an extension of the premises assets of larger capacity (e.g. central heating boilers) may be required.

From what has been said it will be appreciated that different assets may depreciate for different reasons. Whilst leasehold premises depreciate because of the time factor, china, cutlery and kitchen utensils lose in value as a result of wear and tear. Finally, furniture, in common with other assets, depreciates as a result of both. It is mainly for this reason that different methods of depreciation have been evolved to deal with different kinds of assets.

METHODS OF DEALING WITH DEPRECIATION

There are three main methods of dealing with depreciation used in the hospitality industry:

1. the straight-line method;
2. the reducing balance method;
3. the revaluation method.

Straight-line method

Under this method the amount of depreciation to be charged against profits in any one year is calculated by deducting from the initial cost of the asset its scrap value (if any), and dividing the result by the estimated life of the asset in terms of years. The formula for calculating depreciation under this method is, therefore:

$$\frac{\text{INITIAL COST} - \text{SCRAP VALUE}}{\text{ESTIMATED LIFE}} = \text{ANNUAL DEPRECIATION}$$

For example, a hotel buys heavy kitchen equipment for £103,000. It is estimated that the equipment will have an effective working life of ten years and that it will fetch (scrap value) £3,000 at the end of that period. Calculate the annual depreciation that should be debited to the hotel's profit and loss account in respect of the above equipment.

Thus from the equation above: $\dfrac{£103,000 - £3,000}{10} = £10,000$

Two main advantages may be claimed for this method of depreciation. First, it is easy to calculate; second, it is possible to depreciate an asset completely within a definite period. Its disadvantage is that a separate calculation is necessary for every asset and that, consequently, more detailed records of assets have to be kept. The straight-line method is, however, widely used in the hospitality industry in respect of assets such as furniture, heavy kitchen equipment and leaseholds.

Reducing balance method

Under this method the annual depreciation is expressed as a given percentage of the book value of the asset at the beginning of each year. As the book value of the asset diminishes, so does the annual depreciation.

EXAMPLE

For example, a hotel buys two billing machines costing £20,000 and it is decided to write off depreciation at the rate of 20 per cent per annum. Calculate the amount of depreciation to be debited to the profit and loss account of the hotel for the first three years following the acquisition of the billing machines.

	Cost of billing machines		£20,000
less:	Depreciation, year 1, (20% of £20,000)		4,000
	book value – end of first year		16,000
less:	Depreciation, year 2, (20% of £16,000)		3,200
	book value – end of second year		12,800
less:	Depreciation, year 3, (20% of £12,800)		2,560
	book value – end of third year		£10,240

The reducing balance method is easy to apply as all assets of a particular type (furniture, office equipment, kitchen plant) may be lumped together and depreciated at the same rate (percentage). Further, it is often said that the cost of an asset consists of two things:

(a) the actual depreciation;
(b) the cost of repairing and maintaining the asset.

Whilst, under this method, the depreciation charge becomes less and less, the cost of repairs and maintenance tends to rise towards the end of the life of the asset. As a result, it is claimed, the total charge to the profit and loss account tends to be spread evenly over the entire life of the asset. A disadvantage of this method is that it is impossible to write off an asset completely. Even at the end of the nth year, when the book value might be 5p, a depreciation of 20 per cent will only reduce the book value to 4p.

Revaluation method

Assets such as glass, china, cutlery and light kitchen equipment consist of a large number of individual items which require to be replaced at fairly frequent intervals. The simplest method of writing off any losses of such equipment is to revalue it at the end of each accounting period. The decrease in the value of such equipment, as disclosed by the annual inventories, between the beginning and the end of a year, is regarded as the depreciation for that year.

For example, on 31st December 19. . . , a café has a stock of china and cutlery valued at £4,000. A year later on the 31st December 19... , an inventory of the china and cutlery shows that it then has a value of £3,200. The difference of £800 represents losses of china and cutlery in respect of the period and must, therefore, be debited to the café's profit and loss account as depreciation.

PROVISION FOR DEPRECIATION ACCOUNT

The entries in the ledger in respect of depreciation follow the same lines whichever of the three methods is used. This will become evident from the illustrations given below.

A fairly common method of dealing with depreciation in the accounts is to create a provision for depreciation account. Under this method we leave the asset in the ledger at cost in its own asset account and, each year, debit the depreciation charge in the profit and loss account and credit it in the provision for depreciation account. The balance of the latter account will thus increase from one year to another and represent the aggregate amount of depreciation written off to date.

In the balance sheet, we show the asset at original cost less aggregate depreciation written off. This results in a clear picture of the value of the assets owned by the business being given.

When the asset concerned has been completely depreciated the balance of the provision for depreciation account is transferred to the asset account: both balances are thus eliminated. This method of dealing with depreciation may be applied whether we use the straight line or the reducing-balance method.

EXAMPLE 12.1

Using the straight line method

On 1st January 1993, a hotel buys furniture costing £45,000 having an estimated life of fifteen years and no residual value. Show the furniture account of the hotel for three years to 31st December 1995 and give the relevant extracts from the hotel's profit and loss account for the year ended 31st December 1995 and the balance sheet as at that date. Proceed as follows:

Furniture A/c

1993		£	1993		£
Jan 1	Cash	45,000	Dec 31	Balance c/d	45,000
1994			1994		
Jan 1	Balance b/d	45,000	Dec 31	Balance c/d	45,000
1995			1995		
Jan 1	Balance b/d	45,000	Dec 31	Balance c/d	45,000
1996					
Jan 1	Balance b/d	45,000			

Provision for Depreciation A/c

1993		£	1993			£
Dec 31	Balance c/d	3,000	Dec 31	P&L A/c		3,000
		3,000				3,000
1994			1994			
Dec 31	Balance c/d	6,000	Jan 1	Balance b/d		3,000
			Dec 31	P&L A/c		3,000
		6,000				6,000
1995			1995			
Dec 31	Balance c/d	9,000	Jan 1	Balance b/d		6,000
			Dec 31	P&L A/c		3,000
		9,000				9,000
			1996			
			Jan 1	Balance b/d		9,000

(EXTRACT FROM)

Profit & Loss account for year ended 31st December 1995

Less other expenses
Depreciation:
Furniture   £3,000

Balance sheet as at 31st December 1995

FIXED ASSETS	Cost	Dep'n	NBV
Furniture	£45,000	£9,000	£36,000

Notes:

(a) In the balance sheet the meaning of headings used is as follows:

Cost	Original cost of asset.
Dep'n	Aggregate depreciation
NBV	Net book value

(b) If the straight-line method is used, the depreciation debited in the profit and loss account will be constant throughout the life of the asset.

(c) In the balance sheet, the original cost always remains the same but depreciation accumulates each year in order to give the true net book value. At the end of the third year (1995) the asset is still shown at cost (£45,000) less aggregate depreciation to date (£9,000 i.e. @ £3,000 p. a.).

EXAMPLE 12.2

Using the reducing balance method

On 1st January 1993, a catering company operating self-service restaurants buys five computerized cash registers costing £4,000 each. The cash registers are to be depreciated at the rate of 20 per cent per annum. Show the cash register account for the three years ending 31st December 1995, the relevant extracts from the company's profit and loss account for the year ended 31st December 1993, and the balance sheet as at that date.

Proceed as shown below:

Cash Register A/c

1993		£	1993		£
Jan 1	Cash	20,000	Dec 31	Balance c/d	20,000
1994			1994		
Jan 1	Balance b/d	20,000	Dec 31	Balance c/d	20,000
1995			1995		
Jan 1	Balance b/d	20,000	Dec 31	Balance c/d	20,000
1996					
Jan 1	Balance b/d	20,000			

Provision for depreciation account

1993		£	1993		£
Dec 31	Balance c/d	4,000	Dec 31	P&L A/c	4,000
		4,000			4,000
1994			1994		
Dec 31	Balance c/d	7,200	Jan 1	Balance b/d	4,000
			Dec 31	P&L A/c	3,200
		7,200			7,200
1995			1995		
Dec 31	Balance c/d	9,760	Jan 1	Balance b/d	7,200
			Dec 31	P&L A/c	2,560
		9,760			9,760
			1996		
			Jan 1	Balance b/d	9,760

(EXTRACT FROM)

Profit and Loss account for year ended 31st December 1993

Less other expenses:	
Depreciation:	
Cash Registers	£4,000

(EXTRACT FROM)

Balance sheet as at 31st December 1993

FIXED ASSETS	Cost	Dep'n	NBV
Cash Registers	£20,000	£4,000	£16,000

As may be seen the ledger entries are the same whether the straight line or the reducing balance method is used.

EXAMPLE 12.3

Using the revaluation method

On 1st January 1993, a restaurant has glass and china valued at £6,000. During the year ended 31st December 1993, further glass and china are purchased for £1,000. The inventory at 31st December 1993 shows that the stock of glass and china is then worth £5,600. Show the glass and china account for the period concerned and the relevant extracts from the restaurant's profit and loss account and balance sheet.

Proceed as shown below:

Glass and China A/c

1993		£	1993		£
Jan 1	Balance b/d	6,000	Dec 31	P&L A/c	1,400
. . . .	Cash	1,000	" 31	Balance c/d	5,600
		7,000			7,000
1994					
Jan 1	Balance b/d	5,600			

(EXTRACT FROM)
Profit and Loss A/c for year ended 31st December 1993

Less other expenses:
Depreciation:
Glass & China   £1,400

(EXTRACT FROM)
Balance sheet as at 31st December 1993

Fixed assets	Cost	Dep'n	NBV
Glass & China			£5,600

Note: For glass and china, only the net book value is usually shown in the balance sheet because of the different nature of depreciation in this case.

OTHER METHODS OF DEPRECIATION

In addition to the three principal methods of depreciation outlined above there are one or two other methods used in some businesses.

Sinking fund method

Under this method a fixed amount of depreciation is debited in the profit and loss account each year and a corresponding amount of cash is invested in gilt-edged securities each year. As a result, provision is made for the replacement of the asset at the end of its life, when the proceeds from the sale of the securities become available for the purchase of a new asset.

Endowment insurance policy method

Under this method, instead of investing amounts of cash in gilt-edged securities, the cash is used in payment of the premium on what is known as a capital redemption policy, which will mature at the end of the existing asset's life.

Annuity method

Under this method it is assumed that the capital sunk in the purchase of the asset might, if used in some other direction, have earned a certain rate of interest each year. Consequently, interest on the diminishing balance is debited to the account of the asset and a fixed annual depreciation is written off. The balance of the account is completely eliminated at the end of the life of the asset.

DEALING WITH DEPRECIATION IN THE FINAL ACCOUNTS

WORKED EXAMPLE

Willi Brandenburg has been running the Concerto Hotel for many years. Given below is his trial balance for the year ended 30th June 19...

	£	£
Purchases	123,000	
Sales		417,500
Insurance	1,500	
Motor van at cost	27,000	
Provision for depreciation – motor van		8,100
Wages	178,000	
Business rates	38,000	
Kitchen equipment at cost	158,000	
Provision for depreciation – kitchen equipment		79,000
Motor expenses	1,200	
Debtors	35,000	
Creditors		78,500
Cash at bank	56,800	
Heat & light	5,700	
Stock at 1st July 19...	14,600	
Bank loan – 10 year term.		100,000
Printing & stationery	4,900	
Drawings	26,000	
Leasehold premises at cost	280,000	
Provision for depreciation – leasehold premises		130,800
Furniture at cost	78,000	
Provision for depreciation – furniture		39,000
China & utensils at cost	5,900	
Bad debts provision		700
Capital at 1st July 19...		180,000
	1,033,600	1,033,600

Notes:
(a) The year end stock at the 30th June 19... was valued at £12,700.

(b) Depreciation is to be provided as follows:

(i)	Motor van	20 per cent on cost.
(ii)	Furniture	5 per cent on cost.
(iii)	Kitchen equipment	10 per cent on cost.
(iv)	Leasehold premises	£2,500 p.a.
(v)	China & utensils were revalued at £4,600.	

Proceed as shown below:

The student should start with some working notes to calculate depreciation.

Working notes:

1. Depreciation calculations:

Item	Cost	Factor	Annual depreciation
	£	%	£
Leasehold premises	280,000	–	2,500
Kitchen equipment	158,000	10	15,800
Furniture	78,000	5	3,900
Motor van	27,000	20	5,400
			27,600
China & Utensils (£5,900–£4,600)			1,300
To the profit and loss account			28,900

Profit and Loss Account of The Concerto Hotel
for year ended 30th June 19...

	£	£
Sales		417,500
Less Cost of Sales		
Opening stock	14,600	
Add Purchases	123,000	
	137,600	
Less Closing stock	12,700	
Cost of sales		124,900
Gross profit		292,600
Less Other Expenses		
Wages	178,000	
Insurance	1,500	
Rates	38,000	
Motor expenses	1,200	
Heat & light	5,700	
Printing & stationery	4,900	
Depreciation (see note 1 above)	28,900	
		258,200
Net Profit		34,400

Balance sheet of The Concerto Hotel
as at 30th June 19...

Fixed Assets	Cost	Aggregate Depreciation*	Net
	£	£	£
Leasehold premises	280,000	133,300*	146,700
Kitchen equipment	158,000	94,800*	63,200
Furniture	78,000	42,900*	35,100
Motor van	27,000	13,500*	13,500
	543,000	284,500	258,500
China, utensils			4,600
			263,100

	£	£	£
Current Assets			
Stock		12,700	
Debtors	35,000		
Prov. for bad debts	700	34,300	
Cash at bank		56,800	
		103,800	
Less Current Liabilities			
Creditors		78,500	
Net current assets			25,300
			288,400
Less Long-term Liabilities			
Loan (10 year term)			(100,000)
			188,400
Financed by:			
Capital at 30th June 19...			180,000
Add Net profit for year			34,400
			214,400
Less Drawings			26,000
			188,400

* Aggregate depreciation is worked out in the balance sheet as follows: pick up the existing aggregate depreciation figure from the trial balance and add this year's depreciation figure to it, and the result will be the aggregate depreciation as at the end of the current year.

SUMMARY

- Depreciation may be defined as the loss in the value of an asset over its useful working life.
- Depreciation is a legitimate business expense (often described as the cost of using an asset) which should be charged against profit in the profit and loss account.
- There are many factors that cause an asset to lose value, e.g. wear and tear, time, obsolesence etc.
- The three main methods of depreciation are (a) straight-line method (b) reducing balance method and (c) revaluation method.
- The straight line method is easiest to use, resulting in the same amount of depreciation each year of the useful life of the asset.
- The reducing balance method reflects in a more realistic way how depreciation normally takes place, i.e. a large amount of depreciation in the early years followed by a lower slow decline thereafter.
- The revaluation method is usually only applied for china, cutlery and linen, etc. in the hospitality industry.

- When the provision for depreciation account is used, assets are placed in their respective asset accounts and held at original cost, while annual depreciation is aggregated in the provision for depreciation account.
- At the end of useful life of an asset total depreciation is debited in the provision for depreciation account and credited in the asset account. Any difference is a gain or loss on disposal.

PROBLEMS

1. (a) What are the main causes of depreciation?
   (b) What are the main methods of dealing with depreciation?

2. List the main advantages and disadvantages of each of the following methods of depreciation: straight-line method; reducing-balance method; revaluation method.

3. The A-n-B Restaurant purchased heavy kitchen equipment on 1st January 1995 for £30,000. Show by means of ledger accounts how the equipment would be depreciated between this date and 31st December 1998, using the straight-line method and the reducing-balance method.
   Provide in each case depreciation at the rate of 20 per cent.

4. The following trial balance was extracted from the books of the New Acropolis Restaurant on 30th June 19...

	£	£
Capital		600,000
Purchases	270,000	
Sales		706,500
Stock on 1st July 19...	19,500	
Trade creditors		22,500
Banqueting debtors	25,500	
Rent and rates	13,500	
Wages and salaries	149,250	
Loan from X Finance Co.		50,000
Light and heat	23,250	
Repairs and renewals	11,700	
Furniture at cost	75,000	
Provision for depreciation – furniture		18,000
Kitchen equipment at cost	90,000	
Provision for depreciation – kit. equipment		24,000
China and cutlery at cost	24,900	
Drawings	1,650	
Cash at bank	8,250	
Leasehold premises at cost	950,000	
Provision for depreciation – leasehold premises		240,000
Provision for bad debts		1,500
	1,662,500	1,662,500

Required:

Prepare the restaurant's trading, profit and loss account for the year ended 30th June, and a balance sheet as at that date. Take the following into account:

(a) the final stock of food was valued at £21,000;

(b) provide the depreciation as follows:
    furniture 10 per cent;
    kitchen equipment £6,000 per annum;
    leasehold premises £30,000 per annum;
    china and cutlery were revalued at £21,300

(c) the cost of staff meals is estimated at £22,000;

(d) unrecorded invoices in respect of purchases amounted to £1,500;

(e) you are informed that the Society for the Promotion of Neat Book-keeping owes the restaurant £3,000 in respect of a banquet; this has not been recorded in the books;

(f) the item 'repairs and renewals' includes an amount of £2,100 in respect of repairs to the proprietor's house.

5. From the following trial balance prepare a trading, profit and loss account for the year ended 31st December 19..., and a balance sheet as at that date:

	£	£
Stock at 1st January 19...	37,500	
Receipts from visitors		1,057,380
Fuel and light	28,920	
Rent and rates	36,990	
Advertising	21,600	
Purchases	348,480	
China, linen and cutlery at cost	42,810	
Wages and salaries	312,330	
Furniture and fittings at cost	360,000	
Provision for depreciation – furniture & fittings		137,100
Bad debts	6,450	
Drawings	45,900	
Capital		747,000
Visitors ledger balances	39,450	
Creditors		37,500
A Penny – loan account	240,000	
Leasehold premises at cost	600,000	
Provision for depreciation – leasehold premises		285,000
Cash at bank	131,250	
Provision for bad debts		1,200
Repairs to furniture	13,500	
	2,265,180	2,265,180

Notes:

(a) Stocks on hand at 31st December 19... amounted to £28,350.

(b) Provide for depreciation as follows:

    (i)   Furniture and fittings 10 per cent on cost;

    (ii) Leasehold premises £3000 p.a;

    (iii) China, linen and cutlery were revalued at £37,500.

(c) Provide for the outstanding loan interest (£12,000) on the loan to A. Penny.

(d) Treat £5,700 of the advertising as paid in advance.

6. A Gallop is proprietor of the Old Colonial Restaurant and the following trial balance was extracted from his books at 31st December 19...

	£	£
Capital		180,000
Freehold premises	123,000	
Debtors	21,500	
Creditors		28,500
Drawings	31,800	
Cash at bank	37,590	
Purchases	91,680	
Sales		219,060
Restaurant change float	300	
Repairs and renewals	8,130	
Motor van expenses	5,490	
Motor van at cost	18,750	
Provision for depreciation – motor van		6,750
Purchases returns		780
Wages	24,000	
Salaries	19,020	
Stock 1st January 19...	11,550	
Lighting and heating	11,880	
Restaurant furniture at cost	46,800	
Provision for depreciation – rest. furniture		9,300
Printing and stationery	1,710	
Postage and telephone	1,920	
China, utensils and cutlery at cost	7,800	
Insurance	990	
Loan from Sharks Ltd		20,000
Bad debts	480	
	464,390	464,390

Required:

Prepare Gallop's trading, profit and loss account for the year ended 31st December 19... and a balance sheet as at that date. The following are to be taken into account:

(a) Stock at 31st December 19... was valued at £14,940.

(b) Outstanding lighting and heating £570.

(c) Prepaid insurance £240.

(d) Depreciation is to be provided as follows:

    (i)   motor van 20 per cent on cost;

    (ii) restaurant furniture 10 per cent on cost;

    (iii) china, utensils and cutlery were revalued at £6,600.

7. The following trial balance was extracted from the books of the White Eagle Restaurant at 31st March 19.... You are required to prepare the restaurant's trading, profit and loss account for the year ended 31st March, 19... and a balance sheet as at that date.

	£	£
Capital		591,000
Purchases	281,580	
Kitchen equipment at cost	115,200	
Provision for depreciation – kitchen equipment		57,600
Printing and stationery	13,020	
Creditors		30,000
Postage and telephone	9,720	
Stock of food, 1st April 19...	12,660	
Wages and salaries	143,820	
Sales		655,860
National insurance	10,560	
Fuel and light	29,880	
Leasehold premises at cost	618,000	
Provision for depreciation – leasehold premises		157,500
Discounts received		1,140
Cash in hand	900	
Repairs and renewals	18,960	
Bad debts	3,840	
Rates	22,440	
Restaurant furniture at cost	72,000	
Provision for depreciation – restaurant furniture		44,400
Advertising	29,820	
Cash at bank	96,900	
China and utensils at cost	21,000	
Debtors	7,200	
Drawings	30,000	
	1,537,500	1,537,500

Notes:

(a) The stock of food at 31st March 19... was valued at £11,880.

(b) £17,400 of the cost of food consumed is to be treated as the cost of staff meals.

(c) Accrued wages and salaries amounted to £1,680.

(d) Create a provision for bad debts of £300.

(e) Provide for depreciation as follows:

    (i)   Leasehold premises £30,900 per annum;

    (ii) Kitchen equipment 10 per cent on cost;

    (iii) Restaurant furniture £3,600 per annum;

    (iv) China and utensils were revalued at £17,400.

8. The following trial balance was extracted from the books of a restaurant after the compilation of the trading account for the year ended 31st December 19...

	£	£
Gross profit		298,500
Stock	9,450	
Kitchen equipment at cost	97,600	
Provision for depreciation – kitchen equipment		43,800
Drawings	22,500	
Postage and telephone	7,350	
Cash at bank	50,940	
Bank loan – 15 year term		80,000
Wages and salaries	138,030	
National insurance	7,950	
Creditors		24,000
Restaurant furniture at cost	75,800	
Provision for depreciation – restaurant furniture		51,800
Printing and stationery	9,630	
China and cutlery	15,600	
Debtors	16,750	
Advertising	22,390	
Discount received		870
Fuel and light	22,260	
Repairs and renewals	14,550	
Bad debts	2,970	
Rates	17,600	
Leasehold premises at cost	570,000	
Provision for depreciation – leasehold premises		180,000
Cash in hand	3,600	
Capital		426,000
	1,104,970	1,104,970

Required:

Prepare the profit and loss account of the restaurant for the year ended 31st December 19... and a balance sheet as at that date. You are to take into account the information given below.

(a) Provide for depreciation as follows:
    (i)   Leasehold premises £18,000 per annum;
    (ii) Kitchen equipment 10 per cent on cost;
    (iii) Restaurant furniture 12 per cent on cost;
    (iv) China & cutlery were revalued at £13,400;

(b) Make provision for the following accrued expenses:
    (i)   Advertising £750;
    (ii) Audit fee £1,050;
    (iii) Stationery £360;

(c) Treat £300 of the debtors as bad.

(d) Rates paid in advance amounted to £600.

9. The following trial balance was extracted from the books of Allan May at 31st December 19...

	£	£
Capital		400,000
Purchases	158,200	
Sales		482,160
Stock of food, 1st January 19...	16,200	
Bought ledger control account		20,000
Banqueting debtors	39,760	
Rent and rates	24,000	
Wages and salaries	104,600	
Lighting and heating	12,200	
Repairs and renewals	8,040	
Furniture at cost	184,000	
Provision for depreciation – furniture		136,000
Kitchen equipment at cost	128,000	
Provision for depreciation – kitchen equipment		64,000
Plate, china and cutlery at cost	19,320	
Cash at bank	78,680	
Cash in hand	9,160	
Leasehold premises at cost	800,000	
Provision for depreciation – leasehold premises		480,000
	1,582,160	1,582,160

Notes:

(a) Stock of food at 31st December 19... was valued at £15,200.

(b) Depreciation is to be provided as follows:
    (i)   Furniture 10 per cent of cost;
    (ii) Leasehold 15 per cent of cost;
    (iii) Kitchen equipment 15 per cent of cost;
    (iv) Plate china and cutlery were revalued at £18,000.

(c) Of the banqueting debtors £1,760 is considered irrecoverable.

(d) Create a provision for bad debts of 2 per cent.

Required:

Prepare May's trading profit and loss account for the year ended 31st December 19... and a balance sheet as at that date.

Single entry | 13

INTRODUCTION

It is sometimes said that there are two systems of book-keeping: double entry and single entry. Double entry book-keeping – which we have assumed so far in this book – is a system under which we record the **double aspect of each transaction** in the books of a business. Thus for each transaction we have a debit and a credit entry in the ledger. As a result, at the end of each accounting period, we are able to extract a trial balance and then proceed to the preparation of the final accounts.

Single entry book-keeping, though sometimes described as a 'system', is not really a system of book-keeping. Indeed, it is the absence of systematic recording of transactions that characterizes single entry.

OBJECTIVES

On completion of this chapter you should be able to:

- understand the term 'single entry';
- differentiate between single entry and double entry book-keeping;
- reconstruct a workable set of accounts, from information and documentation available, to enable final accounts to be drawn up;
- recognize the importance of the cash book and previous final accounts in the process of preparing final accounts;
- reconstruct bank summary statements and trading accounts where appropriate;
- work out total purchases and total sales figures from available information;
- draw up a trading, profit and loss account and balance sheet from reconstructed accounts.

NATURE OF SINGLE ENTRY

The term single entry (also referred to as 'incomplete records') is usually applied to a set of books which do not amount to a complete double entry system. It will be appreciated, therefore, that – in terms of the books kept –

single entry covers many possibilities. Thus a snack-bar proprietor may keep a cash book only and no other records at all. A guest-house proprietor may keep a cash book, a petty cash book and a simple form of visitors' ledger. A medium-sized restaurant may keep a cash book, a petty cash book and a wages book and some record of purchases and sales. In all these cases some accounting records are kept, but these do not constitute a complete record of all the transactions of the business; accounts of suppliers are not kept; there are no real or nominal accounts. At the end of an accounting period, a trial balance cannot be extracted and, therefore, the preparation of final accounts is difficult.

PREPARATION OF FINAL ACCOUNTS FROM INCOMPLETE RECORDS

From what has been said it will be appreciated that the compilation of final accounts from incomplete records is a more complicated matter than when this is done from an agreed trial balance. The main reason for this is that it is necessary to extract information from several different sources and, sometimes, reconstruct accounts from whatever data are actually available. As the nature and scope of the accounting records kept varies from one establishment to another, it is impossible to suggest a method that can be applied to every set of incomplete records. Provided, however, that the student understands double entry book-keeping he should not find single entry too difficult.

There are several sources of information that usually have to be consulted when compiling final accounts from incomplete records.

Cash book

Even where there are few accounting records kept there is, more often than not, some form of cash book being maintained. Where a cash book is not kept, particulars of cash transactions may be obtained by reference to the bank statements of the business. An analysis of the cash transactions for the period concerned will provide information relating to cash sales, cash purchases and the payment of suppliers, as well as payments in respect of business expenses.

Previous final accounts

As ledger accounts for assets, liabilities and, often, business expenses are not kept it is usually necessary to refer to the final accounts for the previous accounting period. For instance, when preparing the balance sheet, particulars of the assets at the end of the current period may have to be obtained partly from the last balance sheet (to ascertain what was owned at the beginning of the current period) and partly from the cash book (to ascertain what was purchased during the current period). Similarly, particulars of the capital will be compiled by taking from the last balance sheet the opening capital, adding the current net profit and deducting the proprietor's drawings. The latter would be obtained by analysing the cash payments for the period concerned.

Other sources

In addition to the cash book and the previous final accounts there are usually some other records being kept. Thus, there are many smaller establishments which keep an analysed record of purchases and sales under headings such as food, beverages, cigarettes and sundries. Any such records are helpful in the preparation of the trading account. Particulars of the creditors at the end of the current period may be obtained by listing all suppliers' invoices remaining unpaid at the date of the balance sheet. It is often found that many smaller establishments, which do not maintain ledger accounts, keep a reasonably accurate record of any wages paid which, again, is helpful when preparing the profit and loss account.

To sum up, as the nature and extent of the books kept vary from one case to another so must the method used in the compilation of the final accounts. Not infrequently, in the process of preparing final accounts from incomplete records, it is necessary to rely on the proprietor's memory as well as on any records he may have chosen to keep.

EXAMPLE 13.1

On 1st January 19..., A M Field started in business as a snack-bar proprietor with a capital of £50,000 made up as follows:

Cutlery and utensils	£5,000
Furniture	£10,000
Cash	£35,000

There follows a summary of his cash book for the year ended 31st December 19.... You are informed that he pays all expenses by cheque and banks all amounts received.

Cash Book Summary

	£		£
Balance	35,000	Wages	16,000
Sales	70,000	Furniture	5,000
		Rent and rates	6,000
		Light and heat	4,000
		Kitchen equipment	19,000
		Private expenses	5,000
		Purchases	32,000
		Balance c/d	18,000
	105,000		105,000
Balance b/d	18,000		

At 31st December 19..., Field owed £500 in respect of electricity used and £2,000 for the last quarter's rent. His stock of food was valued at £2,000.

You are required to prepare Field's trading, profit and loss account for the year ended 31st December 19... and the balance sheet as at that date.

Depreciate the kitchen equipment and the furniture by 10 per cent and the cutlery and utensils by £1,000.

Proceed as shown:

Trading, profit and loss account
for year ended 31st December 19...

	£	£
Sales		70,000
Purchases	32,000	
Less Closing stock	2,000	
Cost of sales		30,000
Gross profit c/d		40,000
Less other expenses		
Wages	16,000	
Rent & rates	8,000	
Light & heat	4,500	
Depreciation:		
Furniture	1,500	
Kitchen equipment	1,900	
Cutlery etc.	1,000	32,900
Net profit		7,100

Notes:

(a) It will be observed that the information necessary to compile the above trading account is obtained from the cash book summary and other sources, rather than the trial balance.

(b) It is assumed in this illustration that all purchases and sales were on a cash basis.

(c) The debit in the profit and loss account in respect of the rent and rates (£8,000) and the light and heat (£4,500) are arrived at by extracting from the cash book summary the amounts actually paid out and adding the amounts due but unpaid.

(d) It is assumed that the additional furniture purchased for £5,000 was acquired at the commencement of the current year. Depreciation is, therefore, on £15,000.

Balance Sheet as at 31st December 19...

Fixed Assets	Cost £	Dep'n £	Net £
Furniture	15,000	1,500	13,500
Kitchen equipment	19,000	1,900	17,100
Cutlery	5,000	1,000	4,000
	39,000	4,400	34,600
Current Assets			
Stock of food		2,000	
Cash at bank		18,000	
		20,000	
Less Current Liabilities			
Accrued electricity	500		
Accrued rent	2,000	2,500	
Net current assets			17,500
			52,100

Financed by:	£
Capital at 1st January 19...	50,000
Add net profit	7,100
	57,100
Less drawings	5,000
Total capital employed	52,100

Notes:

(a) Particulars of the assets of the business are obtained by reference to the state of affairs at the beginning of the period and to the cash book summary.

(b) The 'capital' section of the balance sheet is written up by ascertaining the opening capital, adding the net profit for the year and deducting the drawings, as shown in the cash book summary.

EXAMPLE 13.2

Mary Price, a restaurant owner, does not keep a full set of books. Her assets and liabilities on 1st January 1997 and 31st December 1997 were:

	1st January 1997	31st December 1997
Cash at bank	£11,000	£23,700
Debtors	1,200	1,400
Stocks	6,000	5,000
Furniture	5,500	5,500
Glass and china	3,500	3,500
Premises	60,000	60,000
Creditors	2,600	3,200
Accrued expenses	600	1,000

Her bank summary for 1997 is as follows:

Bank Summary

	£		£
Balance	11,000	Private expenses	11,000
Cash sales	160,000	Business expenses	41,000
Receipts from debtors	39,900	Wages	55,500
		Payments to suppliers	79,500
		Bank charges	200
		Balance c/d	23,700
	210,900		210,900
Balance b/d	23,700		

You are asked to prepare the restaurant's trading, profit and loss account for the year ended 31st December 1997, and a balance sheet as at that date. Depreciate the furniture by £500, and the glass and china by £300 Proceed as shown below:

Trading Account for year ended 31st December 1997

Cash sales		160,000
Credit sales		40,100
		200,100
Opening stock	6,000	
Purchases	80,100	
	86,100	
Less closing stock	5,000	
Cost of sales		81,100
Gross profit		119,000

What presents some difficulty about the above trading account is that, whilst the opening and the closing stocks are given, the purchases and sales for the year have to be calculated from the information available.

From the particulars given it is clear that all the purchases were on credit. We know how much she owed the suppliers at the beginning and at the end of the period as well as the amount of cash paid to them.

From these data we calculate the credit purchases for the year as follows:

Cash paid to suppliers during 1997	£79,500
Less Amount owing to suppliers at 1st January 1997	2,600
Cash paid to suppliers for 1997 credit purchases	76,900
Add Purchases not yet paid for	
(i.e. creditors at 31st December 1997)	3,200
Total credit purchases in 1997	£80,100

An alternative method of arriving at the amount of credit purchases is to construct a total creditors account, i.e. one personal account for all the suppliers from whom goods were purchased (see below).

Total Creditors A/c

1997		£	1997		£
Dec 31	Cash	79,500	Jan 1	Balance b/d	2,600
" 31	Balance c/d	3,200	Dec 31	Purchases	80,100
		82,700			82,700
			1998		£
			Jan 1	Balances b/d	3,200

The amount of £80,100 (i.e. the purchases) is simply a balancing figure and, had the restaurateur kept a full set of books, would be equal to the total of invoices that would have been credited in the personal accounts of her suppliers.

By reference to the bank summary it may be seen that the restaurant had credit as well as cash sales. The cash sales, assuming that all the cash taken has been banked, may be obtained from the bank summary; here they amount to £160,000.

The credit sales of the restaurant may be calculated in the same way as we calculated the credit purchases above.

Cash received from customers in 1997	£39,900
Less Amount owing from customers at 1st January 1997	1,200
Cash received from customers for 1997 credit sales	38,700
Add Sales not yet settled by customers	
(debtors at 31st December 1997)	1,400
Total credit sales in 1997	£40,100

The total debtors account in respect of the year ended 31st December, 1997 would be constructed as follows:

Total Debtors A/c

1997		£	1997		£
Jan 1	Balance b/d	1,200	Dec 31	Cash	39,900
Dec 31	Sales	40,100	Dec 31	Balance c/d	1,400
		41,300			41,300
1998		£			
Jan 1	Balance b/d	1,400			

Now that we have completed the trading account, we can proceed to show the full trading, profit and loss account, as below:

Trading, Profit and Loss Account
for year ended 31st December 1997

	£	£
Cash sales		160,000
Credit sales		40,100
		200,100
Opening stock	6,000	
Purchases	80,100	
	86,100	
Less closing stock	5,000	
Cost of sales		81,100
Gross profit		119,000
Less other expenses		
Business expenses*	41,400	
Wages	55,500	
Bank charges	200	
Depreciation:		
Furniture	500	
Glass & china	300	800	97,900
Net profit		21,100

* When a profit and loss account is compiled from incomplete records most of the debits in that account will be based on details obtained from the cash book. It must, however, be remembered that in most cases the **cash paid out** during a period does not usually correspond with the **expense** for the period.

In the above illustration the cash paid out in 1997 in respect of business expenses is £41,000 and the amount debited in the profit and loss account, £41,400. This is because accrued business expenses at the end of the year were £400 more than they were at the beginning of the year. It is helpful to construct a (total) business expenses account to decide exactly how much should be charged to the profit and loss account:

Total Business Expenses Account

1997		£	1997			£
Dec 31	Cash	41,000	Jan	1	Balance b/d	600
" 31	Balance c/d	1,000	Dec 31	Expenses		41,400
		42,000				42,000
			1998			£
			Jan	1	Balance b/d	1,000

Balance Sheet as at 31 December 1997

Fixed Assets	Cost	Dep'n.	Net
	£	£	£
Premises	60,000		60,000
Furniture	5,500	500	5,000
Glass & china	3,500	300	3,200
	69,000	800	68,200
Current Assets			
Stocks		5,000	
Debtors		1,400	
Cash at bank		23,700	
		30,100	
Less Current Liabilities			
Creditors	3,200		
Accrued expenses	1,000	4,200	
Net current assets			25,900
			94,100
Financed by:			
Capital as at 1st Jan 1997			84,000
Add profit for year			21,100
			105,100
Less Drawings			11,000
			94,100

The capital of the restaurant at 1st January 1997 was not given and had to be ascertained. Capital has already been defined as the total of assets less any external liabilities. Hence:

			£
Assets at 1st January 1997:	Premises		60,000
	Furniture		5,500
	Glass & china		3,500
	Stocks		6,000
	Debtors		1,200
	Cash at bank		11,000
			87,200
Less Liabilities at above date:	Creditors	2,600	
	Accrued expenses	600	3,200
Capital at 1st January 1997			84,000

ALTERNATIVE SOLUTION TO EXAMPLE 13.2

Sometimes the ascertainment of profit from incomplete records is difficult because the information available is insufficient to construct a profit and loss account. When that is so the net profit for the year has to be calculated by comparing the capital at the beginning and the capital at the end of the period concerned.

In the absence of any drawings, the opening capital increased by the net profit for the year will give the closing capital.

Hence:

CAPITAL AT END − CAPITAL AT BEGINNING = NET PROFIT

Where the proprietor has withdrawn some cash (or goods) it is obvious that this has the effect of decreasing his capital as at the end of the period. Therefore, to arrive at his net profit any drawings must be added to the closing capital and, therefore.

(CAPITAL AT END + DRAWINGS)
                        − CAPITAL AT BEGINNING = NET PROFIT

Applying the above line of approach, we may produce an alternative solution to Example 13.2, as shown below.

		£	£
Capital at 31st December 1997			
	Assets	98,300	
	Liabilities	4,200	94,100
Add Drawings in 1997			11,000
			105,100
Less Capital at 1st January 1997			
	Assets	87,200	
	Liabilities	3,200	84,000
Net Profit			21,100

SUMMARY

- Many small businesses keep only scant records, often only a cash book, and do not operate a double entry book-keeping system.
- This is due partly to the nature of small business entrepreneurs, who often shy away from paper work and partly to the cost of good book-keeping which can be outwith the reach of a small business.
- Without a workable system of double entry book-keeping a trial balance cannot be drawn up and it is difficult to produce meaningful final accounts.
- When a single entry (or incomplete records) book-keeping system is used, it is necessary to reconstruct all the key accounts using the documentation at hand and any other sources available.
- The cash book is one of the key documents necessary in the reconstruction of the accounts. Even in the poorest systems there is likely to be a cash book or the means of reconstructing one.
- Techniques are available for working out total purchases, total sales and other key figures as demonstrated in this chapter.

- Using the techniques and methods described a prefectly acceptable trading, profit and loss account and balance sheet can be drawn up.

PROBLEMS

1. Distinguish between double entry and single entry book-keeping.

2. George Bacon is in business as a restaurateur. His position on 1st January 19... was:

	£
Debtors	1,050
Creditors	10,380
Leasehold premises	103,800
Food stock	3,900
Loan from Wm Penny	15,000
Cash at bank	18,390
Glass and china	3,600
Kitchen equipment	12,000
Restaurant furniture	11,400

On 30th June 19..., you ascertain that his total assets less liabilities amount to £180,000 and that during the half year he withdrew for private purposes £15,600.

Calculate Bacon's net profit for the six months to 30th June 19...

3. A Sloecoach failed to keep proper records from the date of purchasing his snack bar on 1st January 1995. The following details are, however, ascertained:

	1st January 1995	31st December 1997
Food stocks	£1,200	£1,800
Kitchen equipment	6,000	7,500
Cutlery and utensils	1,500	2,100
Creditors	3,000	3,600
Accrued expenses		900
Cash at bank	9,000	12,600

During the years 1995 and 1996, Sloecoach had drawn £300 per week from the snack bar for his private use, and in 1997 this was increased to £450 per week. It is estimated that the profits for the year 1997 were twice as much as those for 1996 and for the last mentioned year twice as much as for 1995. Prepare a statement setting out your calculations of the estimated profit for each of the three years concerned.

4. A Winter is proprietor of the Four Seasons guest house. His balance sheet on 1st January 19... was:

Balance Sheet

Fixed Assets	Cost £	Agg. Dep'n £	Net £
Freehold premises	98,000		98,000
Furniture	42,000	18,000	24,000
Equipment	37,000	15,000	22,000
	177,000	33,000	144,000
Glass & china			8,000
			152,000

Current Assets		
Stock of food	2,000	
Debtors	1,000	
Prepaid expenses	1,500	
Cash at bank	29,600	
	34,100	

Less Current Liabilities		
Creditors	5,000	
Accrued expenses	3,500	
Advance bookings	1,600	10,100

Net current assets	24,000
	176,000

Financed by:	£
Capital at 1st January 19...	176,000
Total capital employed	176,000

The following is a summary of Winter's cash book for the year ended 31st December 19...

Cash Book Summary

	£		£
Balance b/d	29,600	Private expenses	24,000
Receipts from:		Business expenses	157,100
Visitors – cash	501,400	Creditors	180,700
Credit customers	100,600	Wages and salaries	187,000
Sale of furniture	8,000	Bank charges	400
		Furniture	14,500
		Balance c/d	75,900
	639,600		639,600
Balance b/d	75,900		

Required

Prepare Winter's trading, profit and loss account for the year ended 31st December 19..., and a balance sheet as at that date.

Notes:
(a) At 31st December 19... the stock of food amounted to £3,400; debtors were £1,200; advance bookings £800; prepaid expenses were £1,800 and accrued expenses £3,900; creditors were £4,000.
(b) Depreciate furniture by £6,000; equipment by £5,000 and glass and china by £1,500.
(c) The furniture sold during the year stood in the books of the guest house at £12,000 (original cost £16,000).
(d) You are informed that the new furniture purchased during the year includes a wardrobe costing £1,000, for the proprietor's private flat.

5. G H Gupta is the proprietor of the Tandoori Restaurant. His assets and liabilities on 1st January and 31st December 19..., were

	1st Jan 19...	31st Dec 19...
	£	£
Cash at bank	10,000	20,000
Food stocks	2,200	2,000
Furniture	10,000	10,000
Provision for dep'n – furniture	4,000	4,000
China and cutlery	2,000	2,000
Leasehold premises	100,000	100,000
Provision for dep'n – premises	20,000	20,000
Pre-paid expenses	400	600
Creditors	2,400	2,800
Banqueting debtors	1,000	800
Accrued wages		400

The following is his bank summary for the year:

	£	£
Balance on 1st January 19...		10,000
Add Cash sales	£300,000	
Banqueting receipts	100,000	400,000
		410,000
Less Wages	110,000	
Suppliers	184,000	
Expenses	60,000	
Drawings	36,000	390,000
Balance on 31st December 19...		20,000

Required:
Prepare Gupta's trading, profit and loss account for the year ended 31st December 19..., and a balance sheet as at that date. Depreciate his furniture by 10 per cent, his china and cutlery by £600 and the premises by 3 per cent.

6. O Yesser is a café owner. Her assets and liabilities on 1st January 19...,
and 31st December 19..., were as below:

	1st Jan 19... £	31st Dec 19... £
Freehold premises	60,000	60,000
Creditors	1,800	3,800
China and utensils	2,200	2,200
Furniture	9,500	9,500
Provision for dep'n- furniture	3,000	3,000
Stock of food	3,000	3,200
Accrued expenses	6,400	8,800
Pre-paid expenses	800	400
Cash at bank	11,000	13,700

The following is a summary of her bank account in respect of the year
ended 31st December 19...

Bank Account Summary

	£		£
Balance b/d	11,000	Private expenses	11,000
Total receipts	199,900	Business expenses	51,000
		Wages	55,500
		Suppliers	79,500
		Bank charges	200
		Balance c/d	13,700
	£210,900		£210,900
Balance b/d	£13,700		

Required:

Prepare Miss Yesser's trading, profit and loss account for the year ended
31st December 19..., and her balance sheet as at that date, taking the
following into account: depreciate her furniture by £700 and china and
utensils by £600.

7. The balance sheet of Alfons Blumenthal, a café proprietor, on 1st
January 19..., was as follows:

Balance sheet

Fixed assets	Cost	Dep'n	Net
	DM	DM	DM
Leasehold premises	1,562,500	812,500	750,000
Furniture	375,000	225,000	150,000
	1,937,500	1,037,500	900,000
Cutlery etc.			75,000
			975,000
Current assets			
Stocks of food		50,000	
Bank balance		100,000	
		150,000	
Less Current Liabilities			
Creditors	95,000		
Accrued expenses	30,000	125,000	
Net current assets			25,000
			1,000,000

	DM
Financed by:	
Capital at 1st January 19...	1,000,000
Total capital employed	1,000,000

You are informed that Blumenthal pays all receipts into his bank account and pays all expenses by cheque.

His transactions for the year ended 31st December 19..., were:

	DM
Receipts from customers	1,498,500
Payments to creditors	186,000
Cash purchases	448,500
Payments for expenses	184,500
Drawings	64,500

On 31st December 19..., his creditors amounted to DM45,000 and the food stocks were valued at DM39,000.

You are required to prepare:
(a) a summary of his bank account;
(b) his trading, profit and loss account for the year ended 31st December 19..., and a balance sheet as at that date.
   Depreciate Blumenthal's premises by 4 per cent, the furniture by 10 per cent and the cutlery by DM9000.

Accounts of non-profit making bodies

14

INTRODUCTION

We have so far considered the preparation of final accounts by reference to a type of business (the sole trader), where the business is carried on with a view to profit.

There are, however, many organizations which do not seek to make a profit but, primarily, exist to promote their objects. Examples of such non-profit making bodies are: sports clubs, charitable, political, religious and social institutions, professional bodies and several forms of welfare catering. The final accounts of such bodies are prepared according to the principles explained in the previous chapters, i.e. in the same manner as those of a sole trader. What is rather different about these accounts is, however, mainly the terminology used.

OBJECTIVES

On completion of this chapter you should be able to:

- understand the meaning of 'non-profit making bodies';
- draw up an income and expenditure account and balance sheet of a non-profit making body;
- understand and use terms peculiar to this area of accounting, such as accumulated fund, net surplus or net deficit, catering account;
- draw up a catering account of a non-profit making concern;
- comprehend and construct a receipts and payments account;
- deal with subscriptions, entrance fees, donations and similiar items as they arise in the accounts.

INCOME AND EXPENDITURE ACCOUNT

This is the equivalent of the profit and loss account of a trading organization. It is credited (as with the profit and loss account) with all income earned, whether actually received or not, and debited with all expenses incurred, whether actually paid or not.

A credit balance arising in the income and expenditure account is not described as net profit but as 'net surplus' or the 'excess of income over expenditure'. A debit balance arising in the income and expenditure account (the equivalent of the net loss in a trading organization) is described as the 'net deficit' or the 'excess of expenditure over income'.

BALANCE SHEET

The balance sheet of a non-profit making organization is prepared in the same manner as the balance sheet of a trading concern. What is usually described as capital is, sometimes, in a non-profit making organization referred to as 'capital fund' or 'accumulated fund'.

EXAMPLE 14.1

The following trial balance was extracted from the books of the Old Chiswick Club at 31st December 19...

	£	£
Refreshment creditors		4,500
Stock of refreshments on 1st January, 19...	1,500	
Refreshment takings		42,750
Purchases of refreshments	27,000	
Postage and telephone	750	
Furniture at cost	12,000	
Provision for dep'n-furniture		9,000
Leasehold premises at cost	125,000	
Provision for dep'n-premises		50,000
Cleaning	900	
Wages – general	7,500	
Wages – catering	4,800	
Secretary's honorarium	1,500	
Cash at bank	15,450	
Games equipment at cost	12,000	
Provision for dep'n – equipment		6,000
Additions to equipment (28 December 19...)	600	
Printing and stationery	1,050	
Donations		750
Repairs	300	
Prizes	1,500	
Sundry receipts		2,100
Rent	6,000	
Accumulated fund		81,000
Subscriptions		21,750
	£217,850	£217,850

You are required to prepare the club's catering account and income and expenditure account for the year ended 31st December 19..., and a balance sheet as at that date. Take the following notes into account:

(a) The club's stock of refreshments at 31st December 19... was valued at £3,000.

(b) Subscriptions due but unpaid amounted to £750.

(c) Depreciation is to be provided for as follows: furniture 10 per cent, equipment 10 per cent, leasehold 2 per cent.

The catering account, the income and expenditure account and the balance sheet respectively are shown below:

Catering A/c for year ended 31st December 19...

	£	£
Sales		42,750
Opening stock	1,500	
Purchases	27,000	
	28,500	
Less Closing stock	3,000	
Cost of sales		25,500
Gross profit		17,250
Less Catering wages		4,800
Catering profit		12,450

Note: The catering wages are debited in order that the catering account may show the true trading results of the catering facilities provided by the club.

Income & Expenditure A/c for year ended 31st December 19...

Income			£
Catering profit b/d			12,450
Subscriptions			22,500
Donations			750
Sundry receipts			2,100
			37,800
Expenditure			
Rent		6,000	
Printing & stationery		1,050	
Postage & telephone		750	
Sec. honorarium		1,500	
Wages		7,500	
Cleaning		900	
Repairs		300	
Depreciation:			
Furniture	300		
Equipment	600		
Leasehold	1,500	2,400	
Prizes		1,500	21,900
Net surplus			15,900

Students should observe that the above income and expenditure account is prepared in the same manner as the profit and loss account of a profit-making organization. As has been explained above, the construction of an income and expenditure account follows the same lines as that of a profit and loss account; any differences between the two are apparent rather than real and are, in the main, a matter of terminology.

Subscriptions owing but not yet received have been added to those already paid by members because they are due in respect of the period covered by the accounts.

Balance Sheet as at 31st December 19...

Fixed assets	Cost £	Dep'n. £	Net £
Leasehold premises	125,000	51,500	73,500
Furniture	12,000	9,300	2,700
Games equipment	12,600	6,600	6,000
	149,600	67,400	82,200
Current assets			
Stock of refreshments		3,000	
Subscriptions due		750	
Cash at bank		15,450	
		19,200	
Less Current Liabilities			
Refreshment creditors		4,500	
Net current assets			14,700
			96,900
Financed by:			
Accumulated Fund			
Balance on 1st Jan 19...			81,000
Add net surplus			15,900
			96,900

Note: Here again, it will be observed that except for the occasional differences in terminology and one or two items peculiar to clubs, the construction of a balance sheet of non-profit making bodies follows the usual lines.

RECEIPTS AND PAYMENTS ACCOUNT

In addition to an income and expenditure account and a balance sheet, some non-profit making bodies prepare what is known as a 'receipts and payments account'. Some smaller organizations, and these are fortunately few, prepare a receipts and payments account instead of a proper set of final accounts.

A receipts and payments account is simply a summary of all cash received and all cash paid during an accounting period. It does not take into account any accruals or pre-payments of expenditure; similarly it ignores adjustments in respect of income accrued due or received in advance. Often a receipts and payments account includes capital receipts and payments. The balance of this account represents the cash balance available at the end of the period concerned. A specimen receipts and payments account is shown below:

Receipts and Payments A/c for year ended 31 December 19...

	£		£
Balance b/d	3,000	Rent	6,600
Subscriptions	9,000	Furniture	5,400
Donations	1,500	Postage & stationery	1,800
Profit on dances	3,600	Sec. honorarium	1,500
Refreshment takings	6,000	Refreshments	3,600
Sundry receipts	900	Prizes	600
		Balance c/d	4,500
	24,000		24,000
Balance b/d	4,500		

The receipts and payments account is a useful financial statement when it is presented in addition to a set of final accounts (income and expenditure account and balance sheet). On its own it is quite inadequate and a poor substitute for proper final accounts.

ITEMS PECULIAR TO NON-PROFIT MAKING BODIES

Subscriptions

This is usually one of the most important sources of revenue in most clubs and other non-profit making bodies. Ideally, each year should be credited with the subscriptions received in respect of that year. In practice, however, it is often found that a proportion of subscription income is not paid until after the end of the period in respect of which it is due.

The actual treatment of accrued subscriptions depends on the nature of the membership. Where this is stable, it is reasonable to assume that outstanding subscriptions will eventually be recovered. In such circumstances accrued subscriptions are credited in the income and expenditure account. Where, however, the membership of a club is not stable and its composition changes constantly, it is doubtful whether many of the outstanding subscriptions will be paid. Where that is so no credit is usually taken for accrued subscriptions and any subscriptions received in arrears are credited in the income and expenditure account as and when actually received.

Subscriptions received in advance, i.e. before they are due, must, of course, be carried forward to the future years in respect of which they have been paid.

EXAMPLE 14.2

On 1st January 1997, the '66 Club' had subscriptions paid by members in advance (i.e. for the year 1997) amounting to £600. At the same time subscriptions due but unpaid amounted to £1,200. During 1997 the club received subscriptions amounting to £15,150 of which £450 was paid in advance (for 1998) and £1,200 was paid in respect of the year ended 31st December 1996. At 31st December 1997, it was ascertained that current subscriptions due but not paid amounted to £900.

The club's subscriptions account would be adjusted as shown below:

Subscriptions A/c

1997		£	1997		£
Jan 1	Balance b/d	1,200	Jan 1	Balance b/d	600
Dec 31	Balance c/d	450	Dec 31	Cash	15,150
" 31	Inc. & Exp. A/c	15,000	" 31	Balance c/d	900
		16,650			16,650
1998		£	1998		£
Jan 1	Balance b/d	900	Jan 1	Balance b/d	450

Entrance fees

These are payable in some clubs and other bodies on admission to membership. Where the amount of entrance fees received is stable from one year to another they are usually credited in the income and expenditure account.

It is often argued, however, that as such fees are paid by members for benefits extending over a long period of years they should be regarded as capital receipts. Where this view prevails, entrance fees are excluded from the income and expenditure account, and are credited direct to the capital fund account.

Donations

These may be donations received or donations paid. Where there are both kinds, each should be recorded in a separate account and then transferred to the income and expenditure account.

Club catering

Most clubs provide some kind of catering service. Whilst in the smallest clubs the catering facilities usually take the form of refreshments, many of the large clubs operate good-quality restaurants and bars for their members. Whatever the nature of the catering facilities it is desirable periodically to prepare a catering account, showing separate trading results of the catering department.

The catering account will be debited not only with the cost of food used but also other catering costs, i.e. costs directly attributable to the catering department. Such costs will include catering wages, stock-taker's fees (if any), losses of light equipment, depreciation of heavy kitchen equipment, kitchen fuel, etc. At the end of the period the balance of the catering account is transferred to the income and expenditure account.

SUMMARY

- There are a number of organizations which carry on a business but do not primarily wish to make a profit. e.g. sports clubs, political bodies etc.
- The accounts for non-profit making bodies are drawn up according to the same rules as applied to a sole trader, although there is some difference in terminology.
- The income and expenditure account replaces the profit and loss account and a net profit becomes a net surplus. In the balance sheet the capital is called the accumulated fund.
- Where catering takes place it is usual to construct a separate trading account in order to work out the catering profit.
- Subscriptions may be in advance or in arrears and are dealt with in a separate subscriptions account.
- Some smaller organizations produce a receipts and payments account instead of final accounts. This is not in keeping with best accounting practice.

PROBLEMS

1. Prepare from the following trial balance:
   (a) refreshments trading account;
   (b) income and expenditure account of the City Club for the year ended 31st December, 19...;
   (c) balance sheet as at that date.

	£	£
Cash register at cost	1,680	
Provision for dep'n – cash register		780
Refreshment stock at 1st January 19...	1,950	
Stocktaker's fee	180	
Purchases of refreshment	39,450	
Gas and electricity	2,430	
Telephone	690	
Games accessories	270	
Papers and periodicals	300	
Printing and stationery	780	
Refreshments creditors		8,850
Bank loan		51,900
Refreshments takings		54,030
Subscriptions		2,310
Playing fees		930
Rents received		420
Cash at bank	9,630	
Kitchen utensils at cost	3,900	
Provision for dep'n – kitchen utensils		1,200
Secretary's honorarium	1,500	
Furniture at cost	4,500	
Provision for dep'n – furniture		1,650
Catering wages	6,000	
General wages	2,280	
Freehold premises at cost	72,600	
Glass, china and cutlery	3,060	
Sundry receipts		90
Sundry expenses	630	
Accumulated fund at 1st Jan 19...		29,670
	151,830	151,830

You are required to take the following into account:

(a) At 31st December 19..., subscriptions receivable but unpaid amounted to £450.
(b) The stock of refreshments was valued at £2,540.
(c) Accrued gas and electricity amounted to £570.
(d) The stock of unused stationery was valued at £240.
(e) Provide for depreciation as follows:
  (i) cash register £210;
  (ii) furniture £450;
  (iii) kitchen utensils £300;
  (iv) glass, china and cutlery were valued at £2,400.

2. The following is the summary of the cash book of the Mayfair Club for the year to 31st December 1997:

Receipts and Payments Account

	£		£
Balance at bank 1st Jan 1997	10,800	Restaurant & bar supplies	180,000
Members' subscriptions:		Wages	63,600
For year 1996 2,550		Printing, stationery & postage	4,200
1997 77,250		New furniture	19,500
1998 3,000		General expenses	54,900
	82,800	Balance at bank 31 December	
Restaurant & bar takings	240,000	1997	11,400
	333,600		333,600

Additional information is obtained as follows:

	31st December 1996	31st December 1997
	£	£
Freehold premises	150,000	150,000
Stock of restaurant and bar supplies	18,540	16,440
Creditors for restaurant and bar supplies	13,500	14,700
Wages accrued	750	900

Additional information in respect of club's position at 31st December 1996:

(a) Club furniture had following balance:
Cost £185,000, dep'n £76,400, net £108,600.
(b) During 1996, £2,400 had been received in respect of members' subscriptions for 1997.

You are required to prepare:

(a) trading account for the restaurant and bar for the year 1997;
(b) income and expenditure account for the year 1997;
(c) balance sheet as on 31st December 1997.

The gross profit of the restaurant and bar trading account is to be transferred to the income and expenditure account.

It is the practice to take no credit in the annual income and expenditure account for subscriptions in advance at the end of the accounting period.

3. The following is a summary of the cash book of the Beefeaters' Club for the year 1997.

Cash Book Summary

	£		£
Balance at bank and cash in hand 1st Jan 1997	10,200	Payments for restaurant and bar supplies	156,300
Subscriptions:		Rent, lighting & heating	14,700
for 1996	750	New furniture	13,500
1997	21,600	General expenses	12,000
1998	300	Wages	30,000
	22,650	Balance at bank and cash	
Restaurant and bar sales	221,850	in hand, 31st December 1997	28,200
	254,700		254,700

You are given the following information:

(a)	31st Dec 1996 £	31st Dec 1997 £
Restaurant and bar stocks	16,500	15,000
Creditors for restaurant and bar supplies	18,600	21,000

(b) Figures for the club's furniture on 31st December 1996 were:
   Cost £50,000, Dep'n £20,000, Net book value £30,000.

(c) Subscriptions for 1997 received during 1996 amounted to £450.

Required:
Prepare a restaurant and bar trading account, and a general income expenditure account for the year 1997 and a balance sheet as at 31st December 1997. No credit is to be taken for any subscriptions in arrears at 31st December 1997, and you may assume that this principle was followed in the preparation of the accounts for 1996. Ignore depreciation.

4. The Gourmets' Club prepares its accounts annually to 31st December. The restaurant and bar of the club are managed by a firm of outside caterers, Outdoor Catering Ltd, who pay the club by way of rent a percentage of their gross takings. On 1st January 1997 the club's position was as follows:

	£
Bank loan at cost	22,500
Furniture (Cost £88,000, Dep'n £47,800)	40,200
Kitchen plant and utensils (Cost £38,600, Dep'n £13,400)	25,200
Stamps and stationery	450
Rent due from Outdoor Catering Ltd	750

At the same time £3,600 was owing for one quarter's rent and £600 for the telephone. Subscriptions received in advance in respect of 1997 amounted to £1,500.

Given below is the summary of the cash book of the club for the year ended 31st December 1997.

Cash Book Summary

	£		£
Balance at 1st Jan 1997	18,000	Rent (12 months)	14,400
Donations	3,000	Rates	3,900
Green fees	6,300	Sec. Honorarium	6,000
Entrance fees	750	Light and heat	4,500
Sale of furniture	10,200	Cleaning	1,050
Rent – Outdoor Catering Ltd	8,250	Prizes	900
War loan interest	600	Post, stationery & phone	3,300
Subscriptions: 1996	12,000	Furniture	18,000
1997	900	Bank charges	300
		Balance at 31st Dec 1997	7,650
	60,000		60,000
Balance	7,650		

Required:

Prepare the club's income and expenditure account for the year ended 31st December 1997 and a balance sheet as at that date. Take the following into account:

(a) Provide for accrued audit fee of £600.

(b) At the date of the balance sheet £1,050 was owing from Outdoor Catering Ltd; the stock of stamps and stationery unused was valued at £750; and £450 was owing for the telephone.

(c) Provide for depreciation as follows: furniture £2,400; kitchen plant and utensils, £6,000.

5. The following is the receipts and payments account of the Welcome Club for the year ended 31st December 1996.

Receipts and Payments Account

	£		£
Opening balance	7,050	Rent and rates	16,800
Bar takings	121,740	Printing and stationery	3,600
Outside catering receipts		Repairs	2,610
(credit bar account)	7,500	Fuel and lighting	7,800
Subscriptions	13,590	Equipment	6,000
Garden fete net receipts	3,900	Cleaning and sundries	1,950
Investment income	1,500	Barman's wages	22,500
Donations	3,000	Caretaker's wages	7,500
		Additional bar help	3,600
		Bar purchases	74,040
		Closing balance	11,880
	158,280		158,280

Required:

Prepare an income and expenditure account, and a balance sheet as at 31st December, 1996, for presentation to the club members at the general meeting, taking into consideration the following:

(a) A separate bar account should be shown and the net profit on the bar transferred to income and expenditure account.

(b) At 1st January 1996, the club furniture and equipment stood as follows: cost £78,000, dep'n £54,000, net book value £24,000. Depreciation is charged at 10 per cent p.a. on cost.

(c) At 1st January 1996 the value of the furnishings as per the last balance sheet was as follows; cost £29,500, dep'n £22,000, net book value £7,500; furnishings to be depreciated by £1,500 p.a.

(d) At 1st January 1996, the accumulated capital fund stood at £75,000.

(e) At 1st January 1996, the renovations fund stood at £16,050.

(f) The club has investments of £30,000.

(g) The bar stocks were: 1st January 1996, £22,500; 31st December 1996, £24,900.

(h) At 31st December 1996, the following accounts were owing: rent £2,250; printing and stationery £600; repairs £390; fuel £1,350.

(i) At 31st December, rates paid in advance were £1,050.

(j) Of the subscriptions, £300 referred to 1997 and £510 was owing at the end of the year.

(k) One-half of the surplus for the year is to be added to the accumulated fund, and one-half added to the renovations fund.

Accounting for partnerships   15

INTROPDUCTION

People have formed business partnerships over many centuries. They are a sensible way to share the risks of starting a business or in the case of a sole trader wishing to expand, a way of attracting new capital or increasing size quickly.

They are relatively common in the hospitality industry particularly in small scale operations. Partnerships are valuable when they work well but there are also many pitfalls in such dealings, both financial and practical.

OBJECTIVES

On completion of this chapter you should be able to:

- understand the key aspects of partnership agreements, especially the sharing of profits and losses and unlimited liability;
- draw up partnership accounts, including the partners' drawings accounts, salaries accounts and appropriation account;
- construct partnership accounts using the 'fixed capital' method;
- deal with interest on partners' drawings in the accounts;
- explain the meaning of a debit balance on a partners' current account;
- make all necessary end-of-year adjustments to the books of account;
- understand the accounting procedure for when a partner makes a loan to the firm.

NATURE OF PARTNERSHIP

A partnership is defined by the Partnership Act 1890, as 'the relation which subsists between persons carrying on a business in common with a view to profit'. It is possible to form a partnership with only two partners. The maximum number of partners is twenty, except in the case of solicitors, accountants and members of a recognized stock exchange where partnerships of more than twenty persons are allowed.

Two main advantages may be claimed for the partnership over the sole trader type of business unit.

1. It has access to more capital. Other things being equal, two or more people can raise a larger amount of capital than one person.
2. As the partnership is managed by more than one person, it has at its disposal a wider range of ability and experience than a business owned and managed by one person. Thus, in a hotel owned by two partners, the reception, control and accounts may be managed by one partner and the kitchen, restaurant and the bars by the other.

All partners have unlimited liability for the debts of the firm. If the firm ceases business and the assets, when sold, do not realize enough cash to pay the creditors, the partners will be called upon to contribute to the debts of the firm from their private resources. In other words the liability of each partner extends to the whole of the firm's debts irrespective of what each partner has invested as capital.

Partners who take an active part in the running of the business are known as **active partners**. Those who have contributed some capital but do not take an active part in the management are known as **sleeping partners** or **dormant partners**. The distinction between active and sleeping partners is not one made in law. From the legal point of view both kinds of partners are regarded as general partners.

The Limited Partnerships Act 1907, allows what is known as **limited partners**. A limited partner is one who invests money in a firm, shares in the profits but does not take an active part in the management. The liability for the debts of the partnership is limited to the amount of capital contributed by the limited partner. A limited partnership must, in addition to the limited partners, have at least one general partner whose liability is unlimited. As it is relatively easy to form a private limited company (see next chapter) limited partnerships are at present extremely uncommon. We will, therefore, be concerned with ordinary partnerships only.

THE PARTNERSHIP AGREEMENT

It is obvious that the partners must from the outset reach agreement on certain specific points, such as their contributions to the capital, the sharing of profits and losses, etc. In order to avoid possible misunderstandings on such points, it is usual for them to draw up what is known as the partnership agreement (also referred to as the articles of partnership and the deed of partnership). This will be concerned with matters such as:

- the duration of the partnership;
- the capital contributions of the partners and the rate of interest, if any, to be allowed on their capitals;
- the sharing of profits and losses;
- the salaries, if any, to be paid to the partners;
- the amounts which the partners may draw out of the business;

- arrangements for the preparation of final accounts;
- the admission of a new partner and the retirement or death of an existing partner.

Partners may in general make whatever arrangements they please with regard to the above matters. Where, however, there is no satisfactory evidence of the nature of their arrangements and a dispute occurs, it will be settled in accordance with Section 24 of the Partnership Act 1890, which provides, amongst others, that:

(a) Partners share profits and losses equally.
(b) They are not entitled to interest on their capitals or to remuneration for acting in the partnership business.
(c) They are allowed interest at 5 per cent per annum on any loans over and above their capital contributions.

Students should note that where an examination question is silent on the sharing of profits and losses, the provisions of Section 24 should be applied.

ACCOUNTS OF PARTNERS

In general it may be said that the accounts of a partnership do not differ from those of any other type of business. We still keep the same subsidiary books and ledger accounts, and transactions are recorded as explained in the previous chapters.

The only changes that are introduced arise from the fact that there is more than one proprietor and that, in consequence, the profits of the business have to be shared between them. As a result, whilst in the sole trader type of business there is one capital account, in a partnership a separate capital account must be opened for each partner. Similarly, each partner will have to have a separate drawings account and, where partnership salaries are paid, a separate salary account.

In the case of a sole trader, the net profit is transferred from the profit and loss account direct to the capital account. In a partnership the net profit is divided in what is known as the appropriation account before being transferred to the capital or current accounts of the partners. The appropriation account is a continuation of the profit and loss account and, as its name indicates, is used for the purpose of appropriating, or dividing, the profits or losses of the business.

EXAMPLE 15.1

A and B are proprietors of the Metropolitan Hotel. Their capitals at 1st January 19..., were: A – £120,000; B – £90,000. During the year ended 31st December 19..., their drawings amounted to £3,000 and £12,000 respectively, and the net profit for the year was £61,500.

Prepare the hotel's appropriation account for the year ended 31st December 19..., and the partners' capital accounts as at that date, taking the following provisions of the partnership agreement into account:

(a) Partners are entitled to interest on their capital at the rate of 5 per cent per annum.

(b) Partners are allowed salaries as follows: A – £18,000; B – £21,000.

(c) The balance of profit or loss is to be shared by the partners equally.

The appropriation account of the hotel would be drawn up as follows:

Appropriation A/c for year ended 31st December 19...

	£	£	£
Net Profit b/d			61,500
Less Interest on capital			
A	6,000		
B	4,500	10,500	
Less: Salaries			
A	18,000		
B	21,000	39,000	
Less: Share of profit			
A	6,000		
B	6,000	12,000	
			61,500

It should be noted that interest on the partners' capital and partnership salaries are debited in the appropriation account and not in the profit and loss account. This is because these items are not regarded as expenses (charges against profit) but as a convenient means of appropriating or distributing the net profit.

The capital accounts of the partners would be written up as:

Capital A/c -A

19...		£	19...			£
Dec 31	Drawings	3,000	Jan	1	Balance b/d	120,000
" 31	Balance c/d	147,000	Dec 31	Int. on capital	6,000
			"	31	Salary	18,000
			"	31	Net profit	6,000
		150,000				150,000
			19...			£
			Jan	1	Balance b/d	147,000

Capital A/c -B

19...		£	19...			£
Dec 31	Drawings	12,000	Jan	1	Balance b/d	90,000
" 31	Balance c/d	109,500	Dec 31	Int. on capital	4,500
			"	31	Salary	21,000
			"	31	Net profit	6,000
		121,500				121,500
			19...			£
			Jan	1	Balance b/d	109,500

It will be observed that the capital accounts of the partners are written up in the same way as the capital account of a sole trader, except that the net profit is credited to the partners in the form of several separate elements rather than in total.

In the balance sheet of a partnership, it is usual to show all the details affecting the partners' capital accounts rather than the net capitals as at the end of the current period. This is illustrated below:

(EXTRACT FROM)
Balance Sheet as at 31st December 19...

Capital and Reserves
Capital accounts

		Partner A	Partner B	Proprietors'
		£	£	Interest
Balance on 1st Jan 19 . . .		120,000	90,000	
Add	Int. on capital	6,000	4,500	
	Salary	18,000	21,000	
	Net profit	6,000	6,000	
		150,000	121,500	
Less	Drawings	3,000	12,000	
		147,000	109,500	£256,500

'Proprietors' interest' is the total of the capitals of the partners. Alternatively, it may be defined as the total of assets less any external liabilities.

FIXED CAPITAL METHOD

When additions to capital (interest, salary and share of net profit) and deduction from it (drawings) are transferred direct to the capital accounts the balances of those accounts vary from one year to another. Many partners, however, prefer to have a fixed amount of capital invested in their business. Further, it is not uncommon for partnership agreements to provide that the capital contributions of the partners shall be fixed and not varied except by agreement.

In order to keep the capitals of partners fixed it is possible to use the fixed capital method, which has become very popular in recent years. Under the fixed capital method, the capitals of the partners remain constant and no postings to the capital accounts are made.

Any additions to capital and deductions from it are transferred to each partner's current account.

A credit balance on a partner's current account represents a debt from the business to the partner and, conversely, a debit balance on a partner's current account represents a debt from the partner concerned to the business. The capital accounts and current accounts of partners A and B in the illustrations above would, under the fixed capital method, appear as shown below:

Capital A/c - A

19...		£	19...		£
Dec 31	Balance c/d	120,000	Jan 1	Balance b/d	120,000
			19...		
			Jan 1	Balance b/d	120,000

Capital A/c - B

19...		£	19...		£
Dec 31	Balance c/d	90,000	Jan 1	Balance b/d	90,000
			19...		
			Jan 1	Balance b/d	90,000

Current A/c - A

19...		£	19...		£
Dec 31	Drawings	3,000	Dec 31	Int. on capital	6,000
" 31	Balance c/d	27,000	" 31	Salary	18,000
			" 31	Net profit	6,000
		30,000			30,000
			19...		
			Jan 1	Balance b/d	27,000

Current A/c - B

19...		£	19...		£
Dec 31	Drawings	12,000	Dec 31	Int. on capital	4,500
" 31	Balance c/d	19,500	" 31	Salary	21,000
			" 31	Net profit	6,000
		31,500			31,500
			19...		
			Jan 1	Balance b/d	19,500

In the balance sheet, the capitals of the partners and their current accounts are shown as follows:

(EXTRACT FROM)
Balance Sheet as at 31st December 19...

Capital and Reserves

	Partner A	Partner B	Proprietors' Interest
	£	£	£
Capital accounts	<u>120,000</u>	<u>90,000</u>	210,000
Current Accounts			
Interest on capital	6,000	4,500	
Salary	18,000	21,000	
Net profit	6,000	6,000	
	30,000	31,500	
Drawings	3,000	12,000	
	<u>27,000</u>	<u>19,500</u>	46,500
			256,500

INTEREST ON DRAWINGS

Sometimes the partnership agreement of a firm provides that interest shall be charged against the partners on any amounts withdrawn by them on account of profits. In such circumstances the interest is debited in the partners' current accounts and credited in the appropriation account.

Where the dates of withdrawal are given it is possible to calculate the amount of such interest accurately. Where, on the other hand, the dates of withdrawal are not given it is usual to assume that the drawings were spread evenly throughout the accounting period, and charge the interest at half rate.

EXAMPLE 15.2

AB and CD are proprietors of the Esplanade Hotel. Their capitals at 1st January 19 . . ., were £210,000 and £120,000 respectively. Their partnership agreement provided that:

(a) Partners' capitals remain constant.
(b) Partners are entitled to interest on their capitals at the rate of 4 per cent per annum.
(c) Partners are to be charged with interest on drawings at the rate of 5 per cent per annum.
(d) AB and CD share profits and losses in the proportion 2:1.

During the year ended 31st December 19 . . ., AB withdrew £24,000 and CD withdrew £6,000. The hotel's net profit for the year amounted to £60,150. Prepare the hotel's appropriation account and the partners' current accounts. Proceed as follows:

Appropriation A/c for year ended 31st December 19...

	£	£	£
Net Profit b/d			£60,150
Add Interest on drawings			
AB	600		
CD	150		750
			60,900
Less: Interest on capital			
AB	8,400		
CD	4,800	13,200	
Less: Share of net profit			
AB	31,800		
CD	15,900	47,700	60,900

Current A/c - Partner A.B.

19...		£	19...		£
Dec 31	Int. on drawings	600	Dec 31	Int. on capital	8,400
" 31	Drawings	24,000	" 31	Net profit	31,800
" 31	Balance c/d	15,600			
		40,200			40,200
			Jan 1	Balance b/d	15,600

Current A/c - Partner C.D.

19...		£	19...		£
Dec 31	Int. on drawings	150	Dec 31	Int. on capital	4,800
" 31	Drawings	6,000	" 31	Net profit	15,900
" 31	Balance c/d	14,550			
		20,700			20,700
			Jan 1	Balance b/d	14,550

DEBIT BALANCE ON CURRENT ACCOUNT

When a partner's current account shows a debit balance, all particulars relating to it are still shown on the liabilities side of the balance sheet. The net debit balance is then transferred, as a contra entry, to the assets side of the balance sheet. This is illustrated below:

(EXTRACT FROM)
Balance Sheet as at 31st December 19...

Capital and Reserves

	Partner M £	Partner N £	£
Capital Accounts	_____	_____	_____
Current Accounts			
Interest on Capital	6,000		
Salary	12,000		
Net profit	3,000		
	21,000		
Less Drawings	24,000		
Dr Balance*	3,000		

* The net debit balance on partner M's current account will be shown as an asset, under the heading 'current assets'.

Partners' loans

A partner may advance a loan to the business over and above his contribution to the capital. Any sum so received by the partnership will be debited in the cash book, and credited in a loan account.

Any interest paid on the loan would be credited in the cash book, and debited in the loan interest account. At the end of each year the total of loan interest payable should be transferred to the profit and loss account.

END-OF-YEAR ADJUSTMENTS

At the end of an accounting period, it is sometimes found that certain adjustments are necessary in respect of items such as partnership salaries and loan interest due.

When it is found that a partner has not drawn the full salary to which he is entitled, the balance still owing to him must be credited to his current account. Similarly, any loan interest due to a partner but remaining unpaid at the end of the year must be credited to his current account.

From the information given below prepare the appropriation account for the year ended 31st December 19..., and partner B's current account as at that date.

Net profit for the year		£21,940
Capital account	– A	40,000
Capital account	– B	60,000
Drawings	– A	4,000
Drawings	– B	8,000
Salaries actually paid	– A	11,000

Salaries actually paid	– B	7,500
Salaries, accrued due	– A	1,000
Salaries, accrued due	– B	500
Current accounts as 1st January 19 . . .	A Dr	2,000
Current accounts as 1st January 19 . . .	B Cr	4,000

Provide for interest on the partners' capital at 5 per cent per annum, and for interest on drawings at the rate of 6 per cent per annum. Profits and losses are shared in the ratio: 2:1.

Note: interest on B's loan was debited in the profit and loss account as follows:

Interest	£1,500	
Add Accrued	500	£2,000

The appropriation account and Partner B's current account are illustrated below:

Appropriation A/c for year ended 31st December 19 . . .

	£	£
Net Profit b/d		21,940
Add Interest on drawings		
A	120	
B	240	360
		22,300
Less: Interest on capital		
A	2,000	
B	3,000	5,000
		17,300
Less: Salaries		
A	12,000	
B	8,000	20,000
		(2,700)
Add: Share of net loss		
A	(1,800)	
B	(900)	(2,700)

Current A/c - B

19...			£	19...				£
Dec 31	Drawings		8,000	Jan	1	Balance b/d		4,000
" 31	Int. on drawings		240	Dec 31	Int. on capital		3,000
" 31	Net loss		900	" 31	Salary due		500
				" 31	Loan int. due		500
				" 31	Balance c/d		1,140
			9,140					9,140
19...			£					
Jan 1	Balance b/d		1,140					

SUMMARY

- The business dealings of partners are governed by the Partnership Act 1890.
- The maximum number of partners allowed in a partnership is twenty, apart from the listed exceptions – solicitors, accountants, etc.
- When forming a partnership it is sensible, but not compulsory, to enter into a written agreement.
- The absence of a written agreement means that disputes will be settled by Section 24 of the Partnership Act.
- The accounts of a partnership do not differ substantially from those of a sole trader.
- There are clear legal provisions governing interest on drawings and loans from a partner to the firm.
- An important difference in partnership accounts is the use of an appropriation account to appropriate (to divide or distribute) the profit between partners.
- How partners share the profit will be agreed between them either verbally or in a partnership contract. It is normally based on either how much capital each partner contributes or on key skills or other sensible basis.
- Key items dealt with in the appropriation account are: interest on drawings and capital; partners' salaries and the sharing of remaining profits or losses.
- The main changes relate to the appropriation of profits and the capital of the organization. A separate capital account is required for each partner and the net profit is divided up in the appropriation account.

PROBLEMS

1. Write short explanatory notes on each of the following: partnership; partnership agreement; active partner; sleeping partner; limited partner.

2. What are the main provisions of Section 24 of the Partnership Act 1890?

3. (a) X, Y and Z are in partnership as catering contractors. Their capitals are: £80,000, £40,000 and £40,000 respectively. How much should each receive out of the first year's profits of £36,400, if they divide the profits in proportion to capital?

   (b) A Day and B Knight are proprietors of the Battersea Catering Company. Their capitals are: Day £50,000, Knight £90,000. They agreed to allow 5 per cent interest on capital and divide the remaining profits in the proportion 3: 5.

   How much should each receive at the end of a year in which profits are £61,880?

   (c) The proprietors of the Black Rose Hotel are A B Black and C D Rose. Their capitals are £120,000 and £50,000 respectively. They have agreed to divide the firm's profits as follows:
   (i)   Black is to receive a salary of £12,000 per annum;
   (ii) Rose is to receive a salary of £10,000 per annum;
   (iii) each partner is to receive 4 per cent interest on capital;

(iv) the remaining profits are to be divided in the proportion 6: 4. Calculate the total amount due to each partner at the end of 19..., when the hotel's profit amounted to £71,000.

4. Whiting and Herring are partners in a catering business. Their partnership agreement provides that:
(a) partners' capital accounts remain constant;
(b) partners are entitled to 5 per cent interest on their capitals;
(c) Herring is entitled to a salary of £10,000 per annum;
(d) Whiting and Herring share profits and losses in the proportion 3: 1. On 1st January 19..., their capitals were: Whiting, £120,000, Herring £40,000. During the year ended 31st December 19..., they withdrew £6,000 and £4,000 respectively.

The firm's net profit in 19... amounted to £42,400. Prepare the partners' current accounts for the year ended 31st December 19...

5. The following trial balance was extracted from the books of a firm on 30th June 19...

		£	£
Capital	A B Brown		180,000
	C D Brown		90,000
	E F Brown		60,000
Drawings:	A B Brown	12,000	
	C D Brown	9,000	
	E F Brown	6,000	
Purchases		240,000	
Sales			585,000
Stocks on 1st July 19. .		10,500	
Freehold premises		225,000	
Wages and salaries		147,600	
Rates		24,900	
Postage and telephone		9,150	
Kitchen utensils and equipment at cost		37,500	
Provision for dep'n – utensils & equipment etc.			12,000
Cash at bank		132,000	
Printing and stationery		4,950	
Cash in hand		1,350	
Insurances		5,100	
Trade creditors			24,000
Gas and electricity		28,050	
Furniture at cost		42,240	
Provision for dep'n – furniture			15,840
China and linen		9,150	
Office equipment at cost		21,500	
Provision for dep'n – office equipment			15,050
Discount received			3,000
Debtors		3,900	
Repairs and renewals		15,000	
		£984,890	£984,890

Required:

Prepare the firm's trading account, profit and loss account and appropriation account for the year ended 30th June 19 . . ., and a balance sheet as at that date.

The following notes are to be taken into account:

(a) Final stock was valued at £12,000.

(b) Accrued salaries amounted to £2,100.

(c) Accrued electricity amounted to £1,650.

(d) Prepaid insurance amounted to £1,350.

(e) Provide depreciation as follows: furniture 12.5 per cent on cost; kitchen utensils and equipment £1,500 p.a; office equipment 15 per cent on cost: china and linen were revalued at £7,500.

(f) Profits are to be distributed as follows: interest on capital 4 per cent; C D and E F Brown are entitled to salaries of £12,000 and £15,000 respectively; divide remaining profits in the proportion 5: 3: 2.

6. Fox and Hunt are proprietors of the Excelsior Hotel. The following trial balance was extracted from their books on 30th June 19 . . ., after the compilation of the annual trading account.

		£	£
Capitals:	Fox		105,000
	Hunt		90,000
Drawings:	Fox	6,000	
	Hunt	12,000	
Current accounts:	Fox	750	
	Hunt		300
Trading account			182,370
Wages and salaries		68,280	
Deposits – advance bookings			2,250
Trade creditors			12,990
Fuel and light		14,520	
Leasehold premises at cost		390,000	
Provision for dep'n – leasehold			240,000
Cash at bank		68,130	
Cash in hand		990	
Repairs and replacements		5,610	
China, cutlery and linen		13,500	
Discounts received			2,340
Debtors		6,810	
Furniture and fittings at cost		51,000	
Provision for dep'n – furniture etc.			30,600
Advertising		7,530	
Bad debts		1,170	
Loan account – Hunt			15,000
Rates		10,050	
Laundry		6,660	
Postage and telephone		5,520	
Insurance		1,830	
Stock		10,500	
		£680,850	£680,850

Required:

Prepare the hotel's profit and loss account, and appropriation account for the year ended 30th June, 19..., and a balance sheet as at that date.

Notes:

(a) Accrued salaries amounted to £570.

(b) Treat £1,530 of the advertising as paid in advance.

(c) You are informed that £510 of the debtors are definitely bad.

(d) Provide for the depreciation as follows: china, cutlery and linen were revalued at £12,000; furniture and fittings at 10 per cent on cost; leasehold premises at £24,000 p.a.

(e) Provide for interest on Hunt's loan at 5 per cent.

(f) The following provisions of the partnership deed must also be taken into account: partners are entitled to 4 per cent interest on capital; Fox is entitled to a salary equal to 10 per cent of the net profit; Fox and Hunt share profits and losses in the proportion 5: 4.

N.B. All calculations to the nearest £.

7. The following balances appear on 31st December 19..., in the ledger of the Excellent Hotel Co., which is owned by Miss Carla Robson and Miss Helen Carr. They share profits and losses in proportion to their capitals.

    You are required to prepare a balance sheet as at 31st December 19..., in good style. The trading and profit and loss accounts have been completed and show a net profit of £29,079.

			£
Capital accounts:	Miss Robson		180,000
	Miss Carr		90,000
Current accounts			
Balance, 1st January 19...	Miss Robson	Cr	9,750
	Miss Carr	Cr	3,165
Freehold premises, 1st January 19...			180,000
Equipment at cost			81,000
Provision for dep'n – equipment			34,500
Motor van at cost			25,000
Provision for dep'n – motor vans			11,560
Furniture, etc. at cost			95,000
Provision for dep'n – furniture			34,958
Trade creditors			17,838
Cash in hand			1,668
Bank overdraft			30,000
Investment in 4% war loan stock			15,000
Drawings accounts:	Miss Robson		18,000
	Miss Carr		12,000
Sundry debtors			7,380

The following adjustments have been made in the revenue accounts and are required to be included in your balance sheet:

(a) The stocks at 31st December 19... were:

    Food and drink   £14,946

    Cigarettes and tobacco   £2,703

The following are the rates of depreciation:

    Equipment   10 per cent per annum;

    Motor vans   12 per cent per annum;

    Furniture, etc.   15 per cent per annum;

(b) One-half of the advertising account, which totals £30,000, has been charged forward to 19 . . .

(c) The provision for bad debts is 5 per cent on the sundry debtors.

(d) Miss Carr has had goods value £387, which are charged to her account.

(e) A personal telephone bill of Miss Robson, amount £183, has been paid through the business accounts.

(f) Outstanding expenses are:

    Audit and accountancy   £750

    Printing and stationery   £483

(g) £135 of water rates have been paid in advance.

(h) One-quarter interest on the investment in the 4% loan stock has accrued.

(i) £750 has been charged in respect of bank overdraft interest accrued.

8. Ashley, Brown and Cooper are trading under the name of ABC Catering Co. and share profits and losses in the ratio 1/2, 1/3 and 1/6 respectively. The net profit of their business for the year ended 31st December 19..., amounted to £96,000. From the following information you are required to prepare the appropriation account and the partners' current accounts for the year ended 31st December 19...

		Ashley		Brown		Cooper
		£		£		£
Capital accounts		120,000		90,000		60,000
Current accounts on 1st Jan 19...	Cr	6,150	Cr	450	Dr	1,950
Drawings		18,000		9,000		12,000
Partnership salaries: due		18,000		12,000		9,000
paid		15,000		12,000		7,500

On 1st July 19..., Brown advanced a loan of £60,000 to the business at 5 per cent interest per annum. No interest has been paid to him in respect of the loan.

    Provide for interest on partners' capital at 5 per cent and for interest on drawings at 4 per cent per annum.

9. Black and White are partners in the Black and White Catering Co. The following trial balance was extracted from their books on 30th June, 19...

			£	£
Capital accounts:	Black			180,000
	White			90,000
Drawings accounts:	Black		12,000	
	White		10,500	
Current accounts:	Black			3,000
	White		3,000	
Purchases			244,500	
Sales				594,600
Carriage inwards			1,500	
Stock of food on 1st July 19 . . .			11,250	
Repairs and renewals			15,450	
Debtors			4,350	
Creditors				25,500
Freehold premises at cost			270,000	
Discount received				6,900
Cash in hand			600	
Cash at bank			100,200	
Kitchen equipment at cost			76,800	
Provision for dep'n – kitchen equipment				48,000
Rates			17,250	
China and cutlery			10,050	
Furniture at cost			65,000	
Provision for dep'n – furniture				45,500
Gas and electricity			23,100	
Wages and salaries			144,000	
Printing and stationery			9,150	
Postage and telephone			4,800	
Loan account: White				30,000
			£1,023,500	£1,023,500

Required:
Prepare the firm's trading account, profit and loss account and appropriation account for the year ended 30th June 19 . . ., and a balance sheet as at that date.

Take into account the following notes:
(a) The final stock of food was valued at £14,850.
(b) Accrued gas and electricity amounted to £2,400; unused stationery was valued at £750.
(c) Provide depreciation as: furniture 10 per cent; kitchen equipment 12.5 per cent. China and cutlery were revalued at £8,550.
(d) Provide for interest on White's loan at 5 per cent per annum.
(e) Partners are entitled to interest on their fixed capitals at the rate of 4 per cent per annum.
(f) Black and White share profits and losses in proportion to their capitals.

10. Rachel Anley and Elizabeth Burns are proprietors of the Seaside Hotel. The following trial balance was extracted from their books on 31st December 19..., after the compilation of the trading, and profit and loss account.

		£	£
Capital account	Anley		300,000
Capital account:	Burns		300,000
Freehold premises at cost		600,000	
Furniture at cost		285,000	
Provision for dep'n –furniture			60,000
Glass and china		15,000	
Profit and loss account			96,000
City Finance Co. loan account			300,000
Plant and equipment at cost		250,000	
Provision for dep'n – plant & equipment			130,000
Stocks		36,000	
Debtors		13,500	
Current account:	Anley	3,000	
Current account:	Burns		12,000
Trade creditors			19,200
Cash at bank		19,500	
Light and heat			4,800
		1,222,000	1,222,000

You are asked by the partners to verify the figure of net profit above and, in the course of your investigations, you find the following:

(a) Depreciation on plant and equipment was under-provided for to the extent of £6,600.
(b) Two invoices, in respect of advertising, amounting to £5,700, have not been entered in the books.
(c) A customer's cheque for £900, banked on 30th December 19..., was returned by the bank marked R/D.
(d) You find that the total of debtors shown in the above trial balance includes a bad debt of £1,200.
(e) No provision has been made for the annual interest due to the City Finance Co. which amounts to £15,000.

You are also required to prepare the partners' appropriation account for the year ended 31st December 19..., and their balance sheet as at that date, taking the notes below into account:
(a) Allow interest on partners' capital at 5 per cent.
(b) Provide for partnership salaries as follows:
      Anley – £13,500;   Burns – £10,500.
(c) The balance of profit is to be shared by the partners equally.

11. Ashton and Benson are proprietors of the Florida Restaurant. Their balance sheet on 1st January 19..., was:

Balance Sheet 1st Jan 19...

Fixed Assets	Cost	Agg. Dep'n	Net
	£	£	£
Leasehold premises	600,000	180,000	420,000
Restaurant furniture	240,000	75,000	165,000
Kitchen plant	165,000	60,000	105,000
	1,005,000	315,000	690,000
Current Assets			
Stock		19,500	
Banqueting debtors		4,500	
Ashton: current account		3,000	
Prepaid rates		600	
Cash in bank		38,400	
		66,000	
Less Current Liabilities			
Benson: current account	7,500		
Trade creditors	36,000		
Accrued expenses:			
Gas	1,500		
Advertising	2,400		
Repairs	3,600	51,000	
Net current assets			15,000
			705,000
Capital & Reserves.			
Capital accounts:			
Ashton		405,000	
Benson		300,000	
			705,000

You are also given a summary of their cash book for the year ended 31st December 19..., as follows:

Cash Book Summary

	£			£
Balance b/d	38,400	Cash purchases		157,500
Banqueting debtors	66,000	Trade creditors		301,500
Cash sales	849,000	Wages and salaries		283,500
Ashton, current account	3,000	Repairs and renewals		17,100
		Gas and electricity		18,900
		Rates		12,600
		Advertising		9,300
		Partners' salaries		
		Ashton	45,000	
		Benson	30,000	
				75,000
		Balance c/d		81,000
	£956,400			£956,400
Balance b/d	£81,000			

Required:

Prepare the partners' trading, and profit and loss account for the year ended 31st December 19 . . ., and their balance sheets as at that date, taking the following into account:

(a) Stocks at 31st December, 19 . . ., were valued at £16,500.

(b) Trade creditors amounted to £33,000.

(c) Banqueting debtors amounted to £6,000.

(d) Accrued gas was estimated at £1,800.

(e) Rates paid in advance were £750.

(f) Regard £3,000 of the repairs and renewals as paid in advance.

(g) Provide for depreciation as follows:

    (i)   leasehold premises £22,500;

    (ii) restaurant furniture 10 per cent of cost;

    (iii) kitchen plant, etc. 10 per cent of cost.

(h) The partnership agreement provides as follows:

    (i)   partners are entitled to an annual salary of £45,000 each,

    (ii) profits and losses are shared equally.

N.B. All calculations to the nearest £.

12. Alison Anderson and Betty Beaumont are equal partners carrying on business as the proprietors of the Beachside Hotel. At 31st December 19 . . ., the following balances appeared in their books after the compilation of the trading and profit and loss account for the year which ended on that date.

	£	
Hotel premises at cost		600,000
Furnishings at cost		400,000
Provision for dep'n – furniture		100,000
Kitchen equipment at cost		300,000
Provision for dep'n – kitchen equipment		150,000
Plate, cutlery, linen, etc. at cost		240,000
Station van at cost		45,000
Provision for dep'n – station van		12,000
Sundry debtors		8,400
Rates paid in advance		3,600
Cash in hand		2,400
Stocks at 31st December 19. . .		
Food	11,400	
Liquors	60,600	
Cigarettes	15,600	87,600
Sundry creditors		72,000
Bank overdraft		12,000
Provision for outstanding items		
Wages	5,100	
National Insurance	300	
Fire and other insurances	2,100	7,500

	£	£
Reserves for renewals		
Furnishings	60,000	
Plate, cutlery & linen	<u>21,000</u>	81,000
Deposits received for advance bookings		7,500
Partners' current accounts		
Anderson (cr balance)	30,000	
Beaumont (cr balance)	<u>15,000</u>	45,000

You are required to:
(a) compile the balance sheet of A Anderson and B Beaumont as at 31st December 19... The amount necessary to complete the balance sheet is that of the capital, which is owned by the partners in equal shares;
(b) state the total value of the fixed assets;
(c) state the net value of the floating (or current) assets.

Accounting for limited companies 16

INTRODUCTION

The last few decades have witnessed a rapid growth of limited companies. This is, no doubt, mainly due to the privilege of limited liability enjoyed by the shareholders and the ability of limited companies to raise more capital than is usually possible in the sole trader or partnership type of business. As in other industries, a large proportion of hospitality establishments are limited companies.

OBJECTIVES

On completion of this chapter you should be able to:

- list the Acts of Parliament governing limited companies;
- understand the key features which distinguish a limited company from a sole trader or partnership;
- comprehend the following key terms 'separate legal entity', and 'limited liability';
- differentiate between a public company and a private company;
- list the two main documents which need to be registered, and the essential clauses included within each, in order to register as a limited company;
- enumerate the kinds of capital available to a limited company and the types of shares issued;
- understand the procedure for the issue of shares and debentures and the systems for payment either in full or by instalments, with or without a premium;
- know which items to place in the profit and loss account and which in the appropriation account;
- draw up an appropriation account and correctly enter items therein;
- draw up the final accounts for a limited company;
- differentiate between internal and published accounts of limited companies.

Limited company status gives greater protection to its owners than is the case for a sole trader or partnership. Also it should be pointed out that the salient features of any limited company are **the separate legal entity** aspect and **limited liability**.

A SEPARATE LEGAL ENTITY

A limited company, once properly formed, is regarded as a legal person in its own right totally separate from the shareholders of that business. It can own assets and enter into contracts in its own name. Clearly if a limited company fails to pay its debts or is made insolvent, one can sue only the company itself and has no recourse to the shareholders of the business.

LIMITED LIABILITY

The principle of limited liability is without doubt the most important concept underlying the law applying to limited companies.

The owners of a limited company are its shareholders. Any shareholder who invests in a limited company by buying shares is only responsible for the payment of those shares. This means that the most he can lose if the company fails is the price paid for those shares. Compare this with the position of the sole trader who is held responsible for all the debts of his business in case of failure.

THE COMPANIES ACTS

The conduct of limited companies is regulated by the Companies Acts. The legal provisions which currently govern limited companies are: the Companies Act 1985 as amended by the Companies Act 1989.

Over the past twenty years there have been a large number of changes to British company law brought about partly by European Community rulings issued by the Council of the European Community and partly by the evolving needs of the business community.

The Companies Act lays down, in addition to many other items, a formal procedure to be followed in order to register as a limited company.

KINDS OF COMPANIES

There are two types of limited company: the public limited company (PLC) and the private limited company (Ltd).

A company is a private company unless it is registered as a public company and, in this way, becomes subject to the more stringent requirements relating to its capital, the payment of dividends and other matters that apply to public limited companies.

Public Limited Companies

Public Limited Companies or PLCs are usually larger, well-established companies with a good track record in the business world and therefore capable of selling their shares to the public. Shares are quoted on the stock exchange and a PLC is subject to extensive regulation to help protect investors and the public at large from dishonesty.

Under the Companies Act,1985, a public limited company must:

- have at least two members;
- be limited by shares and have a share capital;
- state in its memorandum that it is a public company;
- have a name which ends with 'public limited company' or 'plc'.

A public limited company must have an authorized and issued share capital of at least £50,000. It is also subject to new regulations with regard to payment for its shares, explained later in this chapter.

Private companies

In most cases, people who form a private limited company do so in order to secure the safety that 'limited liability' offers, They are usually, but not always, small companies. They are not subject to such stringent regulation as a PLC, primarily because they cannot, by law, sell their shares to the general public. A private company offers a bit more personal privacy to erstwhile owners of a business.

A good example of the type of person who would profit from limited company status is a husband and wife team who are presently sole traders running a large guest house. By converting to a limited company they may issue all the shares between them. They are now shareholders with the protection of limited liability while retaining full control of their business.

The 1985 Act reaffirms that private companies will continue as limited companies. A private company must have at least two members and is subject to the following principal restriction: it is not a!lowed, directly or indirectly, to offer its shares to the general public.

THE REGISTRATION PROCESS

The majority of companies start life as sole traders or partnerships and simply 'convert' into limited companies when it suits them. There are many reasons why a private concern may wish to convert into a limited company. The following are a few examples:

- smaller businesses will register as limited companies in order to gain the personal protection afforded by limited liability;
- successful, fast growing companies may need to become a PLC in order to raise larger sums of capital by attracting money from shareholders via the stock market;

- in many cases small businesses grow rapidly due to the effort of a highly successful individual owner, who at some point, may wish to realize the fruits of his labour.

How to register as a limited company

Most companies start the process by registering as a private limited company, if and when they expand they may later convert to a PLC.

In order to register as a limited company, one requires a minimum of two directors, they will usually, though not necessarily, complete the registration process using a solicitor/accountant or other specialist in this area.

The procedure is to complete all necessary paperwork. There are two key documents, namely the **Memorandum of Association** and the **Articles of Association**. Both documents plus the fee should be forwarded to the registrar at Companies House. In due course the business will receive a certificate of incorporation which allows it to trade as a limited company.

The Memorandum of Association

This defines the relationship between the company and the outside world and contains five clauses, stating:

1. the name of the proposed company; this must end with the word 'limited';
2. the situation of the registered office of the company, i.e. whether the company is to be situated in England and Wales or Scotland;
3. the objects of the company;
4. that the liability of the members is limited;
5. the nominal capital of the company and its division into shares.

Public limited companies, as defined by the Companies Act 1985, must have names which end with 'public limited company' (plc) or the permitted Welsh equivalent. Also they must state in their memorandum that they are public companies.

The Articles of Association

These are concerned with the internal regulations of the company. They contain clauses dealing with matters such as the issue of shares and debentures, the meetings of shareholders and directors, the rights of shareholders, the powers and duties of directors, etc. A company may have prepared a set of articles of its own, but it is quite usual for companies to adopt a model set of articles (an appendix to the Companies Act 1948) known as Table A.

Re-registration of limited companies

An existing public company may decide to re-register as a private company under the Act and on the other hand a private company may re-register as a public limited company providing it satisfies the requisite criteria.

KINDS OF CAPITAL

In the context of the accounts of limited companies the term 'capital' may be used in several different senses. We may distinguish the following main kinds of capital:

Nominal, authorized or registered capital

This is the amount of capital, stated in the Memorandum of Association, which the company is authorized to issue.

Subscribed or issued capital

This is the amount of capital actually issued to the members of the company. A company may have a nominal capital of 100,000 shares of £1 each but, for one reason or another, issue only 80,000 shares. Its subscribed (issued) capital is then £80,000.

Called-up capital

This is the amount of capital, payment for which has actually been demanded by the company. This applies only where shares are issued and are payable by instalments rather than in full on application. Thus where 80,000 shares of £1 each have been issued by a company and in the meantime only 75p per share called, the called-up capital is £60,000.

Paid-up capital

This is the amount of the called-up capital that has actually been paid by the members. To continue with the above example, if a member holding 1,000 shares failed to pay a call of 25p per share, the paid-up capital of the company would have been (£60,000 less 25p on 1,000 shares) £59,750. Any such unpaid calls are referred to as calls in arrear.

Uncalled capital

This is the amount of capital which, for the time being, has not been called up by the company. In the above example this amounts to (£80,000 less £60,000) £20,000.

Unissued capital

This is the amount of capital which has not been offered to members or has not been subscribed by them. Unissued capital in the above example amounts to (£100,000 less £80,000) £20,000.

Loan capital

This term is sometimes used to describe any capital raised by a company by means of debentures or other long-term loans, rather than by means of shares. Loan capital is quite distinct from the share capital of a company.

SHARES AND DEBENTURES

Shares

A share is a portion of the capital of a limited company owned by a shareholder. The shares of a company may be divided into several different classes. The main ones are described below.

Preference shares

Holders of these shares have a right to a fixed dividend before any dividend is paid to holders of other shares. Preference shares are of different kinds.

Cumulative preference shares

Holders of these shares are entitled to any arrears of dividend unpaid in previous years. Preference shares are assumed to be cumulative unless stated otherwise in the Memorandum of Association or the Articles of Association.

Non-cumulative preference shares

Holders of these shares have a prior claim to a fixed dividend out of the profits of each year. When in any one year no profits are available, any amount unpaid on such shares cannot be recovered by the shareholders in subsequent years.

Ordinary shares

The holders of these shares have no special rights. Dividends on these shares are paid after those on preference shares and vary with the fortunes of the company. In a lean year there may be no ordinary dividend paid at all; when profits are high, the ordinary dividend is usually much more than any preference dividends paid.

Debentures

In addition to any shares, a company may issue debentures. There are some important differences between the two. First of all debentures are loans to the company and do not constitute part of its share capital. As a result, a debenture holder is a creditor and not a part proprietor (shareholder) of the company. The payment of a dividend is dependent on the availability of profits; if there is no profit no dividend may be paid. Debenture interest must, however, be paid even when losses are incurred.

Issue of shares and debentures

The shares and debentures of a company may be issued in several different ways. In the case of a PLC, where the shares will be put on sale to the public at large, it is a complex and risky business. Normally the issue of shares would be handled by specialist companies, known as issuing houses, who for a handsome commission will organize the sale of all shares, the collection of monies due and accept the risk involved. This is often referred to as 'floating a company on the stock exchange', the detail of which is beyond the scope of this textbook.

With regard to the method of payment, they may be: (a) payable in full on application, or (b) payable by instalments.

With regard to the price, they may be issued at par or at a premium. The issue of shares at a discount, allowed by the Companies Act 1948, is now prohibited.

Issue of shares and debentures payable in full on application

In this case prospective members and debenture holders of the company send, when applying for any shares or debentures, the full price thereof. When the shares or debentures have been formally allotted to the applicants, the net effect of the transaction is an increase of the cash balance of the company, and a corresponding increase in the share capital or debentures.

Let us assume that X Hotels PLC offers for subscription 100,000 ordinary shares of £1 each and 5,000 6 per cent debentures of £10 each both payable in full on application. If all the shares and debentures are taken up the net effect of this transaction is shown below:

Cash Book			
	£		
Ordinary Shares	100,000		
6% Debentures	50,000		

Ordinary Shares A/c			
			£
		Cash	100,000

6% Debentures A/c			
			£
		Cash	50,000

Note: Where the company issues several different classes of shares, a separate account is opened for each class.

Issue of shares and debentures payable by instalments

In this case the full amount due in respect of any shares or debentures issued by a company is received over a period of time. Applicants are required to pay so much on application, so much when the shares or debentures have been allotted to them and the balance then due from them is collected by means of periodical calls. A typical arrangement in respect of £1 shares payable by instalments might be:

> 30p per share on application;
> 20p per share on allotment;
> 25p per share on first call;
> 25p per share on second and final call.

Let us assume that the above arrangement has been made by a company offering 20,000 10 per cent preference shares of £1 each. If all shares were subscribed, and all the allotment money paid by the members then, before the first call is made, the position would be as illustrated below.

Cash Book

	£	
10% Pref. Shares	10,000	

10% Preference Shares A/c

			£
		Cash	10,000

The above £10,000 represents a payment of 50p per share (30p and 20p) that is 50p × 20,000 shares equals £10,000

If, a few months later, the first call of 25p per share were made and all the money called by the company received, the cash balance would be increased by £5,000 and so would the called-up (and paid-up) capital:

Cash Book

	£	
10% Pref. Shares	5,000	

10% Preference Shares A/c

			£
		Cash	10,000
		"	5,000

Note: The treatment of the issue of shares and debentures which follows is rather simplified and designed to explain the effect of an issue on the structure of a company's capital rather than to explain the detailed book-keeping entries involved.

After the second and final call the 10 per cent preference shares account would show a balance of £20,000, representing the full nominal value of the preference capital issued by the company.

Calls in arrear and calls in advance

When shares are payable by instalments members sometimes fail to pay the calls due from them. The amounts due but unpaid by members are transferred to the debit of a calls in arrear account.

Let us assume that a company has issued 10,000 ordinary shares of £1 each, payable 25p per share on application, 25p per share on allotment and that all the allotment money has been received. The company then makes a call of 25p per share, and all members pay the calls due with the exception of one holding 100 shares. The calls in arrear are therefore (100 × 25p) £25. In the ledger of the company this would be reflected as:

Cash Book		
	£	
Ord. Shares A/c	2,475	

Ordinary Shares A/c		
		£
	Cash	5,000
	"	2,500

Calls in Arrear A/c		
	£	
Ord. Shares A/c	25	

It will be observed that the ordinary shares account is credited with the full amount of the calls due. The calls in arrears account represents a debt from the members to the company. In the balance sheet of the company, the calls in arrear should be deducted from the issued capital.

Some shareholders do not wish to be troubled with repeated calls, and pay for their shares in advance of any calls actually made by the company. Any such calls paid before they fall due are transferred to a calls in advance account.

Let us revert to the previous example and assume that when the call of 25p per share was made all members paid the amounts due and that, in addition, one member holding 200 shares paid for them in full. The amount of calls paid in advance is therefore (200 × 25p) £50. This would be reflected in the books of the company as follows:

Cash Book		
	£	
Ord. Shares A/c	2,500	
Calls in advance	50	

Ordinary Shares A/c

		£
	Cash	5,000
	"	2,500

Calls in Advance A/c

		£
	Cash	50

Any calls paid in advance do not form part of the share capital of the company and are, for the time being, a liability from the company to the members concerned. In the balance sheet they must, therefore, be shown as a current liability.

Issue of shares and debentures at a premium

We have assumed so far that when shares or debentures are issued the company receives cash equal to their nominal value. This is not always the case. A company which has been successful and paid substantial dividends may issue shares at a premium, i.e. at a price higher than their nominal value. This is often so in the case of companies whose previously issued shares are quoted at a price above nominal value.

Let us assume that a company issues 100,000 ordinary shares of £1 each at a premium of 10p per share. The amount received from the members will therefore be (100,000 × £1.10) £110,000, the share premium being £10,000. The effect of this issue is shown below:

Cash Book

	£		
Ord. Shares and Premium	110,000		

Ordinary Shares A/c

		£
	Cash	100,000

Share Premium A/c

		£
	Cash	10,000

In the balance sheet the share premium account will be shown under the heading 'Reserves'.

Payment for share capital

The Companies Act 1985 stipulates strict procedures relating to the payment for any shares allotted by a limited company. The main points which are relevant in this connection are summarized below.

As a general principle any shares allotted by a company may be paid for either in money or money's worth. The latter may include goodwill and what is described as 'know-how'.

A public company is subject to an additional restriction in this context. It is not allowed to accept payment for its shares (including any premium) in the form of an undertaking given by a person that he, or some other person, should either do work or offer services to the company.

A public company may not allot shares unless they are paid up to the extent of one-quarter of the nominal value together with the whole of any premium, whether in cash or otherwise. However, these provisions do not apply to any shares allotted in connection with an employee share scheme. Where a public company allots shares fully or partly paid by an undertaking to transfer to the company a non-cash asset at a future date, the Act insists that any such transfer must be actually effected within five years.

Finally, a public company is not allowed to allot shares as partly or fully paid up otherwise than for cash, unless the non-cash consideration has been independently valued and an appropriate report submitted to the company and the allottee.

FINAL ACCOUNTS OF LIMITED COMPANIES

The vast majority of the accounting principles and techniques which we used for sole traders and partnerships apply equally to a limited company.

The two main areas of change are the capital account and the appropriation account.

In respect of the final accounts the Companies Act sets out two important points:

1. It requires that the published accounts be set out in a particular way.
2. It sets out what information about the company's financial affairs must be included.

The final accounts of a limited company may be prepared for two main purposes. All companies prepare internal (unpublished) accounts; these are prepared for the same purposes as the final accounts of partners and sole traders. Such internal accounts are, of course, prepared in accordance with current accounting practice. Their form, layout and method of presentation are, however, within the discretion of the company concerned.

In addition to internal accounts, limited companies (both public companies and private companies) have to prepare what is known as **published accounts**. These are the final accounts which are sent to the Registrar of Companies, the shareholders and the auditors of the company. The contents, as well as the method of presentation of such accounts, are regulated by the Companies Acts of 1985 and 1989.

UNPUBLISHED OR INTERNAL ACCOUNTS

The trading account of a limited company is prepared in exactly the same way as that of a partnership or sole trader.

The unpublished profit and loss account would, again, be prepared in the same manner as in other types of business unit, except that it would contain certain items of expenditure peculiar to limited companies, e.g. directors' fees, debenture interest, and auditors' fees and expenses. The net profit from the profit and loss account is, as in the case of the partnership, transferred to the appropriation account.

APPROPRIATION ACCOUNT

Students often find it difficult to decide which items should be debited in the profit and loss account, and which in the appropriation account of a company. The division of items is based on the following principles:

(a) All **charges against profits**, i.e. all current expenditure, as well as expenses which must be paid whether or not there is any profit available (directors' fees, debenture interest, audit fees) must be debited in the profit and loss account. These, it will be appreciated, are items of expenditure which must be taken into account to arrive at the net profit for the period concerned.

(b) All **appropriations of profits**, i.e. items affecting the application or distribution of the profits available are debited in the appropriation account. Examples of such items are dividends, taxation and amounts written out of profits which do not apply to any particular year, e.g. preliminary expenses, goodwill.

The appropriation account will normally be drawn in vertical style, as shown below, and will continue directly from the bottom of the profit and loss account, e.g starts after net profit.

Example of appropriation account

		£		£	£
Net profit	(b)				38,000
Profit & loss account at 1/1/19... b/f	(a)			2,000	
					40,000
Appropriations					
Preference share dividend					
– Interim	(c)	3,000			
– Final	(d)	3,000			
Ordinary share dividend	(e)	8,000		14,000	
Taxation (f)				12,000	
General reserve (g)				7,000	
Prelim. expenses (h)				1,000	34,000
Profit and loss account at 31/12/19... (i)					6,000

Notes:

(a) The profit and loss account at 1/1/19... of £2,000 is the balance of net profit brought forward from the previous accounting period.

(b) The net profit of £38,000 is the current year's net profit from the profit and loss account, The total of profits available in the current year is, therefore, £40,000.

(c) An interim dividend is a dividend which is declared by the directors and paid before the end of the company's accounting year, When the interim dividend of £3,000 was paid the entries shown below were made in the books of the company.

Cash Book

	Pref. Dividend		
	– Interim	£3,000	

Preference Dividend A/c

Cash	£3,000		

At the end of the accounting year the balance of the preference dividend account is transferred to the appropriation account, as follows. The entries then required are a credit in the preference dividend account and a debit in the appropriation account.

Preference Dividend A/c

Cash	£3,000	Dec 31	Appropri'n A/c	£3,000

Appropriation A/c

Pref. Dividend			
Interim	£3,000		

(d) It should be noted that whilst the directors usually have power to **declare** an interim dividend, any final dividend is **recommended** by the directors, and requires the approval of the annual general meeting of the company. Students will appreciate, therefore, that at the date of the balance sheet final dividend is only a recommendation or proposal of the directors in respect of which no cash has yet been paid out. The entries required in respect of the final preference dividend in the above example are shown below.

Preference Dividend A/c

Cash	£3,000	Dec 31	Appropri'n A/c	£3,000
		" 31	Appropri'n A/c	£3,000

Appropriation A/c

Pref. Div. Final	£3,000		

When the annual general meeting approves the final dividend (as it invariably does), the credit balance in the preference dividend account becomes a debt from the company to the members. In the balance sheet the final dividend would be shown as a 'proposed dividend' under the heading of current liabilities. It should be added that the company pays tax on the whole of its profit and any dividends paid are regarded as being paid out of profits already taxed.

(e) The ordinary dividend of £8,000 is also a proposed dividend, and requires the following entries: Dr appropriation account, and Cr ordinary dividend account. The amount provided for this proposed dividend would also be shown in the balance sheet as a current liability.

(f) The full treatment of taxation is outside the scope of this volume, but students should note that companies are subject to 'corporation tax' which will normally appear as an item in the appropriation account.

(g) The corresponding credit entry for the £7,000 in the appropriation account would be made in the general reserve account. In the balance sheet this would be shown under the heading 'Reserves'.

(h) Preliminary expenses are the expenses of forming a limited company and include items such as legal expenses, registration fees, stamp duties and similar costs. Preliminary expenses must be written off quickly. The entries required are a debit in the appropriation account and a credit entry in the preliminary expenses account.

(i) The profit and loss account balance of £6,000 is carried forward to the next accounting period. In the balance sheet it is shown under the heading 'Reserves'.

EXAMPLE 16.1

At 1st January 19..., a hotel company had a credit balance on its profit and loss account of £40,000 and its net profit for the year amounted to £360,000. During the year a half-year's dividend of £50,000 was paid on its preference shares and the directors propose the following distribution of the remaining profits:

1. to pay a final preference dividend of £50,000;
2. to pay an ordinary dividend of £120,000;
3. to transfer £60,000 to general reserve;
4. to write off £40,000 preliminary expenses;
5. to transfer £40,000 to staff welfare fund;
6. to carry the balance of profits to the following year.

Prepare the hotel's appropriation account. Proceed as in the solution below:

Suggested solution

Example of appropriation account.

	£	£	£
Net profit			360,000
Profit & loss account at 1st Jan 19... b/f			40,000
			400,000
Appropriations			
Preference share dividend			
– interim	50,000		
– final	50,000		
Ordinary share dividend	120,000	220,000	
General reserve		60,000	
Staff welfare fund		40,000	
Prelim. expenses		40,000	360,000
Profit and loss account at 31/12/19...			40,000

BALANCE SHEET

The unpublished balance sheet of a limited company may be prepared in several different ways. However, they do tend to follow quite closely the format of the published balance sheet where appropriate.

A typical balance sheet of a limited company will be drawn up as indicated in Figure 16.1.

Fixed assets

These are usually shown at cost less aggregate depreciation to date leading to net book value. This method of writing off the depreciation was explained in Chapter 12.

Investments

Where a company holds shares, debentures or other securities these are shown under this heading.

Current assets

These are listed in the same manner as in other types of business unit. Items should be listed in accordance to their liquidity i.e. starting with the least liquid (usually stock) and working down to the most liquid (cash).

Authorized capital

This is a memorandum note only and shows what shares the company is authorized to issue by its Memorandum of Association.

LODGE INNS Ltd
Balance sheet as at 31 December 19... .

Fixed assets	Cost	Agg. Dep'n	Net
	£	£	£
Freehold premises	X		X
Kitchen equipment	X	X	X
Furniture and Fittings	X	X	X
	X	X	X
China, cutlery, linen etc.			X
			X
Investments			
Shares in Otterbrook Media PLC		X	X
Current assets			
Stocks		X	
Debtors		X	
Prepayments		X	
Cash at bank & in hand		X	
		X	
Less Creditors: due within one year			
Trade creditors	X		
Accrued expenses	X		
Taxation	X		
Proposed dividends	X		
Advance deposits	X	X	
Net current assets			X
Total assets less current liabilities			X
Less Creditors: due after one year			
6% Debentures (2002–2008)			X
			X

Capital and reserves	£	£
Share capital	Authorized	Issued
Ordinary shares of £1 each	X	X
Preference shares of £1 each	X	X
	X	X
Less calls in arrear		X
		X
Reserves		
General reserves	X	
Profit and loss account	X	X
		X

Figure 16.1 Specimen balance sheet

Issued capital

This shows particulars of any shares actually issued. Any calls in arrear should be deducted from the issued capital.

Reserves

Students should be familiar with the main items which are likely to appear under this heading. Reserves may be of a capital nature such as the share premium account or of a revenue nature such as the general reserve which consists of profits set aside in past years. Any credit balance on the profit and loss account will also be shown under this heading.

Creditors: due after one year

This comprises any debentures and other long-term liabilities of the company. The heading is also referred to as 'long-term liabilities', either heading may be used except in published limited company accounts when the formal heading must be used, i.e. creditors: due after one year.

Creditors: due within one year

Under this heading are all the usual items such as trade creditors and accrued expenses, as well as any proposed dividends, taxation etc.

This heading is also referred to as 'current liabilities' and again either heading may be used except in published limited company accounts where the former must be used.

EXAMPLE 16.2

Grand Hotel Ltd has an authorized capital of £1,000,000, consisting of 400,000 ordinary shares of £1 each and 600,000 10 per cent preference shares of £1 each. The following balances were extracted from the books of the hotel after the preparation of the profit and loss appropriation account for the year ended 31st December 19...

	£	£
400,000 ordinary shares, 75p paid		300,000
600,000 preference shares, fully paid		600,000
Stocks	40,000	
Banqueting debtors	20,000	
Trade creditors		32,000
Cash at bank	54,000	
Accrued expenses		30,000
Proposed dividend –ordinary		24,000
–preference		20,000
Prepaid expenses	6,000	
Deposits – advance bookings		6,000
Shares in ABC Ltd	40,000	

	£	£
Shares in DEF Ltd	60,000	
Reserve for future taxation		130,000
China and furnishings, at valuation	40,000	
Profit and loss account		120,000
General reserve		100,000
10,000 9% debentures of £20 each		200,000
Furniture at cost	400,000	
Provision for dep'n – furniture		100,000
Leasehold hotel at cost	900,000	
Provision for dep'n – leasehold hotel		100,000
Kitchen plant at cost	260,000	
Provision for dep'n – kitchen plant		60,000
Calls in arrears	2,000	
	1,822,000	1,822,000

The balance sheet as at 31st December 19... is shown in Figure 16.2.

PUBLISHED ACCOUNTS

As already mentioned, the contents and method of presentation of published accounts are regulated by the Companies Acts 1985 and 1989.

Published accounts are, generally, less informative than internal accounts; this applies particularly to the published profit and loss account. The Companies Acts require limited companies to disclose particular items of income and expenditure and, usually, items which are not expressly required to be disclosed are not shown in the accounts. The effect of this non-disclosure of information is that items such as purchases, sales, wages, salaries, rent and insurance are not disclosed in the published profit and loss account.

The main provisions of the Acts relating to published accounts are given below in summary form.

The profit and loss account must show the following information:

- Loan interest: the amount of interest on loans advanced to the company on bank loans, overdrafts and debentures.
- Taxation: the amount of the charge to revenue for United Kingdom corporation tax.
- Investment income: the separate amounts of income from quoted and unquoted investments.
- Rents: if a substantial part of the company's revenue for the financial year consists in rents from land, the amount, after deducting ground-rents and other outgoings.
- Plant hire: if it is material, the amount charged to revenue in respect of the hire of plant and machinery.
- Dividends: the aggregate of dividends paid and proposed must be shown.

Grand Hotel Ltd
Balance Sheet as at 31 Dec 19...

Fixed assets	Cost	Dep'n.	Net.
	£	£	£
Leasehold premises	900,000	100,000	800,000
Kitchen plant	260,000	60,000	200,000
Furniture	400,000	100,000	300,000
	1,560,000	260,000	1,300,000
China, furnishings etc.			40,000
			1,340,000
Investments			
Shares in ABC Ltd		40,000	
Shares in DEF Ltd		60,000	100,000
Current assets			
Stocks		40,000	
Banqueting debtors		20,000	
Prepaid expenses		6,000	
Cash at bank		54,000	
		120,000	
Less creditors: due within one year			
Trade creditors	32,000		
Accrued expenses	30,000		
Advance deposits	6,000		
Proposed dividends Ordinary	24,000		
Preference	20,000		
		112,000	
Net current assets			8,000
Total assets less current liabilities			1,448,000
Creditors: due after one year			
10,000 9% Debentures of £20 each			(200,000)
			1,248,000
Capital and reserves		Authorized	Issued
Share capital			
Ordinary shares of £1 each		400,000	300,000
Preference shares of £1 each		600,000	600,000
		1,000,000	900,000
Less calls in arrear			2,000
			898,000
Reserves			
General reserves		100,000	
Reserve for future tax		130,000	
Profit and loss account		120,000	350,000
			1,248,000

Notes:

(a) Clearly 'creditors: due within one year' is exactly the same as 'current liabilities' and 'creditors: due after one year' is the same as 'long-term liabilities'.

(b) For the purposes of this textbook, where we are not dealing with published balance sheets of limited companies, the student may use either heading for any of the balance sheets involved, be they sole trader, partnership or limited company.

(c) The authors have decided to use the more formal headings when drawing up balance sheets for the accounts of larger limited companies and to adhere to the traditional headings for sole trader, partnership, etc.

Figure 16.2 Grand Hotel Ltd balance sheet

- Depreciation: all amounts charged to revenue by way of depreciation or diminution in the value of any assets.
- Auditors' remuneration: this must be shown under a separate heading, whether fixed by the company in general meeting or not.
- Turnover: the turnover of the company must normally be disclosed, but there are certain relaxations in the case of small companies.
- Comparative figures: these must be shown, except in relation to the first account laid before the company in general meeting.
- Directors' emoluments: these must be disclosed in the accounts or in a statement annexed to the accounts.

The balance sheet must show the following information:

- Capital: the authorized, issued and paid-up capital.
- Reserves and provisions: particulars of all reserves and provisions must be shown. It is no longer necessary to show separately capital reserves and revenue reserves.
- Loans: particulars of all loans and overdrafts must be given
- Investments: the distinction between trade investments and other investments has now been abolished. Companies must now show separately the aggregate of their quoted investments and unquoted investments.
- UK taxation: the company's tax liabilities and the basis on which any amount set aside for UK corporation tax has been computed must be stated.
- Loans to directors: particulars of these must be given.
- Proposed dividends: the aggregate of any proposed dividends must be shown.
- Assets: particulars of all fixed and current assets must be shown; the basis of valuation of fixed assets must be disclosed. The amount attributable to freehold land and the amount attributable to leaseholds must be shown separately. With regard to the latter, particulars of short leases and long leases must also be given

Reserves and provisions

The terms 'reserve' and 'provision' have been used several times, and it is convenient at this stage to define more accurately what is meant by these terms as well as to explain the main kinds of provisions.

Before the Companies Act 1948 came into force, the terms 'reserve' and 'provision' were used loosely and no clear distinction between them was made.

The Act defines a 'provision' as:

> any amount written-off or retained by way of providing for depreciation, renewals or diminution in the value of assets or retained by way of providing for any known liability of which the amount cannot be determined with substantial accuracy.

The Act defines a 'reserve' as:

> an amount set aside out of divisible profits or other surpluses which is not designed to meet any liability, contingency or diminution in the value of assets known to exist at the date of the balance sheet.'

From the quotations given above it will be appreciated that whilst a provision is a charge against profits (e.g. provision for bad debts, provision for depreciation) a reserve is an appropriation of profits (e.g. general reserve, dividend equalization reserve) .

Reserves are of two main kinds: capital reserves and revenue reserves.

A reserve is a capital reserve if it is regarded as not being available for distribution (payment of dividend). Examples of capital reserves are share premium account and capital redemption reserve fund. The latter is a reserve created in connection with the redemption (repayment) of redeemable preference shares.

All reserves other than capital reserves are revenue reserves, i.e. available for distribution in dividend, e.g. general reserve, dividend equalization reserve, balance of profit and loss account.

SUMMARY

- Limited companies are now governed by the companies acts 1985 and 1989.
- The key features of limited companies are (a) its shareholders have limited liability, and (b) the company itself is a separate legal entity.
- There are two types of limited company: a public company and a private company.
- Larger companies (with a share capital in excess of £50,000) tend to opt for PLC status. This allows them to raise capital by selling shares to the public at large, but also commits them to greater disclosure of business information.
- Private limited companies are more common amongst smaller businesses wishing to avail themselves of limited liability while largely retaining control over their own affairs.
- In order to form a limited company it is necessary, amongst others, to complete two key documents and forward them to the Registrar of Companies and await registration in due course.
- The key documents are the memorandum of association and the articles of association.
- The capital of limited companies consists primarily of share capital and retained profits.
- Payment for shares issued to the public may be by immediate payment in full or for larger issues payment by instalments.
- There are special rules governing shares sold at a premium.
- The internal accounts of a limited company are similiar to those drawn up for a sole trader. The main changes are in the capital account and the appropriation account.

- The balance sheet headings of 'creditors; due within one year' and 'creditors: due after one year' are totally interchangeable with 'current liabilities' and 'long-term liabilities' respectively, except when dealing with published accounts.
- There are certain items of expenditure in the profit and loss account which are peculiar to a limited company: directors' fees, debenture interest and auditors' fees.
- The appropriation account follows on directly from the profit and loss account. This is the account where the net profit is appropriated or divided up usually in three ways. A proportion is:
  (a) paid to the Inland Revenue in the form of taxation;
  (b) paid to shareholders in the form of a dividend;
  (c) put aside in a general reserve to cover special needs;
  (d) the remainder (retained profits) is ploughed back into the business.
- Published accounts must be presented in a standard form as laid out by the Companies Act. In addition there is a large amount of business information disclosure which must be made.

PROBLEMS

1. Explain what is meant by a company limited by shares.

2. Distinguish between public companies and private companies.

3. Write short notes on (a) articles of association; (b) memorandum of association.

4. Explain what you understand by the following:
   (a) nominal capital;
   (b) subscribed capital;
   (c) called-up capital;
   (d) paid-up capital;
   (e) unissued capital;
   (f) loan capital.

5. Distinguish between each of the following:
   (a) shares and debentures;
   (b) ordinary shares and preference shares;
   (c) cumulative preference shares and non-cumulative preference shares.

6. A hotel company issued the following:
   (a) 100,000 ordinary shares of £1 each at a premium of 10p per share; and
   (b) 200,000 10 per cent debentures of £1 each at par.
   Show by means of appropriate extracts how the above would be shown in the balance sheet of the company.

7. Explain the difference between the published and unpublished (internal) accounts of a company.

8. Distinguish between each of the following:
   (a) a charge against profits and an appropriation of profits;
   (b) an interim dividend and a final dividend;
   (c) capital reserve and revenue reserve.

9. The following balances appeared on the books of Cakes-n-Ale Ltd, after closing the profit and loss account for the year ending 31st January 19...

	SFrs
Share capital – authorized, 600,000 shares of SFrs1 each; issued 540,000 shares	540,000
Freehold premises at cost	300,000
Kitchen equipment, at cost	450,000
Provision for dep'n – kitchen equipment	105,000
Creditors	68,640
Prepayments	4,100
Stock as valued by the directors	173,880
Debtors	249,870
Share premium account	30,000
Profit and loss account – accumulated profit at 31st January	68,190
Debentures	120,000
General reserve	150,000
Furniture, etc. at cost	13,500
Provision for dep'n – furniture	6,500
Balance at bank	160,920
Provision for bad debts	4,140
Profit for year to 31st January 19...	259,800

It was resolved that:
(a) general reserve be increased to SFrs225,000;
(b) a dividend of 15 per cent on the issued share capital be declared.

Required:
Prepare the company's appropriation account for the year to 31st January 19... and a balance sheet at that date.

10. The Hertenstein Catering Co. PLC has authorized capital of SFrs 10,000,000 divided into 500,000 10 per cent preference shares of SFrs10 and 500,000 ordinary shares of SFrs10 each. From the following trial balance prepare the company's trading, and profit and loss and appropriation account for the year ended 31st December 19..., and a balance sheet as at that date.

	SFrs	SFrs
Issued capital		
400,000 ordinary shares SFrs10.00 called		4,000,000
500,000 10% preference shares at SFrs8.00		4,000,000
Cash at bank	3,027,500	
Sales		12,500,000
Discounts received		95,000
Glass, china and cutlery	227,500	
Gas and electricity	675,000	
Stock on 1st January 19...	125,000	
Furniture at cost	570,000	
Provision for dep'n – furniture		200,000
Bank interest		15,000
Debtors and creditors	175,000	435,000
Directors' fees	250,000	
Purchases returns		150,000
Repairs and renewals	435,000	
Profit and loss account, 1st January 19...		105,000
Purchases	5,505,000	
Bad debts	60,000	
9% mortgage debentures		1,000,000
Kitchen equipment at cost	2,650,000	
Provision for dep'n – kitchen equipment		300,000
Wages and salaries	2,940,000	
General reserve		500,000
Rent and rates	720,000	
Leasehold premises at cost	6,900,000	
Provision for dep'n – leasehold premises		1,200,000
Calls in advance preference shares		10,000
Travelling expenses	35,000	
Cleaning materials	15,000	
Preference dividend (half year)	200,000	
	24,510,000	24,510,000

Take the following notes into account:
(a) The stock at 31st December, 19... was valued at SFrs150,000.
(b) Accrued gas and electricity amounted to SFrs5,000.
(c) Invoices received from suppliers but not entered in the books amounted to SFrs50,000.
(d) create a provision for bad debts equal to 2 per cent of the debtors.
(e) Provide for depreciation as follows:
    (i)   kitchen equipment, 10 per cent;
    (ii) furniture, 10 per cent;
    (iii) leasehold, 2 per cent;
    (iv) glass, china and cutlery SFrs20,000.
(f) Provide for one year debenture interest due.
(g) Provide for the balance due to preference shareholders and for a proposed ordinary dividend of 10 per cent.
(h) Transfer SFrs 500,000 to general reserve.

11. The Costa Brava Hotel PLC has an authorized capital of Pta7,000,000 divided into 200,000 ordinary shares of Pta10 each and 500,000 preference shares of Pta10 each. After closing the trading, profit and loss account for the year ended 31st December 19..., the balances in the books are:

	Pta	Pta
Ordinary share capital		1,000,000
5% preference share capital		4,000,000
Leasehold premises (cost Pta1,150,000)	750,000	
Kitchen equipment (cost Pta2,630,000)	2,000,000	
Stocks	2,102,400	
Creditors and accrued expenses		319,800
Debtors and prepayments	1,498,700	
Balance at bank	892,700	
Cash in hand	5,000	
Restaurant furniture (cost Pta95,000)	65,000	
General reserve		1,000,000
Profit and loss account 1st January 19...		203,600
Net profit for the year		790,400
	7,313,800	7,313,800

The directors of the hotel recommend that:
(a) The dividend on preference shares be paid.
(b) A dividend of 20 per cent be paid on the ordinary shares.
(c) Pta100,000 be transferred to a general reserve.
Prepare the hotel's appropriation account for the year ended 31st December 19..., and a balance sheet as at that date.

12. The Welcome Hotels PLC has an authorized capital of £1,000,000 divided into 500,000 ordinary shares of £1 each and 250,000 10 per cent preference shares of £2 each. On 31st March 1997, the following balances appeared in the ledger of the hotel after the preparation of the profit and loss and appropriation account for the year ended on that date:

	£
500,000 ordinary shares, 50p paid	250,000
250,000 10% preference shares, £1.50 paid	375,000
Cash at bank	61,500
Calls in advance – preference shares	2,000
Leasehold hotel, at cost	830,000
Provision for dep'n – leasehold premises	200,000
Cash in hand	500
Plate, cutlery and linen at valuation	13,400
Provision for bad debts	100
10% mortgage debentures	50,000
Trade creditors	10,400

Profit and loss account	Cr	30,600
Reserve for future taxation		55,000
Insurance	Dr	200
Shares in XYZ Catering Ltd (unquoted)		22,500
General reserve		85,000
Gas and electricity	Cr	1,050
Banqueting debtors		3,050
Rates	Cr	550
Furniture and equipment, at cost		205,000
Provision for dep'n – Furniture & equipment		45,000
Proposed dividends – ordinary		12,500
– preference		37,500
Stocks at 31st March 1997		18,550

Required:

Prepare the balance sheet of the hotel as at 31st March 1997, taking the following into account:

Depreciation is written off the leasehold hotel at the rate of 2.5 per cent, and furniture and equipment at the rate of 5 per cent pa (both on the straight-line method). All these assets were purchased on 1st April 1993.

13. The Magnificent Catering Co. Ltd was incorporated on 1st January 1997 with a nominal capital of £800,000, divided into 400,000 ordinary shares of £1 each and 400,000 10 per cent preference shares of £1 each. Earlier in that year the company issued all its ordinary shares and 200,000 of the preference shares.

The following is a summary of the cash transactions of the company in respect of the year ended 31st December 1997.

Cash received	£
Sum received for ordinary shares	400,000
Sum received for preference shares	198,000
Cash sales and receipts from debtors	484,950
	1,082,950

Cash paid	
Leasehold premises	400,000
Plant and equipment	148,000
Furniture	51,500
Light and heat	15,200
Postage, stationery and telephone	7,900
Advertising	18,400
Preliminary expenses	5,500
Cash purchases and payments to suppliers	261,150
Wages and salaries	130,050
Directors' salaries	30,000
Balance	15,250
	1,082,950

Required:

Prepare the trading, profit and loss account of the company for the year ended 31st December, 1997, and a balance sheet as at that date. Take the following additional information into account:

(a) The stock of provisions at 31st December, 1997 was valued at £4,500.

(b) At 31st December 1997 debtors amounted to £2,250 and creditors were owed £5,150.

(c) Provide for depreciation as follows:
  (i)   premises, 2 per cent;
  (ii) plant and equipment 10 per cent;
  (iii) furniture 10 per cent.

(d) Accrued lighting and heating amounted to £800; an invoice for £950 in respect of stationery had not been entered in the books and remained unpaid; postage stamps unused amounted to £100.

(e) Carry forward to 1998 £4,000 of the advertising.

(f) Write £1,000 off the preliminary expenses.

(g) Directors' salaries due but unpaid at 31st December 1997 amounted to £5,000; unremitted PAYE and insurance contributions amounted to £700.

(h) You are informed that the £2,000 remaining unpaid on the preference shares represents an unpaid call of 25p per share on 8,000 shares.

Part III
Cost and management accounting in the hospitality industry

Basic costing $\boxed{\mathbf{17}}$

INTRODUCTION

The word costing is not easy to define. It can mean different things to different people. A discussion on this point is beyond the scope of this textbook. It is, however, necessary to choose a definition and for the purposes of this chapter costing will be defined as

a method of ascertaining the costs relating to a specific unit of output.

The unit of output may be an individual menu item, a complete meal or a wedding reception. Indeed costs can be expressed in any number of ways, i.e. per person, as so much per hour, day or week, etc.

Costing is especially important because it underpins profitability. Clearly, if a businessman wants to ensure that he makes a profit, he must know with reasonable accuracy the true cost of what he is selling.

OBJECTIVES

On completion of this chapter you should be able to:

- understand the meaning of the term 'costing';
- explain what is meant by the elements of cost;
- calculate percentages of food cost, gross profit, labour cost, overheads and net profit;
- differentiate between gross profit and net profit;
- comprehend the importance of the gross profit percentage in a hospitality concern;
- calculate the cost of food used and cost of food sold;
- draw up cost of food sold statement and a gross profit statement;
- list the key areas to investigate if the gross profit percentage is less than required;
- draw up a profit statement;
- know how to deal with staff feeding in the profit statement;
- correctly complete a costing sheet;
- calculate the food cost per portion from the costing sheet;
- calculate the selling price per meal using the gross margin method;

- recalculate the selling price per portion following a change in the food cost;
- differentiate between gross profit pricing and mark up pricing.

NATURE OF COSTS

It is important to understand from the start that the price received from the customer for the sale of any item must be sufficient to cover not only the total cost of that item but also an additional sum which represents net profit.

Generally any system of costing will begin with the costs being classified in some manner. How they are classified depends on the type of problem to be solved. The costs of a business may be considered from two main points of view: their nature and their behaviour. (see Chapter 18).

From the point of view of their nature, we may distinguish three groups, often referred to as the 'elements of cost'. They are:

1. **Materials** – in the hospitality industry includes food, beverages, cigarettes and tobaccos.
2. **Labour** – includes the remuneration of the staff employed and consists of wages, salaries, employer's national insurance and staff meals, bonuses, etc.
3. **Overheads** – includes all other costs, such as rent, rates, depreciation, gas, electricity, licences, etc.

Finally, in addition to the above, there is:

4. **Net profit** – this is the reward to the owner for capital invested in the business.

Therefore:

MATERIALS COSTS + LABOUR COSTS + OVERHEAD COSTS + NET PROFIT = SALES

UNIT COST

This means the cost of one unit, such as a meal and frequently an individual menu item.

In the case of a restaurant the selling price set must cover food cost, labour cost, overheads and yield a reasonable net profit. These elements are usually calculated as a percentage of the selling price which always represents 100 per cent.

EXAMPLE 17.1

Let the whole circle represent the selling price of £20 for a dinner at Restaurant X, which is an established restaurant with a consistent and adequate volume of sales.

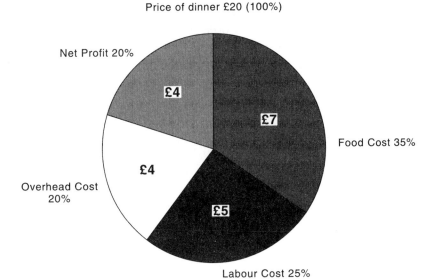

Figure 17.1 Unit cost

In Figure 17.1 above food cost represents 35 per cent of the selling price, labour cost 25 per cent, overhead cost 20 per cent etc.

Net profit is the amount remaining after all costs have been covered. This must not be confused with gross profit which is the amount remaining from the selling price when only the cost of materials (food and beverage costs in the case of a restaurant) has been deducted.

EXAMPLE 17.2

During the month of January Restaurant X achieved sales of £8,600 and had the following costs: food used £3,354; labour £1,892; overheads £1,720.

You are required to work out the gross profit and the net profit for the month of January and show all relevant percentages.

Proceed as shown below:

Suggested solution

		£	%
Sales		8,600	100
Less: food cost		3,354	39
Gross profit		5,246	61
Less: labour costs	1,892		22
overhead costs	1,720		20
		3,612	42
Net profit		1,634	19

How to calculate the Percentages

	Formula	
Food cost %	$\dfrac{\text{Food cost} \% \times 100}{\text{Sales}}$	$\dfrac{3,354 \times 100}{8,600} = 39\%$
Gross profit %	$\dfrac{\text{Gross profit} \times 100}{\text{Sales}}$	$\dfrac{5,246 \times 100}{8,600} = 61\%$
Labour cost %	$\dfrac{\text{Labour cost} \times 100}{\text{Sales}}$	$\dfrac{1,892 \times 100}{8,600} = 22\%$
Overhead cost %	$\dfrac{\text{Overhead cost} \times 100}{\text{Sales}}$	$\dfrac{1,720 \times 100}{8,600} = 20\%$
Net profit %	$\dfrac{\text{Net profit} \times 100}{\text{Sales}}$	$\dfrac{1,634 \times 100}{8,600} = 19\%$

CONCEPT OF GROSS PROFIT

Gross profit and gross profit percentage are very significant terms in hospitality accounting.

We already know that gross profit is simply the surplus left over from sales after paying only the materials used (food and beverage in a catering context).

The gross profit percentage (GP per cent) is widely used as the major control mechanism over food costs, used to ensure we do not overspend on food purchases. In simple terms it works as follows:

If the required gross profit of a restaurant is 65 per cent of sales then food cost will represent 35 per cent of sales, this is because GP per cent and food cost per cent must equal 100 per cent of sales. At the end of an accounting period, say one month, management should check the actual food cost per cent. If it exceeds the budgeted percentage this should lead to an investigation.

The above raises two questions:

1. How do we decide the 'correct' target GP percentage?
2. How do we work out the total amount of food used?

The 'correct' Gross Profit percentage

In an established business the gross profit percentage is usually decided by looking back over a number of years at the actual gross profit achieved and its effect on profit. From a study of these figures a 'correct' gross profit percentage will normally emerge, that is, the gross profit necessary to achieve the desired net profit for that individual business.

For new businesses there are nationwide statistics available which show average gross profit percentages for different grades of restaurants, hotels etc.

Calculating the cost of food sold

The cost of food sold for a month is determined by valuing the stock on hand at the start of the month, to which are added the purchases less returns made during the month; from this total the value of the closing stock at the end of the month and the cost of staff feeding will be deducted giving the cost of food sold during the month. This can be set out in statement form as shown in the example below.

N.B. The cost of staff feeding is part of the cost of employing labour. This is why it is deducted from cost of food used and added on to the cost of labour in the profit statement (shown later). This is merely the transfer of a cost from one cost area to another.

(Students should be familiar with the above from their study of the trading account in Chapter 10.)

EXAMPLE 17.3

	£	£
Opening stock of food 1st Feb 19...		1,960
Add purchases for month	8,700	
Less returns	200	8,500
		10,460
Less closing stock of food 28th Feb 19...		2,200
Cost of food used		8,260
Less staff feeding		700
Cost of food sold		7,560

Assuming food sales of £18,000 in February the gross profit statement would appear as shown below:

The gross profit statement

	£
Sales	18,000
Less cost of food sold (see statement above)	7,560
Gross profit	10,440

Gross profit % $\dfrac{10,440}{18,000} \times \dfrac{100}{1}$ =   58%

Assume that the above business has a target gross profit of 62 per cent.

The GP per cent achieved of only 58 per cent is considerably lower than expected and would certainly require an investigation.

The lower than expected gross profit percentage may be caused by:

(a) An incorrectly set selling price (too low). This problem is dealt with later in this chapter.
(b) The cost of food used being higher than expected.

Providing proper care has been taken in setting the selling price, it is more likely that the cause will be found in the cost of food sold area.

An early investigation and remedial action should follow.

Possible reasons for the increase in food cost are likely to be one or several of the following:

(a) overproduction of meals;
(b) poor portion control;
(c) excessive waste in kitchen;
(d) unexpected increase in suppliers' prices;
(e) bad purchasing system;
(f) pilfering by staff.

Gross profit is the key mechanism for controlling food cost. It is sometimes described in hotels and restaurants as kitchen profit. Most establishments work out kitchen profit on a monthly basis (weekly, if there is a problem in this area).

The procedure starts and ends with a physical stock-taking of all foodstuffs remaining. An accurate record is kept of all foods bought in during the month. Thus the formula is:

STOCK AT START + PURCHASES − STOCK AT END = FOOD CONSUMED DURING MONTH

This is expressed as a percentage of food sales to find the food cost percentage.

THE PROFIT STATEMENT

Many catering concerns produce monthly profit statements for internal use by the management.

The structure of these statements varies from business to business but they all tend to show totals for each element of cost and and key percentages expressed in terms of sales as shown in Figure 17.2 below.

Careful scrutiny of these figures and percentages by management and comparison with past sales periods will produce valuable information for cost control and improved profitability.

Profit statement for February 1997

	£	£	£	%
Sales			18,000	100
Cost of food sold				
Opening stock of food 1st Feb 19 . . .		1,960		
Add: purchases	8,700			
Less returns	200	8,500		
		10,460		
Less: closing stock of food 28th Feb 19 . . .		2,200		
Cost of food used		8,260		
Less: staff feeding		700		
Cost of food sold			7,560	42
Gross profit			10,440	58
Labour cost				
Kitchen wages		1,500		
Restaurant wages		1,000		
Other wages		500		
NI & other costs		620		
		3,620		
Add: staff feeding		700		
			4,320	24
Operating profit			6,120	34
Overhead costs				
Energy costs		580		
Rent & rates		650		
Cleaning materials		190		
Repairs & renewals		270		
Printing & stationery		180		
Laundry		260		
Sundry expenses		880		
Depreciation		1,850		
			4,860	27
Net profit			1,260	7

Figure 17.2 Specimen profit statement

MENU COSTING

Before any selling price can be set in a restaurant or other catering outlet, it is necessary to prepare an individual costing for every menu item that the establishment is likely to produce. This is best achieved by producing a recipe manual which should contain the standard recipe to be used for each menu item with a separate column for the costings which must be updated regularly.

The cost of one portion is arrived at by dividing the total cost of the recipe by the expected number of portions, often referred to as the standard

Costing Sheet

Menu item .... Beef stew   Date ....21/2/96........

Costing for ......6....... portions

Quantity	Ingredients	Unit price	Cost
			£
1.4 Kg	Stewing beef	£5.20/kg	7.28
200 g	Button onions	£2.70/kg	0.54
100 g	Flour	£1.60/kg	0.16
700 g	Onions	£1.92/kg	1.34
500 g	Mushrooms	£3.90/kg	1.95
100 dl	Olive oil	£4.60/litre	0.46
100 g	Butter	£3.40/kg	0.34
1.5 litres	Beef stock	£0.12/litre	0.18
1 bottle	White wine	£3.85/bot	3.85
1	Bouquet garni	£0.15	0.15
	Seasoning		0.08
	Total cost		16.33

Cost per portion $\frac{£16.33}{6}$ =   £2.72

Figure 17.3 Specimen costing sheet

batch. The cost of one portion can then be used as a basis for working out an accurate minimum selling price.

Costing sheet

Whilst the format may differ slightly between establishments they tend to follow a basic pattern – see Figure 17.3.

Costing of menu items

All costing activities require a systematic approach and regular up-dating but none more so than menu costing. A standard recipe for a predetermined number of portions of a particular menu item is established by the food production department, taking into account the quantity, quality and cost of ingredients as indeed the type of customer.

This forms the basis of the costing sheet exercise. The ingredients are listed on the costing sheet, priced from the most recent invoices, extended and totalled.

Particular care must be taken with the following:

(a) The proportions of ingredients should be correct and conform to general standards.

(b) The price of each ingredient should be checked against most recent invoices.
(c) Each costing sheet should be clearly dated – a costing without a date is of limited value.
(d) Name of menu item and number of portions expected must be shown.
(e) Items such as seasoning, parsley, etc. should be estimated in accordance with good kitchen accounting practice.
(f) Calculations should be worked out to 1 or 2 decimal places, in accordance with the practice of the particular establishment.

CALCULATING THE SELLING PRICE

Once we have established the cost of a menu item using the costing sheet, the next step is to calculate the selling price which, subject to the volume of sales, will cover all costs and leave an adequate net profit.

This is not to say that the selling price thus calculated fixes the price to be charged to the customer. When fixing menu prices, in addition to unit costs, we must take into account the attractiveness and popularity of the menu item, competition and the customers' ability to pay.

Establishing a minimum selling price

This involves two key items.

1. The cost of food of the menu item/meal for sale must be known with reasonable accuracy (see costing sheets).
2. An established gross profit percentage must be such as to cover
   (a) the labour costs;
   (b) the overhead costs;
   (c) the net profit.

Thus if experience tells us that one needs a 65 per cent gross profit to cover labour and overheads and achieve the required net profit, the food cost percentage must be 35 per cent. This is illustrated below:
   For example, where required gross profit is 65 per cent:

Sales	100%
Less cost of sales	?
Gross profit (given)	65%

Clearly the missing figure above must be 35 per cent.
   The student should note that sales always represents 100 per cent.

There is a standard formula used to calculate the selling price as follows:

$$\text{Selling price (SP)} = \frac{\text{Food cost}}{\text{Food cost \%}}$$

For example, let us assume that the food cost (FC) of a given dish is calculated at £4.20.

To calculate the selling price the formula is:

Selling price (SP) $\quad = \quad \dfrac{£4.20}{35} \quad \times \quad 100 \quad = \quad £12.00$

Proof:

Selling price	£12.00	100%
Less cost of food	4.20	35%
Gross profit	7.80	65%

The student should return to the costing sheet in Figure 17.3 above for beef stew where the food cost is £2.72 per portion. Using the formula above calculate the selling price necessary to achieve a gross profit of 60 per cent.

$$SP \quad = \quad \frac{FC}{FC\%} \quad = \quad \frac{£2.72}{40} \quad \times \quad 100 \quad = \quad £6.80$$

The charge to the customer

The selling price of £6.80 per portion which was set in the last paragraph represents what the restaurant will gain from each individual sale, but not necessarily what the customer will be charged. Many establishments add a service charge thereafter and of course most restaurants and hotels are subject to VAT.

In the following example we will examine the total charge to the customer for a meal in a restaurant which levies a service charge and is subject to VAT.

EXAMPLE

The Western Restaurant offers a table d'hôte dinner at £15.00 per person, there is a 12.5 per cent service charge. VAT is chargeable at 20 per cent*.

Calculate the total charge for two customers taking table d'hôte dinner.

	£
Table d'hôte dinner (£15.00 × 2)	30.00
Add: service charge @ 12.5%	3.75
	33.75
Add: VAT @ 20%	6.75
Total charge	40.50

The student should note that service charge is also subject to VAT, therefore VAT is charged on £33.75 and not £30.00.

(*An assumed rate of 20 per cent VAT has been used in the above example. The current real rate is likely to change from one year to another.)

Dealing with changes in food cost

When there is a change in the cost of ingredients it is necessary to follow a strict procedure to work out the new selling price.

For example, in the costing sheet for beef stew the total cost for 6 portions was £16.33 or £2.72 per portion. Now assume the total cost increases to £17.43 giving a new cost per portion of £2.90.

You are required to show the following:

(a) If there is no change in the selling price what effect will it have on gross profit percentage?
(b) If one wishes to retain the same gross profit percentage as before, what must be done?

	£	%
Original selling price	6.80	100.0
New food cost per portion	2.90	42.7
Gross profit	3.90	57.3

$$\text{GP \%} = \frac{£3.90 \times 100}{£6.80} = 57.3\%$$

Note that the gross profit percentage has decreased from 60 per cent to 57.3 per cent and of course food cost will have increased from 40 per cent to 42.7 per cent

If one requires the same gross profit percentage (i.e. 60 per cent) as before, there is only one way to calculate a new selling price once the food cost has changed and that is to use the formula:

$$\text{Selling price} = \frac{FC}{FC \%} = \frac{2.90 \times 100}{40} = £7.25$$

A common student error is to attempt to find a new selling price by simply adding the increase in cost (£2.90−£2.72) to the old selling price. It should be clear from the above why that will not work.

MENU COSTING: TABLE D'HÔTE

Once a restaurateur has established a comprehensive recipe manual and calculated accurate costings for each individual item, it is a relatively easy process to price simple table d'hôte menus (with no choice of dishes) and, of course, à la carte menus.

Since each menu item is individually priced on an à la carte menu, the cost of each dish can be easily obtained from the unit costing sheets and grossed up by the required gross profit.

A table d'hôte menu with no choice on courses is equally straightforward – as shown in the following example:

Table d'hôte Lunch

	Unit cost as per costing sheets £
Cream of tomato soup	0.28
Fried fillet of haddock	1.05
Boiled new potatoes	0.20
Garden peas	0.12
Apple pie and cream	0.45
Total cost	2.10

This restaurant works on a kitchen profit (gross profit) of 65 per cent.

$$\text{Minimum selling price} = \frac{FC}{FC\%} = \frac{£2.10 \times 100}{35} = £6.00$$

If there is a choice offered on the table d'hôte menu the calculation becomes more complex and one would require to take account of differential profit margins and sales mix forecasts. This is, however, beyond the scope of this introductory chapter.

METHODS OF PRICING

Basically there are two methods of pricing food items and menus in the hospitality business:

(a) gross profit or gross margin method;
(b) the mark up method, which is less frequently used.

Gross profit method

Gross profit is the most important pricing element in all catering operations. Past experience will indicate at what level it should be maintained. The method works as follows:

Unit cost of meal £2.60

Required gross profit is 60 per cent (therefore food cost is equal to 40 per cent)

$$\text{Formula} \quad \frac{FC}{FC\%} = \frac{£2.60 \times 100}{40} = £6.50$$

Therefore selling price of meal is £6.50

Mark up method

Mark up is the amount which must be added to the cost price in order to arrive at the selling price. This amount, which is in effect the gross profit, is expressed as a percentage mark up on the unit cost price.

The size of the mark up percentage will be a management decision based on past experience.

For example:
Unit cost of dish   £3.20*
Required mark up is 150%

Formula for $\dfrac{FC \times 150}{100}$ $\dfrac{£3.20 \times 150}{100}$ =   £4.80
Mark up   (mark up)

Cost price   +   mark up   =   Selling price
£3.20   +   £4.80   =   £8.00

(*In food costing, as a general rule, the selling price always equals 100 per cent. However the one exception is with mark up pricing where the the cost price is treated as 100 per cent.)

SUMMARY

- The elements of cost consist of: food cost, labour cost and overhead cost.
- The selling price of any item must cover the elements of cost plus a reasonable amount for net profit.
- Gross profit and net profit are different concepts of profit.
    Sales − food and beverage cost = gross profit:
    Sales − all costs = net profit.
- Gross profit is used both as a control mechanism and a pricing instrument.
- If gross profit percentage is materially different from the expected level an investigation should follow. Key areas are: overproduction, wastage and portion control amongst others.
- Profit statements are widely used by management, usually on a monthly basis, to assist in controlling business performance.
- The costing of each individual menu item is an important exercise for all catering businesses and necessary for accurate pricing.
- A recipe manual and costing sheets provide a systematic approach to menu item costing.
- A minimum selling price can be calculated using the required gross profit percentage for an individual business. This gross profit percentage must be sufficient to cover all expenses and leave an adequate net profit.
- The formula for arriving at the selling price is:

$$\text{Selling price} \quad = \quad \frac{\text{Food cost}}{\text{Food cost \%}}$$

- If the food cost per unit changes there is no short cut for adjusting selling price. You must use the original formula.
- Simple table d'hôte and à la carte menus can be priced from the individual costing sheets.

- The selling price, calculated via the formula shown above, should represent the minimum selling price. However, many other factors will effect pricing decisions such as competition, loss leaders, etc.
- There are two methods of pricing menu items (a) the gross profit method and (b) the mark up method.

PROBLEMS

1. Explain what you understand by the 'elements of cost'.
2. Define the term 'overhead'. List five items of overhead.
3. Explain the terms 'gross profit' and 'net profit'.
4. Every business must establish a suitable gross profit percentage for its needs. Why is this important? How is the percentage established?
5. The following details relate to the food costs of the Elf Restaurant:
   (a) Opening stock at 1st Feb £2,600.
   (b) Purchases during month £14,400.
   (c) Closing stock at 28th Feb £3,100.
   (d) Purchases returns £650

   From the above details you are required to produce a cost of food used statement.

6. The following details relate to the food costs of the Dwarf Restaurant:
   (a) Purchases during June £11,500.
   (b) Opening stock at 1st June £2,860.
   (c) Purchases returns £400.
   (d) Closing stock at 30th June £2,600.
   (e) Staff feeding £580.

   From the above details you are required to produce a cost of food sold statement.

7. The following information relates to the Munchkin Restaurant for the month of September.
   (a) Opening stock £2,400. •
   (b) Closing stock £2,150.
   (c) Staff feeding £540.
   (d) Purchases for month £13,200.
   (e) Sales for month £28,000. •
   (f) Purchases returns £410. •

   Prepare a gross profit statement for the month and show the gross profit percentage. Explain what happens to the staff feeding cost which you have excluded.

8. The following information was extracted from the accounts of the Hobbit Restaurant for the month of January:

	£
Sales in January	36,000
Food stocks at 1st January	5,100
Food stocks at 30th January	4,850
Purchases of food in January	18,150
Purchases returns	360
Wages for month	7,440
Rent and business rates	1,760
Energy costs	980
Repairs and renewals	1,180
Sundry expenses	660
Depreciation	1,200

It is estimated that the cost of staff feeding amounted to £520.

You are required to produce a profit statement for the month of January for the Hobbit Restaurant, showing all key percentages.

9. Heaven Sent Restaurant had the following results for August.
   (a) Purchases for August   £28,560
   (b) Closing stock 31st August 19...   £3,270
   (c) Sales for August   £56,490
   (d) Purchases returns   £340
   (e) Opening stock at 1st August 19...   £4,220

It is estimated that staff feeding cost £810 for the month of August.

Prepare a gross profit statement statement for August showing all relevant percentages.

10. Most large-scale catering companies devote considerable resources to the operation of some method of menu costing. Why is this considered so important in the control of food cost and profit?

11. Listed on the dinner menu of a local restaurant were three items, priced to sell as follows:
   Menu item A   £5.00
   Menu item B   £2.40
   Menu item C   £7.50

Assuming that the selling price is calculated on the basis of a gross profit of 60 per cent, calculate the food cost of each item.

12. Calculate the values of the missing amounts

Sales	Food cost	Gross profit
£	£	£
9,600	4,350	?
6,500	?	2,800
?	7.500	6,250
9,550	?	4,450

13. The Matchstick Restaurant Company has operated a budgeting system for many years. The following are the budgeted results expected from the restaurant for the month of March:

	Budget figures
Sales	£71,250
Cost of sales	35%
Labour costs	23%
Overhead costs	20%
Net profit	22%

The following are the actual results for the Matchstick Restaurant Company for the month of March.

	£
Sales	70,650
Opening food stock 1st March	3,340
Purchases returns	400
Purchases for month	28,910
Wages & salaries	13,875
Employer's NI	1,875
Energy costs	3,750
Laundry and cleaning materials	935
Printing and stationery	1,015
Telephone and postage	675
Rent and business rates	3,750
Repairs and renewals	1,500
Depreciation	3,000

Notes.
(a) A stock-taking shows that the food stock at 31st March is £2,750.
(b) Staff feeding for March is estimated at £1,840.

Required:
Prepare a profit statement of the trading results for the Matchstick Restaurant Company for the month of March, showing clearly any deviations from the budgeted results.

14. Calculate the values of the missing amounts (All percentages are expressed in terms of sales)

Sales	Food cost	Gross profit
£9,800	38%	?
?	£5,400	68%
£11,500	?	65%
?	40%	£6,600
£7,800	?%	£5,226
?	£7,300	75%

15. Calculate the required figures in the following exercises:

    (a) If the sales of a restaurant are £25,000 and the food costs are £8,500, what is the percentage gross profit being made?
    (b) A meal sells at £7.80 and the restaurant management expects a gross profit of 65 per cent. What is the maximum ingredient cost which can be spent?
    (c) If the ingredient cost of a dish is £2.70 and the management require a gross profit of at least 70 per cent on everything they sell, what is the minimum selling price which can be charged to the customer?
    (d) The table d'hôte menu of the Chenon Restaurant is charged at £11.75 and the food cost is £3.76. What percentage gross profit is being made?

16. Prepare a standard recipe card for 24 portions of Sole Fourrees from the following information:

24 × 400 g	Lemon Sole	@ £8.00 per kg
800 g	Prawns	@ £6.85 per kg
400 g	Butter	@ £2.60 per kg
600 g	Flour	@ £1.55 per kg
2	Bread loaves	@ £0.46 each
600 g	Mushrooms	@ £3.60 per kg
1 carton	Cream	@ £1.10 per carton
8	Lemons	@ £0.28 each
2 bunches	Parsley	@ £0.42 per bunch
	Seasoning etc.	@ £0.30

    Required:
    (a) using a costing sheet show the total cost and the cost per portion;
    (b) calculate the total selling price and the selling price per portion required to obtain a gross profit of 65 per cent (answer to nearest whole penny);
    (c) illustrate the inclusive selling price to the customer, assuming a 10 per cent service charge and the current rate of VAT.

17. Prepare a standard recipe card for 20 portions of Moussaka from the following information:

180 g	Butter	@ £2.60 per kg
300 g	Onions	@ £1.45 per kg
3 bulbs	Garlic	@ £0.48 per bulb
750 g	Mushrooms	@ £3.35 per kg
90 g	Tomato puree	@ £5.25 per kg
9 dl	Demiglace	@ £0.90 per litre
3 kg 750 g	Cooked mutton	@ £3.95 per kg
9 dl	Vegetable oil	@ £1.10 per litre
1 kg 300g	Aubergines	@ £3.40 per kg
200 g	Flour	@ £1.40 per kg

900 g	Tomatoes	@ £1.85 per kg
450 g	Breadcrumbs	@ £1.65 per kg
1 bunch	Parsley	@ £0.55 per bunch
	Seasoning, etc.	@ £0.20

Required:
(a) Using a costing sheet show the total food cost and the cost per portion.
(b) Calculate the total selling price and the selling price per portion required to obtain a gross profit of 65 per cent.
(c) Calculate the inclusive selling price to the customer assuming a service charge of 15 per cent and the current rate of VAT.

All calculations to nearest whole penny.

18. Prepare a standard recipe card for 12 portions of Irish stew from the following information:

2.250 kg	Stewing Lamb	@ £4.10 per kg
400g	White cabbage	@ £0.98 per kg
350g	Leeks	@ £1.65 per kg
250g	Celery	@ £1.40 per kg
500g	Onions	@ £1.40 per kg
350g	Button onions	@ £1.55 per kg
1.600 kg	Potatoes	@ £0.75 per kg
2 bunches	Parsley	@ £0.45 per bunch
1	Bouquet garni	@ £0.70 each
	Seasoning etc.	@ £0.45

Required:
(a) using a costing sheet show the total cost and the cost per portion;
(b) calculate the selling price per portion required to obtain a gross profit of 68 per cent;
(c) assume an increase of £0.50 in the food cost per portion. Recalculate the selling price needed to retain the same gross profit per cent as above.

All answers to nearest whole penny.

19. Prepare a standard recipe card for 15 portions of Bitoks à la Russe from the following information:

3.500 kg	Beef – thick flank	@ £5.90 per kg
1.500 kg	Pork shoulder	@ £5.05 per kg
0.600 kg	Onions	@ £1.45 per kg
0.160 kg	Beef dripping	@ £1.80 per kg
0.75 litres	Milk	@ £0.48 per litre
0.100 kg	Chopped parsley	@ £2.55 per kg
4	Eggs	@ £2.80 per doz.
0.060 kg	Salt	@ £0.95 per kg

0.030 kg	White pepper	@ £4.15 per kg
0.015 kg	Nutmeg	@ £6.80 per kg
0.300 kg	Plain flour	@ £1.90 per kg
0.500 kg	Cooking butter	@ £2.85 per kg

Required:

    (a) using a costing sheet show the total cost and the cost per portion;

    (b) calculate the total selling price and the selling price per portion required to obtain a gross profit of 62 per cent;

    (c) calculate the total selling price and the price per portion if the restaurant required a gross profit of 70 per cent;

All answers to nearest whole penny.

Basic cost behaviour | 18

INTRODUCTION

The division of total cost into materials, labour and overheads has been used in hospitality operations for a long time. It is useful for some purposes but it does not take into account the dynamics of business, i.e. the effect on costs of changes in the volume of turnover (sales).

This chapter is primarily concerned with how different types of cost behave when the number of customers (sales volume) increases or decreases. This technique is particularly useful in planning, estimating, pricing and decision-making.

OBJECTIVES

On completion of this chapter you should be able to:

- explain what is meant by cost behaviour;
- understand and state the difference between fixed and variable costs;
- give examples of variable costs and fixed costs;
- define the terms 'volume of sales' and 'number of units';
- comprehend the term 'contribution' and understand its significance;
- define and use the C/S ratio;
- understand the difference between contribution and gross profit;
- draw up a contribution statement;
- calculate contribution per unit;
- define the break-even point;
- use correctly the break-even formulae;
- draw a break-even chart.

FIXED AND VARIABLE COSTS

We may divide all costs into three groups:

1. **Fixed costs** – these costs tend to remain constant irrespective of changes in the volume of business, e.g. rent, rates, insurance, depreciation of premises, licences, etc. A characteristic feature of fixed costs is that they

accrue with the passage of time; hence, they are sometimes described as 'period costs'.

2. **Semi-fixed costs** – (also described as semi-variable costs). These move in sympathy with, but not in proportion to, the volume of sales. Examples of semi-fixed costs are: gas, electricity, cleaning materials and breakages and replacements. When the turnover of a business increases by 50 per cent it is quite certain that the cost of kitchen fuel will also increase; the increase will, however, be much less than 50 per cent.

3. **Variable costs** – these tend to move in proportion to sales and include all commodity costs such as food, beverage, tobaccos, etc. Provided that a close check is kept on the gross profit margins, all these costs will move almost in direct proportion to any changes in the volume of business.

CLASSIFICATION OF COSTS INTO FIXED AND VARIABLE

The student should note that we are primarily considering costs from the point of view of their behaviour in response to changes in the volume of sales. By this we mean the physical changes in the number of customers or meals served or produced.

Before we can proceed to examine cost behaviour in any detail it is absolutely necessary to classify all costs as either fixed or variable. In the case of many cost items it is relatively straightforward.

Fixed costs such as rent or rates are quite simple. These costs remain the same no matter how many or few customers one serves.

In a restaurant, for example, any costs which increase simply because more customers have been served must be somewhat 'variable'. A good example is food. Clearly, the more customers one serves the more food will be used and in an efficient establishment, one would expect food costs to rise or fall in proportion to the number of customers served. For this reason we regard food as a fully variable cost.

Other costs are less easy to classify. The cost of electricity or gas, for example, is much more difficult to classify. These costs will of course increase as the number of customers served increases, but our common sense tells us that the increase should be small and certainly not in proportion. These are semi-fixed costs and are a mixture of fixed and variable costs.

There are tried and tested techniques available to classify semi-fixed costs into their separate elements which the student will study at a later point. One simple technique is illustrated below.

CONTRIBUTION AND THE C/S RATIO

Contribution is a key concept in the study of cost behaviour. Contribution is defined as sales less total variable costs. The C/S ratio is simply the contribution expressed as a percentage of sales, for example:

	£
Sales	40,000
Less variable costs	28,000
Contribution	12,000

The C/S ratio (contribution/sales ratio) is always expressed as a percentage using the following formula:

$$\frac{\text{Contribution} \times 100}{\text{Sales}} = \frac{£12,000 \times 100}{£40,000} = 30\% \text{ (C/S Ratio)}$$

Contribution must not be confused with gross profit (sales–cost of sales). Although there are some similiarities they are very different concepts. Variable costs are made up of food and beverage costs **plus** variable labour and overhead costs. The c/s ratio will, therefore, always be lower than the gross profit percentage.

In order to understand and operate cost behaviour techniques, it is necessary, as a first step, to separate all costs into either fixed or variable costs.

EXAMPLE 18.1

Consider the trading, profit and loss account of the Whitehouse Restaurant, below:

Trading, Profit and Loss Account
of Whitehouse Restaurant

	£	£
Sales		100,000
Less cost of sales		40,000
Gross profit		60,000
Less other expenses		
Wages	20,000	
Rent and rates	6,000	
Light and heat	4,000	
Telephone	3,000	
Laundry	4,000	
Sundry expenses	5,000	42,000
Net profit		18,000

Notes on profit and loss account:
(a) Cost of sales is **always** a variable cost.
(b) 50 per cent of labour costs are variable with sales, the remainder are fixed costs.
(c) Telephone costs £3,000, of which £1,000 is variable and £2,000 is fixed.
(d) Laundry costs £4,000, of which £3,000 is variable and £1,000 is fixed.
(e) Sundry expenses £5,000, of which £4,000 is variable and £1,000 is fixed.

You are required to convert the above profit and loss account into a 'contribution statement' (also known as a marginal costing statement). Proceed as shown below:

Contribution Statement
Whitehouse Restaurant

	£	£	
Sales		100,000	100%
Less Variable costs			
Cost of sales	40,000		
Variable – Labour costs	10,000		
– Telephone	1,000		
– Laundry	3,000		
– Sundry expenses	4,000	58,000	58%
Contribution		42,000	42%
Less Fixed Costs			
Fixed labour costs	10,000		
Rent & rates	6,000		
Light & heat	4,000		
Fixed – Telephone	2,000		
– Laundry	1,000		
– Sundry expenses	1,000	24,000	24%
Net profit		18,000	18%

The C/S ratio is calculated as follows: $\dfrac{£42,000 \times 100}{£100,000}$ = 42%

The meaning of contribution

Contribution is simply the surplus remaining after paying the variable costs and which can now contribute to the payment of fixed costs and profit thereafter.

CONTRIBUTION PER UNIT

When we look at cost behaviour, we are interested in how costs behave when the number of customers (sales volume) either increases or decreases. The key principles are sometimes easier to grasp in a unit cost context.

EXAMPLE 18.2

Assume that the owner of a restaurant sells only steaks. All other costs (labour and overheads) are fixed and amount to £1,375 per week.
Each steak costs £4.50 and is sold for £10.00.

Clearly the contribution per unit (or per steak) is £5.50:

	£
Selling price	10.00
Variable costs	4.50
Contribution per unit	5.50

It should also be clear that every time the owner makes a sale it costs £4.50 (the cost of the steak). Therefore from each sale the restaurant owner is left with £5.50 to contribute firstly to the payment of fixed costs (£1,375 per week) and once they are paid every additional £5.50 for that week is clear profit.

Question
How many customers does one need to serve in order to pay the fixed costs of £1,375?

Answer
Since each customer contributes £5.50, then simply divide the fixed cost figure of £1,375 by £5.50 to get the answer

$$\frac{£1,375}{£5.50} = 250 \text{ units or customers}$$

This is known as the break-even point in number of units and is of immense value to any business person. We will study this in more detail later in this chapter.

Question
If the above business sells 400 steaks in a given week, how much profit will be made?

Answer
We know the business receives a contribution of £5.50 per customer. We also know from the calculations above, that the restaurant needs to sell 250 steaks to cover all fixed costs. So clearly every £5.50 received thereafter is net profit and the answer is a profit of £825, being 150 steaks (400–250 steaks) at £5.50.

Proof:		£
	Sales (400 × £10.00)	4,000
	Less variable costs (400 × £4.50)	1,800
	Contribution	2,200
	Less Fixed costs	1,375
	Net profit	825

The above illustrations demonstrate the importance of separating costs into fixed and variable elements. Once one has accurately assessed the variable costs for any given level of sales one can work out the break-even point or the expected profit/loss at any other level of sales. This is explained more fully later in this chapter.

TURNOVER, COSTS AND PROFITS

An appreciation of the relationship between the volume of turnover, costs and profits is indispensable to those responsible for the running of a business. For, as will have been appreciated, a given change in sales will not affect all costs in the same manner: some will remain constant; some will change less than proportionately; others will change in proportion.

EXAMPLE 18.3

Let us assume that the turnover, costs and profits of two restaurants are as shown below:

	Restaurant A		Restaurant B	
	£		£	
Turnover	1,000	(100.00%)	1,000	(100.00%)
Variable costs	500	(50.00%)	300	(30.00%)
Contribution	500	(50.00%)	700	(70.00%)
Fixed costs	400	(40.00%)	600	(60.00%)
Net profit	100	(10.00%)	100	(10.00%)

Let us now assume that the turnover of both restaurants decreases by 10 per cent. The effect on the trading results of the restaurants will be as follows:

	Restaurant A		Restaurant B	
	£		£	
Turnover	900	(100.00%)	900	(100.00%)
Variable costs	450	(50.00%)	270	(30.00%)
Contribution	450	(50.00%)	630	(70.00%)
Fixed costs	400	(44.40%)	600	(66.70%)
Net profit	50	(5.60%)	30	(3.30%)

It may be seen that the relatively small decrease in the sales of the restaurants of 10 per cent has reduced the net profit of Restaurant A by 50 per cent (i.e. from £100 to £50) and the net profit of Restaurant B by 70 per cent (i.e. from £100 to £30).

A consideration of the figures given in this example enables us to draw the following conclusions:

1. A given change in turnover will **not** result in a proportionate change in costs.
2. When sales increase/decrease, net profit tends to increase/decrease more than in proportion.
3. The higher the proportion of fixed costs the greater the effect on net profit (or net loss) of any given change in turnover.

4. There is no change in the C/S ratio. Any increase/decrease in turnover caused by a change in volume (number of customers) will not alter the C/S ratio.

Turnover and unit costs

Changes in the volume of turnover of a business affect unit costs in the same manner as they do the costs of the establishment as a whole.

An increase in sales increases the total variable cost of the establishment, but the variable cost per unit remains constant. Thus when the number of meals sold increases from 1,000 to 1,500 per week, the variable cost (food cost) increases by 50 per cent, yet the cost of food per meal served remains the same.

On the other hand, whilst an increase in sales will not affect the total fixed costs of a restaurant, the fixed cost per unit will be decreased. The total fixed cost is now spread over a larger number of meals sold.

As a result, every increase in turnover will have the effect of reducing unit costs and thus increasing the net profit per unit sold.

EXAMPLE 18.4

The fixed costs of the Old City Restaurant amount to £6,000 per week. The restaurant serves between 1,800 and 2,600 meals weekly and the average amount spent by the customers is £5.00 per meal. The variable cost (food cost) per meal is £2.00.

Find the total cost per meal served and the net profit or loss per meal when the restaurant serves 1,800, 2,000, 2,200, 2,400 and 2,600 meals per week.

Proceed as shown below:

Total cost and net profit per meal

No. of meals served per week	1,800	2,000	2,200	2,400	2,600
	£	£	£	£	£
Selling price per meal	5.00	5.00	5.00	5.00	5.00
Variable cost per meal	2.00	2.00	2.00	2.00	2.00
Fixed cost per meal	3.33	3.00	2.72	2.50	2.30
Total cost per meal	5.33	5.00	4.72	4.50	4.30
Net profit per meal	–	–	28p	50p	70p
Net loss per meal	33p	–	–	–	–

Note carefully the effect on 'total cost per meal' as sales increase. This is caused exclusively by a decrease in fixed cost per unit. Clearly any fixed cost when expressed as so much per unit must decrease as numbers increase with a positive effect on profit.

BREAK-EVEN POINT

Break-even point is that point in a business's trading when it makes neither a profit nor a loss: in other words when the sales (turnover) exactly equal the total costs. At the break-even point and at no other point in the business's trading will the contribution exactly equal the fixed costs.

There are two formulae for calculating the break-even point. The C/S ratio and the contribution per unit form part of these formulae and the student should ensure that they understand each before proceeding.

Formulae:

1. Break-even point in sales (£)

$$\frac{\text{Fixed costs}}{\text{C/S ratio}}$$

2. Break-even point in number of units

$$\frac{\text{Fixed costs}}{\text{Contribution per unit}}$$

These formulae can be adapted to calculate the turnover necessary for any level of desired profit as follows:

3. Sales (in £) needed to achieve a specific profit

$$\frac{\text{Fixed costs + specific profit}}{\text{C/S ratio}}$$

4. Number of units needed to achieve a specific profit

$$\frac{\text{Fixed costs + specific profit}}{\text{Contribution per unit}}$$

EXAMPLE 18.5

The results of the Tullamore Restaurant for year end 31st March 19... are set out in a contribution statement below:

Number of covers served: <u>10,000</u>

	£	£	
Sales		200,000	
<u>Less variable costs</u>			
Cost of sales	80,000		
Variable labour costs	24,000		
Variable overhead costs	<u>16,000</u>	<u>120,000</u>	
Contribution		80,000	40% (C/S Ratio)
Less fixed costs		<u>60,000</u>	
Net profit		<u>20,000</u>	

Using the above information we can now calculate the business's break-even point or the volume of sales necessary to give any level of net profit.

Using the formulae to forecast the break-even point:

$$\frac{\text{Break-even}}{\text{in sales (£)}} \quad \frac{\text{Fixed costs}}{\text{C/S ratio}} \quad = \quad \frac{£60,000}{40} \times \frac{100}{1} = £150,000$$

$$\frac{\text{Break-even}}{\text{in units}} \quad \frac{\text{Fixed costs}}{\text{Contribution per unit}} \quad = \quad \frac{£60,000}{£8} \quad = 7,500 \text{ covers}$$

Note: Contribution per unit is calculated as follows: Total contribution/ number of covers served – £80,000/10,000 covers = £8 per cover.

Using the formulae to forecast sales required for a specific level of profit

The management of the Tullamore Restaurant wish to know what sales figure they would require to produce a profit of £35,000

$$\frac{\text{Sales(£) needed to}}{\text{achieve a profit of £35,000}} \quad = \quad \frac{\text{Fixed costs + specific profit}}{\text{C/S ratio}}$$

$$= \quad \frac{£60,000 + £35,000}{40} \times \frac{100}{1} = £237,500$$

$$\frac{\text{Number of units needed to}}{\text{achieve a profit of £35,000}} \quad = \quad \frac{\text{Fixed costs + specific profit}}{\text{Contribution per unit}}$$

$$= \quad \frac{£60,000 + £35,000}{£8} = 11,875 \text{ covers}$$

GRAPHICAL PRESENTATION OF COST BEHAVIOUR

Break-even charts

In order to construct a break-even chart the costs of a business must be clearly separated into fixed and variable costs, according to their behaviour in response to changes in the volume of turnover.

EXAMPLE 18.6

The Verona Restaurant had the following results for the half year ended 31st March 19...

Number of meals sold	5,000
ASP	£12
	£
Sales	60,000
Less total variable costs	30,000
Contribution	30,000
Less fixed costs	20,000
Net profit	10,000

You are required to present the above account in the form of a break-even chart.

Proceed as shown in Figures 18.1, 18.2 and 18.3.

Guide to drawing graphs

If you are new to graphs then a good rule to remember is that the horizontal axis (X) normally relates to activity such as number of meals sold, number of dishes produced, hours worked, etc. whereas the vertical axis (Y) relates to money values such as sales and costs in £.

Basically there are three steps to producing a simple break-even chart.

In order to draw any line on a graph one requires a minimum of two separate points (known as co-ordinates on a graph) which should be a reasonable distance apart: using a ruler and pencil join them together to form the line.

Please note that in reality many more than two co-ordinates are used.

Stage One Insert the fixed cost line:

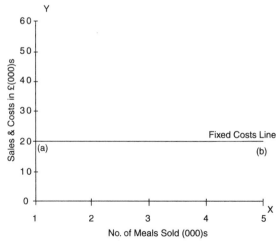

Figure 18.1 Fixed cost line

Note the two points shown:

(a) When meals sold is zero (X=0),fixed costs are £20,000 (Y=20)

(b) When meals sold is 5,000 (X=5), fixed costs are still £20,000 (Y=20)

Thus by joining the two points you form the fixed cost line. This conforms to our view that as meals served increases fixed costs remain constant.

Stage Two On the same graph place the total cost line:

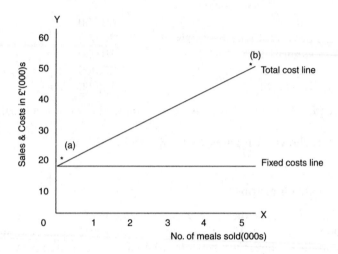

Figure 18.2 Total cost line
Notes: the two points shown are:
(a) When meals sold is zero then total costs are £20,000 (fixed costs only) Using co-ordinates, that is represented by X=0, Y=20.
(b) When meals sold are 5,000 then total costs are £50,000 (fixed plus variable). Using co-ordinates, that is represented by X=5, Y=50.

Stage Three Still using the same graph place the sales line as shown:

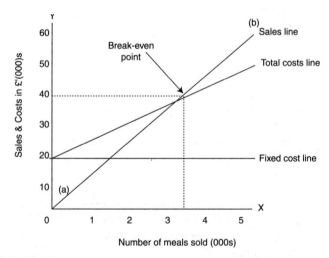

Figure 18.3 Sales line
Notes: the two points shown are:
(a) When meals sold are zero (X=0), naturally sales in £ value are also zero (Y=0).
(b) When meals sold are 5,000 (X=5), then sales in £ are £60,000 (Y=60).

This completes the break-even chart. All that remains is to read off the information given as follows:

1. Where the sales line crosses the total cost line this marks the break-even point. The dotted lines on the chart show the key co-ordinates; that is, at break-even sales are £40,000 and the number of meals sold equals 3,333.33 meals.
2. When sales are less than £40,000 total costs are greater than sales producing a loss. This loss can be ascertained by measuring the vertical distance between the two lines against the vertical scale, e.g. the net loss at sales of £30,000 is £5,000 (see chart above). Similarly the net profit can be ascertained from the distance between the sales and total cost lines for any level in excess of £40,000.

The purpose of a break-even chart is to show how much profit or loss will be made by a business at different levels of turnover. The term 'break-even chart' is unfortunate in that it stresses a particular – and not necessarily the most important – purpose of the chart, i.e. the ascertainment of the break-even point. It should be appreciated that the object of a break-even chart is to project the profitability of a business *vis-à-vis* changes in its turnover and not merely to find the turnover which results in a condition where all costs are covered and no profit is achieved.

EXAMPLE 18.7

The Belle Vue Restaurant serves up to 2,000 customers per week. The average spending power is £5.00.

The costs of the restaurant are:

(a) fixed costs (rent, rates, insurance, wages and salaries) £2,500 per week;
(b) variable costs (food and beverages) 50 per cent of sales.

Calculate:

(a) the amount of profit/loss per week when the restaurant serves 400, 800, 1,200, 1,600 and 2,000 customers per week.
(b) the break-even point of the restaurant.

The relationship between the turnover of the restaurant, its costs and profits may be represented in two ways: by means of a simple tabular statement or by means of a break-even chart.

The tabular statement could be drawn up as shown below:

Belle Vue Restaurant

Weekly profit/loss at different levels of turnover

NOC*	Sales	Fixed Costs	Variable Costs	Total Cost	+ Profit −Loss
	£	£	£	£	£
400	2,000	2,500	1,000	3,500	−1,500
800	4,000	2,500	2,000	4,500	−500
1,200	6,000	2,500	3,000	5.500	+500
1,600	8,000	2,500	4,000	6,500	+1,500
2,000	10,000	2,500	5,000	7,500	+2,500

*NOC = Number of covers

The break-even chart of the restaurant could be prepared either from the tabular statement given above or from the information shown in Example 18.7.

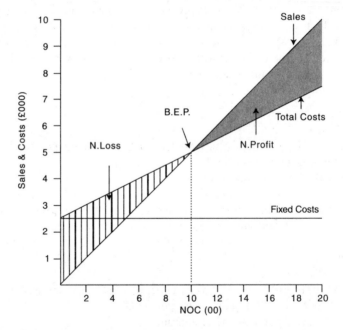

Figure 18.4 Belle Vue Restaurant break-even chart

By reference to the break-even chart, it may be seen that:

1. No profit can be made by the restaurant unless it serves 1,000 customers per week.
2. When the restaurant serves 2,000 customers per week, its net profit is £2,500 per week.
3. Once the break-even point (1,000 customers) has been reached, every increase of 100 customers increases the net profit of the restaurant by £250 per week.

Margin of safety

An interesting and useful concept connected with break-even analysis is that of the margin of safety. This may be defined as the range of output over which a net profit must be made, i.e. the range of output between the break-even point and the total of sales.

Where the margin of safety is narrow a small drop in sales will reduce profits considerably or convert any net profit made into a loss. When, on the other hand, the margin of safety is wide, a considerable decrease in turnover has to take place for the business to incur a loss. In general, the higher the ratio of fixed costs to variable costs the narrower the margin of safety, and vice versa.

EXAMPLE 18.8

The capital invested in the Pagoda Restaurant is £150,000. The proprietors' policy is to aim at a net profit target of 20 per cent on all restaurant sales.

The restaurant has a seating capacity enabling it to serve up to 5,000 customers per month, i.e. a maximum of 60,000 customers per annum. The ASP of the restaurant is £5.00. Fixed costs amount to £90,000 p.a. and variable costs account for 40 per cent of the sales revenue. From this information a break-even chart is prepared as shown in Figure 18.5. This indicates:

(a) the break-even point;
(b) the margin of safety;
(c) the volume of sales required to achieve the net profit target.

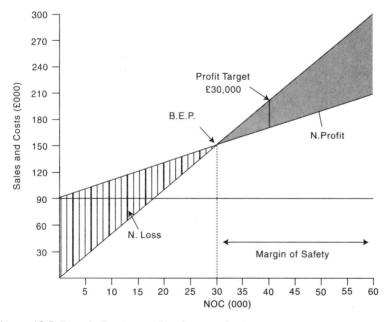

Figure 18.5 Pagoda Restaurant break-even chart

SUMMARY

- The standard division of costs into materials, labour and overhead does not take account of the dynamics of the business and/or its cost–volume–profit implications.
- In order to understand how costs behave as volume of sales increases or decreases one must first separate them into their fixed and variable elements.
- Fixed costs remain fixed irrespective of changes in the volume of sales. By volume we mean the number of units sold.
- Variable costs tend to move in proportion to the sales volume. For the purposes of these exercises we will assume that they move in exact proportion.
- Sales less all variable cost equals contribution. This is a very important concept in terms of cost behaviour.
- The C/S ratio is written as a percentage (often referred to as the P/V ratio). It is simply the contribution expressed as a percentage of sales.
- Food and beverage cost or cost of sales is the most important variable cost. It is often expressed in a question as the difference between sales and gross profit which many students fail to recognize.
- A contribution statement is a profit and loss account where the costs are grouped according to their behaviour (either fixed or variable). It is sometimes called a marginal costing statement.
- Contribution per unit is total contribution divided by number of units sold, or selling price less variable cost per unit.
- Break-even point is where sales are exactly equal to total costs. The business makes neither a profit nor a loss.
- There are formulae for calculating break-even point both in sales value or the number of units required. These formulae can be adjusted to forecast any desired profit level.
- Break-even charts are a popular way of expressing, in a visual way, how much profit or loss is made at different levels of turnover.

PROBLEMS

1. Explain what is meant by: fixed cost; semi-fixed cost; variable cost.

2. (a) Define the term 'break-even';
   (b) Explain fully the different sorts of information which may be elicited from a break-even chart;
   (c) Why are break-even charts thought to be popular amongst managers?

3. Complete the following table:

Average spend £	Average food cost £	Other variable costs £	Total variable cost %	Contribution £	C/S ratio %
15.00	6.00	5.25			
20.00	7.00		70%		
	8.75	6.25			40%
17.50	7.00			7.50	
12.50		2.50			35%

4. The following are the trading results of a restaurant in respect of Year 1:

	£
Sales	400,000

Less:

	£	
(a) Fixed costs (rent, rates, insurance, salaries, etc.)	100,000	
(b) Semi-fixed costs (fuel, telephone, laundry, etc)	100,000	
(c) Variable costs (food, beverages, tobacco, etc.	160,000	360,000
Net profit		40,000

It is estimated that in Year 2 the sales of the restaurant will increase by 10 per cent. It is also estimated that semi-fixed costs will rise by $2\frac{1}{2}$ per cent. It is intended to keep the variable costs in the same ratio to sales as in Year 1.

Prepare an estimate of the trading results for Year 2.

5. Complete the following table:

	Selling price per cover £	Variable costs per cover £	Contribution per cover £	Fixed costs £	Break-even point Units
(a)	1.75	1.05			35,000
(b)	22.50	15.00		11,250	
(c)	11.25	8.25			3,000
(d)	18.00	9.00		27,000	
(e)		17.25		6,750	750
(f)	9.75			6,500	26,000
(g)	5.10			24,000	12,000
(h)		4.50		52,000	13,000

6. The capital invested in the Norus Hotel is £1,000,000 and the following are the sales and costs of the hotel at different rates of occupancy.

Occupancy	65%	75%	85%	95%
Sales	£630,000	£740,000	£850,000	£960,000
Total cost	£580,000	£640,000	£700,000	£750,000

(a) comment on the relationship between sales, total cost and the net profit of the hotel;

(b) calculate the return on the capital invested in the hotel in relation to each rate of occupancy given above;

(c) comment on your results in (b) above.

7. The Hartfelt Restaurant Company operates three restaurants. From the information given below you are required to calculate for each restaurant:

(a) the C/S ratio;
(b) the sales necessary to break even;
(c) the sales required to achieve a 15% return on capital invested.

	Riverford Restaurant	Waterford Restaurant	Seaford Restaurant
Gross profit	65%	60%	55%
Variable labour & overhead	15%	17%	20%
	£	£	£
Fixed labour/overhead	200,000	375,000	250,000
Capital invested	350,000	750,000	500,000

8. High-class and Low-class are two restaurants with an identical volume of turnover.

From the information given below you are required to:
(a) prepare a break-even chart of each restaurant;
(b) explain which restaurant is likely to earn greater profits in conditions of: (i) heavy demand; and
　　　　　　　　　　(ii) low demand

	High-class		Low-class	
	£	£	£	£
Sales		200,000		200,000
Less Fixed costs	120,000		60,000	
Variable costs	60,000	180,000	120,000	180,000
Net profit		20,000		20,000

9. A canteen serves between 1,800 and 2,200 main meals weekly. Its fixed costs (labour costs and overheads) are £3,700 per week and it operates at a gross profit of 50 per cent. The charge per main meal is fixed at £4.00. You are required to find:

(a) how many main meals the canteen has to serve each week to break even;
(b) The net profit/loss when 2,000 main meals are served weekly;
(c) Explain the relationship between the volume of sales and the net profit/loss of a business by reference to the information given above.

10. The Ryan Hotel Company owns two restaurants in a medium sized town in middle Britain. They have been operating for many years and the information given below is a summary of the trading results for the year ended 31st December 19...

	The Saw and Dust Restaurant		The Sand and Pit Restaurant	
Average spend per cover	£24		£12	
	£		£	
Sales	218,400		218,400	
Less Cost of sales	67,900		87,200	
		150,500		131,200
Less Labour costs Fixed	49,800		30,480	
Variable	5,400		29,320	
Overheads Fixed	56,200		10,000	
Variable	3,140	114,540	25,440	95,240
Net profit		35,960		35,960

Required:

(a) For each of the two restaurants above, calculate:
 (i) the C/S ratio;
 (ii) the break-even point in sales(£);
 (iii) the break-even point in number of covers;
 (iv) the sales value(£) and number of covers necessary to produce a profit of £60,000.
(b) Construct a break-even chart for each restaurant.

11. Dix Catering Co. operates at a C/S ratio of 60 per cent. Its fixed expenses are £60,000. Calculate:
 (a) the value of sales required for the company to break even;
 (b) the value of sales required for the company to achieve a net profit of £15,000.

12. The Acropolis Restaurant serves between 3,000 and 4,000 customers per month. The average spending power is £5.00. The restaurant operates at a fixed margin of gross profit of 60 per cent. Other variable costs are 20p per cover. Its fixed costs are as follows:

	£
Wages, salaries, national insurance, etc.	4,500
Proportion of rent, rates and depreciation	2,400
Postage, telephone and stationery	1,000
Other fixed costs	1,900

You are required to:

(a) prepare a break-even chart for the restaurant;
(b) explain the significance of the break-even point;
(c) comment on the 'margin of safety' of the restaurant.

13. Hyfix and Lofix are two restaurants with an identical volume of turn-over. The estimated profits and loss accounts of the restaurants are:

	Hyfix		Lofix	
	£	£	£	£
Sales		520,000		520,000
Less Fixed costs	312,000		156,000	
Variable costs	156,000		312,000	
		468,000		468,000
Net profit		52,000		52,000

Required:

(a) calculate the break-even point of each restaurant;

(b) comment on their respective 'margins of safety'.

14. Barnardo's Snack Bar operates at a C/S ratio of 60 per cent. Its fixed expenses are £50,000.

(a) find the value of sales required for the snack bar to cover its fixed and variable costs only;

(b) also find the value of sales necessary to give the snack bar a net profit of £20,000.

15. The Riverside Restaurant has been run by Mr Trad for many years. He has never been sure as to how many customers he needs to serve to break even or the rate of increase of profit as numbers served increase. From the following information you are required to:

(a) Prepare a break-even tabular statement and

(b) Draw a break-even chart showing the results.

The Riverside Restaurant serves between 900 and 1,500 customers per week. The average spending power is £12.00; the fixed costs are £8,000 per week and total variable costs amount to 35% of sales.

16. The following is a summary of the Avery Restaurant's trading results for the year ended 30th June 1995:

Existing position		£
Sales		500,000
Less cost of sales		225,000
Gross profit		275,000
Less labour	130,000	
overheads	100,000	230,000
Net profit		45,000

Of the total labour and overhead costs, £180,000 is fixed and £50,000 is variable.

Proposed changes – for projected results 1995/96
The general manager proposes to introduce certain changes in the operation of the restaurant which will affect the operating results as follows:

(a) the cost of sales is to be reduced to 35 per cent;
(b) labour costs are to be increased to £150,000 p.a., and overheads to £130,000 p.a.;
(c) it is anticipated that the volume of sales will remain as in 1994/95, but it is considered that, of the total of labour and overheads, £255,000 will be fixed and £25,000 will be variable.

You are required:
(a) prepare two break-even charts, one portraying the trading results for 1994/95, and the other showing the projected results for 1995/96;
(b) comment on the effects of the proposed changes on the sales/cost/profit relationships of the restaurant.

17. Thomas Blake is a successful restaurant owner who already operates four restaurants in his home town. He is considering the purchase of a fifth restaurant in an out of town location where a purpose built structure already exists.

Capital costs would be as follows:

Premises	£250,000
Equipment, furniture etc.	150,000
Working capital	310,000

Mr Blake works on an expected return on capital employed of 18 per cent p.a.

Given below are his forecast figures for the coming year.

Wages and salaries (fixed)	£89,000
Business rates	40,000
Insurance and other fixed expenses	8,000
Depreciation	10,000

Other variable costs (excluding cost of sales) amount to 18 per cent of sales.

This restaurant will be expected to achieve a gross profit of 65 per cent and an average spending power of £22.50.

Required:
(a) calculate the break-even point in sales (£) and in number of covers;
(b) calculate the sales(£) and the number of covers for the restaurant to achieve the required return on capital employed;
(c) construct a contribution statement showing sales, costs and profit in (b) above;
(d) using the above information, prepare a break-even chart.
All calculations to the nearest whole number.

Basic decision accounting 19

INTRODUCTION

In the previous chapter on cost behaviour we introduced many new cost concepts such as contribution, C/S ratio and break-even formulae and charts, often referred to as tools of marginal costing.

Marginal costing techniques are not only used as a means of establishing the break-even point or profit level, but also as a method of deciding on one of a number of different strategies open to management. The aim of the present chapter is to illustrate several specific and typical applications of accounting for business decisions.

OBJECTIVES

On completion of this chapter you should be able to:

- understand the meaning of 'decision accounting';
- list the accounting techniques available for use in a decision accounting context;
- use the marginal costing approach (contribution approach) to solve pricing problems and produce profit estimates;
- use other concepts such as C/S ratio, contribution per unit, ASP, etc. where appropriate;
- employ break-even analysis and charts to a variety of decision-making problems;
- decide on a definitive course of action when faced with alternative business proposals, based on sound cost accounting practice;
- decide on issues such as off-season closure or department closure from a firm costing perspective.

BASIC TECHNIQUES OF PROFIT MANAGEMENT

Business decisions relate to a large number of operational, financial, marketing and other matters. From the point of view of profitability such decisions may affect operating costs, the sales volume or both. Ultimately, every business decision will have a 'bottom line consequence' that is to say an effect on the net profit of the business.

The relevant costing techniques will be illustrated by reference to the profit and loss account of the Station Restaurant which is reproduced below:

Contribution Statement of the Station Restaurant

	£	£	%
Sales		300,000	100
Less Variable Costs			
Cost of sales	120,000		
Variable – labour costs	30,000		
– telephone	3,000		
– laundry	9,000		
– sundry expenses	12,000	174,000	58%
Contribution		126,000	42%
Less Fixed Costs			
Fixed labour costs	30,000		
Rent & rates	18,000		
Light & heat	12,000		
Fixed – telephone	6,000		
– laundry	3,000		
– sundry expenses	3,000	72,000	24%
Net profit		54,000	18%

From the point of view of decision-making this form of presentation is more appropriate in that one can see immediately the division of all costs into fixed and variable. Also, the relevant percentages, including the C/S ratio, are shown. You are informed that, for the purposes of the calculations which follow, the ASP of the restaurant is £15.

Business decision 1 – effect of a reduction in permanent labour

Let us assume that the restaurant manager has decided to reduce his permanent labour and, in this way, secure an annual saving of £6,000. This reduction in labour costs lowers the total fixed cost and, in effect, means that a lower level of contribution (and hence fewer covers) need now be secured to break-even.

The break-even number of covers (NoC) was 11,429 covers (to nearest whole cover) and this is now reduced to:

$$\frac{\text{Fixed costs } (£72,000 - £6,000) \; £66,000}{\text{Contribution per unit } £6.30} = 10,476 \text{ (covers)}$$

In terms of the number of covers the effect of this decision is as follows:

	Annual	Weekly
Original NoC required to break-even	11,429	220
New NoC required to break-even	10,476	202
Resulting improvement	953	18

This means that the Station Restaurant now requires 953 fewer covers to reach the break-even point. This can be of real significance in recessionary times when covers are likely to drop.

The effect of the above improvement on the net profit of the restaurant is quite obvious. Total cost is now £6,000 less and this means a corresponding increase in net profit, which will now be £62,000 and represent 20.67 per cent of the sales figure.

Business decision 2 – increase in selling prices

The restaurant manager is planning to increase all his food and beverage prices by 5 per cent, and wants to know the effect of this on the break-even point and net profit of the restaurant. On the assumption that there are no other changes, the whole of the price increase will materialize as additional net profit, as shown below:

	Present		Proposed	
	£	%	£	%
Composition of sales				
Fixed costs	72,000	24	72,000	22.86
Variable costs	174,000	58	174,000	55.24
Net profit	54,000	18	69,000	21.90
Sales	300,000	100%	315,000	100.00%

The effect of a 5 per cent price increase is to decrease the variable cost percentage from 58 per cent to 55.24 per cent. The new contribution per cover will, therefore, be:

	£	%
Average selling price (£15 + 5%)	15.75	100.00
Less variable cost	8.70	55.24
Contribution and C/S ratio	7.05	44.76%

We may now calculate the new break-even point, which will be as follows:

$$\frac{\text{Fixed costs}}{\text{Contribution per unit}} = \frac{£72,000}{£7.05} = 10,213 \text{ covers}$$

In terms of the number of covers, the improvement achieved through the 5 per cent price rise may be summarized as follows:

	Annual	Weekly
Original NoC required to break-even	11,429	220
New NoC required to break-even	10,213	197
Resulting improvement	1,216	23

(All figures are rounded up to next whole number.)

From the point of view of the overall profitability of the restaurant the effect of the price increase is very powerful indeed. The new level of net profit, £69,000, is 27.77 per cent higher than the original figure of £54,000.

PROFIT ESTIMATES

Another useful application of the division of costs into fixed, semi-fixed and variable is the estimating of future profits.
    Profit estimates are necessary in various circumstances, e.g.:

1. when planning the operations of a business for a future period;
2. when commencing a new business;
3. when planning to extend the premises;
4. when planning to take over a business as a going concern;
5. when contemplating a change in the type of service, e.g. from self-service to waiter service.

The method to be applied in profit estimates is illustrated in the example below:

EXAMPLE 19.1

The following is a summary of the trading results of the Mulberry Restaurant for the quarter ended 31st March 19...

Mulberry Restaurant
Trading results for the quarter ended 31st March 19...

		£	£
Sales:	Restaurant		320,000
	Bar		180,000
			500 000
Less Variable costs:		£	
	Cost of food sold	144,000	
	Cost of beverages sold	72,000	216,000
	Gross profit		284,000
Less Fixed costs			
	Wages and salaries	130,000	
	Rent and rates	30,000	
	Light and heat	16,000	
	Depreciation	24,000	
	Repairs and replacement	12,000	
	Advertising	10,000	
	Other costs	14,000	236,000
	Net profit		48,000

The turnover of the restaurant has remained constant in the last two years, and the proprietors think that by eliminating waste and by improving menu planning the cost of food sold could be decreased from the usual 45 per cent to 40 per cent of the respective figure of sales. They also consider that an increase in press advertising costing £40,000 should raise the turnover for the next quarter to £600,000.

You are required to prepare:

(a) a summary of the estimated trading results for the next quarter on the assumption that the cost of food sold is decreased to 40 per cent of restaurant sales, but that no increase in press advertising takes place.

(b) a summary of the estimated trading results for the next quarter on the assumption that the cost of food sold is reduced and that the proposed increase in press advertising does take place.

(a)   Mulberry Restaurant
Estimated trading results (a) for quarter ended 30th June 19...

Sales	Restaurant		£320,000
	Bar		180,000
	Total		500,000
Less Variable costs:		£	
	Cost of food sold	128,000	
	Cost of drink sold	72,000	200,000
Gross profit			300,000
	Less Fixed costs		236,000
Net profit			£64,000

(b)   Mulberry Restaurant
Estimated trading results (b) for quarter ended 30th June 19...

Sales:	Restaurant		£384,000
	bar		216,000
Total			600,000
Less Variable costs:		£	
	Cost of food sold	£153,600	
	Cost of drink sold	86,400	240,000
Gross profit			360,000
	Less Fixed costs		276,000
Net profit			£84,000

It seems, therefore, that as a result of the two proposed measures the net profit of the restaurant may be improved considerably, i.e. by £36,000. Of the total increase in net profit £16,000 is due to the reduction in the cost of food sold and £20,000 is due to the effect of the proposed advertising.

PRICING – THE MARGINAL COSTING APPROACH

The usual method of fixing prices in the hospitality industry is to calculate the variable cost (e.g. food and beverage costs) and increase it by a percentage of gross profit. The gross profit added to the variable cost must be sufficient to cover all other expenses such as labour costs and overheads and leave a satisfactory margin of net profit. Thus, another way of defining selling price is:

TOTAL COST + NET PROFIT = SELLING PRICE

There are, however, particular circumstances which may justify selling at a price below total cost and this is illustrated below.

EXAMPLE 19.2

The Montrose Restaurant is divided into three separate sections; self-service, waitress service and banqueting. The annual fixed costs of the banqueting section are:

	£
Proportion of rent and rates	16,500
Depreciation	8,400
Repairs and maintenance	3,600
Salaries and wages	41,000
Other fixed costs	3,500
	73,000

The banqueting section is open all the year round and the fixed cost per day is therefore:

$$\frac{£73,000}{365} = £200$$

Taking into account the fixed cost per day and the variable cost (see below) in respect of a menu already agreed with your clients, calculate the charge per cover.

Assume that a net profit of 20 per cent is required on all banqueting sales.

Variable costs for 100 covers

	£
Food cost	330
Extra labour (waiting staff)	110
Variable overheads—(linen, laundry, electricity, gas, etc.)	60
Total variable cost	500

The charge per cover is:	
Fixed cost	200
Variable cost	500
Total cost of banquet	700

$$\frac{\text{TOTAL COST OF BANQUET}}{\text{NUMBER OF COVERS}} = \frac{£700}{100} = £7.00$$

Therefore total cost per cover = £7.00

$$\frac{£7.00 \times 100}{80*} = £8.75 = \text{Selling price per cover}$$

*Note: Since we require a net profit of 20 per cent then total costs must be 80 per cent.

Let us now assume that, for one reason or another, it is necessary to offer the above banquet at a reduced price and that if the banquet is not undertaken no other banqueting business can be secured for that particular day:
    The position then is this:

1. If the banquet is not undertaken the banqueting section will suffer a net loss equal to its fixed cost per day, i.e. £200;
2. If a reduced charge is made the banqueting section may cover its variable costs and some of its fixed costs, and in this way suffer a loss of less than £200. This second alternative is, clearly, preferable to the first.

The minimum charge per cover – which will recover all variable costs and leave no contribution to fixed costs – is calculated as follows:

$$\frac{\text{TOTAL VARIABLE COST}}{\text{NUMBER OF COVERS}} = \frac{£500}{100} = £5.00$$

Assuming that a charge of £6.50 per cover is made, then

	£
Sales 100 @ £6.50	650
Less variable cost	500
Contribution to fixed costs	150

As a result, the net loss of the banqueting section for that day will be £50 (£200 less £150).

DECISION-MAKING AND SEASONAL ESTABLISHMENTS

Decision-making techniques can be extremely useful in managing seasonal establishments. Important questions which arise from time to time are: (a) should the establishment be closed during the low season? (b) if so, what additional factors should one consider?

Closure in off-season

EXAMPLE 19.3

The Four Seasons Restaurant is a seasonal establishment. At 31st December 19... the book-keeper of the restaurant prepared the following summary of trading results:

Trading, Profit & Loss Account

Quarters	1	2	3	4
	£	£	£	£
Sales	96,000	144,000	192,000	128,000
Food & beverage costs	38,400	57,600	76,800	51,200
Wages	40,000	48,000	64,000	44,000
Rent & rates	4,800	4,800	4,800	4,800
Advertising	2,400	2,400	2,400	2,400
Depreciation: lease	12,800	12,800	12,800	12,800
Depreciation: other	5,600	5,600	5,600	5,600
Repairs & replacements	1,200	1,600	2,000	1,200
Light & heat	2,800	2,400	2,000	2,800
Miscellaneous expenses	400	400	400	400
	108,400	135,600	170,800	125,200
Net profit/(loss)	(12,400)	8,400	21,200	2,800

Notes:

(a) The policy of the restaurant is to maintain food and beverage costs at 40 per cent of sales.
(b) Wages are allocated to each period as they accrue.
(c) Rent, rates and advertising are apportioned on a time basis.
(d) Depreciation of lease is also apportioned on a time basis; other depreciation is, however, regarded as 50 per cent variable.
(e) Repairs and replacements consist of a fixed element of £800; the balance being fully variable.
(f) Light and heat are allocated to each period on the basis of actual metered consumption.
(g) Miscellaneous expenses: this consists of a large number of small items and is regarded as a fixed cost.

The proprietors of the restaurant expect that the trading results for the following year will not materially differ from those shown above.

They are anxious to improve the profitability of the restaurant and would like you to advise them on the desirability of closing the restaurant during the first quarter of the forthcoming year.

Suggested solution
Basically there are two different methods of deciding whether or not closure during the off-season should be contemplated:

1. To compare the net loss resulting from operations with that which would result in the event of closure (shown in **A** below).
2. To compare the gain resulting from closure (i.e. savings in variable costs) with the loss resulting from closure (i.e. loss of sales revenue). Hence (shown in **B** below):

A

		£
Net loss if restaurant remains open		12,400
Net loss if restaurant closes – i.e. the sum		
of the fixed costs for that period:	£	
Rent & rates	4,800	
Advertising	2,400	
Depreciation-lease	12,800	
Depreciation-other	2,800	
Repairs & replacements	800	
Miscellaneous expenses	400	24,000
		11,600

By closing down the restaurant would therefore be £11,600 worse off.

B

	£	£
Loss of revenue resulting from closure		96,000
Gains resulting from closure (i.e. savings in variable costs):		
Food and beverage costs	38,400	
Wages	40,000	
Depreciation	2,800	
Repairs & replacement	400	
Light & heat	2,800	84,400
		11,600

The result is again as before and at least on the face of it, there is no sound financial reason for closing the restaurant during the first quarter of the following year.

In practice, however, the proprietors of the restaurant would have to take into account some other factors when making this kind of decision. Some of the questions they would have to ask themselves are: (a) How easy or difficult will it be to replace the labour force? (b) Is it desirable to offer key staff a retainer? (c) What will be the effect of closure in the off-season on the volume of sales during the season? (d) Is it possible for the employer to take up alternative employment during the period of closure? Thus the calculations shown above are only the first step.

Closure of a department

EXAMPLE 19.4

Situated in the foyer of the Galway International Hotel is a kiosk, open seven days a week, from 08.00 hrs to 20.00 hrs.

The hotel controller insists that all departments should make a contribution to the general overheads of the hotel and show a satisfactory net profit. Each department is, therefore, charged with a proportion of: administrative and general expenses; advertising and sales promotion; rent and occupancy costs; depreciation; light and heat. The charge has been fixed at 20 per cent of departmental sales.

At 31st December 19... the trading results of the kiosk were ascertained as shown below:

Kiosk
Trading, profit & loss Account

	£	£
Sales		125,000
Less: cost of sales		110,000
Gross profit		15,000
Less: wages	10,000	
Proportion of overheads	25,000	35,000
Net loss		(20,000)

The hotel controller is considering the possible closure of the kiosk and you are asked to comment on the financial consequences of this decision.

Suggested solution

Following the first method in the the previous example, the position is this:

	£
Net loss if kiosk remains open	20,000
Net loss if kiosk closes -i.e. the sum of general overheads whose level would not be affected.	25,000
	(5,000)

It is clear that the hotel would be £5,000 worse off by closing the kiosk.

Following the second method:

	£	£
Loss resulting from closure (sales)		125,000
Gain resulting from closure:		
Cost of sales	110,000	
Wages	10,000	120,000
		(5,000)

Here again we see that, following closure, the hotel would be worse off to the extent of £5,000.

The decision on the possible closure of the kiosk should be made in the light of a strong likelihood that the opportunity cost of the space occupied is nil, i.e. if the kiosk was closed down the space could not be used by another department. Finally one must ask: is the kiosk providing an important service to guests?

There seems therefore to be very strong arguments for not closing the kiosk. The above example demonstrates how the arbitrary apportionment of overheads to all departments may lead to wrong conclusions and incorrect management decisions.

SUMMARY

- Decision accounting is perhaps the most important aspect of accounting from a manager's point of view. Good use of the techniques available can improve profitability and reduce business risk.
- The division of costs into fixed and variable, contribution statements (marginal costing statements) and break-even analysis are the basic tools of decision accounting.
- As a starting point for the decision-making process, all profit and loss accounts should be restructured as contribution statements.
- A contribution statement used with break-even formulae and other such techniques can be used, for example, to forecast profit at any level of sales or to estimate changes to the break-even point caused by cost or price structure changes.
- The student should note that the C/S ratio remains constant (same percentage) whatever the volume of turnover. The only items which change the C/S ratio are: (a) a change in the selling price with no equivalent change in the variable cost; (b) a change in the variable cost with no corresponding change in the selling price.
- Decision accounting can highlight situations where it may be justifiable to sell at a price below total cost.
- The techniques used in this chapter will help managers to make sensible decisions in respect of off-season closure or removal of a department within a hotel or restaurant complex.

PROBLEMS

1. What do you understand by the term 'decision accounting'?

2. List three key areas where decision accounting techiques can be of assistance to management.

3. The Venus Restaurant is a 75 seater restaurant situated close to a town centre.
   The average number of covers served daily is as follows:

Monday	50	Thursday	90
Tuesday	60	Friday	150
Wednesday	70	Saturday	220

   The ASP is £12.00 and the variable costs are 45 per cent of sales. Fixed costs for the six day week are £3,000.
   Using the above information, prepare a tabular statement (using the headings shown below) showing each day's contribution and the total profit for the week.

NoC	ASP	Sales	Variable costs	Contribution
	£	£	£	£

Three proposals for improving the performance of the restaurant have been put forward to management:

(a) To impose a cover charge of £1.75 per cover. It is believed that this measure will reduce the number of covers (NoC) by 15 per cent.

(b) To introduce a cost reduction programme with the aim of reducing variable costs to 40 per cent of sales. This move will not affect the number of covers served during the week.

(c) In addition to proposal (b) it is suggested that improved decor and fittings in the restaurant (adding £250 per week to fixed costs) would increase existing business by 10 per cent.

Required:

(a) calculate which of the above proposals will result in the highest net profit;

(b) show the margin of safety, in covers, for each of these proposals.

4. The Maplin Holiday Camp is considering the replacement of an existing waiter service coffee shop with a self-service coffee shop (alternative service)

Existing Situation

Waiter service

(a) Sales: Tea   2,800 cups @ 18p per cup.
             Coffee   3,500 cups @ 27p per cup.
             Soft drinks 4,800 @ 36p each.
             Cakes etc. 5,000 @ 40p each.
    A gross profit mark-up of 50 per cent on cost is expected.

(b) Direct fixed costs: £1,200 (avoidable if the service is not offered)

(c) Indirect fixed costs: £300 (will remain whether or not the service is offered).

Alternative Service

Self service

(a) The gross profit mark-up on cost will be reduced to 33.33 per cent for drinks in order to stimulate demand, the revised estimates being:
       Tea: 5,000 cups; Coffee: 7,000 cups; Soft drinks 10,000.
       The mark-up on cakes, etc. will remain at 50 per cent and demand is expected to be 8,000 units.

(b) Direct fixed costs: £1,500 (avoidable if the service is not offered)

(c) Indirect fixed costs: £2,000 (will remain whether or not the service is offered).

Required:

(a) calculate the net profit or loss for each strategy and advise the management whether or not the proposed changes to the coffee shop are financially worthwhile;

(b) give specific examples of items which may make up the direct and indirect fixed costs referred to in the question.

5. The Greenacre Restaurant has been suffering losses for the last two

years and this is causing the management considerable concern. The following statement relates to the last three months' trading:

Number of covers		2,500
	£	£
Sales		40,000
Cost of sales	16,000	
Other variable costs	6,000	22,000
Contribution		18,000
Less fixed costs		20,000
Net loss		(2,000)

The owners feel that with better marketing they would be able to increase the covers per quarter to 4,000 without having to alter the selling price. The extra marketing costs would amount to £5,000 per quarter.

Alternatively, they could combine the marketing exercise with an increase in menu prices, although this would have an effect on the quarterly covers as follows:

Increase in menu price per cover £	Estimated covers per quarter
0.50	3,800
1.00	3,600
1.50	3,300
2.00	3,000

Required:
Prepare a table to show (by calculation) which of the above alternatives would maximize profits.

6. Vitamins Ltd operate a works canteen for the provision of meals to their employees. They serve an average of 500 meals per day, 5 days per week for 50 weeks of the year, several choices being offered each day. The annual cost of food is £93,750, wages £62,500, overheads £78,120. The company wish to provide meals at an average charge of £1.25 each and are willing to subsidize the canteen to the extent of £50,000 per annum. The company occupying an adjoining factory have approached Vitamins Ltd and asked if they would be prepared to serve their employees with meals (400 per day) of the same quality at £1.25 each. They are prepared to take the meals at a different time from the Vitamins employees, so there would be no difficulty regarding accommodation. Additional labour costing £25,000 per annum would be required in the canteen.

As canteen manager, you are asked to suggest a pricing policy (i.e. the percentages to be added to the cost of each dish) and give your recommendation as to whether the company should be prepared to supply the meals to the neighbouring firm on the terms suggested.

You should supply detailed figures to support your recommendation.

7. (a) How important is the distinction between fixed and variable costs?
   (b) From the information given below calculate the charge per cover in respect of a menu already agreed with your clients.

Costs for 50 covers

		£
Food stores:		60
Fishmonger		65
Butcher		85
Dairy		15
Greengrocer		30
Other costs:	Proportion of fixed salaries	100
	Wages of part-time labour	90
	Proportion of fixed overheads	180
	Variable overheads	95

Your intention is to achieve a net profit of 10 per cent on all sales.
   (c) From the information given above, calculate the lowest acceptable charge per cover, assuming that there is no alternative business for that day.

8. The Bonheur Hotel has been established for many years and can cater for a maximum of 12,000 covers per quarter. The average spend is £15.00, of which £12.00 is in respect of food, and £3.00 in respect of beverages. Food is costed to give a gross profit of 60 per cent, and beverages to give a gross profit of 55 per cent. Other variable costs amount to 15 per cent of total sales and fixed overheads are £60,000 per quarter.

A new manager has recently been appointed with a brief to improve profitability and he has put forward the following proposals:

   (a) to reorganize the layout of the restaurant, with a view to increasing the maximum capacity to 14,000 covers per quarter;
   (b) to significantly increase the number of permanent staff at the expense of part-timers, thus increasing fixed overheads to £78,000 per quarter and reducing the other variable costs to 10 per cent of sales;
   (c) to increase menu food prices by 10 per cent and beverage prices by 5 per cent.

Required:
   (a) calculate for both the current and proposed operation of the restaurant:
   (i) the contribution/sales ratio.
   (ii) the quarterly break-even points in sales revenue and number of covers.

(iii) the net profit arising from the maximum sales per quarter.

(iv) state if you would make the changes and any problems you may foresee.

(b) draw up two break-even charts to illustrate your answer; one for the current situation and one for the proposed.

9. Jax Café is a seasonal establishment. The proprietor informs you that his takings are satisfactory between the beginning of April and the end of September, but that the rest of the year is very slack. He thinks his business makes a net loss in the off-season and asks you whether he should close down between October and March. He further explains that if he closed down in the off-season he would be able to work in his brother's business for a period of three months at a salary of £120 per week.

On checking his accounts you find that his sales and expenses for the past year were:

	Total	April to September	October to March
	£	£	£
Sales	101,000	72,000	29,000
Cost of food used	40,650	28,750	11,900
Wages and National Insurance	25,950	18,250	7,700
Gas and electricity	7,600	3,250	4,350
Depreciation: lease	8,200		
Depreciation: other assets	2,000		
Other expenses: rates, insurance, accountant's fees, telephone, etc.	7,300		

Advise the proprietor.

10. The El Peso Restaurant is a seasonal establishment. Its accounts are prepared twice yearly at 30th September and at 31st March. The following information is extracted from the books of the restaurant in respect of the year ended 31st March 19...

	Season (half year to 30th September)	Off-season (half year to 31st March)
	£	£
Restaurant sales	228,070	104,960
Bar sales	71,940	34,050
Cost of restaurant sales	91,510	43,490
Cost of bar sales	27,460	12,620
Wages and salaries	106,030	63,510
Rent and rates	15,000	15,000
Depreciation: lease	16,000	16,000
Depreciation: other assets	9,000	6,000
Lighting and heating	2,600	8,000
Cleaning materials	3,060	2,500

	£	£
Postage and stationery	2,540	1,490
Laundry	5,810	4,520
Fire insurance, etc.	1,000	1,000
Sundry expenses	2,000	1,500

Required:

(a) prepare a trading and profit and loss account for the year ended 31st March 19..., showing a separate result for each half year;

(b) state whether or not, in your opinion, the restaurant should be closed down in the off-season.

11. The Ebb-n-Flow Restaurant is a seasonal establishment in a seaside resort. It was opened on 1st January, 19..., and at the end of its first year's operation the following analysis of its trading results was prepared:

	Jan. Feb. £	Mar. Apr. £	May June £	July Aug. £	Sept. Oct. £	Nov. Dec. £
Sales	24,000	32,000	36,000	48,000	38,000	30,000
Less Cost of sales	9,600	12,800	14,400	19,200	15,200	12,000
Gross profit	14,400	19,200	21,600	28,800	22,800	18,000
Wages	10,000	11,000	12,000	16,000	14,000	12,000
Rent and rates	1,200	1,200	1,200	1,200	1,200	1,200
Advertising	600	600	600	600	600	600
Depreciation: lease	3,200	3,200	3,200	3,200	3,200	3,200
Depreciation: other	1,400	1,400	1,400	1,400	1,400	1,400
Repairs and replacem't	300	300	400	500	400	300
Light and heat	700	700	600	500	600	600
Miscellan's expenses	100	100	100	100	100	100
Total expenses	17,500	18,500	19,500	23,500	21,500	19,400
Profit		700	2,100	5,300	1,300	
Loss	(3,100)					(1,400)

Notes on allocation and apportionment of expenditure:

(a) Rent and rates are apportioned on a time basis.

(b) Advertising is a fixed annual allocation.

(c) Depreciation of lease is apportioned on a time basis; other depreciation is regarded as 50 per cent variable.

(d) Wages—actual cost is allocated to each period.

(e) Repairs and replacements: this contains a fixed element of £200; the balance is regarded as variable.

(f) Light and heat, metered consumption allocated to each period.

(g) Miscellaneous expenses: this consists of a large number of small items and is treated as a fixed cost.

The proprietors are of the opinion that the trading results for the second year should not materially differ from those for the first year. They are, however, concerned about the losses incurred in the off-season. Advise them as to whether or not it is desirable to close the restaurant during any particular part of the year.

Departmental accounting $\boxed{\textbf{20}}$

INTRODUCTION

The larger an organization grows the more important control mechanisms become as part of the overall business structure. Most larger hospitality operations break down into departments with a head of department in charge of each. Departmental accounts are aimed at producing an accounting statement which is useful to this process, for example, by separating costs into costs controllable by the head of department and costs that are not.

A well-designed system of departmental accounting will promote cost consciousness and enable a fair assessment of the contribution of each departmental manager to overall profits.

OBJECTIVES

On completion of this chapter you should be able to:

- understand the need for departmental accounting;
- differentiate between controllable and uncontrollable costs from the departmental manager's point of view;
- state the objectives of departmental accounting;
- know the meaning of direct costs and indirect costs;
- list the main methods of departmental accounting;
- draw up departmental accounts using each of the three listed methods;
- understand the arguments for and against each of the methods used;
- deal with the apportionment of cost as applied to the net profit method;
- use correctly the two methods of apportionment described in this chapter.

DEFINITION AND AIMS

Departmental accounting may be described as a method of book-keeping and accounting, the purpose of which is to find how much profit (or loss) is produced by each section or department of a business. In this context the term 'department' means a revenue-producing department, as trading results cannot be obtained for non-revenue producing departments such as maintenance, marketing or administration, etc.

One of the major benefits of departmental accounts is that costs are divided into direct and indirect costs. Direct costs are those costs incurred exclusively by the department in question (e.g as food costs would be to the food sales department) whereas indirect costs are general costs incurred by the establishment as a whole and shared between departments on some arbitrary basis (e.g rent and rates). Direct and indirect costs are often referred to as controllable and uncontrollable costs respectively. This is because direct costs should be fully controllable by the departmental manager whereas indirect costs are normally not controllable by him.

In addition, in a business consisting of several departments, it is clearly necessary to find the separate results of each department. Otherwise, the fact that some departments are being operated at a loss will not be revealed, and over a long period the position might be as shown below:

ABC Catering Ltd

	Dept A £	Dept B £	Dept C £	Total £
Sales	30,000	60,000	75,000	165,000
Less Costs	18,000	42,000	78,000	138,000
Profit/ (Loss)	12,000	18,000	(3,000)	27,000

Note: The overall profit on sales, namely £27,000 on a turnover of £165,000 is probably quite satisfactory; yet in the absence of departmental accounting the loss incurred by Department C would not be revealed.

Book-keeping records

In order to be able to ascertain the profit (or loss) of each department, suitably analysed records – subsidiary books and ledger accounts – must be kept. The exact analysis of income and expenditure depends on the particular circumstances of each business and on the degree of departmentalization desired. The following analytical records show how an analysis may be undertaken in the case of a large licensed restaurant. It is assumed that the restaurant has three revenue producing departments, namely, food, drink and tobaccos.

In addition to the purchases, sales and stocks, possibly other items would have to be analysed and recorded in the same manner.

Purchases Day Book

Date		F.	Inv.	Total	Food	Bev.	Tobacco
19...				£	£	£	£
Jan 1	A B Brown & Co.	16	001	480	480		
" 2	Irish Whiskey Ltd	27	002	840		840	
" 3	N O Nicotine Ltd	53	003	270			270
" 4	B M Grocer & Son	19	004	720	720		
	etc.						
" 31	To Purchases a/c	116		48,000	33,000	12,000	3,000

Purchases Account

Date		Total	Food	Bev	Tobac							
		£	£	£	£							
Jan 31	Purchases DB	48,000	33,000	12,000	3,000							

The columnar purchases account shown above can be used to collect separate totals for food, beverage, tobacco, etc.

DEPARTMENTAL TRADING AND PROFIT AND LOSS ACCOUNT

There are three main methods by which departmental final accounts may be prepared. These are the:

1. Gross profit method;
2. Departmental profit method;
3. Net profit method.

Gross profit method

This is the method most commonly used in hospitality establishments. It entails an analysis of purchases, sales and stocks only, i.e. items affecting the gross profit of each department. Its aim is to control the gross profit (kitchen profit, bar profit, etc.) of each department. Expenses such as wages, salaries, gas, electricity, etc. are not analysed and are debited in the profit and loss account against the total of gross profit plus any other income such as room sales, discounts received, and investment income.

The main advantage of this method is its simplicity. Its disadvantages are: first, no attempt is made to control departmental expenses such as wages, salaries, lighting, heating, etc. Second, a department may earn a high percentage of gross profit yet, if its overheads are high, contribute little to the net profit of the business.

The application of the gross profit method is illustrated in Figure 20.1 by the trading, profit and loss account.

The Magic Carpet Restaurant
Trading and profit and loss account for year ended 31st December 19 . . .

	Food £	Drink £	Tobaccos £	Total £
Sales	240,000	140,000	20,000	400,000
Less: Cost of sales				
Opening stock	5,000	7,800	1,200	14,000
Purchases (net)	120,000	80,400	19,600	220,000
	125,000	88,200	20,800	234,000
Less Closing stock	7,000	7,400	1,600	16,000
Cost of goods sold	118,000	80,800	19,200	218,000
Gross profit	122,000	59,200	800	182,000
Add other income				
Discounts received				4,000
				186,000
Less other expenses				
Wages and salaries			98,000	
Rent and rates			19,200	
Lighting and heating			12,600	
Depreciation			10,000	
Repairs and replacements			7,000	
Printing and stationery			6,000	
Miscellaneous expenses			1,200	154,000
Net profit				32,000

Figure 20.1 Magic Carpet Restaurant trading and profit and loss account

Departmental profit method

This second method, excellent as it is, requires a rather elaborate set of records and a high degree of departmentalization, and therefore can only be applied in large hospitality operations. The aim of this method is to ascertain and control the departmental (controllable) profit of each section of a business.

Departmental profit may be defined as the total revenue of a department less the cost of goods sold (if any), departmental wages, salaries and any other expenses attributable to (and controllable by) that department. All other expenses – those incurred on behalf of the business as a whole – such as rent, rates, advertising, etc. are debited against the total of departmental profits in the general profit and loss account.

A specimen general profit and loss account, illustrating this particular method, is shown in Figure 20.2.

Grand Hotel Ltd
Profit and loss account
for year ended 31st December 19...

Department	Net sales	Cost of sales	Wages	Direct dept. expenses	Departmental profit
	£	£	£	£	£
Room sales	590,000		(110,000)	(172,000)	308,000
Food sales	425,000	(140,000)	(105,000)	(110,000)	70,000
Bev. sales	165,000	(48,000)	(45,000)	(26,000)	46,000
Other sales	39,000	(20,000)	(9,000)	(8,000)	2,000
Rents receivable	24,000				24,000
Misc. income	10,000				10,000
	1,253,000	(208,000)	(269,000)	(316,000)	460,000

Less: Undistributed expenditure: £

Rent and rates	55,000
Repairs and maintenance	27,000
Depreciation	89,000
Heat, light and power	12,000
Advertising	52,000
Administration expenses	85,000
Miscellaneous expenses	34,000
	354,000
Net profit	106,000

Figure 20.2 Specimen hotel profit and loss account

In addition to the profit and loss account, it is usual to prepare for each revenue-producing department a separate, detailed statement of operating results.

It will be appreciated that this method is both good accounting and good management as, in effect, each departmental manager is made responsible for all income and expenditure he is capable of controlling. In order to produce an adequate amount of departmental profit, he must control not only the cost of goods he sells but also other direct expenses incurred by his department.

The departmental method divides all costs into controllable and uncontrollable costs. This means 'controllable' by the departmental manager. This is an aspect of 'responsibility accounting', where the managers are only responsible for the costs which they should be able to control and not fixed costs or apportioned costs over which they have largely no control. Apart from being a much fairer approach to management assessment it is also widely recognized that it motivates managers better.

The student should note that the terms 'controllable' and 'uncontrollable' costs are basically the same as 'direct' and 'indirect' costs and indeed very similiar to 'variable' and 'fixed' costs.

Net profit method

Under this method all expenses are debited to the revenue-producing departments in order to arrive at a figure of net profit for each of them.

Expenses which are attributable to, or originate from, a certain department are allocated to that department. Thus, the cost of kitchen wages would be debited against food sales; barmen's wages would be debited against bar sales, etc.

Expenses which are incurred on behalf of the business as a whole are apportioned (split) on some fair and reasonable basis as between the departments concerned. Thus, rent and rates could be apportioned on the basis of the floor space occupied by each department; general manager's salary could be apportioned on the basis of the turnover of each department, etc.

The net profit method is illustrated by the profit and loss account shown in Figure 20.3.

The Bombay Duck Restaurant
Trading and profit and loss account for year ended 31st December 19...

	Ceylon Room £	Kashmir Room £	American Bar £	Total £
Sales	199,600	254,200	223,600	677,400
Less: Cost of sales				
Opening stock	2,500	3,500	6,500	12,500
Purchases(net)	99,500	142,600	101,400	343,500
	102,000	146,100	107,900	356,000
Less closing stock	2,000	3,100	6,400	11,500
	100,000	143,000	101,500	344,500
Gross profit	99,600	111,200	122,100	332,900
Less: other expenses				
Wages and salaries	46,500	64,100	22,100	132,700
Rent and rates	9,300	12,100	3,000	24,400
Gas and electricity	4,300	6,100	1,200	11,600
Repairs and renewals	8,100	12,400	6,700	27,200
Depreciation	6,700	8,500	4,600	19,800
Miscellaneous exp.	5,300	6,200	1,300	12,800
Total other expenses	80,200	109,400	38,900	228,500
Net profit	19,400	1,800	83,200	104,400

Figure 20.3 Bombay Duck Restaurant trading and profit and loss account

Arguments in favour of this method are:

(a) expenditure which has to be apportioned benefits all the departments concerned; each department should, therefore, be charged with a fair proportion of the total;

(b) a department may produce a large amount of gross profit, yet, if its fixed expenses are high, show little or no net profit;

(c) the main purpose of business is to make profit; an attempt should, therefore, be made to find how much net profit has been made by each department.

Arguments against this method are:

(a) whatever method of apportionment is chosen it is always an arbitrary method;

(b) apportioned (indirect) expenses are incurred to benefit the business as a whole – if a particular department were closed down many of these expenses would remain unchanged;

(c) the apportionment of expenses may give a misleading picture of the results achieved by departments.

The net profit method is shown here simply to explain how it is applied in what is hoped is a small minority of establishments. Most certainly, the intention is not to recommend it as good accounting practice.

Balance sheet

Whatever method of departmental accounting is in use the balance sheet of the business is not affected, except that it is usual to show separately the stocks of each department.

APPORTIONMENT OF COSTS

In order to complete the departmental profit and loss account using the net profit method it will be necessary to apportion all the indirect expenses, that is to say, expenses which are not specific to one of the departments.

Kitchen wages are obviously a direct expense of the food department – clearly the whole output of the kitchen is used to generate food sales. However, there are many expenses which cannot be directly related to any one department. The salary of the hotel manager is a good example; the manager's time will be divided between all the departments of the hotel and it would be extremely difficult to divide time between departments with any real accuracy. Many other expenses fall into this category, e.g. wages clerks, hotel accountants and other similiar employees; also items such as rent and rates, gas and electricity (unless individually metered) are most difficult to apportion.

All apportionment of costs is arbitrary. It is important therefore to use as fair a basis as possible. Hence rent and rates should normally be apportioned on a floor area basis; a manager's salary is perhaps best apportioned on a turnover basis.

METHODS OF APPORTIONMENT

There are a number of different methods of apportionment, but for our purposes we will confine ourselves to the two main methods, the first based on turnover, the second based on floor space used.

Apportionment based on turnover

Using this method costs are divided in proportion to sales. It may be considered equitable in the sense that the departments generating the highest revenue will bear the highest share of costs.

EXAMPLE 20.1

The total sales of the Hotel California amounted to £700,000. This was made up as follows: Room Sales £322,000, Food sales £231,000, Drink sales £147,000. After allocating all direct expenses to each department it is necessary to apportion administration salaries of £28,000 and miscellaneous expenses of £33,500.

Proceed as shown below:

Suggested solution
Stage 1
Work out the sales mix vis à vis departments

	Rooms £	Food £	Drink £	Total £
Sales	322,000	231,000	147,000	700,000
Sales mix %	46%*	33%	21%	100%

$$*\text{Rooms } \% = \frac{322,000 \times 100}{700,000} = 46\%$$

Stage 2
Apportionment (using sales mix %)

		Admin Salaries £	Misc. Expenses £
Total cost for apportionment	100%	28,000	33,500
Rooms	46%	12,880	15,410
Food	33%	9,240	11,055
Drink	21%	5,880	7,035
		28,000	33,500

Apportionment based on floor area

Many people believe this method is a fairer method of apportionment of general costs because it takes into account the amount of space occupied and the opportunity cost of that space.

The student should note that the only floor areas we take into account are those floor areas which are used exclusively by the departments concerned. This means that any public areas (shared by all departments) will be excluded from the calculation. In a hotel, for example, areas such as reception, main lounge, service areas, etc. will normally be excluded. Corridors on the 1st and 2nd floor, etc. are usually judged as being exclusive to the Rooms department.

EXAMPLE 20.2

The following details relate to the Abraham Hotel.

Floor areas occupied:

	Sq. m	Index
Restaurant	1,700	(1)
Bar	500	(2)
Wine cellar	300	(3)
Reception, offices etc	600	(4)
Kitchen, food stores	900	(5)
Lounge	700	(6)
Bedrooms (1st & 2nd floors)	3,800	(7)
Corridors on 1st & 2nd floor	800	(8)

After allocating all direct costs to each department It is necessary to apportion rent and rates of £67,000 and gas and electricity of £42,000 using an equitable method.

Proceed as shown below:

Suggested solution

The relevant floor areas are as follows

	Index	Sq.m	%
Rooms dept	(7) + (8)	4,600	57.5%
Food dept	(1) + (5)	2,600	32.5%
Drink dept	(2) + (3)	800	10.0%
Total floor space for allocation purposes		8,000	100.0%

Note: Items (4) and (6) above are regarded as 'shared areas' and as such are excluded from the calculation.

Apportionment (using floor space)

		Rent & rates £	Gas & electric. £
Total cost for apportionment	100.00%	67,000	42,000
Rooms	57.50%	38,525	24,150
Food	32.50%	21,775	13,650
Drink	10.00%	6,700	4,200
		67,000	42,000

SUMMARY

- The main purpose of departmental accounting is to assist in the control of costs. The larger the establishment the more important these accounts become.
- Departmental accounts promote fairness in the sense that costs are divided into controllable and uncontrollable costs. This, in turn, allows departmental managers to be judged/appraised by their general manager against the costs and revenues they can control.
- There are three methods of departmental accounting:
  (a) gross profit method;
  (b) departmental profit method;
  (c) net profit method.
- In larger establishments the departmental profit method is the most widely used, due to flaws in the other two methods.
- It is necessary to apportion the indirect costs when using the net profit method. Apportionment by its very nature is always arbitrary.
- There are many different methods of apportionment of which only two are dealt with in this chapter.
- The two main methods of apportionment are:
  (a) on the basis of turnover
  (b) on the basis of floor space.

PROBLEMS

1. Write short explanatory notes on the following methods of departmental accounting:
   (a) gross profit method;
   (b) departmental profit method;
   (c) net profit method.

2. Distinguish between the allocation and the apportionment of expenditure.

3. What method of apportionment would you use in respect of the following:
   (a) rent and rates;
   (b) depreciation of premises;
   (c) depreciation of equipment;
   (d) general manager's salary;

(e) advertising;

(f) administration expenses?

4. Explain the purposes of departmental accounting and state what modifications it entails in the layout of the subsidiary books and the ledger.

5. The following balances were extracted from the accounts of the Blue Moon Restaurant at 31st December 19. .

		£
Stocks at 1st Jan 19. . .	food	20,300
	beverages	16,700
	cigarettes	3,080
Purchases:	food	394,700
	beverages	189,420
	cigarettes	24,600
Sales:	food	847,480
	beverages	472,500
	cigarettes	28,140
Wages and salaries		299,060
Light and heat		38,940
Cleaning materials		6,380
Postage and stationery		3,120
Laundry		9,880
Rates		17,460
Advertising		10,000
Repairs and replacements		2,680
Depreciation		28,520

Required:

Stocks at 31st December 19 . . . were valued as follows: food – £16,900; beverages – £12,680; cigarettes – £2,520. You are informed that the capital invested in the restaurant amounts to £400,000.

(a) Prepare the restaurant's trading, profit and loss account for the year ended 31st December 19 . . . The form and presentation of the account must be such as to convey the maximum information to the proprietor.

(b) Comment on the trading results of the restaurant on the basis of the information available.

6. The following figures relate to a factory canteen for the six months ending 31st March 1997. Prepare, in tabular form, a trading and profit and loss account, showing the contribution each type of sale makes towards the general expenses and profit.

	£
1st October 1996 Opening stocks	
food	18,150
minerals	2,900
tobacco	8,200
Purchases for the six months	
food	35,750
minerals	8,450
tobaccos	15,750
31st March 1997 Closing stocks	
food	14,900
minerals	2,450
tobaccos	7,400
Fuel	5,050
Wages: kitchen	20,150
counter and clerical	16,900
Receipts:	
food	96,100
minerals	10,050
tobaccos	17,900
General expenses	2,650

7. The Supreme Hotel is owned by J Smythe and T Brown, and their capitals are £400,000 and £300,000 respectively. The following balances have been extracted from their books at 31st December 19...

	£	£
Stock—1st January 19...		
food	16,800	
liquor	42,000	
cigarettes and tobacco	7,000	
sundries	4,800	
Purchases for the year:		
food	1,056,000	
liquor	415,000	
cigarettes and tobacco	96,000	
sundries	34,000	
Wages	257,200	
National Insurance	24,800	
Discounts	1,560	5,500
Rates and water	19,200	
Fuels, etc.	56,400	
Lighting and heating	92,000	
Interest received		2,400
Partners' salaries paid during the year:		
J Smythe	35,000	
T Brown	36,000	
Office salaries	123,200	
Rent	155,000	
Printing and stationery	14,400	

	£	£
Dividends received		4,000
Advertising	18,800	
Cleaning materials	13,800	
Laundry	22,000	
Drawings:		
J Smythe	104,000	
T Brown	90,000	
Income		
apartments		1,573,600
restaurant		479,200
liquors		516,600
cigarettes and tobacco		130,560
sundries		55,600

Required:

Prepare a trading and profit and loss account for the year and the partners' current accounts as they would appear in the ledger, taking into account the following additional matters:

(a) Partners share profits and losses in proportion to their capitals.

(b) Partners are entitled to interest on capital at 5 per cent per annum.

(c) Partners are entitled to salaries as follows: J Smythe – £50,000 per annum; T Brown – £40,000 per annum.

(d) J Smythe has loaned the firm £100,000 and is entitled to interest on this at 5 per cent per annum.

(e) On 1st January 19 . . ., the credit balances on current accounts were: J Smythe – £5,000 and T Brown – £2,000.

(f) The stocks at 31st December 19 . . . were:
food	£15,200
liquors	£60,000
cigarettes & tobacco	£8,400
sundries	£2,000

(g) Make provision for depreciation as follows:
premises (valued at £220,000) at 5 per cent per annum;
equipment (valued at £160,000) at 10 per cent per annum;
linen and cutlery £10,000 for the year.

(h) Provide £1,500 against doubtful debts.

(i) Accounts owing:
| stationery | £5,000 |
| laundry | £3,400 |

(j) Rates paid in advance £3,200.

8. The Troika Catering Co. Ltd operates an establishment consisting of:
- restaurant;
- banqueting department;
- bar.

The company operates a system of departmental accounts and, periodically, separate trading results are obtained for each department of the business.

(a) From the following information you are required to prepare the company's departmental trading, profit and loss account for the year ended 31st December 19 . . .

(b) If, having arrived at the net profit/loss for each department, you find that the results are misleading, suggest an alternative method of arriving at the necessary departmental results.

		£
Sales:	restaurant	750,000
	banqueting	450,000
	bar	300,000
Cost of food and beverages sold:	restaurant	300,000
	banqueting	150,000
	bar	112,500
Wages and salaries:	restaurant	217,500
	banqueting	112,500
	bar	22,500
Repairs and replacements:	restaurant	31,500
	banqueting	19,500
	bar	6,000
Gas and electricity		45,000
Rent and rates		90,000
Depreciation		105,000
Postage and telephone		7,500
Advertising		60,000
Laundry and cleaning		9,000
Office and administration expenses		90,000

Note: Expenses which cannot be allocated to particular departments are apportioned as follows:

(a) Gas and electricity: restaurant   60 per cent
banqueting   35 per cent
bar   5 per cent

(b) Rent, rates and depreciation are apportioned on the basis of floor space occupied: restaurant   60 per cent
banqueting   30 per cent
bar   10 per cent

(c) All other expenses are apportioned on the basis of turnover.

US uniform system of accounts for hotels

21

INTRODUCTION

Since the last edition of this volume, we have witnessed a great deal of interest in the US Uniform System of Accounts for Hotels. Whilst until the late 1970s, the main users of the system were the large US based international hotel corporations, there are now many medium-sized and large hotels which have adopted the uniform system as it stands or adapted it somewhat to suit their particular circumstances.

As explained later in this chapter, the popularity of the uniform system is due to its main characteristics: it is simple and easy to understand; it is flexible and adaptable; it represents the best hotel accounting practice.

OBJECTIVES

On completion of this chapter you should be able to:

- appreciate the importance of the Uniform System – both to the individual hotel and the hospitality industry;
- use the correct terminology relevant to the Uniform System;
- understand the structure of the Departmental Statement of Income, its compilation and relationship to the departmental schedules;
- see clearly the principal advantages of the Uniform System;
- prepare a Departmental Statement of Income and write up the appropriate schedules.

DEVELOPMENT OF UNIFORM SYSTEMS

The development of systems of uniform accounting (and uniform costing systems) is by no means a recent development. Probably the most successful uniform system was the one introduced by the Federation of Master Printers in 1911. Subsequently, a number of industries introduced uniform systems and, inevitably, some of these were more successful than others.

In 1969, HM Stationery Office published, on behalf of the Economic Development Committee for Hotels and Catering, a scheme of uniform accounts for hotels – *A Standard System of Hotel Accounting*. Two years later, HM Stationery Office published a companion volume, entitled *A Standard System of Catering Accounting*. Regrettably, neither the hotel nor the catering system enjoyed a great deal of acceptance in the hotel and catering industry.

Corresponding developments on the other side of the Atlantic were, however, more fruitful. In March 1926, the Hotel Association of New York City adopted and recommended to its members a newly formulated *Uniform System of Accounts for Hotels*. In September of that year, the American Hotel Association of the United States and Canada adopted the Uniform System. The system has been revised from time to time and the latest, the eighth version, was approved in 1985 and became effective in 1986.

TERMINOLOGY

Students should note the following differences between British and American terminology:

1. American accountants (including hotel accountants) do not use the term 'profit' – the term 'income' is used instead. Hence, throughout the Uniform System net profit is described as net income and departmental profit as departmental income. The only exception is gross profit which is still in use. Also, it should be noted that the term 'revenue' is used instead of 'sales'.
2. Many British accountants and hotel executives continue to use the term 'gross operating profit'. It should be pointed out that this term was discontinued at the seventh revision of the Uniform System. It is important to use the correct terminology: students should avoid the term 'gross operating profit' and use the correct term 'income before fixed charges' or 'income before management fees and fixed charges' – as the case may be.

DEPARTMENTAL STATEMENT OF INCOME

In Figure 21.1 we show the Departmental Statement of Income. It should be noted that it consists of three parts:

• The upper portion relates to departmental operations. From the net revenue of each department we deduct the cost of sales (if any), departmental payroll and related expenses as well as other departmental expenses in order to arrive at the resulting figure of departmental income or departmental loss.
• The second (middle) part of the Departmental Statement of Income lists the 'Undistributed Operating Expenses'. The total of these is deducted from the total of departmental incomes (less, of course, any departmental losses) to arrive at the 'Income before Fixed Charges'.
• Finally, in the third part fixed charges are deducted, such as rent, taxes,

DEPARTMENTAL STATEMENT OF INCOME

		Current Period				
Operating Departments	Schedule	**Net Revenues**	**Cost of Sales**	**Payroll and Related Expenses**	**Other Expenses**	**Income (Loss)**
Rooms	1	$	$	$	$	$
Food and beverage	2					
Telephone	3					
Garage and Parking	4					
Guest laundry	5					
Golf course	6					
Golf pro shop	7					
Tennis – racquet club	8					
Tennis pro shop	9					
Health club	10					
Swimming pool – cabanas – baths	11					
Other operated deptartments						
Rentals and other income	12					
Total Operating Deptartments						
Undistributed Operating Expenses						
Administrative and general	13					
Data processing	14					
Human resources	15					
Transportation	16					
Marketing	17					
Guest entertainment	18					
Energy costs	19					
Property operation and maintenance	20					
Total Undistributed Operating Expenses						
Income before Management Fees and Fixed Charges		$	$	$	$	
Management fees					$	
Rent, taxes and insurance	21					
Interest expenses	21					
Depreciation and amortization	21					
Income before Income Taxes						
Income taxes	22					
Net Income						$

Figure 21.1 Departmental Satement of Income (reproduced courtesy of The Hotel Association of New York City, Inc.)

insurance, interest, depreciation and amortization (as well as any management fees), to arrive at 'Income before Income Taxes'. Any income taxes are then deducted before we finally show the figure of 'Net Income'.

Treatment of operating departments

It should be noted that all operating departments are treated in a uniform manner. Whether the department is the rooms department, food and beverage department, health club or whatever, the method of arriving at the departmental income (or loss) is exactly the same.

Flexibility and adaptability

The Uniform System is both flexible and adaptable: whatever the type of the hotel operation and whatever the range and variety of services provided, the Departmental Statement of Income will always accommodate any differences from one hotel to another. Thus a hotel which does not operate a health club will remove schedule 10. If it operates a department not listed under 'Operating Departments', e.g. boat trips, this will be shown in the space provided for 'other Operating Departments'.

Aspects of responsibility

The layout of the Departmental Statement of Income is such as to indicate responsibility for operating results. Persons immediately responsible for departmental incomes are, presumably, department heads; income before fixed charges is ordinarily the responsibility of the general manager. Finally, net income (which is arrived at after deducting fixed and uncontrollable expenses) should be regarded as the responsibility of top management (board of directors).

DEPARTMENTAL SCHEDULES

As may be seen from Figure 21.1, there is a large number of departmental schedules, and it would be impossible in the space available here to describe them all. We are, therefore, showing two specimen schedules – one for an operated (i.e. revenue producing) department, the Food and Beverage schedule, and one for another (a non-revenue producing department or a cost centre) the Administrative and General schedule. As all departments are treated in the same manner there is, in fact, little difference from one schedule to another. Further schedules will be illustrated in the numerical example – the Grand Hotel – later in this chapter.

Our second illustration is a departmental schedule for food and beverage shown below in Figure 21.2:

In Figure 21.2, we show the departmental schedule for Food and

Schedule 2

FOOD AND BEVERAGE

Current
Period
19

Revenue
  Food
  Beverage $
    Total   ————

Allowances   ————

Net Revenue

Other Income   ————
    Total Revenue   ————

Cost of Sales
  Cost of food consumed
    Less cost of employee meals   ————
  Net cost of food sales
  Cost of beverage sales
  Other cost of sales   ————
    Net Cost of Sales   ————

Gross Profit   ————

Expenses
  Salaries and wages
  Employee benefits   ————
    Total Payroll and Related Expenses   ————

  Other Expenses
    China, glassware, silver and linen
    Contract cleaning
    Laundry and dry cleaning
    Licenses
    Music and entertainment
    Operating supplies
    Uniforms
    Other   ————
    Total Other Expenses   ————

Total Expenses   ————

Departmental Income (Loss) $ ————

Figure 21.2 Departmental Schedule for Food and Beverage (reproduced courtesy of The Hotel Association of New York City, Inc.)

Beverage. It should be noticed that food and beverage is treated as one department. The basic pattern here is:

1. We show some analysis of total revenue, from which we deduct any allowances to arrive at the figure of net revenue.
2. We deduct:
   (a) the cost of sales (to arrive at the combined figure of food and beverage gross profit;
   (b) total payroll and related expenses; and
   (c) other expenses to obtain the figure of departmental income (loss).

In Figure 21.3, we show the departmental schedule for Administrative and General Expenses. This is not a revenue producing department, but one where costs are incurred, i.e. a cost centre. The total cost of administrative and general expenses will consist of two cost categories:

(a) Total Payroll and Related Expenses; and
(b) Total Other Expenses.

Only these two totals will appear in the Departmental Statement of Income.

The reader will have noticed that our consideration of the Uniform System has been limited to the profit and loss account (income statement). We have had, in fact, nothing to say about the balance sheet. The reasons for this are twofold. First, the balance sheet is, in most situations, prepared infrequently – annually or half-yearly – whilst the control and reporting procedures based on the income statement take place more frequently. Second, the structure of the balance sheet as such is not in any way affected by the Uniform System.

Schedule 13

ADMINISTRATIVE AND GENERAL

Current
Period
19

Salaries and wages $

Employee Benefits

    Total Payroll and Related Expenses

Other Expenses

    Cash overages and shortages

    Credit card commissions

    Credit and collection

    Data processing

    Donations

    Dues and subscriptions

    Executive office

    Human resources

    Insurance

    Internal audit

    Internal communication systems

    Loss and damage

    Operating supplies

    Postage and telegrams

    Professional fees

    Provision for doubtful accounts

    Security

    Telephone

    Transportation

    Travel and entertainment

    Other

        Total Other Expenses

Total Administrative and General Expenses $

Figure 21.3 Departmental schedule for Administration and General Expenses (reproduced courtesy of The Hotel Association of New York City, Inc.)

WORKED EXAMPLE

We have now introduced the uniform system and our next task is to look at a practical example. The Grand Hotel is a four-star hotel with 150 rooms. In the example which follows we show the hotel's Departmental Statement of Income and departmental schedules for Rooms, Food and Beverage and Administrative and General Expenses in Figures 21.4, 21.5, 21.6 and 21.7.

Grand Hotel Ltd
Departmental Statement of Income for year ended 31 December 1996

	Net Revenues £000	Cost of Sales £000	Payroll & Rel. Exps £000	Other Expenses £000	Dept. Income £000
Rooms	2,766		486	180	2,100
Food & Beverage	2,670	912	1,038	276	444
Telephone	156	108	24	12	12
Garage & Parking	108		48	12	48
Rentals	84				84
	5,784	1,020	1,596	480	2,688
Undistributed Operating Expenses:					
Administrative & General			210	270	
Marketing			60	156	
Guest Entertainment			30	12	
Property Operation & Maintenance			60	54	
Energy Costs			42	150	
			402	642	1,044
Total Income before Fixed Charges					1,644
Rent and Insurance				138	
Interest				276	
Depreciation				300	714
Income before Tax					930

Figure 21.4 Departmental statement of income

Grand Hotel Limited
ROOMS

Revenue	£000
Transient – regular	2,334
Transient – group	450
Total Revenue	2,784
Allowances	18
Net Revenue	2,766

Expenses:

Salaries and Wages	402
Employee Benefits	84
Total Payroll and Related Expenses	486

Other Expenses

China, Glassware and Linen	28
Commissions	2
Contract Cleaning	13
Laundry and Dry Cleaning	47
Operating Supplies	30
Other Operating Expenses	9
Reservation Expense	43
Uniforms	8
Total Other Expenses	180
Total Expenses	666
Departmental Income	2,100

Figure 21.5 Departmental schedule – rooms

Grand Hotel Limited
FOOD AND BEVERAGE

Revenue	£000
Food	1,914
Beverage	762
Total Revenue	2,676
Allowances	6
Net Revenue	2,670
Cost of Sales	816
Less Cost of Employees Meals	84
Net Cost of Food Sales	732
Cost of Beverage Sales	180
Net Cost of Sales	912
Gross Profit	1,758
Expenses	
Salaries and Wages	900
Employee Benefits	138
Total Payroll and Related Expenses	1,038
Other Expenses	
China, Glassware, Silver and Linen	38
Contact Cleaning	18
Kitchen Fuel	10
Laundry and Dry Cleaning	26
Licences and Taxes	3
Music and Entertainment	86
Operating Supplies	59
Other Operating Expenses	23
Uniforms	13
Total Other Expenses	276
Total Expenses	1,314
Departmental Income	444

Figure 21.6 Departmental schedule – food and beverage

Grand Hotel Limited
ADMINISTRATIVE AND GENERAL EXPENSES

	£000
Salaries and Wages	180
Employee Benefits	30
Total Payroll and Related Expenses	210

Other Expenses:

Cash Overages and Shortages	1
Commissions and Credit Card Charges	82
Credit and Collection	2
Data Processing Service	29
Donations	3
Insurance – General	35
Other Operating Expenses	11
Postage and Telegrams	7
Printing and Stationery	12
Professional Fees	26
Provision for Doubtful Accounts	10
Security Service	28
Trade Association Dues, Publications	14
Travelling Expenses	10
Total Other Expenses	270
Total Administrative and General Expenses	**480**

Figure 21.7 Departmental schedule – administrative and general expenses

SUMMARY

We complete our description of the uniform system with a summary of its principal advantages.

- The system is simple, easy to understand and, therefore, of particular benefit to all non-accountants in the hotel industry.
- As all hotels use the same concepts and terminology, the Uniform System enables the compilation of hotel statistics – both nationally and internationally.
- The Uniform System represents the 'best practice' in the hotel industry and, therefore, results in better quality of financial statements.
- There is no need for tailor-made systems, which saves time and money (and, of course, some tailors are better than others!).
- The Uniform System facilitates the training of accounting and control personnel: only one, generally accepted system has to be learnt.
- The system facilitates managerial mobility: there is no need to learn a new system when moving from one company to another.

PROBLEMS

1. Describe the principal advantages of the US Uniform System of Accounts for Hotels.
2. The exercise which follows consists of four parts. You are required to prepare, in accordance with the US Uniform System of Accounts for Hotels, the following schedules:
   (i)   Departmental Income Statement.
   (ii) Rooms Department Schedule.
   (iii) Food and Beverage Department Schedule.
   (iv) Property Operation and Maintenance Department Schedule.

Part I – Departmental and Income Statement

	£000
Net Revenues:	
Rooms	4,140
Food and Beverage	4,005
Telephone	235
Rentals	125
Cost of Sales:	
Food and Beverage	1,370
Telephone	160
Payroll and Related Expenses:	
Rooms	730
Food and Beverage	1,560
Telephone	35
Other (Departmental) Expenses:	
Rooms	270
Food and Beverage	415
Telephone	15
Undistributed Operating Expenses – Payroll and Related Expenses:	
Administrative and General	315
Marketing	90
Guest Entertainment	45
Property Operation and Maintenance	155
Undistributed Operating Expenses – Other Expenses:	
Administrative and General	405
Marketing	235
Guest Entertainment	20
Energy Costs	186
Property Operation and Maintenance	119
Property Tax and Insurance	205
Interest	415
Depreciation	450

Part II – Rooms Department Schedule

	£000
Revenue:	
Transient – Regular	3,500
Transient – Group	665
Allowances	25
Expenses:	
Salaries and Wages	605
Employee Benefits	125
China, Glassware and Linen	41
Commissions	4
Contract Cleaning	20
Laundry and Dry Cleaning	70
Operating Supplies	45
Other Operating Expenses	13
Reservation Expense	65
Uniforms	12

Part III – Food and Beverage Department Schedule

	£000
Revenue:	
Food	2,870
Beverage	1,145
Allowances	10
Cost of Sales:	
Cost of Food Consumed	1,225
Employee Meals	125
Cost of Beverage Sales	270
Expenses:	
Salaries and Wages	1,350
Employee Benefits	210
China, Glassware, Silver and Linen	60
Contract Cleaning	25
Kitchen Fuel	15
Laundry and Dry Cleaning	40
Licenses and Taxes	4
Music and Entertainment	130
Operating Supplies	88
Other Operating Expenses	35
Uniforms	18

Part IV – Property Operation and Maintenance Schedule

	£000
Salaries and Wages	126
Employee Benefits	29
Building	6

Curtains and Drapes	2
Electrical and Mechanical Equipment	42
Elevators	28
Floor Covering	1
Furniture	11
Grounds and Landscaping	12
Other Operating Expenses	2
Painting and Decorating	2
Refrigeration Supplies	7
Removal of Waste Matter	5
Uniforms	1

3. From the balances listed below prepare a Departmental Statement of Income of the Cracow City Hotel for the year ended 31 March 1997.

	£000
Net Revenues:	
Rooms	4,550
Food and Beverage	4,400
Telephone	265
Rentals	140
Cost of Sales:	
Food and Beverage	1,510
Telephone	175
Payroll and Related Expenses:	
Rooms	810
Food and Beverage	1,720
Telephone	40
Other Departmental Expenses:	
Rooms	310
Food and Beverage	455
Telephone	20
Undistributed Operating Expenses – Payroll and Related Expenses:	
Administrative and General	345
Marketing	105
Guest Entertainment	65
Property Operation and Maintenance	170
Undistributed Operating Expenses – Other Expenses:	
Administrative and General	445
Marketing	255
Guest Entertainment	35
Energy Costs	205
Property Operation and Maintenance	130
Property Tax and Insurance	235
Interest	475
Depreciation	515

Comment, as far as is possible, on the profitability of the hotel.

Interpretation of accounts 22

INTRODUCTION

There can be little doubt that it is a considerable advantage for all aspiring business managers to be able to understand and analyse company accounts. This chapter shows you how. It demonstrates how to analyse the data found in a set of accounts and to use this information to help you understand how the business is performing, covering the key areas of profitability, liquidity and operations.

Of all the accounting topics that management students may study, this area is widely regarded as amongst the most important in respect of their long-term careers.

OBJECTIVES

On completion of this chapter you should be able to:

- know the meaning of interpretation of accounts;
- identify the key ratios/percentages from the trading account, profit and loss account and balance sheet;
- understand the terms: sales mix, gross profit margin and others;
- list and comprehend the key profitability ratios, liquidity ratios and operational ratios;
- carry out a detailed ratio analysis;
- determine the return on capital employed, its importance and the difficulties attached to its calculation;
- comment in detail on the ratio analysis carried out;
- understand the different concepts of profit.

INTERPRETATION OF ACCOUNTS

The process of reviewing, appraising and criticizing accounts is known as the interpretation of accounts.

We said in Chapter 16 that there are different parties interested in the accounts and that, consequently, they all look at the accounts from different points of view. The creditors, before they grant credit, want to be satisfied

with the liquidity of the business. The proprietors are primarily interested
in the profits earned and the dividends paid.

The management of a business have, obviously, a much greater and
comprehensive interest in the accounts than any other party. It is, therefore,
primarily from the point of view of the management that we shall deal with
the interpretation of accounts.

In order to be able to interpret a set of accounts, it is necessary to
examine not only many individual figures in the accounts, but also several
important relationships between such figures.

Trading account

There are three main things that should be considered when reviewing the
trading account:

1. the volume of sales;
2. sales mix;
3. gross profit margins;

Volume of sales

The level of sales is important for several reasons. First, a business which
does not sell enough cannot make a profit. Second, the higher the volume of
sales the lower the incidence of fixed costs per unit sold (be it meal,
banquet or room) and the higher, therefore, the profit per unit. Similarly,
because most hospitality establishments have a high proportion of fixed
costs, any given increase in sales invariably results in a more than propor-
tional increase in total net profit. Finally, it is important to compare the
current volume of sales with the corresponding figure of sales for the
previous accounting period.

Sales mix

The term 'sales mix' refers to the composition of total sales, and is usually
expressed in percentage terms, and so the total sales of a restaurant consist
of food, beverage and other (cigarettes, tobaccos etc) sales. Given below is
the sales mix percentage of a restaurant with total sales of £150,000.

	Sales in £	Sales mix %
Food sales	82,500	55%
Beverage sales	52,500	35%
Other sales	15,000	10%
Total sales	150,000	100%

It will be appreciated that, because there is a different margin of profit on
each section of the sales, the sales mix of a business must be watched very
closely. An increase in the sales of cigarettes of £100 (typical cost of sales
92 per cent) will usually result in an increase in gross profit of about £8.

The same increase in food sales may well bring an additional gross profit of over £65.

Gross profit margins

Finally, attention should be paid to the gross profit margins of the various revenue producing departments. Past experience will indicate whether or not the current percentages of gross profit are what they should be.

Gross profit margins vary from one type of establishment to another. In general, it is true to say that the better the type of business the higher the percentage of gross profit and vice versa. This is necessary in order to cover the relatively higher cost of labour and overheads entailed by the provision of a better type of service.

As between the various components of the sales mix the position is this: beverage sales will usually produce a percentage of gross profit which is very similar to that on food sales. The gross profit on cigarettes is normally very modest and invariably under 10 per cent.

Needless to say, gross profit margins are one of the important determinants of the profitability of a business and should, therefore, be reviewed carefully and frequently.

Profit and loss account

However satisfactory the total amount of gross profit of a business, its net profit will not be adequate if the labour costs and overheads are too high. When examining the profit and loss account it is, therefore, important to relate each of the following to total sales:

Labour costs

These costs are usually in the region of 25 per cent of sales in restaurants, about 30 per cent in most hotels and between 30 and 35 per cent in industrial canteens.

Overheads

These tend to be about 5 per cent less than the labour costs in most hospitality establishments. They may appear to be very low in industrial canteens, where many fixed charges are sometimes not debited but borne by the company.

Net profit

The percentage of net profit on sales varies considerably and may be anything from a very small percentage to over 20 per cent. Past experience will, however, indicate what this percentage should be in each particular case.

Balance sheet

A review of the balance sheet of a business tends to centre around two main problems: the profitability of the business, and the adequacy or otherwise of its liquid resources.

Profitability

This is usually measured by expressing the net profit as a percentage of the capital of the business.

It is pointed out that whilst the percentage of net profit on sales is an appropriate measure of the operating efficiency of a business from one trading period to another, it is not an adequate index of its profitability. A restaurant which has a capital of £100,000, a turnover of £10,000 and a net profit equal to 20 per cent of its sales is not a profitable business by any means. What matters, from the point of view of the proprietors, and what is important in the long run, is the percentage return on the capital.

What the percentage return on capital should be can only be determined by reference to the particular circumstances of each individual business. As a general rule it may, however, be taken that a business will aim at a return which:

(a) is in excess of the return obtainable on government securities and other more or less riskless investments such as debentures and preference shares of well established companies;

(b) compensates for the risks inherent in the nature of the business concerned; generally, the more risky the business the higher the expected return on capital;

(c) is not so high as to be prejudicial to the quality of service and standard of comfort expected by the customers. It is, surely, bad policy to earn a high return in the short run at the expense of loss of customers due to inadequate portions, badly presented food, inefficient service, etc.

When calculating the return on capital, it should be remembered that, more often than not, the fixed assets are shown in the accounts as historical costs, which do not correspond with current economic values. A freehold hotel purchased thirty years ago for £10,000 may now be worth twenty times as much, and yet be shown in the balance sheet at cost. Similarly, equipment purchased five years before a balance sheet date may have a replacement cost well above its book value. It is, therefore, often necessary to adjust the values of the fixed assets to arrive at the **true** return on capital.

Fixed Asset Utilization is a measure of how efficiently a company is using its fixed assets and is an important component in any examination of profitability. If the ratio is low it means that the management may not be utilizing its fixed assets very efficiently.

To improve fixed asset utilization the business needs to use the money invested in fixed assets more efficiently. This can be acheived by making more sales from the existing fixed assets. This is measured by the fixed asset utilization ratio shown later in this chapter.

Liquidity

The liquidity of a business is usually measured by relating its current assets to its current liabilities. The excess of current assets over current liabilities is known as 'working capital'.

Whilst the current assets represent a source of liquid funds, current liabilities represent a claim on such funds. Clearly, therefore, the former should stand in some relationship to the latter. What this exact relationship should be depends on the circumstances of each business. In general, however, we may say that:

(a) each business requires an excess of current assets over current liabilities, i.e. some working capital;
(b) the amount of working capital depends on factors such as the period of credit obtained from suppliers and granted to customers; the degree to which the business is seasonal; the level of stocks it has to carry, and the way heavy fixed expenses are spread over the calendar year.

A business which allows a long period of credit to its customers needs a relatively larger working capital; it takes longer to convert the debts into cash, which may be urgently required. The opposite applies to the length of credit received from the suppliers. In seasonal hospitality establishments, the pattern of sales (and the consequent cash inflow) tends to differ quite considerably from the pattern of expenditure. Often heavy expenses are payable when the volume of sales is low. This calls for a larger excess of current assets over current liabilities. A licensed business has a higher proportion of its total capital invested in (beverage) stocks and, therefore, will tend to have a relatively larger working capital. Finally, a business where heavy expenses are spread reasonably evenly over the year needs rather less working capital than one where expenses are bunched.

In addition to the examination of the overall amount of working capital, it is essential to review the components of working capital. The cash position should be considered in relation to the immediate commitments of the business. The debtors should be related to credit sales to ensure that the period of credit allowed to them is reasonable. Stock levels should be reviewed to see if they are reasonable in relation to the volume of business. Finally, creditors should be related to credit purchases to ensure that the amount owing to them is reasonable. Where it is not, it is quite likely that cash discounts are being lost through dilatory payment of suppliers.

Other matters

There are one or two other points to consider when interpreting a balance sheet. Thus, it is important to examine the basis of the valuation of fixed assets and ensure that depreciation charges have been adequate. Where there are any long-term loans, it is essential to ascertain the date of repayment and its effect on the liquidity of the business. In the case of a limited company, it is important to review the reserves available and the profits earned in relation to the dividends payable.

ACCOUNTING RATIOS

Reference has already been made to the desirability of ascertaining the relationship between various figures in the accounts, e.g. sales and gross profit, current assets and current liabilities. A convenient way of achieving this is to apply what are known as 'accounting ratios'.

A ratio is, simply, one figure expressed in terms of another.

Though it is possible to calculate dozens of different ratios from a set of final accounts, only some of them are of practical value. From the point of view of the management of a business two sets of ratios are especially valuable in the interpretation of accounts. These are the ratios showing the profitability and the ratios showing the liquidity of the business.

Ratios measuring profitability

The student should note that all profitability ratios are expressed as percentages. In fact, whether we speak of ratios or percentages makes no notable difference.

Gross profit percentage

This measures the relationship between gross profit and net sales, e.g.

$$\frac{\text{Gross profit} \times 100}{\text{Net sales}} \quad \frac{£6{,}000 \times 100}{£10{,}000} = 60\%$$

In most hospitality establishments, it is more usual to speak of the 'gross profit percentage' rather than the 'gross profit ratio'.

This is a key ratio and you should review the paragraph on Gross Profit Margins earlier in this chapter for further information.

Net profit percentage

This measures the relationship between net profit and net sales, e.g.

$$\frac{\text{Net profit} \times 100}{\text{Net sales}} \quad \frac{£10{,}000 \times 100}{£100{,}000} = 10\%$$

This is not strictly speaking a profitability ratio, rather an efficiency ratio. As a general rule the higher the percentage the more efficient the business.

Labour/Overhead cost percentage

This measures the relationship between labour costs or overhead costs and sales.

$$\frac{\text{Labour costs} \times 100}{\text{Net sales}} \quad \frac{£28,000 \times 100}{£100,000} = 28\%$$

$$\frac{\text{Overhead costs} \times 100}{\text{Net sales}} \quad \frac{£22,000 \times 100}{£100,000} = 22\%$$

A low net profit percentage coupled with a reasonable gross profit percentage means that labour and/or overheads are too high and need to be examined for overstaffing, unnecessary expenditure etc.

Asset turnover ratio

This measures the relationship between net sales and capital employed.

$$\frac{\text{Net sales}}{\text{Capital employed}} \quad \frac{£100,000}{£380,000} = 0.26 : 1$$

The ratio 0.26: 1 means that the business is producing 26p of sales for every £1 invested in the assets.

Management often put a great deal of effort into cost cutting to improve profitability when the real problem is poor utilization of assets.

Fixed asset utilization ratio

This measures the relationship between net sales and net fixed assets.

$$\frac{\text{Net sales}}{\text{Net fixed assets}} \quad \frac{£100,000}{£300,000} \quad 0.33 : 1$$

The ratio 0.33 : 1 again means that only 33p of sales is produced for every £1 of fixed assets owned. Students will note that this ratio is very similar to the asset turnover ratio mentioned above.

Return on capital employed

Capital employed in a business is usually regarded as the issued share capital plus reserves for a limited company and the opening capital plus profit less drawings for a sole trader and partnership.

Return on capital employed, therefore, means return (before or after tax) on the capital of a business. The formula for this ratio is illustrated below:

$$\frac{\text{Net profit (before tax)}}{\text{Capital employed}} \quad \frac{£5,000 \times 100}{£50,000} = 10\%$$

This is a seemingly straightforward calculation, but the question arises as to the figure to be used as capital employed. Is it the opening or the closing capital or some average of the two? This is the subject of much debate and beyond the scope of this chapter. For the purpose of simplicity, however, this textbook will always use the closing capital figure for its calculations.

Ratios measuring liquidity

The current ratio

This measures the relationship between current assets and current liabilities, and is therefore an indication of the short-run solvency of the business. The ratio is calculated as follows:

$$\frac{\text{Current assets}}{\text{Current liabilities}} \quad \frac{£15,000}{£10,000} = 1.5:1$$

In simple terms this means that for every £1.50 of current assets owned by the business it owes £1 in current liabilities.

The acid test ratio

This measures the relationship between the liquid assets (cash, debtors, temporary investments) and current liabilities. A business may have an adequate current ratio but, if too high a proportion of its current assets is represented by stocks rather than cash balances and debtors, insufficient liquid funds remain for current operations. In the acid test ratio only liquid assets are related to the current liabilities. The formula is:

$$\frac{\text{Liquid assets}}{\text{Current liabilities}} \quad \frac{£12,500}{£10,000} = 1.25:1$$

The average collection period

This, strictly speaking, is not a ratio but a measure of how quickly or otherwise debts are collected by the business. The formula is:

$$\frac{\text{Debtors}}{\text{Av. daily credit sales*}} \quad \frac{£1,000}{£50} = 20 \text{ days}$$

This means it takes on average 20 days for debtors to pay their bills.
   * Average daily credit sales is worked out by dividing total credit sales p.a. by 365 days.

The average payment period

This ratio shows how quickly or otherwise the business pays its suppliers.

$$\frac{\text{Creditors}}{\text{Av. daily credit purchases*}} \quad \frac{£1,800}{£60} = 30 \text{ days}$$

This means that the business takes on average 30 days to pay its suppliers.
   * Average daily credit purchases is worked out by dividing total credit purchases p.a. by 365 days.

The rate of stock turnover

This measures the speed with which stocks move through the business. A high rate of stock turnover indicates that stocks are low in relation to the turnover and, usually, means efficient buying. A low rate of stock turnover indicates that high stocks are kept in relation to the volume of turnover and, usually, points to over-buying. The formula is:

$$\frac{\text{Cost of sales}}{\text{Av. stock at cost}} \quad \frac{£40,000}{£1000} = 40 \text{ times p.a.}$$

This means that on average the stock turns over 40 times in a year

It is often expressed in number of days as follows:

$$\frac{\text{No. of days in year}}{\text{Turnover time p. a.}} \quad \frac{365 \text{ days}}{40 \text{ times}} = 9.12 \text{ days}$$

This means that the business holds enough stock at any one time to keep it going for approximately 9 days.

Important note: Stock turnover is normally worked out separately for food and beverage stocks because of the markedly different levels of stock holding acceptable for each commodity. In fact the rate of stock turnover varies from one section of sales to another, as indeed from one business to another.

In respect of food sales the rate varies from about 25 to 50. In other words the average stock held represents from one to two weeks' consumption. The amount of wines, spirits, minerals, etc. held depends, amongst others, on the type of business. Usually, the better the type of business the larger the relative size of the beverage stocks. Cigarettes and tobaccos are usually purchased monthly; this would indicate a rate of stock turnover of about twelve. The relevant formulae are:

$$\frac{\text{Cost of food sales}}{\text{Average food stock}} \quad = \quad \begin{array}{l}\text{Stock turnover} \\ \text{for food}\end{array}$$

$$\frac{\text{Cost of beverage sales}}{\text{Average beverage stock}} \quad = \quad \begin{array}{l}\text{Stock turnover} \\ \text{for beverages}\end{array}$$

For examination question purposes, the average stock is usually worked out by adding the opening stock and closing stock together and dividing by two.

Operating ratios

In addition to selecting the correct measures of profitability, a business will adopt several operating ratios, i.e. ratios which measure the current operating efficiency of a business. An advantage of operating ratios is that they can be applied at frequent intervals (daily, weekly) to check the progress of the business.

Rate of room occupancy

This shows the number of rooms occupied in relation to the number of rooms available, and it is usually expressed as a percentage. Thus a hotel which has 200 rooms and, on a particular day, sells 150 rooms, has a room occupancy of:

$$\frac{\text{Rooms occupied}}{\text{Rooms available}} = \frac{150 \times 100}{200} = 75\%$$

Room occupancy is somewhat misleading when there is a high proportion of double or twin-bedded rooms let as singles.

Rate of guest occupancy

This is also referred to as the rate of 'bed occupancy'. It shows the number of guests staying in the hotel in relation to the guest capacity. The formula for calculating guest occupancy is:

$$\frac{\text{Actual number of guests}}{\text{Guest capacity}} = \frac{120 \times 100}{200} = 60\%$$

Guest occupancy is a more accurate indication than room occupancy of the extent to which the capacity of the hotel is used.

Room density index

This measures the relationship between the number of guests and occupied rooms. When we have 120 guests in 100 rooms, the RDI is

$$\frac{\text{Number of guests (120)}}{\text{Occupied rooms (100)}} = 1.2$$

The room density index is normally used as an alternative to the percentage of double occupancy, which is described below.

Percentage double occupancy

The percentage double occupancy shows the proportion of rooms sold as doubles rather than singles. If we sell 200 rooms, and of these 50 are doubles, our percentage of double occupancy is 25%. It should be noted that we are not concerned with available but occupied rooms only. An easy formula for calculating double occupancy is given below.

Number of guests	120
Less: Occupied rooms	80
Double occupied rooms	40

In this particular case we sold 80 rooms and of these 40 are doubles: our double occupancy percentage is, therefore, 50 per cent.

Room yield

This expresses actual room sales as a percentage of potential room sales. This indicator is especially useful in situations where substantial discounts are offered by hotels to tour operators, industrial and commercial clients. For this purpose 'room sales potential' means the volume of room sales which would be achieved if all the rooms were sold at published tariffs. Where, for example, a hotel may potentially take £8,000 per day, and its actual room sales are £6,000, the percentage room yield is:

$$\frac{\text{Actual room sales (£6,000)} \times 100}{\text{Potential room sales (£8,000)}} = 75\%$$

Average room rate

This measures the relationship between room sales and rooms occupied, e.g.

$$\frac{\text{Room sales}}{\text{Rooms occupied}} \quad \frac{£4,000}{200} = £20$$

Rate of restaurant occupancy

This shows the number of meals sold in relation to the normal seating capacity of a restaurant. Thus if a restaurant, which serves luncheons and dinners, has a seating capacity of 100, it has a total daily capacity of 200. If, on a particular day, it serves 300 meals its rate of restaurant occupancy is:

$$\frac{\text{Meals served}}{\text{Seating capacity}} \quad \frac{300}{200} = 1.5$$

The rate of 1.5 shows that on that particular day the average seat available was relaid 1.5 times. Quite obviously the higher this rate, the more economical the utilization of the fixed equipment and other facilities of the restaurant.

Average spending power

The total turnover of a business depends on two factors: the number of customers, and the average amount spent by them. Many hospitality establishments review the average spending power at regular intervals to ensure that it is adequate and that menus are planned in accordance with what customers want to spend. Average spending power is calculated by dividing sales by the number of meals served, e.g.:

$$\frac{\text{Sales}}{\text{Number of covers}} \quad \frac{£3000}{200} = £15$$

Average spending power may be calculated on total sales or separately in relation to food sales, beverage sales and other sales.

Gross profit percentage

This is, traditionally, one of the most important indicators of the efficiency of food and beverage operations.

Net margin

This is also referred to as 'after wage profit'. This ratio is important in establishments employing a high proportion of part-time or casual staff.

INTERPRETATION OF ACCOUNTS QUESTIONS

Interpretation questions usually consist of one or two sets of final accounts plus notes and the student is asked to analyse and comment on the accounts in respect of profitability, liquidity, etc.

It is important to have the right strategy to tackle such questions and the following steps are suggested.

1. Examine the given accounts carefully for any key changes over the year.
2. Work out a detailed ratio analysis under headings of profitability, liquidity and operations.
3. Comment briefly on all key ratios; then concentrate on the trouble areas highlighted by the analysis; be sure to suggest ways of remedying the problems.
4. Always finish with a conclusions and recommendations paragraph.

Students should note that the ratios/percentages that they have worked out are of little use on their own: to have value they must be compared with something, e.g. budgeted figures.

WORKED EXAMPLE

The balance sheet below has been prepared by the book-keeper of a small city hotel.

Balance Sheet
as at 31st December 19...

Fixed Assets	Cost	Agg. Dep'n	Net
	£	£	£
Leasehold premises	276,000	15,500	260,500
Restaurant furniture	21,000	4,500	16,500
	297,000	20,000	277,000
China and cutlery			15,750
			292,750

	£	£	£
Current Assets			
Stock: food	18,000		
drink	20,000	38,000	
Debtors		37,420	
Cash in bank		17,340	
Cash in hand		1,750	
		94,510	
Current Liabilities			
Trade creditors	65,000		
Less Provision for disc. received	3,500		
	61,500		
Expense creditors	1,500	63,000	
Net current assets			31,510
			324,260
Capital and Reserves;			
Capital at 1st Jan. 19...			331,850
Add net profit			45,660
			377,510
Less drawings			53,250
			324,260

You are required to comment on the financial position of the hotel, taking the following additional information into account:

(a) The trading account for the year in question was as follows:

	Rooms	Food	Drink	Total
	£	£	£	£
Sales	150,000	600,000	200,000	950,000
Less cost of sales				
Opening stock		28,000	34,500	62,500
Add purchases for year		242,000	87,500	329,500
		270,000	122,000	392,000
Less closing stock		18,000	20,000	38,000
Cost of sales		252,000	102,000	354,000
Gross profit	150,000	348,000	98,000	596,000

(b) The sales of the hotel for the year end in question were:

Cash sales	£750,000
Credit sales	200,000
Total sales	£950,000

The purchases for the same period were:

Cash purchases	£29,500
Credit purchases	300,000
Total purchases	£329,500

(c) The hotel works on a budgetary control system and for the year in question management have set the following targets

Target GP	Food GP%	66%
	Drink GP%	55%
	Overall GP%	72%
Labour cost %		29%
Overhead cost %		25%
Net profit %		20%
Return on capital employed %		21%

Proceed as shown in the suggested solution

Suggested solution
Ratio analysis:
A sensible place to begin is with the trading account given in note (a). Work out the sales mix percentage and then the GP percentage for food and drink separately and the overall gross profit. The student should note that there is no cost of sales for accommodation and therefore the room GP percentage is 100 per cent.

	Rooms	Food	Drink	Total
Sales Mix Formula	£150,000	£600,000	£200,000	
	£950,000	£950,000	£950,000	
Sales Mix %	16%	63%	21%	100%
Gross Profit Formula		£348,000	£98,000	£596,000
		£600,000	£200,000	£950,000
Gross Profit	100%	58%	49%	62.7%

Profitability ratios

Sales mix %	Rooms	16.00%
	Food	63.00%
	Drink	21.00%
Gross Profit	Food GP%	58.00%
	Drink GP%	49.00%
	Overall GP%	62.70%

Labour/Overhead %* $\dfrac{£550,340}{£950,000}$ = 57.93%

Net profit % $\dfrac{£45,660}{£950,000}$ = 4.81%

Return on capital employed $\dfrac{£45,660}{£324,260}$ = 14.08%

Asset turnover $\dfrac{£950,000}{£324,260}$ = 2.93 : 1

* The labour/overhead figure is the difference between gross profit and net profit (£596,000 − £45,660) £550,340

Liquidity Ratios

Current ratio $\dfrac{£94,510}{£63,000}$ 1.50 : 1

Acid test ratio $\dfrac{£56,510}{£63,000}$ 0.89 : 1

Average collection period $\dfrac{£37,420.00}{£547.94}$ 68.3 days

Average payment period $\dfrac{£65,000.00}{£821.91}$ 79.08 days

Rate of stock turnover

Food $\dfrac{£252,000}{£23,000*}$ 10.96 times

Drink $\dfrac{£102,000}{£27,250*}$ 3.74 times

* Average stock is arrived at by adding the opening stock and closing stock together and dividing by two.

Comments

The net profit amounts to only 4.81 per cent which suggests that operations are not as efficient as they should be.

The overall working capital position is thus:

Working capital	
Current assets	£94,510
Less current liabilities	£63,000
Working capital	£31,510

The current ratio of the hotel is about 3 : 2, which seems reasonably adequate.

The acid test ratio is slightly below expectations at 0.89 : 1

This means that for every one pound owing to suppliers the business has only 89p in liquid assets. This means that if all the short-term creditors needed to be paid at once the business might be short of the required cash.

Steps should be taken to improve the position to at least a ratio of 1 : 1

Components of working capital

Stocks The total cost of sales for food is £252,000. Assuming that the hotel is non-seasonal, this indicates a monthly cost of sales of about £21,000. The average food stocks of £23,000 are, therefore, equal to about five weeks' consumption, which appears quite excessive. This would indicate a rate of stock turnover of about 11, which again is very much less than is normally the case in the majority of hotels. Also the rate of stock turnover for drinks, 3.74, is considerably lower than would have been expected.

Debtors The credit sales of the hotel were £200,000 and, assuming that the hotel is non-seasonal, this would indicate monthly credit sales of £16,667. The £37,420 owing from the debtors amounts, therefore, to just over two months' credit sales. As the figure of debtors certainly includes a proportion of visitors' ledger balances, it is quite possible that the hotel does not collect its debts quickly enough. It is quite likely that some of the debts have been owing for more than two or three months.

This is supported by the average collection period time of 68 days.

Cash position The total of cash available is £19,090. This is quite inadequate in relation to the current liabilities of £63,000. It is imperative for the hotel to run down its stocks and collect its debts more speedily in order to improve its cash position.

Trade creditors As the hotel buys on credit at the rate of about £25,000 per month, the debts owing to the suppliers represent considerably over two months' credit purchases. This may be bad as it is quite likely that cash discounts are being lost. Second, in view of the usual level of cash discounts, it seems that it is too optimistic to hope for £3,500 cash discounts on £65,000, a proportion of which has been outstanding for more than two months.

Again this is supported by the average payment period of approximately 79 days.

Expense creditors The nature of this debt is not known and no comment is therefore possible.

Profitability
Assuming that the fixed assets are shown in the balance sheet at realistic values and that adequate proprietor's remuneration has been debited in the hotel profit and loss account, the return on capital employed is:

$$\frac{\text{Net profit}}{\text{Capital employed}} \quad \frac{£45,660}{£324,260} \quad \times\ 100 \quad = 14.08\% \text{ (before tax)}.$$

This ratio is below expectation (budgeted return is 21%), but it would have to be considered in conjunction with the corresponding ratios for past years.

The net profit is considerably lower than expected; this can be traced back to the poor food GP% of 58 per cent (against an expected 66 per cent) and the drink GP% of 49 per cent (against an expected 55 per cent) reducing the overall gross profit. An early investigation should centre on food and beverage control. In addition the labour/overhead costs are higher at 57.9 per cent of sales (54 per cent budgeted).

If, as already assumed, the profit and loss account of the hotel contains a debit in respect of the proprietor's salary, the drawings of £53,250 are excessive in view of the unsatisfactory cash position of the hotel.

The net profit percentage is very poor at 4.81 per cent and reflects poor gross profit and high labour costs as outlined above. In reality this is an efficency ratio, which means that if management had been efficient in their control of food and beverage costs, labour and overheads and achieved the expected targets then a very healthy net profit percentage would have emerged.

Fixed assets

No information is available on how the fixed assets have been valued and, therefore, it is difficult to comment on them.

EXAMPLE 22.1

The following information was extracted from the records of a large unlicensed restaurant:

	May £	June £	July £
Food sales	200,000	220,000	240,000
Cost of sales	80,000	92,400	105,600
Labour costs	50,000	57,200	64,800
Overheads	40,000	41,800	43,200
Number of covers served	20,000	24,444	30,000

From the information given above it is possible to construct a comparative table of trading results as shown below.

Comparative trading results for quarter ended 31st July 19...

	May £	%	June £	%	July £	%
Food sales	200,000	100	220,000	100	240,000	100
Less cost of sales	80,000	40	92,400	42	105,600	44
Gross profit	120,000	60	127,600	58	134,400	56
Less labour costs	50,000	25	57,200	26	64,800	27
After-wage results	70,000	35	70,400	32	69,600	29
Less overheads	40,000	20	41,800	19	43,200	18
Net profit	30,000	15	28,600	13	26,400	11
Number of covers	20,000		24,444		30,000	
Av. spending power	£10.00		£9.00		£8.00	

Having analysed the trading results we may offer the following comments:

Food sales These show a substantial upward trend, which would have to be compared with the trend for the same quarter of the previous year. Though the volume of sales seems satisfactory, it is clear that the rise over the three months is due to an increasing number of covers rather than any increase in the customers' spending power.

Cost of sales The percentage of cost of sales in relation to the turnover is rising and this could be due to higher prices being paid to suppliers, inefficient kitchen operations or other reasons. Immediate action is now required to keep this percentage in line with the volume of sales.

Gross profit Although this is increasing in absolute terms, as a percentage of sales it is becoming less and less. As a result the restaurant does not obtain much benefit out of the increasing turnover.

Labour costs These are rising both absolutely and in relation to sales. This is bad as, normally, when sales are rising labour costs tend to lag behind. Reasons for this must be sought and the appropriate action taken.

After-wage percentage This has declined from 35 per cent to 29 per cent due to increased labour and commodity costs.

Overheads These show a moderate rise, which is to be expected in conditions of rising turnover.

Net profit This, in spite of the increase in sales, shows a downward trend. Quite obviously, what the restaurant gains in a lower incidence of fixed overheads due to a larger turnover is more than offset by higher food costs and labour costs.

Average spending power This has declined more than seems reasonable over a period of three months. It is important that reasons for this unfavourable trend are found and some corrective action taken as soon as possible.

CONCEPTS OF PROFITABILITY

We said earlier in this chapter that the usual and most appropriate method of measuring profitability is to relate the net profit to the capital (net worth) of the business. There are, however, one or two other possible measures of profitability and the purpose of this section is to list and explain them in some detail.

Profit in relation to capital employed/net worth

This, as already indicated, is the most common and appropriate method. There are few profit-making hospitality establishments to which this method could not be applied.

Profit in relation to turnover

In most establishments this is simply a method of assessing the operating efficiency over a period of time. There are, however, some businesses which have a substantial turnover but, at the same time, relatively little capital. This applies to a number of catering contractors who organize and manage the catering departments of their clients without supplying any of the fixed equipment. In such businesses the return on net worth is rather meaningless, and it is more appropriate to measure profitability in relation to turnover.

Profit per unit sold

This is a useful additional measure of profitability. The 'unit' may be a meal, banquet or room sold.

Profit in relation to time factor

This is also a useful additional method of assessing profitability. It would be applied in cases where the time factor is of paramount importance, e.g. in particular forms of outdoor catering for functions of limited duration such as exhibitions, flower shows, etc. and, possibly, in highly seasonal establishments, where it is known that so much profit must be made during the season to provide a reasonable annual return on capital.

SUMMARY

- Interpretation of accounts is the process of reviewing, appraising and criticizing a set of final accounts.
- As a first step it is necessary to perform a ratio analysis, this means producing a series of percentages and ratios from a given set of accounts.
- Interpretation will usually cover three key areas
  (a) Profitability
  (b) Liquidity
  (c) Operations.
  By profitability we mean the ability to make profits over the coming years; by liquidity we mean the cash position of the business and its abitity to pay its short term debts; by operations we mean the general efficiency and use of resources.
- Key profitability ratios are: return on capital employed; gross profit percentage; labour cost percentage; overhead cost percentage; net profit percentage; asset turnover rate.
- Key liquidity ratios are: current ratio; acid test ratio; debtors ratio; creditors ratio; stock turnover.
- Key operating ratios are: rate of room occupancy; rate of guest occupancy; room density index; room yield; rate of restaurant turnover.
- A set of ratios by themselves is of limited value. To make them useful they must be compared with something. Most businesses compare this year's ratios against last year's. They may also be compared to budget figures. Larger companies will have their own company standards and ratios to adhere to. Finally, it is possible to use national statistics where average ratios are produced from returns from a large number of businesses.
- It is important to comment in detail on your ratio analysis. Where the actual ratio falls below that expected/required, you are expected to make

an educated guess at what may have caused the shortfall and how to remedy it for the future.

PROBLEMS

1. Enumerate the main points that you would examine when interpreting a set of final accounts.

2. Explain what is meant by the 'liquidity' and 'profitability' of a business.

3. Comment on the usefulness of accounting ratios. Explain what is meant by the following: gross profit ratio; net profit ratio; return on capital employed; current ratio; acid test ratio; average collection period; rate of stock turnover.

4. 'There is not one but several concepts of profitability.' Comment.

5. Enumerate the most important operating ratios that would be of value in:
   (a) a hotel;
   (b) a restaurant;
   (c) a luncheon club.

6. The following is the balance sheet of a small hotel, drawn up as at 31st December 19...

Balance sheet of the Black Rose Hotel
as at 31st December 19...

Fixed assets	Cost	Agg. Dep'n	Net
	£	£	£
Leasehold hotel	800,000	160,000	640,000
Furniture	240,000	48,000	192,000
	1,040,000	208,000	832,000
Glass, china, etc.			20,000
			852,000

Current assets			
Stock food	16,800		
drink	33,200	50,000	
Debtors		34,000	
Cash at bank		7,500	
Cash in hand		500	
		92,000	
Less current liabilities			
Trade creditors	32,000		
Expense creditors	18,000		
Advance bookings	2,000	52,000	
Net current assets			40,000
			892,000

Financed by:

	Mr Black	Mr Rose	Total
	£	£	£
Capital at 1st January 19...	480,000	400,000	880,000
Current account balances	5,000	7,000	12,000
	485,000	407,000	892,000

You are also given the following information:

(a) Sales for the year ended 31st December 19... were £1,600,000, of which:

room sales	£800,000
food	£500,000
liquor	£300,000

The total sales figure divides as follows: cash sales £1,500,000; credit sales £100,000.

(b) (i) Purchases in the same period amounted to £400,000; of the total purchases cash purchases were £40,000.

(ii) The total purchases figure is broken down as follows:

food purchases	£250,000
liquor purchases	£150,000

(c) The net profit of the hotel was £60,000.

(d) You may assume that opening and closing stocks are equal.

Comment on the financial position of the hotel as disclosed by the above balance sheet.

7. The following information relates to two catering businesses of very different background.

Summary of trading and profit and loss account.

		Leo's Hospitality Co.		Barry's Hospitality Co.	
		£	£	£	£
Sales	Food	30,000		150,000	
	Beverage	7,500	37,500	100,000	250,000
Less: Cost of sales					
	Food	22,500		60,000	
	Beverage	2,500	25,000	65,000	125,000
Gross profit					
	Food	7,500		90,000	
	Beverage	5,000	12,500	35,000	125,000
Less: Labour/overheads					
	Labour cost	3,750		62,500	
	Overheads	6,250	10,000	37,500	100,000
Net profit			2,500		25,000

You are given the following additional information in respect of the two companies:

	Leo's	Barry's
Capital employed	£5,000	£87,500
Average stocks: food	£225	£4,800
beverage	£50	£6,400
Debtors	£150	£9,375
Credit sales (as % of total sales)	5%	20%

Required:

Analyse and compare the results of the two businesses using relevant percentages and ratios.

8. Below are the financial results of The Classic Hotel Ltd for the years 1993 and 1994. The hotel has been operating since 1986 and is accommodation sales biased.

Balance sheets as at 31st December 19...

	1993		1994	
Fixed assets (net)	£	£	£	£
Freehold property		960,000		1,170,000
Equipment and furniture		210,000		300,000
		1,170,000		1,470,000
Current assets				
Stocks of food and beverage	60,000		225,000	
Debtors	36,000		150,000	
Cash	159,000		6,000	
	255,000		381,000	
Less Current liabilities				
Creditors	24,000		45,000	
Taxation	120,000		180,000	
Proposed dividend	75,000		90,000	
Overdraft	6,000		36,000	
	225,000		351,000	
Net current assets		30,000		30,000
Less long-term liabilities				
10% Debenture		(180,000)		(180,000)
(secured on property – 2003)				
		1,020,000		1,320,000
Financed by:				
Capital and Reserves				
Ordinary share capital		750,000		960,000
Retained profits		270,000		360,000
		1,020,000		1,320,000

Profit and Loss Accounts for Year ended 31st December 19...

	1993 £	1993 £	1994 £	1994 £
Sales		1,500,000		2,100,000
Less: Cost of sales		300,000		420,000
Gross profit		1,200,000		1,680,000
Less: Labour	420,000		600,000	
Other expenses	540,000	960,000	720,000	1,320,000
Net profit before tax		240,000		360,000
Less: Corporation tax (50%)		120,000		180,000
Net profit after tax		120,000		180,000
Less: Proposed ordinary share dividend		75,000		90,000
Retained profits for the year		45,000		90,000

You are requested to:
(a) calculate six key accounting ratios for 1993 and 1994; and
(b) comment on the strengths and weaknesses revealed by the ratios
and any other information you consider relevant.
State clearly any assumptions you make.

9. Briefly explain the following accounting ratios and their importance in
terms of profitability, liquidity and operational efficiency.
(a) current ratio;
(b) acid test ratio;
(c) sales mix;
(d) net profit percentage;
(e) room yield;
(f) room density index;
(g) return on capital employed.

10. The following information relates to the Chatsworth Restaurant, a sole
owned establishment in a provincial city:

Balance sheet as at 31st May 1995

	Cost £	Dep'n £	Net £
Fixed assets			
Leasehold building	320,000	16,000	304,000
Kitchen equipment	60,000	6,000	54,000
Restaurant furniture	40,000	4,000	36,000
Loose equipment (china, etc.)	16,000	2,000	14,000
	436,000	28,000	408,000

	£	£	£
Current assets			
Food and beverage stocks		12,000	
Trade debtors		10,000	
Prepaid expenses		2,000	
Cash at bank		6,800	
Cash in hand		1,200	
		32,000	
Current liabilities			
Trade creditors	11,200		
Advance deposits	1,400		
Accrued expenses	4,600	17,200	
Net current assets			14,800
			422,800

	£
Financed by:	
Capital and Reserves	
Capital on 1st June 1994	360,800
Add: Net profit for year	76,000
	436,800
Less: Proprietor's drawings	14,000
	422,800

Additional information:
(a) The owner/manager has been paid a salary of £28,000, which has already been charged against profits.
(b) Sales for the year were:

Cash	£260,000
Credit	£112,000
	£372,000

(c) Purchases for the year were all on credit and totalled £98,400.
(d) On 1 June 1994 food and beverage stocks, trade debtors and trade creditors were valued at £17,600, £12,400 and £14,400 respectively.
(e) The restaurant is open 312 days per year.
(f) This type of establishment is expected to achieve a 16 per cent return on capital employed.

You are requested to examine the above data, from the point of view of a prospective purchaser, for profitability and liquidity and state, giving reasons supported by relevant calculations, if the restaurant would be a viable proposition at an asking price of £480,000.

Ignore income tax and VAT.

Management of working capital and the cash flow statement

23

INTRODUCTION

The owners of any enterprise make two major investments of capital in their business. The first is when they buy it: the capital invested in the building, furniture and fittings, kitchen equipment, etc. The second is the capital (in the form of cash) that they need to invest in stocks (food and drink for resale) and, particularly in a business with a large volume of credit sales, a further amount of cash is necessary to pay wages and running costs whilst awaiting payment from debtors.

Working capital may be defined as the necessary investment in stocks and cash to cover day-to-day running costs of the business.

It is important to realize that money tied up in working capital is a cost to the business in terms of either lost interest or overdraft charges and therefore must be controlled and kept at the minimum.

OBJECTIVES

On completion of the chapter you should be able to:
- understand the meaning of 'working capital';
- know why the need for working capital arises;
- list the key items affecting working capital;
- differentiate between the working capital needs of service industries and manufacturing industries;
- know how to control working capital;
- recognize transactions which affect working capital and those that do not;
- understand the term 'cash flow statement';
- comprehend the need for the production of a standard cash flow statement;
- draw up correctly a cash flow statement incorporating all key headings;
- extract the correct information from the profit and loss account and the balance sheet and place it in the cash flow statement;
- comment on the completed statement in terms of any increase/decrease in cash.

WHAT IS WORKING CAPITAL?

In simple terms working capital is the difference between current assets and current liabilities.

Working capital can be easily identified in the balance sheet as shown below:

EXTRACT FROM A BALANCE SHEET

Current Assets

	£	£	£
Stock		11,000	
Debtors		17,000	
Cash at bank		10,500	
		38,500	

Less Current Liabilities

Creditors	21,000		
Accruals	2,500	23,500	
Working capital			15,000

Students should note that all the above items are created by 'trading' activities, e.g.

- the business acquires stocks of food and drink which creates creditors and subsequently uses up cash at bank;
- stocks are processed and served to customers who, when they pay, increase the cash at bank (cash sales) or create debtors (credit sales);

Then the process starts all over again: more stock is bought, creating more creditors, which requires a cash outlay.

This is often referred to as the working capital cycle and may be expressed in diagrammatic form as shown in Figure 23.1:

Clearly the circulation of working capital is an oversimplification of

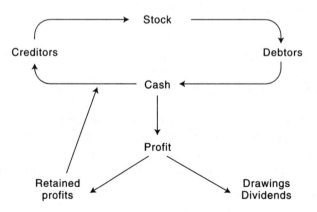

Figure 23.1 The working capital cycle

events – for instance, other expenses must be paid, but the basic idea is there. To enable the business to grow profits cannot be siphoned out completely. Some profits must be ploughed back into the business so that more stock can be bought to expand sales, increase profit and so on. In times of inflation it must be remembered that stock cannot be replaced at the same price as before so prices must be raised to provide additional cash resources, sometimes just to maintain the same quantity of stock.

THE WORKING CAPITAL CYCLE

The size of the investment in working capital depends largely on the type of business one operates, in particular the length of the working capital cycle. This means the length of time a business has to wait between **expending** its cash on materials and labour etc. in order to sell goods or services and **receiving** payment from its customers.

The hospitality industry has traditionally a relatively short working capital cycle. This is because, as a general rule, there is a high level of cash transactions (includes payment by cheque or credit card). In a number of establishments, for example, a public house or restaurant, one is likely to encounter a negative working capital because of the high levels of cash transactions, i.e. the business receives the cash from sales straightaway but may be allowed up to six weeks before paying for their purchases. In such a situation working capital may be completely financed by suppliers. Compare this to a brewery, which must expend large sums on materials and labour, wait many months or years for their product to mature, followed by distribution to sellers who will need a credit period of at least six weeks. All of the above will require a sizeable investment in working capital to cover wages/working expenses during that long time-lag between expending and receiving cash.

In a hospitality context, the sector to suffer most from the 'working capital cycle' effect, is the large city hotel with high accommodation sales which are mostly charged to companies. This is somewhat offset, because the most important sales in hotels are accommodation and service, which are not supported by stocks of materials.

CONTROLLING WORKING CAPITAL

Management must control the amount of cash tied up in working capital. This is because investment in working capital does not add value to anything, e.g. if more money is invested in fixed assets, the company can usually sell more goods and services as a result; but more money invested in working capital produces no more of anything.

The amount of working capital needed by a business normally depends on three things:

1. the level of trade;
2. the length of the working capital cycle;
3. the level of stocks required.

As explained earlier, when trade expands more stock is required, more debtors created, etc. therefore more money will have to be invested in working capital.

The working capital cycle is traditionally fairly short in the hospitality industry because of the nature of the product, i.e. the sale of a service (rooms) which does not have to be supported by stocks of raw materials.

Importance of control

Many hospitality managers regard working capital control and stock control as synonymous. The level of stocks held is of increasing importance because of the modern trend for hotels and restaurants to have large wine cellars. This can tie up a substantial amount of working capital. The best way to control working capital is to manage carefully the key items of debt collection and level of stocks held.

Controlling the key items

Systems will vary from business to business but the following are fairly general:

Stock: Regular stock-taking, reviewing the system of stock receipt and quality of suppliers (the more dependable the supplier the less need for large stocks). Regular analysis of fast and slow moving items.
Debtors: A good system of sales ledger control is essential with:
(a) age analysis and two-week reminder system;
(b) offer of discounts.
Creditors: Reduction of the number of suppliers and negotiate terms.

CHANGES IN WORKING CAPITAL

It is possible to think of the balance sheet as consisting of current and non-current items. If we draw a horizontal line after fixed assets and before the long-term liabilities and capital section, we will have, between the lines, current assets and current liabilities and, above and below the horizontal lines items of a non-current nature as illustrated below:

Balance Sheet

Fixed assets
Premises
Furniture & fittings   Non-Current
Kitchen equipment

Current Assets
Stock
Debtors
Cash
                                              Current

Less Current liabilities
Creditors
Accruals
Net current assets (Working Capital)

Long-term liabilities   Non Current

Financed by:
Capital A/c   Non Current
Add Net profit

Now that we have separated the current and non-current elements of the balance sheet, we can trace the effect of any one transaction on the working capital.

From the point of view of the impact on the working capital, transactions may be divided into three groups.

1. transactions which increase working capital;
2. transactions which decrease working capital;
3. transactions which have no effect on working capital.

Transactions which increase working capital

If the owners of a business introduce more capital then the effect is as follows:

Capital (below the horizontal line) is increased and cash (between the lines) is also increased. As current liabilities are unchanged and current assets have increased, we have an increase in working capital.

The same effect is obtained if we raise a long-term loan:

Long-term liabilities are increased (below the line). There is an increase in current assets (cash) between the lines and an increase in working capital.

Any withdrawal/reduction of capital will have the opposite effect:

Thus any drawings will decrease the current assets and, as current liabilities are not affected, the effect will be to decrease the working capital.

All profitable transactions have the effect of increasing working capital:

If we sell for £200 cash, beverages costing £100, the effect is this: current assets will increase by £100 (stock decreased by £100, but cash increased by £200). Net profit (below the line) will increase by £100. As current liabilities are not affected by the transaction, the working capital is increased by £100.

Transactions which decrease working capital

The purchase of fixed assets for cash will decrease current assets (cash) and increase fixed assets (above the line). As current liabilities are unchanged the effect will be to decrease working capital. Any withdrawal of owners' capital will, as already explained reduce working capital.

The effect of unprofitable transactions is to decrease working capital. If we sell food, costing £50, for £25 on credit, the effect is as follows. Current assets are decreased by £25 (food stocks having decreased by £50 and debtors increased by £25). Net profit (profit & loss account – below the line) will be decreased by £25. The working capital of the business will be decreased by £25.

Transactions which have no effect on working capital

There are several transactions which have no effect on working capital:

Thus if we purchase fixed assets and finance the transaction by a long-term loan, both effects are recorded outside the horizontal lines and neither current assets nor current liabilities are in any way affected.

When we pay suppliers, there is a decrease in current assets (cash) and a corresponding decrease in current liabilities (creditors) and the amount of working capital remains unaffected.

If we purchase goods on credit, we have an increase in current assets (stocks) and an increase in current liabilities (creditors) and hence no change in working capital.

Finally, when we write off depreciation we reduce both the fixed assets and the net profit. Both these items are non-current and the effect on the working capital is nil.

EXAMPLE 23.1

The balance sheet of a restaurant drawn up on 1st May 19 . . . is shown below:

Balance Sheet as at 1st May 19 . . .

Fixed Assets	£	£	£
Sundry fixed assets			460,000
Current Assets			
Food and beverage stocks		44,000	
Debtors		4,000	
Cash		12,000	
		60,000	

Less Current Liabilities	£	£	£
Creditors	32,000		
Accruals	8,000	40,000	
Net current assets (working capital)			20,000
			480,000
Financed by			£
Capital A/c			400,000
Add net profit			80,000
			480,000

On 2nd May 19 . . ., the following transactions took place:

(a) Beverage stocks, costing £800, were sold for £1,600 cash.
(b) The proprietor withdrew cash, £2,000, for private use.
(c) Cutlery was purchased for cash, £4,000.
(d) Food was purchased on credit, £8,000.
(e) Cash, £2,000, was received from debtors.
(f) Unwanted kitchen equipment was sold for cash, £1,600.

Required:

(a) to show the effect of each of the above transactions on the working capital;
(b) to prepare a statement, explaining the change in the total working capital between 1st and 2nd May 19 . . . ;
(c) to prepare the balance sheet of the restaurant as at 2nd May 19 . . .

Suggested Solution
Effect of transactions on working capital

(a) Current assets increased by £800; no change in current liabilities; working capital increased by £800.
(b) Current assets decreased by £2,000; no change in current liabilities; working capital decreased by £2,000.
(c) Current assets decreased by £4,000; no change in current liabilities; working capital decreased by £4,000.
(d) Both current assets and current liabilities increased by £8,000; no change in working capital.
(e) Current assets unchanged as decrease in debtors of £2,000 offset by corresponding increase in cash; hence no change in working capital.
(f) Current assets increased by £1,600; no change in current liabilities; increase in working capital of £1,600.

Statement explaining changes in working capital
From the analysis of the impact of the six transactions on working capital we may prepare a simple statement explaining the change in the overall working capital position between 1st and 2nd May 19 . . . as shown below:

		£
Working capital at 1st May 19 . . . (£60,000–£40,000)		20,000
Add Items which increase cash funds:		
Net profit (see note a)	800	
Sale of equipment (note f)	1,600	2,400
		22,400

Less Items which decrease cash funds

Drawings (note b)	2,000	
Purchase of cutlery (note c)	4,000	6,000
Working capital at 2nd May 19 . . . (£64,400–£48,000)		£16,400

Students should note that of the six transactions in Example 23.1, two increased the working capital, two decreased it and, finally, two had no effect at all on the working capital of the restaurant. Transactions (d) and (e) operated wholly outside the horizontal lines and were thus neutral. Each of the other four transactions operated across the horizontal line and had some effect on the working capital.

Balance Sheet

We may now show the balance sheet of the restaurant on 2nd May 19... as follows:

Balance sheet as at 1st May 19...

	£	£	£
Fixed assets			
Sundry fixed assets			462,400
Current assets			
Food and beverage stocks		51,200	
Debtors		2,000	
Cash		11,200	
		64,400	
Less Current liabilities			
Creditors	40,000		
Accruals	8,000	48,000	
Net Current assets (working capital)			16,400
			478,800
Financed by			£
Capital A/c			400,000
Add net profit			80,800
			480,800
Less drawings			2,000
			478,800

WORKING CAPITAL AND CASH FLOW

Changes in working capital can have a major effect on 'cash flow' (this means in simple terms how and when cash flows in and out of a business's bank account). Understanding cash flow is important to any business as it is widely recognized that it is often poor cash flow and not poor profitability which causes business failure.

Before moving on to cash flow statements it is useful to examine a situation as shown below where the cash funds have improved dramatically (from £3,000 to £6,500) but with no year-on-year increase in working capital (remains at £4,800) which would normally indicate a poor profit performance in that year.

EXAMPLE 23.2

	Extract from balance sheet end of year 1	Extract from balance sheet end of year 2
	£	£
Current assets		
Stock	15,000	17,000
Debtors	14,800	13,800
Cash at bank	3,000	6,500
	32,800	37,300
Current Liabilities		
Creditors	25,000	30,000
Accrued expenses	3,000	2,500
	28,000	32,500
Working capital	4,800	4,800

Assumption: The figures shown above for stock, debtors, creditors etc. represent the average value held over the year.

You are required to explain the mysterious increase in cash funds using the following framework:

(a) Show clearly how an increase/decrease in each item of working capital will affect cash funds.
(b) Reconcile the balance of cash at bank between the two years.

Stage 1
Examine each item individually, except cash at bank, and ask what effect an increase/decrease from year 1 to year 2 will have on cash, all other factors remaining equal.

Stock
Cause: There has been an increase in stock of £2,000 (£15,000–£17,000).
Effect: Clearly if we increase the value of stock held, this will ultimately reduce cash at bank by £2,000 – all other factors being equal.

Debtors
Cause: Debtors have decreased, the business is owed £1,000 (£14,800–£13,800) less at the end of year 2 than at the beginning.
Effect: The average amount owing in year 2 is £1,000 less than in year1. This should increase cash at bank by £1,000 over the year – all other factors being equal.

Creditors
Cause: Creditors have increased by £5,000 (£25,000–£30,000) between year 1 and 2.
Effect: This should increase cash at bank – all other factors being equal, i.e. If a business owes on average £5,000 more at the end of year 2 than at the beginning, theoretically the cash balance should be better off by £5,000.

Accrued expenses
Cause: Accrued expenses have decreased by £500 (£3,000–£2,500) over

the year. Please note that accrued expenses are simply creditors by another name and therefore behave in the same way.

Effect: If the business owes £500 less on average than a year ago obviously cash at bank will also be £500 less – all other things being equal.

Stage 2
Reconciliation Statement

		£	£
Balance of cash at bank at end of year 1			3,000
Add:	Decrease in debtors	1,000	
	Increase in creditors	5,000	
			6,000
			9,000
Less:	Increase in stock	(2,000)	
	Decrease in accrued expenses	(500)	
			(2,500)
Balance of cash at bank at end of year 2			6,500

Comment on statement

It is unusual for cash to increase over the year if not accompanied by an increase in profits, but the above statement demonstrates clearly how it occurred.

Note to student: it is important to understand clearly the technique used in the above example as you will need to use a similiar approach as part of your construction of a cash flow statement below.

THE CASH FLOW STATEMENT

Many accountants and analysts consider this to be the most important statement found in the accounts. It can reveal more about the business than the profit & loss account or balance sheet. After all, cash is the one thing that cannot be 'created'. A close examinination of the movement of cash in a business provides a considerably clearer idea of the business's financial stability and long-term viability. In addition cash flow statements offer a useful starting point for interpretation of accounts or financial analysis.

Purpose of the statement

All limited companies over a certain size are obliged to produce a cash flow statement as part of their presentation accounts registered annually with the Registrar of Companies. The pre-set structure of the statement ensures uniformity of approach and facilitates inter-company comparison from year to year. Its overriding purpose is to explain the changes in the financial position of a company which cannot be explained by the profit and loss account alone.

In Figure 23.2 there is an example of the standard layout of the statement:

	£	£
Cash flow from:		
Operating Activities		
Operating profit before tax	X	
<u>Add</u> back depreciation	<u>X</u>	X
<u>Add</u> increase in creditors	X	
<u>Less</u> increase in stock	(X)	
increase in debtors	<u>(X)</u>	(X)
Net cash flow from operating activities		X
Returns on Investment and Servicing of Finance		
Dividends paid	(X)	
Interest	<u>(X)</u>	(X)
Net cash outflow from returns on investments		
and servicing of finance		X
Taxation		
Tax paid	<u>(X)</u>	
Net cash outflow from taxation		(X)
Investing Activities		
Purchase of fixed assets	(X)	
Sale of investment	<u>X</u>	
Net cash outflow from investing activities		(X)
Net cash outflow before financing		(X)
Financing		
New share issue	X	
Repayment of loan	<u>(X)</u>	
Net cash inflow from financing		X
Increase (Decrease) in cash or cash equivalents		X

Figure 23.2 Specimen cash flow statement

The student should note that the presentation cash flow statement, in Figure 23.2 above, will usually carry additional notes at the end of the statement to further explain items within the statement and will, for example, help to identify how the shortfall was funded and whether the company used its cash balances or increased its overdraft.

The effect of depreciation on cash flow

Depreciation is a legitimate expense of the business and as such is written off in the profit and loss account before arriving at net profit.

However, when the net profit is placed in the cash flow statement it is necessary to add back depreciation. Why should this be so?

Depreciation is different from all other expenses in the sense that it is the only expense where money does not change hands. For example, compare the two expenses of rent and depreciation. Both are legitimate expenses of the business, both are entered in the profit and loss account. The difference is that the rent money must physically change hands from the business to the landlord which means the business bank balance is reduced. Depreciation on the other hand is a non-cash expense because it does not entail an external payment and does not reduce funds; therefore depreciation must be added back in order to arrive at the real increase in cash funds from net profit.

Key headings in the statement

The statement shows in summary form the cash flows in and out of the business during the accounting year. It identifies the main sources of cash and shows how the cash has been spent.

Cash flows are shown functionally and are grouped together as follows:

Cash flows from:	Example
1. Operating activities.	Trading profit plus current depreciation and takes account of cash increases/decreases by changes in working capital items.
2. Interest on investments/ servicing of finance	Items such as interest paid and on loans and dividends paid.
3. Taxation	Tax paid.
4. Investing Activities	Buying and selling of fixed assets.

These cash flows are totalled, identifying whether the business has generated a surplus or deficit of cash. The resulting cash flow total is referred to as 'cash flows before financing'. Having shown whether the business is living within its means or not, the statement then identifies where the company has applied the surplus or how it has dealt with the deficit. This is represented by:

5. Cash flows from financing	New share issues or loans acquired.

Note on first heading in statement – operating activities

There are two different methods of presenting this information in the statement, known as the direct and indirect methods. Both methods express the same information in a different way. The direct method shows cash receipts and payments. On the other hand the indirect method reconciles the operating profit to the operating cash flow. Whichever method is used a reconciliation statement must be shown in the statement. The authors have chosen to use only the indirect method shown below:

Cash flow from operating activities	£	£
Operating profit		18,000
Add back depreciation		31,000
		49,000
Less: Increase in stock*	(25,000)	
Add: Decrease in debtors*	24,000	
Increase in creditors*	17,000	16,000
Net cash inflow from operating activities		65,000

* These figures are calculated using two consecutive balance sheets, e.g. the increase in stock is the difference between this year's and last year's figure for stock in the relevant balance sheets.

In the above example, this business has only generated £49,000 from this year's trading operations but has managed to generate £65,000 during the year – the balance coming from changes in working capital. This is because, although stock has increased, this has been more than offset by a decrease in debtors and an increase in creditors.

WORKED EXAMPLES

1. Given below are details of the balance sheet and profit and loss accounts of the Breakpoint Hotel Ltd which has been operating for a number of years.

Balance Sheet of the Breakpoint Hotel Ltd
as at 31st March

	1995 £	1995 £	1995 £	1996 £	1996 £	1996 £
Fixed assets at cost			80,000			100,000
Less Depreciation			30,000			40,000
			50,000			60,000
Current assets						
Stock		10,545			14,135	
Prepayments		500			500	
Debtors		3,900			4,605	
Bank		2,100			1,738	
		17,045			20,978	
Less Current liabilities						
Creditors	2,305			2,470		
Accruals	500			500		
Taxation	765			1,025		
Proposed dividend	1,250			1,875		
		4,820			5,870	
			12,225			15,108
Less Long-term liabilities						
Debenture loan			(10,000)			(15,000)
			£52,225			£60,108

Financed by	£	£
Issued share capital	32,500	35,000
Profit and loss account	19,725	25,108
	£52,225	£60,108

Profit and Loss Account for year ended 31st March 1996

	£
Operating profit before tax	8,283
Tax on operating Profit	1,025
	7,258
Profit and loss account b/f	19,725
	26,983
Proposed dividends	1,875
Profit and loss account c/f to balance sheet	25,108

Proceed as shown below:

Suggested solution

Cash flow statement
for year ended 31st March 1996

Cash flow from:	£	£
Operating Activities		
Operating profit before tax		8,283
Add back depreciation		10,000
		18,283
Add Increase in creditors	165	
Less Increase in stock	(3,590)	
Increase in debtors	(705)	(4,130)
Net cash flow from operating activities		14,153
Return on Investments and Servicing of Finance		
Dividends paid		(1,250)
Taxation		
Tax paid		(765)
Net cash flow before investing and finance		12,138
Investing Activities		
Purchases of fixed assets		(20,000)
Net cash flow before financing		(7,862)
Financing		
Issue of shares	2,500	
New loan	5,000	7,500
Reduction in cash and cash equivalents		(362)

Notes:

(a) The usual practice of the Breakpoint Hotel is to show all inflows of cash as positive and all outflows as negative (in brackets).

(b) Analysis of cash balances in balance sheet (and a means of checking the correctness of your answer).

	£
Bank balance at 31st March 1995	2,100
Reduction in cash/cash equivalents	(362)
Bank balance at 31st March 1996	1,738

(c) Analysis of changes in finance during year.

	Share capital £	Long term loans £
Balance at 31st March 1995	32,500	10,000
New issue of shares/loan	2,500	5,000
Balance at 31st March 1996	35,000	15,000

(d) Dividend paid: The dividend in this year's profit and loss account (£1,875) is only proposed and will not be paid until next year. Thus the only dividend paid in the last year is £1,250 from the balance sheet ended 31st March 1995.

(e) Taxation paid: Taxation on this year's accounts will be paid next year and so on. Therefore the tax paid during the current year will be the £765 from the balance sheet of 31st March 1995.

Comments on cash flow statement.

This statement shows a business that is generating more than enough cash to pay its dividends and tax commitments and has a £12,138 surplus before investing activities.

The new issue of shares and the new loan would appear to have been the result of the need for additional cash to pay for new fixed assets of £20,000. This purchase has dramatically reduced the cash surplus and perhaps a somewhat larger new share issue may have been prudent, assuming the demand for shares was there.

2. Given below in summary form is the profit and loss account of P J Finnegan (Hotels) Ltd and the balance sheets for 1995 and 1996:

P J Finnegan (Hotels) Ltd
Profit and Loss account for year ended 31st December 1996

	£
Operating profit before tax	55,000
Tax on profit	11,000
	44,000
Add retained profits at 1st Jan	48,000
	92,000
Less proposed dividends	10,000
Retained profits carried on to next year	82,000

During 1996 no leasehold property or plant was disposed of. The managing director is puzzled by the fact that although he made a profit of £55,000 during 1996 his bank balance appears to have fallen by £68,000 during the year.

The balance sheets of P J Finnegan (Hotels) Ltd, for the years ended 31st December 1995 and 1996 were as follows:

Balance sheets

Fixed assets	Cost	1995 Dep'n	Net	Cost	1996 Dep'n	Net
	£	£	£	£	£	£
Leasehold	320,000	270,000	50,000	320,000	300,000	20,000
Kitchen equip.	250,000	210,000	40,000	420,000	218,000	202,000
Furniture etc.	100,000	60,000	40,000	100,000	62,000	38,000
	670,000	540,000	130,000	840,000	580,000	260,000
Investments						
Trade investment at cost			40,000			–
Investment in Distillers & Co.		–				80,000
Current assets						
Stock		44,000			86,000	
Debtors		28,000			60,000	
Cash at bank		16,000			–	
		88,000			146,000	
Less current liabilities						
Creditors	18,000			23,000		
Taxation	10,000			11,000		
Proposed divs	8,000			10,000		
Bank overdraft	–	36,000		52,000	96,000	
Net current assets			52,000			50,000
Loan from Castle Brewers			–			(100,000)
			222,000			290,000
Financed by						
Share capital at 1st January			174,000			208,000
Retained profit			48,000			82,000
			222,000			290,000

Assuming that all the above figures are correct, you are required to tabulate briefly the main points you would make in explaining to Mr Finnegan the reasons for the fall in his bank balance despite the high profit earned in 1996.

Proceed as shown below:

Suggested solution

Cash Flow Statement
for year ended 31st December 1996

Cash flow from:	£	£
Operating activities		
Operating profit before tax		55,000
Add Back depreciation	40,000	
Add Increase in creditors	5,000	
Less Increase in stock	(42,000)	
Increase in debtors	(32,000)	(29,000)
Net cash flow from operating activities		26,000
Return on investments and servicing of finance		
Dividends paid		(8,000)
Taxation		
Tax paid		(10,000)
Net cash flow before investing and finance		8,000
Investing activities		
Purchases of fixed assets	(170,000)	
Sale of investment	40,000	
Purchase of investment	(80,000)	(210,000)
Net cash flow before financing		(202,000)
Financing		
Issue of shares		34,000
New loan		100,000
Reduction in cash and cash equivalents		(68,000)

Report

1. The cash increase from sale of investment (£40,000) was more than offset by the purchase of a new one (£80,000) in 1996.
2. The money received from the sale of a new share issue (£34,000) and a new loan (£100,000) did not cover the purchase of a major fixed asset (£170,000). Therefore the difference (£36,000) is required to come from cash in hand.
3. The dramatic increase in stock (from £44,000 to £86,000) and debtors (from £28,000 to £60,000) decreases cash available for use.
4. The year on year increase in creditors increases cash available.

Footnote

Most limited companies, with the exception of small private companies, are required to publish a cash flow statement in their published accounts, to show the movement of cash in the business. The procedure is laid down by the accounting standard known as FRS 1.

This statement replaces the old sources and application of funds statement and more clearly identifies the cash flows in the business. It is widely regarded as easier to understand and interpret.

SUMMARY

- The hospitality industry is characterized by high fixed costs and low working capital
- Working capital is the difference between current assets and current liabilities.
- The working capital cycle illustrates the time-lag between investing in stocks and receiving the money from sales.
- Hospitality businesses in general have a short working capital cycle.
- Large city hotels with high bed occupancy from business people will be the most seriously affected by time-lag factor.
- Management must exercise control to keep working capital to a minimum.
- The key items to control are stock value, debtors and cash in current account.
- The amount of funds flowing into working capital from profit is not likely to be the same as net profit. Adjustments must be made for items which do not involve any movement of funds, e.g. depreciation.
- The balance sheet can be divided into current and non-current items.
- It is important to differentiate between transactions which increase working capital, decrease it and have no effect on it.
- Most larger limited companies are required to produce a cash flow statement in addition to the normal final accounts.
- The cash flow statement links the net cash flow from operating activities to other inflows in order to explain the movement of cash resources.
- The aim of the statement is to ensure that all companies follow the same format and make it easier to identify and compare cash flows in and out of a company.
- The cash flow statement has a strict format required by FRS 1. It contains a series of headings under which cash inflows and outflows are grouped.
- One of the main reasons for this statement is that changes in the financial position of a company cannot be properly explained by the profit and loss account alone.
- The main headings of the statement are cash flows from:
  (a) operating activities;
  (b) returns on investment and servicing of finance;
  (c) taxation;
  (d) investing activities; and
  (e) financing.
- It is important to have a clear understanding of what is taking place in the cash flow statement and to comment on it.

PROBLEMS

1. What do you understand by the term 'working capital'?

2. Describe the working capital cycle and state to what degree it affects the hospitality industry.

3. List three ways of controlling the amount of cash invested in working capital.

4. Describe the effect of transactions on working capital. Give examples of transactions which:
   (a) increase;
   (b) decrease; and
   (c) have no effect on working capital.

5. Explain what you understand by the term 'cash flow'.

6. Name three key items of information which you would expect to elicit from a completed cash flow statement.

7. List the five key headings which make up the cash flow statement.

8. The directors of the Haywood Hotel Co. Ltd have been worried for some time about the cash flow position of their hotel since their bank balance appears to be decreasing despite increases in profit.
   Two consecutive balance sheets have been produced in summary form as follows to facilitate the preparation of a cash flow statement:

Balance sheets

	1996 £	1996 £	1997 £	1997 £
Fixed assets				
Assets at cost	80,000		104,000	
Less Agg. depn	20,000	60,000	24,000	80,000
Current assets				
Stock	15,000		11,000	
Debtors	50,000		48,000	
Prepayments	2,000		4,000	
Cash at bank	40,000		36,000	
	107,000		99,000	
Less current liabilities				
Creditors	25,000		5,000	
Accrued expenses	4,000		2,000	
Taxation	2,000		3,000	
Proposed dividends	8,000		7,000	
	39,000		17,000	

Net current assets	68,000	82,000
	128,000	162,000
Financed by:		
Ordinary shares	120,000	150,000
Profit and loss account	8,000	12,000*
	128,000	162,000

* Before drawing up the statement the student will need to calculate the operating profit for 1997. This entails finding this year's profit (difference between profit & loss account figures) and adding back this year's proposed dividends and taxation.

Required:

(a) Prepare a cash flow statement in accordance with good accounting practice.
(b) State, with reasons, if you believe there is cause for concern over the cash flow position of this business.
(c) Write a brief note on the purpose of the cash flow statement.

9. Given below are the balance sheets of the Mayo Hotel Ltd for the years ended 31st March 1995 and 1996 respectively. There were no purchases of fixed assets during the current year.

   Using the balance sheets given below you are required to draw up a cash flow statement in accordance with good accounting practice.

Balance sheet as at 31st March

1995 £		1996 £
	Fixed assets	
450,000	Premises (net)	450,000
360,000	Kitchen equipment (net)	315,000
45,000	Fixtures, etc.	36,000
855,000		801,000
	Current assets	
135,000	Stock at cost	270,000
315,000	Debtors (net)	360,000
22,500	Cash at bank	–
472,500		630,000
	Less current liabilities:	
400,000	Creditors	355,000
–	Bank overdraft	22,500
40,000	Taxation	35,000
10,000	Dividends	15,000
450,000		427,500
22,500	Net current assets	202,500
(360,000)	Long-term loan	(270,000)
517,500		733,500

	Financed by:	
375,000	Issued share capital	517,500
142,500	Retained profits	216,000
517,500		733,500

Students should note that here again they are required, as a pre-requisite to preparing the cash flow statement, to work out the operating profit for 1996. To achieve this one needs to add back the appropriations which, in this case, are taxation (1996) and dividends (1996).

The above information will apply equally to other questions in this chapter.

10. The Taverno Hotel Ltd has been trading successfully for many years. The owner has always recognized the importance of cash flow to business success, but he could never elicit enough information from the balance sheet. He has provided two comparative balance sheets as shown below.

Balance sheets

	1994		1995	
	£	£	£	£
Fixed assets				
Leasehold building	1,200,000		1,560,000	
Less Agg. dep'n	300,000	900,000	360,000	1,200,000
Equipment and fittings	100,000		130,000	
Less Agg. dep'n	70,000	30,000	85,000	45,000
		930,000		1,245,000
Current assets				
Stock	150,000		90,000	
Debtors	750,000		720,000	
Prepayments	30,000		60,000	
Cash at bank	600,000		540,000	
	1,530,000		1,410,000	
Less current liabilities				
Creditors	450,000		150,000	
Accrued expenses	60,000		30,000	
Proposed dividends	30,000		45,000	
	540,000		225,000	
Net current assets		990,000		1,185,000
		1,920,000		2,430,000

Financed by:	£	£
Ordinary shares	1,800,000	2,250,000
Profit and loss account	120,000	180,000
	1,920,000	2,430,000

You are required to draw up a cash flow statement in accordance with good accounting practice.

Write a brief note to the owner highlighting the types of useful information which one can elicit from the cash flow statement but not necessarily from the balance sheet.

11. Given below are the balance sheets of the Robertas Hotel as at 31st December 1996 and 1997. The owner of the hotel cannot understand how a profit of £60,750 has resulted in a bank balance of £20,250 at the beginning of the year becoming an overdraft of £21,000 by the end of the year.

Balance Sheets

		1996			1997	
Fixed assets	Cost	Dep'n	Net	Cost	Dep'n	Net
	£	£	£	£	£	£
Premises	87,000		87,000	87,000		87,000
Kitchen equip.	126,000	80,000	46,000	126,000	83,900	42,100
Furniture, etc.	96,000	40,000	56,000	96,000	43,000	53,000
	309,000	120,000	189,000	309,000	126,900	182,100
Current assets						
Stock		50,100			66,525	
Debtors		40,500			66,000	
Cash at bank		20,250			–	
Cash in hand		150			375	
		111,000			132,900	
Less current liabilities						
Creditors	29,250			26,250		
Bank overdraft	–	29,250		21,000	47,250	
Net current assets			81,750			85,650
			270,750			267,750
Financed by			£			£
Capital at 1st January			255,000			270,750
Add: net profit for year			49,500			60,750
			304,500			331,500
Less drawings			33,750			63,750
			270,750			267,750

Required:

(a) Show by means of a cash flow statement how the above situation has arisen.

(b) Write a short report to the owner of the hotel by way of explanation.

12. The Sirocco Leisure Complex Ltd makes up its accounts to 31st December each year.

   Given below are two consecutive balance sheets for the restaurant complex for the years 1995 and 1996.

Balance sheets

	1995		1996	
Fixed assets	£	£	£	£
Assets at cost	180,000		228,000	
Less Agg. dep'n	30,000	150,000	36,000	192,000
Current assets				
Stock	15,000		9,000	
Debtors	75,000		72,000	
Prepayments	3,000		6,000	
Cash at bank	60,000		54,000	
	153,000		141,000	
Less current liabilities				
Creditors	45,000		15,000	
Accrued expenses	6,000		3,000	
Proposed dividends	10,000		12,000	
	61,000		30,000	
Net current assets		92,000		111,000
Less long-term loan		(50,000)		(60,000)
		192,000		243,000
Financed by:				
Ordinary shares		180,000		225,000
Profit and loss account		12,000		18,000
		192,000		243,000

You are required the draw up a cash flow statement in accordance with good accounting practice.

   Comment briefly on the advantages of producing a cash flow statement; use examples from your completed statement to illustrate your answer.

Budgeting and budgetary control 24

INTRODUCTION

More and more attention is being attached to budgeting in the hospitality industry. Virtually all businesses of any size now use budgeting as a major instrument in their controlling, planning and forecasting strategy.

Budgeting techniques have been widely used in Britain for over twenty five years now and have received much praise and criticism over that period.

A budget is, at best, only an educated guess at what results a business may achieve in the coming year. Used sensibly it can be of great assistance with revenue and cost control, planning and dissemination of information. It can improve cash flow and motivate staff. Its critics say, however, that it is often a rigid forecast, imposed on the middle managers by senior management and used, in effect, as a weapon to discipline them. Nevertheless most young managers entering the industry today can expect a budget to loom large in their day-to-day activities.

OBJECTIVES

On completion of this chapter you should be able to:

- understand the terms 'budget' and 'budgetary control';
- appreciate the significance of the terms: budget committee; budget period and budget review period;
- list the different types of budget;
- differentiate between capital budgets and operating budgets;
- comprehend the meaning of the 'limiting factor';
- build up an operating budget in a systematic and logical manner;
- use budgeting techniques to determine the budgeted sales target;
- place the following budgets meaningfully in an overall budget plan: labour cost; overhead cost; office and administration; marketing;
- draw up a cash budget and correctly enter transactions therein.

DEFINITIONS, AIMS AND TERMS

A **budget** is a plan, expressed in monetary or other terms, which governs the operation of a business over a predetermined period of time. Whereas most budgets (e.g. sales budget, labour cost budget) are expressed in terms of money, some are expressed in terms of units or percentages. A personnel budget may be expressed in terms of numbers of employees to be replaced or engaged over a period of time. A sales budget invariably shows the budgeted value of sales; it may, in addition, show the budgeted number of covers or the budgeted rate of room occupancy.

Budgetary control is a means of control by which responsibility for various budgets is assigned to the managers concerned and a continual comparison is made of the actual results with the budgeted results. Where there are discrepancies between the two, appropriate corrective action is taken.

From the definitions given above it will be realized that a budget is the plan on which a system of budgetary control is based. The budget sets standards of performance (targets) for the managers of a business. Budgetary control is a means of ensuring that the objectives set for the managers are fulfilled.

The main objectives and the consequent advantages of budgeting may be summarized as follows:

- the budget is a detailed plan of action which guides and regulates the progress of a business;
- budgeting results in a better co-ordination of all activities of a business;
- the budget sets standards against which the performance of those responsible may be measured and assessed;
- budgeting is an important method of expense and revenue control; it establishes clear lines of cost responsibility and promotes cost consciousness;
- budgeting ensures an economical utilization of the resources of a business and thus helps to maximize profits.

FORMULATION OF THE BUDGET

Budget committee

Where there is a system of budgetary control in operation there is invariably constituted a budget committee. This consists of the senior executive of the business (managing director or general manager), several senior managers (e.g. the food and beverage manager, executive chef, executive housekeeper, banqueting manager) and the accountant. The senior executive usually acts as chairman and the accountant as secretary of the budget committee.

Before any budgets are drawn up the budget committee must decide how the overall system of budgeting will fit into the existing structure of the business. This entails a review of the organizational structure of the business and a definition of each manager's authority and responsibility. It is only when this preliminary work has been done that it is possible to draw up the necessary budgets for the various departments of the business. The departmental, as well as other, budgets will set appropriate targets expressed in terms of turnover, profit margins, operating ratios and cost limits.

The main function of the budget committee is to prepare budget proposals (draft budgets) for submission to the board of directors. When preparing the budget proposals the budget committee will take into account the following:

(a) Past performance – this entails a thorough analysis of past income, expenditure, trends in income and expenditure, etc.
(b) Current trends – this necessitates a review of the current position with regard to the items mentioned in (a) above.
(c) Other information – would include a consideration of the prosperity of the particular sector of the hospitality industry, the condition of local industries, the degree of unemployment, if any, and the degree of competition.

The budget period

Another function of the budget committee is to choose an appropriate budget period. This, in most hospitality establishments, is one calendar year.

All businesses whether large or small have budgets covering a period of one year. Where the budget year runs from January to December work on the following year's budget will start early in October so that budget proposals are ready for submission to the board of directors early in December.

The review period

In addition to determining the budget period the budget committee must choose the most appropriate review period (also referred to as 'control period').

As already mentioned, an essential part of budgetary control is the continual comparison of the actual with the budgeted results. Budget reports will be submitted at various intervals: some will cover one week, others will cover a period of one month. In addition there will be quarterly and half-yearly reports.

KINDS OF BUDGETS

There are several kinds of budgets used in hospitality establishments.

From the point of view of the subject-matter budgeted for we may distinguish:

- **Capital budgets** – these are budgets dealing with the assets and the capital funds of a business. Examples of capital budgets are budgets dealing with equipment and plant, cash, any proposed issue of shares or debentures.
- **Operating budgets** – these are budgets concerned with the day-to-day running of the business. Examples of operating budgets are those dealing with sales, purchases, labour costs, office and administration expenses, maintenance, etc.

From the point of view of the comprehensiveness of budgets, we may distinguish:

- **Master budgets** – a master budget may be a budgeted profit and loss account, incorporating all income and all expenditure of a business; it may also be a budgeted balance sheet, incorporating all assets and liabilities of a business.
- **Departmental budgets** – these are concerned with particular departments of a business. Examples of such budgets are: banqueting budget, maintenance budget, rooms division budget; food and beverage budget.

From the point of view of the level of sales assumed we may distinguish:

- **Fixed budgets** – these remain unchanged irrespective of the level of sales achieved. Thus a sales promotion budget may be a fixed budget in that the expenditure (press advertising, printing of brochures, etc.) may be a fixed amount allocated before the commencement of the budget period.
- **Flexible budgets** – a flexible budget predetermines costs in relation to several possible volumes of sales. The cost of sales budget of a resort restaurant relying on day trippers – and therefore dependent on weather conditions – will normally be a flexible budget. In seasonal hotels the labour cost budget will also be a flexible budget in that the budgeted labour costs will be planned in relation to the changing rate of occupancy. It is pointed out that a particular establishment may have some fixed and some flexible budgets. A hotel may have a flexible labour cost budget and fixed budgets for sales promotion, maintenance and office and administration expenses. Second, students should realize a particular budget does not necessarily fall under one of the types given above. A labour cost budget is an operating budget but it may also be a departmental budget and a flexible or fixed budget.

THE LIMITING FACTOR

The first step in the preparation of a budget is to forecast the volume of sales, as it is this that affects most other parts of the budget. Thus, the forecast volume of sales will determine the level of all variable and semi-fixed costs; also it will affect the cash position of the business which, in turn, may determine the amount of capital expenditure planned for the period.

When forecasting the future volume of sales it is important to remember what is known as the 'limiting factor' (also referred to as the 'key factor', 'governing factor' and 'principal budget factor'). This is the factor that limits the volume of sales and makes a further increase in sales impossible.

The following limiting factors will be found operating in hospitality establishments.

1. **Accommodation available** – this operates in residential establishments, namely, hotels, motels, hostels, etc. Once all the accommodation available has been let it is impossible to increase the volume of sales except by raising prices.
2. **Seating capacity** – this applies particularly to restaurants where the seating capacity is fixed; also to banqueting sales, as insufficient seating capacity may well result in loss of potential sales.
3. **Insufficient capital** – in a multiple catering business an expansion of sales through the acquisition of further units may be impossible due to insufficient capital.
4. **Shortage of efficient labour** – many hospitality establishments could increase their sales by improving the efficiency of their labour. Thus the speed with which cash is taken by the cashier in a self-service restaurant has an important bearing on the volume of sales; similarly, the speed with which waiters serve customers can affect the volume of sales considerably. The abilities of the chef and other kitchen staff are equally important in this respect.
5. **Shortage of efficient executives** – this, obviously, is even more important than a shortage of efficient labour. Inefficient management makes an expansion of sales difficult through bad organization, unimaginative menu planning and failure to take advantage of any opportunities to increase sales that may present themselves.
6. **Management policy** – an increase in sales may be impossible as a result of the deliberate policy of a business. Thus a restaurant may discourage the 'wrong' type of customer; a hotel may refuse to accept coach tour business, football teams, etc.
7. **Consumer demand** – this is a limiting factor the operation of which is most difficult to remove. Consumer demand may be limited in several ways: by the prices charged; through competition, as a result of a fixed potential demand, e.g. in industrial canteens. When an increase in sales proves difficult it is important to identify the limiting factor(s). The nature of the limiting factor will then indicate the most appropriate method of dealing with the problem.

OPERATING BUDGETS

A full and detailed description of all the operating budgets used in the hospitality industry is, clearly, outside the scope of this textbook. We will, therefore, deal with one operating budget (sales budget) at some length and only refer in a general way to other operating budgets.

Sales budget

This is the most important and the most difficult budget to prepare. It is the most important budget because it affects the accuracy of most other budgets. Thus, if budgeted sales are forecast inaccurately, budgeted variable and semi-variable costs will also be inaccurate. Similarly, the cash budget, which is obviously affected by the volume of sales, will be inaccurate. It is difficult to produce as, naturally, there are many external and therefore uncontrollable factors that influence the actual level of sales.

The sales budget is prepared on the basis of the following:

Past performance: (a) actual sales of previous periods; (b) sales mix; (c) trends in sales and sales mix.

Current trends: (a) trends in sales and sales mix; (b) bookings received for accommodation, banquets, etc.

Limiting factors: Where the increase in sales is considered inadequate, limiting factors should be identified and dealt with accordingly.

Other information: (a) condition of local industries; (b) state of employment and prosperity in the locality concerned; (c) political situation, government policy, etc. and their effect on future turnover.

EXAMPLE 24.1

The Essex Restaurant is a large, licensed establishment and budgets its sales a year in advance; actual sales are reviewed in the light of the budgeted figures at the end of each four-weekly period. The sales of the restaurant for the past three years have been as follows:

Analysis of past sales

	1993 £	1994 £	1995 £
Restaurant sales	179,500	186,500	190,200
Percentage increase on previous year	7%	4%	2%
Bar sales	91,000	95,500	102,200
Percentage increase on previous year	4%	5%	7%
Sundry sales	30,500	32,000	34,000
Percentage increase on previous year	5%	5%	6%
Total sales	301,000	314,000	326,400
Percentage increase on previous year	6%	4.3%	4%

The following supplementary information is also made available.

(a) **Restaurant sales**: the rate of increase in this section of the turnover is falling off. This is due to the limited dining room space available. It is thought that, in the circumstances, little increase in sales is possible.
(b) **Bar sales**: the turnover has been rising satisfactorily but in view of the limiting factor restricting restaurant sales a higher rate of increase cannot be expected.
(c) **Sundry sales**: this is expected to increase at least as well as in 1995.

Determination of sales target

Having due regard to the past trends in sales and all other relevant factors the following sales targets are set for 1996.

(a) Restaurant sales: it is decided that these ought to be increased by 4 per cent. In view of the limited space available the increase in sales is to be achieved through increased prices. To this end, all restaurant prices are to be revised early in the year.

(b) Bar sales: these ought to show an increase of 7 per cent on the previous year.

(c) Sundry sales: in view of the past trend, an increase of 7 per cent should be aimed for. The budgeted sales for 1996 are therefore:

	£		£
Restaurant sales	190,200	+4%	197,800
Bar sales	102,200	+7%	109,350
Sundry sales	34,000	+7%	36,380
			£343,530

The budgeted sales for each four-weekly period are:

Restaurant sales	$\dfrac{£197,800}{13}$	=	£15,215	say £15,200
Bar sales	$\dfrac{£109,350}{13}$	=	£8,411	say £8,400
Sundry sales	$\dfrac{£36,380}{13}$	=	£2,798	say £2,800
	Total monthly sales			£26,400

At the end of each four-weekly period the actual sales would be compared with budgeted sales; any discrepancies (variances) would then be investigated and the necessary corrective action would be taken. The following is a monthly sales report, based on the figures given above:

Essex Restaurant
Monthly sales report for 4 weeks ended 28th January 1996
To: 1. Managing director
    2. General manager
From: Catering controller

	Budgeted sales £	Actual sales £	Variances + or −
Restaurant sales	15,200	14,400	− 800
Bar sales	8,400	8,500	+ 100
Sundry sales	2,800	2,950	+ 150
Total	26,400	25,850	− 550

Note: Only a partial revision of restaurant prices has taken place; a complete revision is called for.

Labour cost budget

This would be evolved in relation to the budgeted volume of sales. When an increase in sales is budgeted for it is necessary to establish how much of the increase can be dealt with by the existing staff of the establishment. A labour cost budget cannot be realistic unless it is based on a detailed analysis of the staffing of each department *vis-à-vis* the budgeted turnover. The budget will have to take into account the following:

(a) the number and grades of staff in each department;
(b) the current rates of pay for each grade of staff;
(c) casual labour and authorized overtime;
(d) proposed changes in staffing, rates of pay and grading of staff;
(e) staff meals, holiday pay and other labour costs.

Overhead cost budget

Whilst a smaller hospitality establishment would tend to have an overhead cost budget covering all overheads, larger establishments would tend to have separate budgets for the various component parts of overhead expenditure, e.g. maintenance, office and administration costs, marketing, etc.

The overhead cost budget is also evolved in relation to the budgeted sales. It must, therefore, clearly distinguish between fixed overheads (rates, depreciation of premises, licences, etc.) and variable and semi-variable overheads (gas, electricity, telephone, laundry, cleaning materials, etc.)

Office and administration budget

This budget will tend to change little from one year to another. The most important items covered by the office and administration budget are:

(a) office salaries;
(b) depreciation of office equipment;
(c) telephone;
(d) printing and stationery;
(e) insurances, bank charges and audit fees.

As with all other budgets the office and administration budget will distinguish between fixed and variable costs. This is particularly important in seasonal establishments.

Maintenance budget

Whilst most smaller hospitality establishments include maintenance costs in a total expense budget or overhead cost budget, larger units tend to have a separate maintenance budget.

A well-prepared maintenance budget will do two things: first, it will predetermine the maintenance costs; second, it will show the sequence of the work to be done over the budget period.

Budgeted maintenance costs will be arrived at by reference to:

(a) the state of the premises, kitchen plant, furniture and other equipment;
(b) the standard of comfort which it is necessary to provide, having regard to the type of customer catered for; and
(c) the current availability of funds.

The costs which have to be taken into account are:

(a) maintenance materials and supplies – items such as paints, wallpaper, electrical components, loose tools and other supplies required by the maintenance department;
(b) maintenance labour costs – this includes all wages and salaries payable to the maintenance staff; and
(c) other costs such as depreciation of maintenance department's equipment, stationery, office supplies, etc.

The sequencing of maintenance work is necessary to ensure that it does not interfere with current operations (e.g. the selling of rooms, banqueting business) and that all budgeted maintenance work is completed in a thought-out, logical manner.

Finally, when planning a maintenance budget it is necessary to distinguish between and itemize separately (a) routine maintenance work and (b) maintenance work to be carried out by outside parties in respect of any maintenance contracts. Provision must also be made for emergency repair work which, though quite unpredictable, always presents a claim on the staff of the maintenance department.

Marketing budget

In smaller establishments any marketing and sales promotion expenditure would be included in the overhead cost budget. In larger businesses – hotels rather than restaurants – the marketing budget will involve a large amount of expense and include amongst others:

a) salaries of the marketing staff;
b) cost of press and television advertising;
c) cost of printing brochures and other promotional material;
d) other expenditure such as office expenses, travel, entertainment etc.

CAPITAL BUDGETS

Capital budgets, as already explained, are budgets concerned with the assets and capital funds of a business. More specifically, they are budgets in respect of matters such as: capital expenditure on new fixed assets, cash, debtors, stocks; the raising of fresh capital by the issue of shares or debentures, etc. In practice, the most important of such budgets is the cash budget.

CASH BUDGET

This is prepared from the various operating and capital budgets. Particulars of cash receivable over the budget period will be obtained from the sales budget and other sources. Particulars of cash payable over the budget period will be extracted mainly from the operating (expense) budgets and budgets in respect of any planned acquisition of fixed assets.

Students should note that cash budgets may look similiar to operating budgets because they use much of the same information. They are, however, very different.

Operating budgets forecast income, expenditure and the level of profits over the coming year whereas cash budgets are concerned only with the actual receipt and payment of cash.

Depreciation, for example, will never feature in a cash budget because no cash changes hands. It is, however, a legitimate expense in an operating budget.

The important thing to remember in connection with cash budgeting is that the receipt of cash will not always coincide with the sale of goods: nor, of course, the payment of cash with the purchase of goods.

Take, for example, the case where a credit sale is made in June. The business will not receive the cash from this sale until July or August depending on the terms of credit.

EXAMPLE 24.2

Forecast receipt of cash

The following is the forecast sales budget for a restaurant for 6 months starting in January:

	Jan	Feb	Mar	Apr	May	Jun
Forecast	£	£	£	£	£	£
Sales	4,000	5,000	6,000	7,500	6,000	6,500

Past experience has shown that 40 per cent of sales are for cash and 60 per cent are on a credit basis with the cash from the above sales being received as follows:

		Expected Receipt of Cash
Cash sales	(40%)	Straight away
Credit sales 1	(50%)	after 4 weeks
Credit sales 2	(10%)	after 6 weeks
Total sales	100%	

Using the above information, you are required to complete the cash received section of the cash budget statement for April, May and June.

Cash Budget for 3 Months ending 30th June
(Forecasted cash receipts only)

	April	May	June
	£	£	£
Cash Receipts:			
Sales – Cash			
Credit 1			
Credit 2			
Total cash received			

Proceed as shown below:

Suggested solution

Cash Budget for 3 Months ending 30th June
(Forecast cash receipts only)

	April	May	June
	£	£	£
Cash Receipts:			
Sales – Cash	3,000	2,400	2,600
Credit 1	3,000	3,750	3,000
Credit 2	500	600	750
Total cash received	6,500	6,750	6,350

The figures in the solution above were calculated as follows:

					April £	May £	June £
Cash –	40%	(from April)	of	£7,500	3,000		
	40%	(from May)	of	£6,000		2,400	
	40%	(from June)	of	£6,500			2,600
Credit 1–	50%	(from March)	of	£6,000	3,000		
	50%	(from April)	of	£7,500		3,750	
	50%	(from May)	of	£6,000			3,000
Credit 2–	10%	(from Feb)	of	£5,000	500		
	10%	(from March)	of	£6,000		600	
	10%	(from April)	of	£7,500			750

Now that we are familiar with the pattern of cash receipts and payments we can now proceed to complete a full cash budget statement as shown in Example 24.3 below.

EXAMPLE 24.3

From the information given below prepare a cash budget for the six months commencing 1st April 19...

Month	Food sales	Bev. sales	Food purchases	Bev. purchases	Labour cost	Over-heads
	£	£	£	£	£	£
February	30,000	9,000	12,000	4,400	12,000	10,400
March	31,000	9,600	12,200	4,800	12,400	10,400
April	34,000	10,800	13,600	5,400	13,000	10,800
May	35,600	12,600	14,000	6,400	13,800	11,200
June	46,000	13,800	14,600	6,800	15,000	11,600
July	50,000	16,200	16,600	8,200	14,800	11,400
August	45,000	14,200	14,600	7,200	13,400	10,600
September	40,800	13,000	14,200	6,400	12,200	10,200

Notes:

(a) Assume that 80 per cent of total food sales are for cash, with the remaining 20 per cent on a credit basis of one month. All beverage sales are on a cash basis.

(b) The annual interest on the company's investments, £1,600, will be received in July.

(c) The time-lag in the payment of all suppliers is two months; in the payment of overheads the time-lag is one month: in the case of the labour costs it is nil.

(d) New kitchen plant costing £45,000 will be purchased in May and paid for the following month.

(e) The bank balance of the company on 1st April 19... was £8,000.

The cash budget would be drawn up as shown in Figure 24.1.

Cash Budget Statement
for 6 Months ending 30th September

	April	May	June	July	Aug	Sept
Cash receipts	£	£	£	£	£	£
Food sales- cash	27,200	28,480	36,800	40,000	36,000	32,640
credit	6,200	6,800	7,120	9,200	10,000	9,000
Beverage sales	10,800	12,600	13,800	16,200	14,200	13,000
Other receipts				1,600		
Total cash received	44,200	47,880	57,720	67,000	60,200	54,640
Cash payments						
Food purchases	12,000	12,200	13,600	14,000	14,600	16,600
Bev. purchases	4,400	4,800	5,400	6,400	6,800	8,200
Labour costs	13,000	13,800	15,000	14,800	13,400	12,200
Overheads	10,400	10,800	11,200	11,600	11,400	10,600
Other payments			45,000			
Total cash payments	39,800	41,600	90,200	46,800	46,200	47,600
Surplus/deficit for month	4,400	6,280	(32,480)	20,200	14,000	7,040
Opening Balance	8,000	12,400	18,680	(13,800)	6,400	20,400
Closing Balance	12,400	18,680	(13,800)	6,400	20,400	27,440

Figure 24.1 Cash budget statement

Notes on cash budget:

(a) The data shown in the cash budget are extracted from the operating and capital budgets.
(b) Eighty per cent of food sales and all beverage sales are cash sales, which represents an immediate cash inflow for that month. In respect of the credit food sales there is a time-lag of a month before the receipt of cash for such sales.
(c) From the cash budget it is possible to determine whether or not the future cash position is going to be satisfactory. It is also easier to plan capital expenditure and, generally, ensure a more economical use of the cash resources of the business.

MASTER BUDGETS

When all the operating and capital budgets have been completed it is possible to prepare the master budgets of the business, i.e. the budgeted profit and loss account and the budgeted balance sheet.

The budgeted profit and loss account will incorporate the sales budget, all the expense budgets and will show the budgeted net profit. The budgeted balance sheet will be compiled by reference to the last balance sheet (to ascertain the state of affairs at the beginning of the budget period), the capital budgets (with regard to any new acquisitions of assets) and the expense budgets (with regard to budgeted amounts of depreciation).

SUMMARY

* A budget is a plan, expressed in monetary or other terms.
* Budgetary control is a means of control by which responsibility for various budgets is assigned to the managers concerned. Actual results are compared with the budgeted figures and if there is a variance an inquiry and corrective action should follow.
* The main objectives of budgeting are; improved planning; better co-ordination of all activities; clearer standards of business performance; improved contol of income and expenditure; clearer lines of cost and profit responsibility.
* A budget committee consisting of senior managers and an accountant usually oversees budgeting and budgetary control.
* Capital budgets deal with assets and the capital funds of the business.
* Operating budgets are concerned with revenue/expense matters and the day-to-day running of the business.
* The limiting factor is any key feature which by its very nature limits the volume of sales and thereby sets a ceiling on budgeted sales e.g. if a hotel has only 10 single bedrooms there is no point in budgeting for 20 guests per night – the limiting factor is 10 bedrooms.
* When formulating an operating budget the most important budget is the sales budget as all the cost budgets are reckoned in relation to sales.
* The cash budget is prepared from the various capital and operating budgets. It not only helps to control and forecast cash needs but provides valuable information on the liquidity position of the business in advance.

PROBLEMS

1. Explain what you understand by: (a) budget; (b) budgetary control.

2. What are the objectives and advantages of budgetary control?

3. Write short explanatory notes on:
   (a) budget committee;
   (b) budget period;
   (c) review period.

4. Distinguish clearly between the following:
   (a) operating budgets and capital budgets;
   (b) departmental budgets and master budgets;
   (c) fixed budgets and flexible budgets.

5. Explain what you understand by 'limiting factor'.

6. Write short notes on how you would prepare the following:
   (a) sales budget;
   (b) cash budget;
   (c) maintenance budget;
   (d) marketing budget;
   (e) budgeted balance sheet.

7. The Leaning Tower Restaurant is a large, unlicensed restaurant and operates a system of budgetary control. Its bank balance on 1st April 19... is £16,000. From the information given below you are to prepare a cash budget for the quarter ending 30th June 19...

Budgeted sales

	February £	March £	April £	May £	June £
Cash sales	12,000	13,000	15,600	17,200	20,400
Credit sales	6,400	7,000	8,400	8,800	9,000
Total	18,400	20,000	24,000	26,000	29,400

Notes: You are informed that 80 per cent of credit sales are settled by clients within one month; the balance of 20 per cent is settled with a time-lag of two months.

Budgeted food cost

The restaurant operates at a food cost of 40 per cent. Thirty per cent of food cost represents current cash purchases. Seventy per cent of food cost is purchased on credit and settled in the month following purchase.

Budgeted labour costs

	April £	May £	June £
Kitchen staff	2,430	2,830	3,350
Waiting staff	1,870	2,150	2,470
Other	1,100	1,220	1,220
	5,400	6,200	7,040

Note: The time-lag in the payment of labour costs is nil.

Budgeted overheads

	January £	February £	March £	April £	May £	June £
Rent				1,400	1,400	1,400
Rates				700	700	700
Depreciation				1,640	1,640	1,640
Insurance				20	20	20
Gas	150	150	160	160	170	180
Electricity	150	100	80	70	80	90
Telephone	20	20	30	30	30	40
Total				4,020	4,040	4,070

Notes:
(a) The rent of the restaurant is payable in two half-yearly instalments, each March and September.
(b) Half-yearly demand notes in respect of rates are received each April and October.
(c) The full annual insurance premium is payable on 17th April.
(d) The gas, electricity and telephone accounts are payable quarterly each January, April, July and October.
(e) The time-lag in the payment of overheads is one month; this does not apply to the insurance premium.

8. From the following information prepare a cash budget for the months of June, July, August and September 19...

	£
1st June 19. . . bank balance	51,269
Sales for April 19...	31,465
Sales for May 19...	29,658
Estimated sales for – June 19...	42,147
– July 19...	58,393
– August 19...	61,215
– September 19...	52,147
Investment income due 30th June 19..., £1,000 – receivable in July, 19...	
Estimated expenses for June 19... (including wages and salaries)	10,213
Estimated expenses for – July 19...	10,869
– August 19...	11,019
– September 19...	10,542
Purchases for May 19...	49,251
Estimated purchases for – June 19...	52,375
– July 19...	19,142
– August 19...	11,641
– September 19...	16,842
Rent payable on 30th June 19...	1,200
Rent payable on 30th September 19...	1,200
Interim dividend of 5 per cent on capital of £50,000 payable on 1st July 19...	

Allow for 2 months' credit on sales.
Allow for 1 month's credit on purchases.

Discuss briefly the use of such a cash budget.

9. From the following forecasts of income and expenditure prepare a cash budget for the six months commencing 1st April 19...

Notes:
(a) Assume that all sales are on a cash basis.
(b) The time-lag in the payment of suppliers' accounts is two months.

(c) The time-lag in the payment of overheads is one month; in the case of labour it is nil.

(d) New furniture, costing £6,000, will be purchased in June and paid on delivery.

(e) The annual interest on the company's investments will be received in August; the amount is £1,000.

Month	Sales Food	Sales Bevs	Purchases Food	Purchases Bevs	Labour	Overhead
	£	£	£	£	£	£
February	20,000	6,000	8,000	3,000	8,000	7,000
March	22,000	6,200	8,800	3,100	8,400	7,000
April	24,000	7,200	9,600	3,600	8,400	7,200
May	28,000	8,400	11,200	4,200	9,200	7,200
June	32,000	9,600	12,800	4,800	10,000	7,400
July	36,000	10,800	14,400	5,400	10,000	7,400
August	32,000	9,600	12,800	4,800	9,600	7,400
September	26,000	7,800	10,400	3,900	8,800	7,200

You are informed that the company's bank balance on 1st April 19... was £20,000.

10. A large, licensed seasonal restaurant is managed by two partners, A and B. The restaurant was opened on 1st January 19... and at the end of the first year of its operation, the following accounts were prepared.

Trading, profit and loss appropriation account
for the year ended 31st December 19...

		£	£
Sales:	Food	660,000	
	Beverages	340,000	1,000,000
Less: Cost of sales	Food	268,000	
	Beverages	112,000	380,000
Gross profit			620,000
Add rent receivable			10,000
			630,000
Less: other expenses			
Wages and salaries		296,000	
Rates		48,000	
Insurance		4,000	
Advertising		16,000	
Printing and stationery		10,000	
Laundry and cleaning		8,000	
Depreciation		64,000	
Repairs and renewals		22,000	
Light and heat		24,000	
Miscellaneous expenses		4,000	496,000
Net profit			134,000

Less: appropriations:	A	B	Total
Partners:	£	£	£
Salary	30,000	30,000	60,000
Share of profit	37,000	37,000	74,000
			134,000

Balance sheet as at 31st December 19...

Fixed assets	Cost	Dep'n	Net
	£	£	£
Leasehold	950,000	650,000	300,000
Kitchen plant	400,000	320,000	80,000
Furniture	450,000	350,000	100,000
	1,800,000	1,320,000	480,000
China and cutlery			10,000
			490,000

Current assets			
Stocks		15,000	
Debtors'		8,000*	
Prepayments		13,000**	
Cash at bank		14,000	
		50,000	

Less Current liabilities***			
Creditors	8,000		
Accrued advertising	6,000	14,000	
Net current assets			36,000
			526,000

Financed by			
Partners	A	B	
	£	£	£
Capital accounts	250,000	250,000	500,000
Current accounts	13,000	13,000	26,000
	263,000	263,000	526,000

* Receivable in month 1
** Consists of prepaid rates £12,000 and prepaid insurance £1,000
*** Payable in month 1

The partners are anxious to introduce from the beginning of the following year a simple system of budgetary control. They have prepared the following sales budget for the year commencing 1st January 19...

	Sales	
	Food	Beverages
	£	£
Month 1	20,000	10,000
" 2	30,000	15,000
" 3	40,000	20,000
" 4	60,000	30,000
" 5	80,000	40,000
" 6	110,000	55,000
" 7	110,000	55,000
" 8	100,000	50,000
" 9	90,000	45,000
" 10	70,000	35,000
" 11	40,000	20,000
" 12	30,000	15,000
" 13	20,000	10,000
	800,000	400,000

Notes on sales budget:
(a) All beverage sales are on a cash basis.
(b) Half the food sales are cash sales: the other (credit) sales are settled by customers with a time-lag of one month.

You are required by the partners to prepare the following draft budgets for their consideration:
(a) an expense budget;
(b) a cash budget (showing the balance available at the end of each month);
(c) a budgeted profit and loss account;
(d) a budgeted balance sheet.

You are given the following information on the various draft budgets you are to prepare:

Expense budget: this, as well as the cash budget, is to cover the ensuing financial year of twelve calendar months.

Wages and salaries: the partners intend to employ additional labour to cope with the budgeted increase in sales and, having analysed the staffing of the restaurant, inform you that the budgeted cost of wages and salaries for the coming year should be:

	£
Month 1	18,000
" 2	18,000
" 3	22,000
" 4	24,000
" 5	24,000
" 6	28,000
" 7	32,000
" 8	28,000

"	9	24,000
"	10	24,000
"	11	24,000
"	12	20,000
"	13	18,000
Total		304,000

All wages and salaries are paid by the restaurant weekly.

Rates: the rate in the £ is expected to remain constant in the coming year. The rates are paid half-yearly in advance each month 4 and month 10.

Insurance: this will remain unchanged. The premiums are paid half-yearly in advance – in months 3 and 9.

Advertising: this consists of press advertising only. The partners have decided to spend the same amount as in the previous year. Of the £16,000 one-half will be spent in month 3 and £4,000 will be spent in months 4 and 5.

Printing and stationery: owing to an increase in printing costs and the partners' intention to introduce more attractively printed menus the budgeted expenditure on this item is expected to increase by £2,000. Of the £12,000 one-half will be spent in month 1 and the rest of the expenditure will be incurred in the remaining months.

Laundry and cleaning: the amount budgeted by the partners for this item is £9,000. In months 6, 7 and 8 the cost of this item will be £1,000 per month, in the remaining ten months it will be £600 per month. The time-lag in the payment of this expenditure is one month.

Depreciation: This will remain as in the previous year, i.e.

Leasehold	£38,000
Kitchen plant	14,000
Furniture	12,000

Repairs and renewals: the partners budget to spend £26,000 on this item. Of this, £12,000 is to be paid out in month 3 in respect of urgent external repairs and the balance is to be made available for other repairs to be carried out towards the close of the season and paid out in month 12.

Light and heat: it is anticipated that as a result of the additional volume of sales the budgeted amount for this item should be £25,000. The cash payments will be as follows:

		£
Month	4	7,000
"	7	6,000
"	11	5,000
"	13	7,000
Total		25,000

Miscellaneous expenses: this item consists of a large number of small items. The budgeted amount for the ensuing year is £5,200 and, you are informed, there is no time-lag in the payment of these items.

Cash budget: the partners have decided to leave the balances owing to them (see current accounts) until month 6, when they hope the cash position of the restaurant will warrant withdrawing these sums.

They also intend to draw cash from the business in anticipation of profits at the rate of £2,000 each per month, commencing in month 7.

The rent receivable is in respect of the premises sub-let to a travel agency and is payable in full at the end of each calendar year.

Budgeted profit and loss account: it is intended by the partners that the restaurant should operate at an overall gross profit margin of 60 per cent.

It is planned that half the cost of sales for any one period should be cash purchases, the other half being credit purchases to be settled the month following purchase.

The net profit of the restaurant is to be divided between the partners in the same manner as in the previous year.

Budgeted balance sheet: no new acquisitions of fixed assets are planned by the partners.

It is intended that the stocks should be maintained at the same level as at the end of the first year of operation.

Hospitality accounting and computerization: an overview

Bruce Braham

INTRODUCTION

The 1980s and 1990s have seen great strides in the implementation of computerization in businesses and homes alike. The hospitality industry has been slow to computerize especially the smaller hotels and restaurants. It is only in the 1990s that any serious inroads have been made in this area, indeed there is still a long way to go. In many respects the accounting function is ideal for computerization: it is systematic by concept and well understood and many aspects are repetitive by nature. There are many exciting and easy to use computer accounting packages available off the shelf to businessmen and women. However, there is no substitute for a good working knowledge of the accounting concepts and structures behind the computing packages to which the whole of this textbook is dedicated.

OBJECTIVES

On completion of this chapter you should be able to:

* know the meaning of the term 'computerization';
* be familiar with the evolution of computerized accounting systems;
* understand what is meant by an 'integrated computer package';
* demonstrate how individual double entry transactions are entered via a computer package;
* define 'input' and 'output' data;
* comprehend clearly that an accounting computer package is always made up from a manual system;
* understand that by the simple entry on computer of one transaction all relevant double entry is completed;
* recognize a transaction history document;
* list the advantages of computerization as against a manual system.

HISTORY

Since their earliest usage in business in the 1950s computers have been described as 'number crunchers' because they are basically fast calculators

---

Candidate functions for hotel computerization
- Reservations handling
- Guest Registration
- **Guest Accounting, including charge recording and bill settlement and cash sales.**
- **City Ledger billing**
- Function room usage
- Food and beverage control
- **Accounts payable handling**
- **Payroll preparation**
- **General accounting functions**
- **Reporting for management control**

Figure 25.1 Candidate functions for hotel computerization
(*Source*: The Cornell HRA Quarterly, Anon, 'Automation for hotels'.)

and therefore ideally suited to handling figures. Early evidence of the recommended usage of computers in hotels clearly illustrates that the software writers or programmers of the day acknowledged this, as is illustrated in Figure 25.1.

It may be seen in Figure 25.1 that six of the then recognized computer functions are purely mathematical and if one examines present day hotel computer packages the same is still basically true.

In those early days of business computers the systems were both large and cumbersome and the costs of the equipment (hardware) and the programs (software) were out of reach of all but the multi-national hotel groups – usually those linked to parent airlines. Much of the system development, though, took place at that time and it is only now with the enhanced microprocessor personal computers widely on offer that economies of scale have brought enhanced accounting hardware and software within easy reach of even the smallest of hotels at a reasonable price.

COMPUTERIZED ACCOUNTING SYSTEM

The computerized hotel accounting system will provide management with a number of immediate advantages, for example:

(a) it does away with the need for repetitive chores;
(b) it will considerably reduce errors due to transposition;
(c) it speeds up accounting operations, i.e. updates all files with one entry;
(d) it produces key documents at the flick of a switch, e.g. trial balance, trading accounts, profit & loss accounts, etc.

In addition, computerization gives management three distinct facilities:

(a) the ability to control internal operations;
(b) an improved cash flow;
(c) a wide ranging selection of management reports on the business.

The use of a computerized accounts package in these areas is attractive because it will remove much of the drudgery of book-keeping. This is provided the system is set up correctly at its inception, by taking great care over the process by which data is input. The intention will always be for data to be input just once and for the computer to manipulate this data into the various reports and formats that are subsequently required by customers (bills), staff (working records), management (operational accounts and reports) and suppliers (purchase documents). Whoever is entering data, whether it be the waiting staff in the restaurant, the receptionist at the front desk or the purchasing clerk in the back office, must be doubly careful as the computer will do exactly what it is told. If the receptionist mistakenly enters £300.00, instead of £30.00, then £300.00 is what the computer will manipulate! According to the age-old computer phrase, therefore, if you put '**garbage in**' then you will receive '**garbage out**'!

ACCOUNTING AND COMPUTER PACKAGES

Throughout this book instruction is given on the theory of how to create accounts manually. Most computerized accounts packages will undertake all of that for you but you need to know both how and why, not only for peace of mind but also in case the system lets you down; this, though, does not mean that you have to have the skills of a programmer. Whilst the computer will provide you with information quickly, you need to know what it actually means and it is then up to you to make the business decisions that only you can from the available data. You should therefore always regard a computer system as a tool that assists you with your day-to-day work and not as an end in itself.

Another important concept is that the computer system should be tailored to the individual hotel's business and not vice versa. Whilst the system may well reveal streamlined ways of undertaking certain procedures, every business is slightly different and the computer package selected must be flexible enough to cope with this. That is not to say that applying the logic built into computerized accounting software may not reveal improved methods of operation in some establishments!

Ideally an accounts package should be versatile and easy to use so that a smooth operation is possible. The operators must be able to access all of its features rapidly so that it is 'user friendly', whilst it must not be forgotten that there may have to be built-in security in the form of passwords to maintain confidentiality in places.

Input data

Nowadays it will be very unlikely for the accounts, or Back Office package, to be a 'stand alone' system, which means that it will undoubtedly be integrated with other hotel-wide applications such as the Front Office system which will be handling such tasks as enquiries, reservations and check-in. This area of the hotel will in effect be creating 'input data' for the

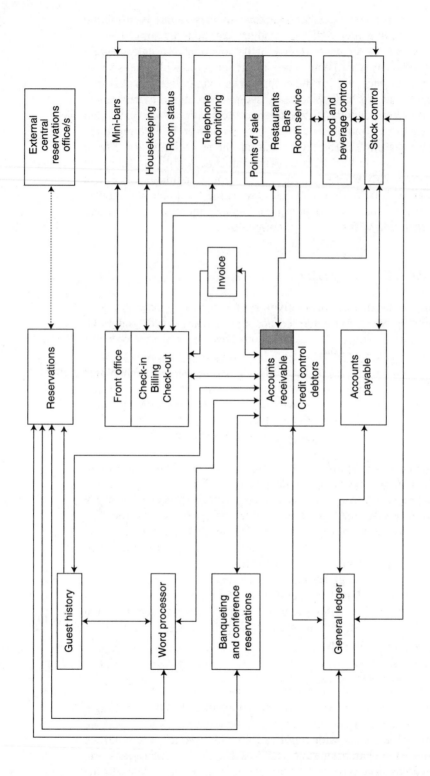

Figure 25.2 A typical integrated hotel computer system
Source: Bruce Braham *Hotel Front Office*, 2nd Edition,
Stanley Thornes 1993: 61

overall computer system. It is after all at the front desk that the financial tracking of customers starts, whether this be when deposits are received in advance or when the individuals actually arrive at the hotel and start to incur charges from the tariff. It makes sense for the Front Office staff – receptionists and cashiers – to actually input their information directly into the integrated accounting system so that what in other business might be called 'sales' are recorded at the time the transactions occur, instead of historically. In fact most hotel computer systems revolve around the 'Reservations' package which prompts many of the other computer applications with the initial information that they need to manipulate including the payment or tariff detail that the customer, whether as an individual or as part of a group, is expected to make for their stay. It should be appreciated too that reservations may be immediate or advance with the latter allowing the business to plan ahead, whilst also having to handle some advance payments in the form of deposits.

An illustration of the potential links for an integrated computer package is shown in Figure 25.2.

It may be perceived from Figure 25.2 that there is the possibility for hundreds of transactions to be generated for and then posted to a single bill. All of those transactions need to be verified to avoid inaccurate postings and a good accounts package will spot obvious errors such as charges going to the wrong room number.

Double entry

A computerized accounting system is no different from its manual predecessor in that, as explained elsewhere, it too relies on debits and credits to record financial transactions. Electronically as well as manually every debit boasts a corresponding credit, and vice versa; and the omission of either will lead a good computerized accounting system to the automatic detection of an error should the account not balance. For example, when a guest arrives at reception and 'books in', say for one night, the guest's details/room charge are typed into the computer. By pressing a single key the room-price will be automatically charged to the sales ledger – **debit customer account** – by opening an account in the guest's name and at the same time recording an identical amount in the sales account in the nominal ledger, thus **credit sales account** and complete double entry.

Output data

Most accounts packages are ledger accounting systems that cover the sales ledger, purchase ledger and nominal ledger functions that when integrated with other software applications, such as those in the front office, allow automatic credit account transfers to the sales ledger as well as daily revenue posting to the nominal ledger. These ledgers may on occasions be handled by the front office system but there may also be a need for remote accounts sites, such as, in the case of an individual hotel within a group, to communicate with its head office and this facility may need to be built into the system.

INTEGRATED COMPUTER PACKAGE

Typically an integrated accounts system will provide:

Type	Meaning
• Sales Ledger	Customers' accounts
• Purchase Ledger	Suppliers' accounts
• Nominal Ledger	All other accounts, e.g. sales a/c purchases a/c, rent a/c, etc.
• Management Information	Revenue a/cs, forecasts, etc.

Sales ledger

The sales ledger records all payments whether these arrive in the form of advance deposits, cash or credit transactions (subsequently paid as bills or as invoices). The sales ledger allows a close control to be kept over both cash and debtors in a business where so much is undertaken on credit. Also included will be transactions incurred in the hotel, such as cash restaurant sales, which permit a comprehensive ledger to be maintained.

The input screen for the sales ledger may be shown as in Figure 25.3:

THE SHIP INN

Sales Ledger Input Screen

Title: Mr **Initials**: S **Surname**: Calver

Address: 12 Amberley Road **Acc Ref**: NBG Ltd
Canford Cliffs **Acc Name**:
Town: Poole
County: Dorset
Postcode: BH55 2ZX **Telephone**: 01202 818203
Nationality: British **Passport**:

Arrival Date: 11/02/96 **Nights**: 5 **Room**: 8 **Extra Rooms**: 0
Room Type: Double **Position**: Front

Adults: 2
Children 0–2: 0 **2–12**: 0
Meal: Y **Rate Code**: S **Rate**: £118.00
Cots: 0 **Total**: £594.00
Deposit: 0.00 **Method**: **Pay Ref**:
Confirmation Letter: N **Booking Form Received**: N
Reference: **Misc**:

Figure 25.3 Sample sales ledger input screen
(*Source*: Fylde Business Technology)

In Figure 25.3 Mr Calver's Account Reference is NBG Ltd – the name of his company. A distinct benefit of a computerized accounts system is that when the details of the invoice are transferred to the hotel's accounts for payment the system will automatically locate the details of the account's department at NBG Ltd to whom the request for payment should be sent.

Within the sales ledger there will be the need to handle a number of applications. These will include:

Type	Meaning
• Receipts	Payments from customers
• Refunds	Overcharges, poor service etc.
• Bad debts	Non-payment by customer
• Statements	Total balance owing by customer
• Day books	List of credit sales from bar etc.
• Transaction histories	See Figure 25.4 below

Figure 25.4 shows what NBG Ltd's current transaction history might look like.

THE SHIP INN

Transaction History   **11th February 1996**

A/C Ref: NBG   **A/C Name**: NBG Ltd.

No.	Tp	Date	Ref	Details	Value £	Debit £	Credit £
8	SI	110296	000003	Inv. (Accom)	425.00		
9	SI	110296	000003	Inv. (Meals)	169.00		
10	SI	110296	000003	Call to 0253 867047	2.40		
11	SI	110296	000003	Call to 0253 825229	1.60		
12	SI	110296	000003	Call to 0229 869585	4.00		
13	SI	110296	000003	Drinks	1.90		
14	SI	110296	000003	Drinks	8.60	612.50	

Amount Outstanding   : 612.50   **Credit Limit:**   0.00
Amount paid this period   :   0.00   **Turnover YTD**: 521.27

Figure 25.4 Sample transaction history
(*Source*: Fylde Business Technology)

In Figure 25.4 it is apparent that NBG Ltd have been invoiced on 11.02.96 under invoice reference number 3 with all the payments itemized – a facility that will make NBG Ltd's accountant's life that much easier, allowing close control of their payments. Statements too may be issued at the conclusion of accounting periods.

Usually, as in this example, the payment data is taken initially from the reservation where payment types are identified, such as those customers who are having their bills paid by their company. A good computer system will transfer the individual guest charges into the company account in the sales ledger ready for payment from a company transaction history (guest bill). This would break charges down into accommodation, meals and any other relevant charge headings. The turnover for the year for the company would be shown, either inclusive or exclusive of VAT, and account balances would be available at any time to maintain a strict credit control. Monthly statements may be automatically created too.

Customer invoices or bills can be produced at any time because computerization (via integrated package) means that the customer's bill is always up to date. Payment may be required either on arrival in some hotels or more typically on departure. In other situations it must also be acknowledged that many sales will be on a credit basis and therefore, according to the hotel's policy, these accounts will be recorded as debtors and automatically sent out to the relevant firm/company after guest departure. Sales accounts for credit customers may well have been set up at the reservation stage. A single invoice may be produced too to cover a group booking, which is something that would previously have been very tedious when using manual accounting procedures. The important benefit is that any deposits received or bills paid should be automatically maintained within the sales ledger so that sales reports may be produced, analysing income by payment types. Additionally, the projected turnover for any given period of time may be a budgetary or managerial information outcome allowing greater financial control.

Purchase or bought ledger

The function of the purchase ledger is to enable the hotel to keep up-to-date with payments to suppliers once invoices and discounts have been agreed. The accounts established for each supplier, of which there may be many hundreds in a large hotel, must continually be kept under control and such items as VAT calculations and cheques may be automatically generated.

Within the purchase ledger there will be the need to handle a number of applications. These might include:

Type	Meaning
• Supplier details	Name, address, etc.
• Payments	Amounts outstanding
• Refunds	For returns, etc.
• Account balances	Net amounts outstanding
• Day books	For credit transactions
• Transaction histories	Invoices
• Remittance advice notes	as stated

Nominal or general ledger

This provides the facility that enables an analysis of all the hotel's sales and purchases as well as information concerning those guests who pay by cash.

Within the nominal or general ledger there will be the need to handle a number of applications. These will include:

- nominal account structure;
- bank transactions;
- petty cash transactions;
- journal entries;
- prepayments and accruals;
- depreciation;
- trial balance;
- transactions history;
- control accounts;
- day books;
- VAT return analysis;
- monthly accounts;
- asset valuation.

By using the transaction history facility within the nominal ledger it would be possible to examine the current situation under a particular cost head. For example Figure 25.5 shows the situation with telephones:
Figure 25.5 shows that three telephone calls have been made to the total value of £6.80.

THE SHIP INN

		Transaction History			**11th February 1996**		

A/C Ref: 4064   **A/C Name**: Telephones

No.	Tp	Date	Ref	Details	Value £	Debit £	Credit £
3	SI	110296	000003	Call to 0253 867047	2.04		
4	SI	110296	000003	Call to 0253 825229	1.36		
5	SI	110296	000003	Call to 0229 869585	3.40	6.80	
				Totals:		0.00	6.80
				Balance:			6.80

Figure 25.5 Sample transaction history
(*Source*: Fylde Business Technology)

Additionally a trial balance may be quickly produced at any time – a great advantage over manual systems – using the facility within the nominal ledger as shown in Figure 25.6.
Figure 25.6 shows the total business for each of the Ship Inn's categories that has been nominated – a full trial balance would possess many more categories than this. It is obvious that, for example, the hotel is still owed £1198.20 by the total against the Debtors' Control Account.
At the conclusion of each month or any defined accounting period the

THE SHIP INN

Trial Balance   11th February 1996

Ref.	Accounts Name	Debit £	Credit £
1100	Debtors' Control Account	1198.20	
1200	Bank Current Account	220.00	
2100	Creditors Control Account		317.50
2200	Tax Control Account		164.96
4000	Accommodation		723.40
4010	Meals		287.66
4010	Deposits		200.00
4060	Bar		17.88
4064	Telephone Calls		6.80
5000	Linen Purchases	200.00	
7200	Electricity	100.00	
		1718.20	1718.20

Figure 25.6 Sample trial balance
(*Source*: Fylde Business Technology)

automated system can produce a profit and loss account, a balance sheet and complete budget reports which are not only swift, but also accurate; this is essential to the successful managerial control of the hotel. It should be a natural feature that last year comparisons and year-to-date figures are included in any output. Equally important is that at the conclusion of each quarter a calculation of the input and output figures for the VAT return may be automatically produced.

SUMMARY

- Any computer system is only as good as the input information typed into it, remember 'garbage in, garbage out'.
- Hotel accounting packages simply replicate the manual system which they supercede, but handle the information much faster and more effectively.
- Computer packages are especially suitable for repetitive work such as removing the drudgery of book-keeping entries.
- Computerization is, in simple terms, the replacement of a well-understood manual system with an electronic one.
- Hotel operations lend themselves to use of integrated packages. This means that all the business departments of the hotel are linked by computer and that charging, etc. is instantaneous.
- Accurate customer bills depend on correct input data, e.g. restaurant bills, room service charges, drinks bills, etc.

- 'Input data' once processed produces 'output data' in the form of customer bills, total debtors, creditors, profit statements, etc.

PROBLEMS

1. Discuss what you understand by the term 'garbage in, garbage out'.

2. Produce a brief outline, including definitions, of the key elements of a computerized integrated hotel accounting package.

3. What are the main advantages of a computer accounting system over a manual one?

4. What do you understand by the following terms:
   (a) input data;
   (b) output data;
   (c) transaction history document?

5. As a concept, you are required to attempt to improve the layout of the sales ledger input screen in Figure 25.3.

Index